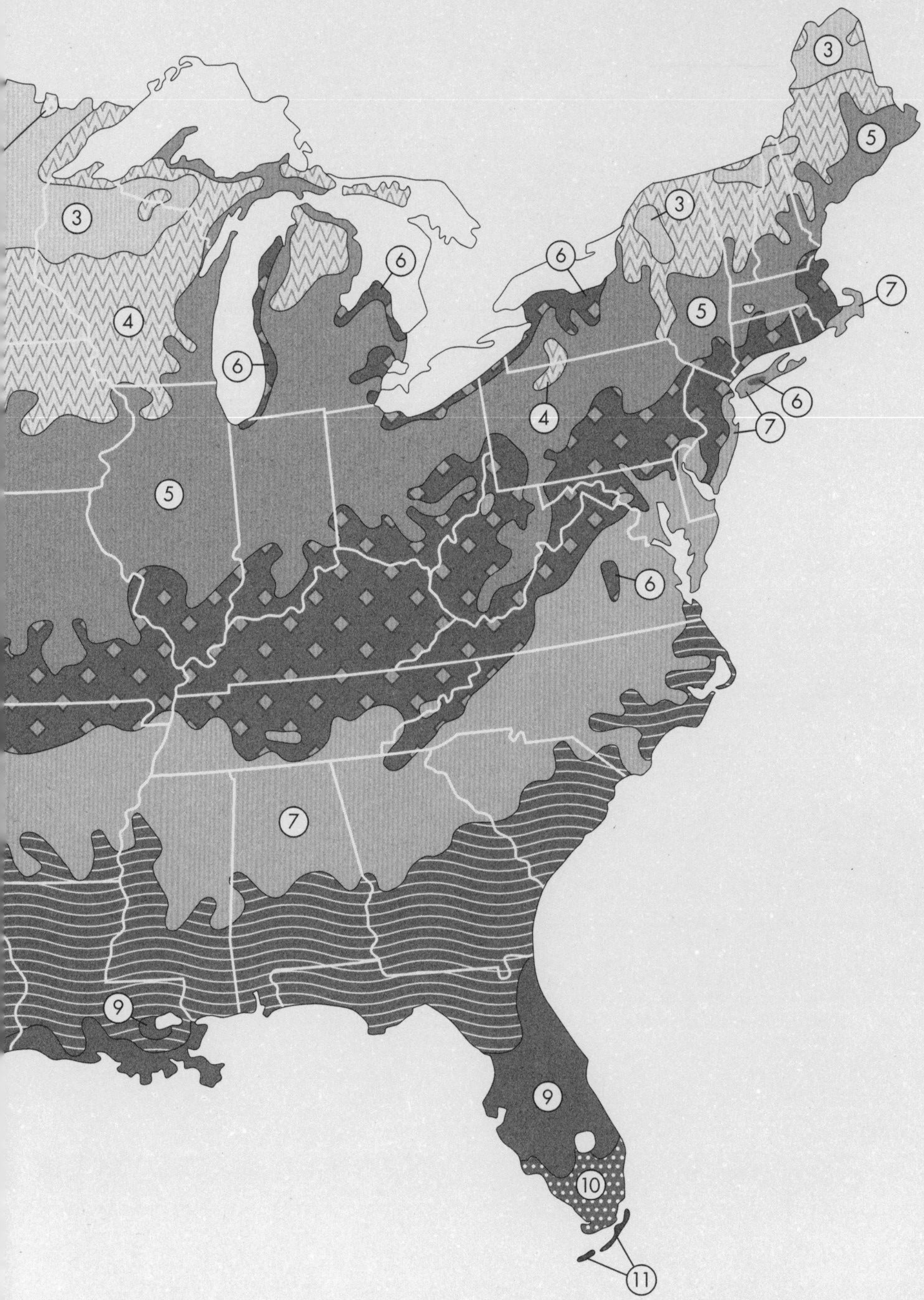

	Fahrenheit	Celsius
Zone 1	below -50°	below -46°
Zone 2	-50° to -40°	-46° to -40°
Zone 3	-40° to -30°	-40° to -34°
Zone 4	-30° to -20°	-34° to -29°
Zone 5	-20° to -10°	-29° to -23°
Zone 6	-10° to 0°	-23° to -18°
Zone 7	0° to 10°	-18° to -12°
Zone 8	10° to 20°	-12° to -7°
Zone 9	20° to 30°	-7° to -1°
Zone 10	30° to 40°	-1° to 4°
Zone 11	above 40°	above 4°

Hardiness Across America

Zones in the United States are based on average minimum temperatures, with Zone 11 rated warmest, and Zone 1 coldest. Plants in this book are rated according to the coldest temperatures they survive. Summer heat and humidity, and lack of winter chilling in warmer climates may limit the ability of some plants to thrive. Because of this, and the fact that within each Zone are microclimates that can be colder or warmer, we suggest that you use the Zones as a guide, but feel free to experiment with plants rated marginally hardy.

THE No-Garden GARDENER

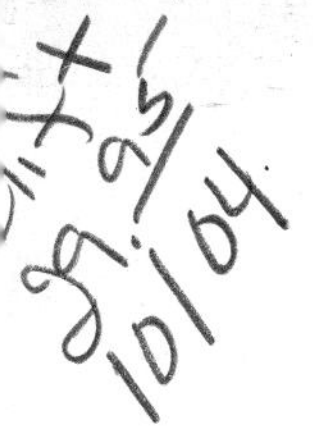

THE No-Garden GARDENER

Creating gardens on patios, balconies, terraces, and in other small spaces

JANE COURTIER

Gardening Consultant Ruth Clausen

The Reader's Digest Association, Inc.
Pleasantville, New York • Montreal

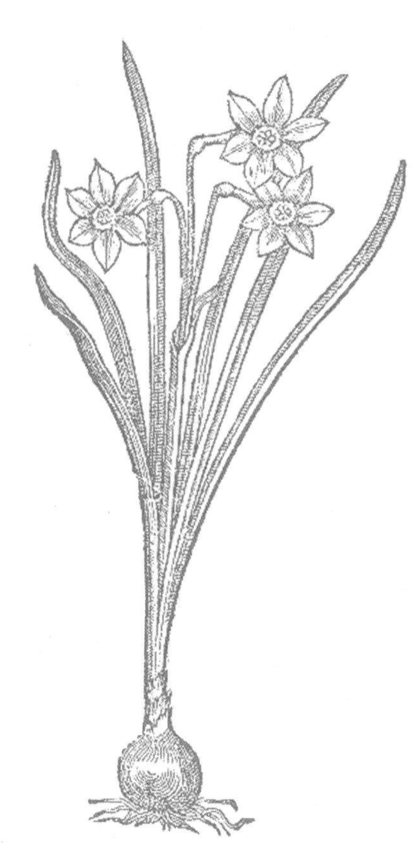

A READER'S DIGEST BOOK

Conceived, edited and designed by Marshall Editions Ltd

Project editor	Gwen Rigby
Designer	Gary Ottewill
Picture editor	Zilda Tandy
DTP editors	Lesley Gilbert, Keith Bambury
Production	Nikki Ingram
Managing editor	Clare Currie
Managing art editor	Patrick Carpenter
Art director	Sean Keogh
Editorial director	Sophie Collins
Editorial coordinator	Rebecca Clunes
Editorial assistant	Sophie Sandy

Library of Congress Cataloging-in-Publication Data.

Courtier, Jane.
No garden gardener / Jane Courtier : consulting editor,
Ruth Clausen
p. cm.
Includes index.
ISBN 0-7621-0127-X
1. Gardening. 2. Container gardening. I. Clausen, Ruth Rogers.
1938- . II. Title.
SB473,C6845 1999
635.9'86—dc21 98-30453

Printed and bound in Italy

Contents

Introduction

We live in a crowded world. As populations continue to grow, our lifestyles have changed accordingly. Although commerce, business and industry have taken over from agriculture, many of us still have a desire to see things flourish that we have grown ourselves. The fact that we have chosen the benefit of living in a city or a housing development does not mean we have lost that desire. There is no reason at all why we cannot combine the benefits of the two and provide ourselves with a very pleasant environment.

Where land is at a premium, and city living is increasingly the norm, the maximum number of dwellings must fit into the minimum amount of space. That often means blocks of high-rise apartments and streets of close-set houses where garden space often consists of small yards, balconies, or roof gardens.

The more crowded our living conditions become, the greater is our desire for our own space to keep in touch in some small way with the natural world. Growing plants fulfils a basic, instinctive need, and it can also help relieve stress by providing a calm, refreshing oasis in our busy lives.

Houseplants have rarely been more popular, but they are obviously not the whole answer for a homeowner who craves a garden to tend. While they provide welcome greenery and flowers to enhance our living space, outdoor plants give us something extra. Rather than thriving in an artificial and protected environment, they speak to us of fresh air and open spaces, sunlight, and sweet summer scents. Outdoor plants attract birds, butterflies, and a host of other small creatures, and as

they flourish can give a sense of satisfaction disproportionate to their size. As they transform themselves with the changing seasons, outdoor plants remind us of the patterns of nature.

If you think all this is denied you because you don't have a garden, think again. The pleasures of growing plants are available to everyone who cares to enjoy them, no matter how restricted the available space. Even those would-be gardeners who have chosen life in upper-story apartments, with no ground space, may be able to use window boxes, hanging baskets, and wall pots to make all the difference in their view. House walls and boundary fences can support prolific climbers and wall plants, and the variety of containers available means that paths, patios, steps, porches, balconies, and basement entries can become green havens.

All you need is to understand the requirements of your situation and to be aware of the various options open to you—which is just what this book will help you to do. In this way, you can enter into partnership with your environment, and achieve results that will not only give you great satisfaction but may also benefit the whole neighborhood.

Gardening in a small space is both challenging and rewarding. Each plant assumes greater importance, and a true sense of achievement is gained as you raise each one to maturity. Make the most of the space you have and you'll be surprised at just how much pleasure you can get from gardening without a garden!

About this book

To help you get started, Chapters 1 and 2 discuss the basics of design and planning and suggest practical ways of making your own garden space work for you, be it a window box, a balcony or a roof garden. There are inspiring examples of "no-garden" situations, and planting plans to help you create the particular style that appeals to you.

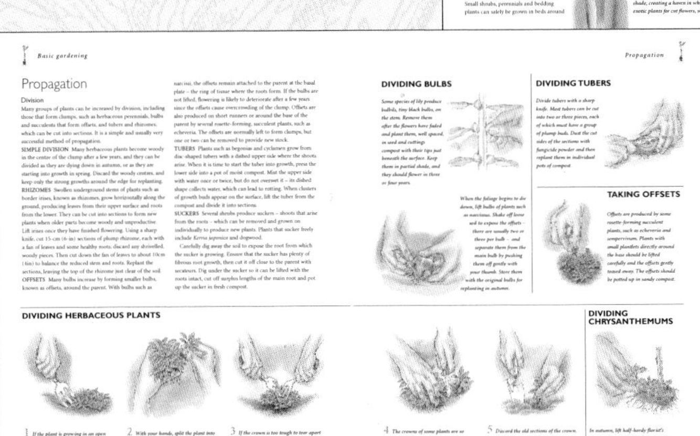

Once you have decided how you want your garden to look, Chapter 3 provides the practical information you need to put your ideas into practice. There are step-by-step guides to all the main techniques, and a wealth of tips on propagation, plant maintenance, pests and diseases, tools, soil and buying plants.

An invaluable section called "Plants for Special Places" provides an alphabetical list of plants for special purposes. Whether you are looking for a conifer to grow in a container, some hardy groundcover, scented plants, or plants that provide year-round interest, you are sure to find something here to suit your needs.

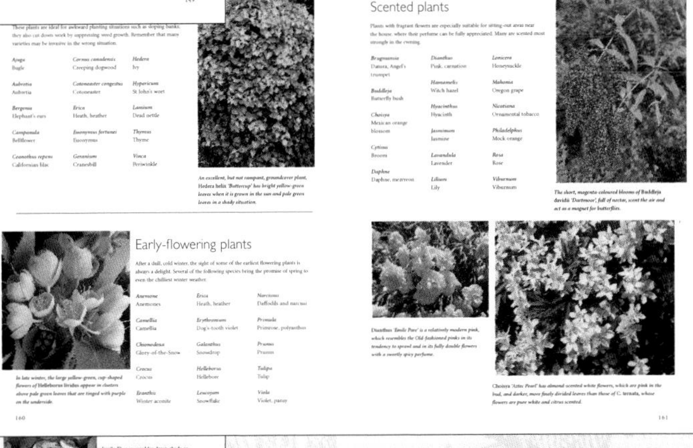

The directory of plants lists them alphabetically by their botanical names and also gives their family and common names. Each plant's main features are described, and the species and cultivars most appropriate for growing in confined spaces are highlighted, along with information on cultivation, care and propagation.

Chapter One

Homes without gardens

The first step in turning an unpromising plot into a special area filled with plants is to take a good, hard look at exactly what you are faced with. In this chapter we define precisely what we mean by homes without gardens and see what the possibilities—and the resulting benefits—are.

Having taken a general look at the many types of "no-garden" gardens that can successfully be turned into plant havens (with some inspiring examples to show just what can be done), you can now begin a thorough assessment of your own situation and decide what you can achieve with what you have. There are many points to bear in mind, but this chapter will guide you through the main considerations one by one, until you have a much clearer idea of the task ahead.

The wonderful examples of "no-garden" gardens shown in this book, such as this tiny, flower-filled balcony, will inspire and encourage you to make your own oasis in what may now seem an impossible and desolate spot.

Examining the possibilities

Garden: A piece of ground on which flowers etc. are cultivated; a pleasant spot; a fertile region.

(Chambers Everyday Dictionary)

For most people, the very word "garden" conjures up an image of colorful flowers, leafy trees, spreading lawns—a green and beautiful place of peace and tranquillity. How different from the surroundings that many of us are faced with in reality. Modern urban dwellers look from their front windows straight on to the street and the houses opposite; at the back there may be rows of tiny yards between the tightly packed homes. The noise of traffic is often constant; the very air seems gritty and stale. Those living in high apartments look out over a sprawl of roofs and chimneys, their elevated position giving an increased sense of unreality and detachment from the real world. Frequently there is no tree or green space as far as the eye can see.

Limited space does not mean that you cannot grow plants. With imagination, a small, flat roof can be turned into a garden; a walkway bounded by a high brick wall (at right) can be made to seem wider by the repeated use of shaped trellis and regular planting.

Even in rural areas, modern housing developments are often tightly packed with homes, with no yard space. Communal playgrounds are provided for children, with nonslip safety surfaces replacing grass and abstract wooden and metal "sculptures" instead of trees. Everything must be safe, indestructible, and low maintenance.

Even where builders have been more generous with the land allotted to each home, often the extra space could by no stretch of the imagination be called a garden. Surfaces are usually solid paving or asphalt to avoid problems with weed growth and wet-weather mud. Increasingly, front yards in older properties have disappeared under blacktop to provide room for cars to be parked off the street. Such a plot is far from "a pleasant spot" or "a fertile region."

As far as this book is concerned, these are the homes without gardens. They include the obvious candidates, such as upper-story apartments that have no ground space at all, and also those homes with small, hard-surfaced yards and patios, steps, porches, and paths, which may have a little ground space but no growing space. A garden, by our definition, needs to have a reasonable area of fertile soil into which

plants can be set directly; the soil must be sufficiently deep for the plants to obtain most of the water and nutrients they need to develop. If you do not have such a growing area, you qualify for full membership in our club—the "no-garden" gardeners.

Having accepted that you have no yard, you may also have begun to think that you can't enjoy growing plants outdoors. You have probably decorated the interior of your home with an array of well-cultivated, expensive houseplants that bring you pleasure with their lush foliage and bright flowers; these are your garden substitutes, and you may think that you will have to be satisfied with them.

But, as this book will show, it is possible to garden without a yard. Even the most unpromising situation can be made to bloom, with only a small amount of skill and dedication. The question is, is it worthwhile? Is there really any point in battling against nature?

Why grow plants?

There are many advantages to growing plants, even in the most challenging locations. First and foremost, there is the sheer satisfaction of raising a plant and seeing it develop and mature; this satisfaction is evident in any situation, but particularly so when the odds are stacked against you. In a "no-garden" situation you know that the plants are almost entirely dependent on you for their needs, from the soil in which they grow to the last drop of water. So you can take all the credit when things go right!

In sterile, barren surroundings, plants provide a contrast that makes them an even greater joy. They can provide ever-changing color and form; the gradual development of their shape, the formation and unfolding of flower buds, the fall color changes of their foliage—no nonliving decoration can ever compete. Many plants also have the bonus of fragrance, either from their foliage or flowers, which is even better appreciated at close quarters. Houses are often all identical; plants provide an easy way to give your home its individuality and set it apart from its neighbors. Plants soften harsh outlines and mellow uncompromising building materials; they can disguise flaws and imperfections and give a rapid facelift to almost any building.

If you crave vegetables, you can grow them in a hanging basket—and they are very decorative, too. Even in the tiniest area, there is room for a small pond (at right) surrounded by a few flowering shrubs.

A living screen

A major problem of living in densely populated areas is the lack of privacy. Plants can offer a perfect screen, helping to provide breathing space and some privacy from your neighbors. This is probably most valuable in warm weather, when you want to open your windows and make the most of the little outdoor space you have, but evergreens will enable you to maintain a screen all year-round. There is often a particular pleasure to be had in the seasonal changes your plants show and in the challenge of making the display look good at all times. Plants can also be used to hide unsightly views so that the scene from your windows is uplifting rather than depressing.

The colors and perfumes of flowers are always a delight, but if you long to harvest your own home-grown food, don't let

Gardening in containers (above) means that you can grow unusual plants side by side—here calla lilies and calamondin orange—and offers the chance to add plants to any space that is attractive architecturally (left) but offers little soil.

lack of space deter you. Fruit and vegetables can be grown in containers with great success, and while you are not likely to produce large crops, your enjoyment of them will probably be out of all proportion to their size. Careful choice of varieties will enable you to sample delicacies that are not available in the supermarket, and they will certainly be fresher than anything else you are likely to buy.

Encouraging wildlife

Plants growing outside will be visited by a number of wild creatures, some of them more welcome than others. There will be pests, of course, but there will also be a range of more welcome creatures. Bees will visit flowers for both pollen and nectar; ladybugs, lacewings, and a variety of other insects—beneficial or otherwise—will be seen. Miniature water gardens may be graced by dragonflies, and nectar-rich blooms will attract butterflies. Where plants provide cover, perching positions, and a free food supply in the form of berries, seeds, or insect life, birds will often follow.

It is, perhaps, especially important that children be given the chance to find out firsthand about living things, particularly when they live in an otherwise sterile urban environment. Gardening on such a small scale will be very appealing to them: they will not be overwhelmed as they might be by larger areas. At the other end of the age spectrum, elderly people, too, may find their "no-garden" garden easier to enjoy and to keep under control when they no longer have the strength, stamina, or dexterity to maintain a larger plot. This applies also to a range of people with physical limitations on their abilities.

There are few environments that cannot be improved by plants. Boost your confidence by starting with something cheap and cheerful, such as nasturtiums from seed or a few pots of bright bedding plants. In this book you should find all the guidance you need on choosing plants and techniques to suit your situation, but be prepared to experiment. No one can say exactly how a plant will react to a particular set of conditions, and you could have some pleasant surprises. At the very least, it will make life more interesting.

"No-garden" situations

We have broadly defined "no-gardens" as areas where there is little or no soil in which to plant, but that still leaves a number of widely differing situations. What they all have in common is the restriction on space and planting possibilities that needs to be overcome. The types of situation can be conveniently split into three main categories: no ground space *(pp.16–19)*; little ground space, such as terraces *(pp.20–25)*; and slightly larger ground space, such as roof gardens and patios *(pp.26–33)*.

No ground space

There can be no argument that this fits the description of having no yard. It is a situation probably most typical of an upper-floor apartment, where the dwelling has no horizontal surface outdoors except, perhaps, for a window ledge. Vertical walls have to provide all the growing space for plants.

Restricted as it is, this situation can still support an attractive plant display. Obviously, containers are essential,

Begonias, petunias, and trailing lobelia (above) have been used for this brilliantly colorful window box outside a country cottage. A similar grouping (right), but with a different color scheme, helps to mask an unattractive view from a town house.

and they will have to be fairly small containers, too, which means that extra attention will need to be paid to feeding and watering. The containers must be secured firmly to the wall, not balanced on window ledges. While they may appear quite safe when the plants in them are small, they will become increasingly top-heavy as the plants grow. In hot weather, soil mixes dry out quickly, and the rootball and pot become much lighter in weight as the day goes on, so that the slightest breeze or movement nearby may cause the container to topple over. Not only will this ruin your plants, it could cause damage and injury to properties or people below.

A large variety of wall pots and troughs is available *(see pp.84–85)*, many of which have mounting holes so that they

"No-garden" situations

can be screwed to the wall, but the number and position of these holes is sometimes inadequate for good support. Only small, lightweight containers are suitable for attaching directly to a wall without additional support, and adding a metal bracket beneath the container gives extra security and peace of mind. If there is a suitable downspout, special rings that hold small pots can sometimes be clipped around it.

Window boxes and hanging baskets

These often give some of the most eye-catching displays and with careful planting, can be attractive all year-round. The types of window ledge and window opening need to be taken into account when deciding on the style of window box *(see pp.84–85)* and the way it is attached. Brackets are essential; a fully planted window box is heavy, even when lightweight materials and soil mixes are used.

Hanging baskets are always popular, and again there are many styles available. Because the basket is viewed in the round, it is held away from the wall on a bracket or hung from an overhead support. Don't underestimate the weight of a basket filled with soil and plants, especially when it is freshly watered. Because the security of the baskets is so important, examine the wall on which they are to be fixed carefully. Old crumbling brickwork or loose plaster will not provide good anchor points, and special fasteners may be needed for hollow walls. A good hardware store will be able to advise you on the best type.

Where possible, use a ladder outside the building to gain access to the wall in order to fit the container supports, rather than lean out of a window. But remember that you will need access to the containers for watering, feeding, deadheading, and replanting, so you must be able to reach them easily and safely from inside—it may be safer and simpler to pay a handyman to set the brackets in place. Consider also whether you want to decorate the outside of the building for the benefit of passers-by or whether you want to be able to see the display from inside. Remember, if you hang pots and baskets where they can be enjoyed from indoors, they will reduce the amount of light entering rooms through the windows.

Walls reflect a great deal of heat, and in sunny locations, plants will dry out rapidly, especially if it is windy. Little rain is likely to reach the containers, and they may need watering several times a day in hot weather. Surplus water must be free to drain away without causing a problem for people and

These large, well-grown baskets show how varied planting can be while still following the scheme of bedding plants—geraniums, busy lizzie, petunias, and trailing lobelia—in hot or cool shades; taller plants such as fuchsia; and trailers such as variegated vinca, with cream-and-green leaves.

Barely visible from inside the building, these hanging baskets (above), uniformly massed with summer annuals, are a treat for people walking past on the street below. Watering such hanging baskets can be a problem, best solved by using a pulley to raise and lower them or by using a watering wand, which is a rigid extension to a hose.

Planters set on the retaining wall of this balcony and well filled with geraniums and petunias provide brilliant color and extra privacy, while cascades of Virginia creeper break the starkness of the white walls.

properties below, so choose containers with capacious drip saucers or self-watering planters, or hanging baskets on a pulley system that makes watering easier.

Choosing your plants

The most popular plants for wall pots, hanging baskets, and window boxes are free-flowering bedding plants, with some upright specimens and trailers. You can also grow climbers, either self-clinging or supported on a trellis, but because there is relatively little soil in a container, perennial climbers are likely to be short-lived and annuals are probably better.

An advantage of smaller containers is that the plants can be replaced quite cheaply as they pass their best. Individual plants can also be removed easily if they are kept in their own pots inside a window box. Keeping wall containers attractive during the winter in cold regions can be a challenge. The small volume of soil mix means plant roots are subject to damage from exposure and frost-heaving, even though the warmth coming through house walls can help to protect them.

AVOIDING STRUCTURAL DAMAGE

When drilling holes in outside walls, use a power drill fitted with the correct size and type of bit. With brick walls, it may be safer to drill into the brickwork than into the mortar if the mortar is soft or crumbling. But if the container is going to be removed later, you will be left with a permanent hole in the brick; making the hole in the mortar allows it to be filled in more easily.

The best device to use in walls are wall anchors, such as lead or expansion anchors that open up to grip the wall as the bolt is tightened. Another method is to drill holes, insert pieces of wooden dowelling, then screw directly into the dowelling. For extra security, attach a flat piece of wood to the wall using wall anchors and screw the bracket to the wood—this helps to spread the load. Always put any extra screws into the top of a bracket rather than the base, since it is the top that has to bear the maximum load.

Walls, fences, alleys, and walkways

There is a world of difference between having only a vertical wall on which to grow your plants and having even the tiniest area of horizontal space in which to place a few containers. Some very unlikely corners can be brightened up with a little imagination and some well-chosen plants.

A narrow bed against the house wall filled with climbing roses, bedding plants, and a few plants in pots enlivens this walkway.

Walls and fences

These have an important role to play in supporting wall pots and hanging baskets, but if it is possible to use the ground at the base of the wall, many more opportunities are opened up. It may be feasible to make planting holes by lifting pavers or breaking up small areas of concrete so that plants can be set directly into soil at the base of the wall. This makes growing perennial plants and shrubs possible. With room for roots to spread under the hard surface, plants should have better access to nutrients and moisture and so grow larger and be easier to care for. It is often the case, however, that there is no soil to speak of beneath the surface, but even if you cannot add suitable soil to make a planting pocket, climbers can still be grown in containers placed at the base of the wall. The size and weight of containers is less restricted when they are placed on the ground, which allows more ambitious planting.

Massed hydrangeas (above) fill beds at the base of the wall on each side of the door, which opens right onto the street.

Climbers and plants in a variety of pots, on a trellis, and on the ground turn the alleyway (right) into a lush, inviting garden.

Shrubby wall plants such as firethorn or cotoneaster and climbers like clematis, Boston ivy, and honeysuckle are all possibilities. Make sure that the plants will have sufficient air circulation when positioning containers.

As well as your own house wall, there may be garden walls, boundary walls, sheds, and adjoining property walls that you can use to support plants. But where the structures do not belong to you, make sure you have the permission of their owners before attaching any hardware such as bolts, nails, or trelliswork to any wall or fence, as this could be viewed as having damaged the structure.

Alleys and walkways

Such areas are commonly found between blocks of apartments and pairs of semidetached houses, as well as at the end of row houses and between a house and its garage. They are designed to allow outside access to the rear of the properties, generally with the minimum waste of space, so they are nearly always narrow and often shaded. Wind tunnels can form in narrow passageways, making them less than ideal places for growing plants, but this effect can be prevented or decreased by adding a gate at one or both ends of the alley.

Where space allows, set plants in containers along the walkways and use the walls to support climbers and wall plants; shade-lovers and foliage plants are probably the best choice. Sometimes it is possible to span the top of the walkway with timbers supported on sturdy uprights or attached to the walls to make a sort of pergola on which climbers can be trained to form a green roof. They are likely to grow more vigorously in the better light there, but they will cut down the amount of light that filters through to plants below. In sunny locations, the shade they give may be welcome; enclosed spaces in full sun can become uncomfortably warm as the heat is bounced off the adjoining walls.

But don't forget that the purpose of the walkway is to allow access, often for bulky loads, and it is easy to obstruct it with too many containers or overgrown plants.

Paths, entrances, and steps

A path—usually leading to the front door of a house, but also sometimes to the back—is frequently flanked by railings, walls, or hard-surfaced areas unsuitable for planting. Its individual shape, design, and material needs to be considered when deciding on how to plant it.

The path should look pleasing, and it may be worth replacing one that is old, damaged, or simply unattractive. Depending on its width, containers of plants can line each side or be staggered along it. Spreading alpines can be planted at the sides if space allows, but remember that the path's primary purpose is to give access and impeding it with mounds of creeping plants can be a hazard. If there are walls or fences beside the path, you can train climbing plants up them, but avoid prickly specimens whose stems may scratch passers-by or rampant growers that will restrict room on the path.

Clothed with creeping foliage plants, steps up to an entrance (above) blend in with their surroundings. The soft color of the brick path, the geraniums, and the flowering shrub (left) echo the shade of the walls, creating an inviting entrance, while an eclectic selection of plant containers (right) up wooden porch steps provide instant appeal.

Entrances

Front paths and entrances are particularly important because they give visitors their first impression of your home. Often, a front path runs straight from the pavement a relatively short distance to the front door; in this instance, the door will naturally form the focal point to which the eye is drawn. Planting along the path should usually reinforce this. A short path can be made to look longer by planting larger specimens near the road and decreasing the size of plants and their containers as they approach the door, while smaller plants at the front and larger plants closest to the door will make the entrance appear more imposing and give it extra emphasis. Formality is often favored in this situation, with symmetrical plantings on either side of the door and path; a pair of identical plants, such as juniper or boxwood, are favorite subjects to stand guard at each side of the entrance.

Steps

The entrance to a house often consists of a flight of steps, whether it is going up to the front door or down to a basement. The tiered arrangement is ideal for displaying plants, and groups of containers placed here are attractive. Keep them well to the sides of the steps and take care that they do not make access to the handrail difficult.

Back paths and porches

At the back of the house, the path will usually be viewed from the building. There is unlikely to be an obvious focal point at the far end, so interest will be centred on the path itself, and since this area is more frequently viewed by the home owner than a visitor, a less formal approach is often better. Although the main object with small spaces is normally to make them appear larger, a long narrow area may benefit from some foreshortening by placing staggered groups of plants on the path rather than emphasizing its narrowness by setting plants along each side.

By framing the door with greenery and flowers, plants can be used to emphasize the path's arrival at the house. There is usually the opportunity to spread upward, using the house walls, and there may be a porch that climbers can scramble over. If this is simply a roof attached to the doorway by brackets, it will bear less weight than if it is supported by uprights, so choose the plants carefully, avoiding very dense, vigorous specimens. Plants with scented flowers or aromatic foliage are ideal here, and they will also make it a pleasant place to sit on a sunny evening.

Terraces

The ornate woodwork forms an attractive frame for the troughs and hanging baskets on this terrace. Although the terrace is too small to sit on, the colorful plantings can be viewed and enjoyed from indoors.

Although terraces are most often a feature of apartments, houses may also have terraces on an upper story, especially if there is a good view to be enjoyed. Some terraces are constructed primarily to afford access to the outside of the building for maintenance; these are usually narrow, with just enough room to step out on to them. Others can serve as an extra room, with enough space for several people to sit outside comfortably.

The construction of the terrace must be taken into account when deciding what plants you can grow there; the most important aspect is its load-bearing capability. It may be of a cantilevered design, jutting out from the building with no visible means of support; it may be supported by pillars or posts from ground level; or be built as a flat roof to a room below. A supported terrace usually looks safer to the unqualified eye, but this is not necessarily the case, and if you have any doubts about a terrace's load-bearing capacity, you should arrange for a structural engineer to inspect it.

Plastic and fiberglass containers can mimic terra-cotta or glazed pottry. Their attractive style and light weight are suitable for a terrace garden.

The floor of the terrace should be waterproof, particularly if there is living space immediately below. And since there is likely to be considerably more run-off where regular watering is taking place than from a terrace on which there are no plants, you should check that provision for drainage is adequate. Take particular care where the living space below does not belong to you, since you will be held responsible for any damage to the property caused by your activities. Third-party insurance cover should be arranged, and you should check that your terrace garden is covered by your homeowner's or renter's insurance. If the property is rented, it is always a good policy to obtain the landlord's agreement to your proposals first.

If the terrace of a reasonably modern dwelling is large enough to be used as a living area, with access through full-length doors, it is fairly safe to assume that it has been constructed to a sufficiently high standard to be used as a container garden. On older properties, however, this may not be the case; building standards were lower, and wear and tear may have weakened the structure further.

Lightweight materials

However sturdy the terrace, it makes sense to keep the load to a minimum by using lightweight plastic containers rather than those of terra-cotta or clay and soilless potting mixes rather than soil-based types. But these have their drawbacks; soilless mixes require more frequent watering, and you may need to secure the containers to the floor or walls to prevent them being blown over. Remember that freshly watered soil mix weighs considerably more than that which is just moist and that as plants grow they will not only weigh more themselves but will demand increasing amounts of water. It may be tempting to construct raised beds on the terrace rather than to use containers, but the extra weight, plus drainage problems and the risk of damage to the property through penetrating dampness, may make this a less desirable option.

The more attractive you make the terrace, the more use it is likely to get and

Tempting though it may be to fill your entire terrace area with plants, leave enough space for a couple of chairs and a table so that you can sit out and enjoy your surroundings.

the greater the potential for accidents. Before using any terrace as a minigarden, check the surrounds. These may be solid walls, but railings are also common; on older properties, particularly, they may not be safe—make sure the space between them is not wide enough for a child to squeeze through. Safety glass can be used as a barrier that will not obstruct light or detract from the view.

As with any situation where floor space is limited, climbing plants are valuable, but because many terraces are exposed to strong winds, supports for climbers need to be well secured. Keep the plant growth thinned so that wind can filter through; if wind meets a solid wall of foliage, the plants and their supports are likely to be blown over. Make sure that containers can be moved fairly easily so that access to the outside of the building is still possible and resist the temptation to balance pots on the edges of surrounding walls or railings. Sooner or later they will fall, and they are almost bound to do some damage in the process.

Roof gardens

Skillfully sited supports and plantings help to mask unattractive features without obstructing the view from this roof garden.

Some city dwellers are lucky enough to have a slightly larger ground space to cultivate. A flat roof, for instance, offers a tempting prospect for making a garden, and roof gardens can be spectacularly successful, often offering a degree of privacy difficult to find elsewhere in a densely populated urban location. The sheer unexpectedness of a plant haven so far from the ground gives it the feeling of an oasis, a truly secret garden.

Who does the roof belong to?

A flat roof often tops a block of apartments, and the first step is to find out who owns the roof and/or is responsible for its maintenance; before going farther you will need to come to an arrangement with all the interested parties. The other occupants of the block may be more than happy to allow you sole use of the roof in return for taking the responsibility for its upkeep, or they may wish to share the roof garden, with everyone contributing to the expenses. Either way, you will need to get legal advice and arrange suitable insurance for both yourself and third parties.

Much of what has already been said about terraces also applies to roof gardens. The roof may have been constructed with a garden in mind, but it is more likely that you will want to convert a presently unused roof.

Gaining access

Take a good look at the access. It may be fairly simple to clamber out on to the roof, but will you be able to carry equipment and plants up to it? And how about a water supply? The expense of installing a faucet and water supply to the roof is probably a wise investment, and you should also consider installing a power supply if you want to use the roof garden in the evening.

The roof surface must be waterproof and in good repair. Under a roof garden it will probably have to stand up to more

A feeling of space, of two "rooms," is created here by the contrast between the shady back wall and the sunny seating area.

On this roof garden, shaped trellises and raised beds filled with shrubs and climbing plants help to hide an unsightly wall and drain pipe.

wear and tear than was envisaged when it was laid. Check the drainage and ensure that nothing you do will impede it. Options for suitable flooring material range from conventional or lightweight paving slabs to gravel, shredded bark, artificial turf, and attractive wood decking.

Windbreaks

Because the garden will be relatively high up, strong winds are likely to damage plants and their supports and accelerate moisture loss. Some form of windbreak will improve this and can often be combined with extending the walls, which for safety reasons should reach at least waist height. The barrier can take the form of brickwork, screening, or railings; above this height, trelliswork to support climbing plants or wind-resistant hedging plants can provide shelter. Safety-glass panels, professionally installed, are also excellent, or you can use small-mesh screening on the windward side only.

The patterned paved floor is in itself an attractive feature of this sunny roof garden, which leads down to the one shown above.

Weight distribution

Raised beds are possible on a roof garden, but, as with terraces, weight distribution and drainage problems usually make containers a better option. Wooden pallets help to spread the load of large and heavy containers. It is always a good idea to raise containers off the ground, both to ensure good drainage and to prevent root growth emerging through the base of the pot from damaging the roof surface. Ask a structural engineer to advise you on load bearing and also to identify, if possible, where the load-bearing supports are so that you can set the heaviest items in the safest place.

Enclosed gardens

An enclosed patio can be crowded with plants, as if it were an outdoor conservatory, to be viewed from inside the house.

Alternatively, it can be a secluded corner in which to sit in the sun and enjoy a few plants chosen for their fragrance and color.

A paved area, usually adjoining the house, a patio is a place for relaxation and enjoyment. It may form a small part of a larger garden, but often the patio is all there is—a self-contained area that becomes a "patio garden."

Patio gardens

Enclosed patios can often be sun traps, especially where boundary walls provide shelter from the wind. The paved surface reflects the sun's warmth, and the temperature inside the patio garden can be much higher than that outside. This can present difficult conditions for plants, which may suffer from moisture stress and sun scorch; in warm, sunny climates some form of shade is essential. Pergolas or similar structures over which vines, roses, or wisteria can climb offer both shelter from wind and pleasant dappled shade below. Where patio gardens are not on the sunny side of the house, high walls can cast permanent shade and can be a delightful cool retreat in which to relax at the end of a grimy, city day. Although the choice of plants is more restricted, some choice specimens need shade to grow well.

The formal design of this courtyard is emphasized by the central fountain and pool, clipped evergreens, and palms in pots.

Courtyard gardens

The distinctions between a courtyard and a patio are rather blurred. Originally a courtyard was a square or rectangular open space entirely surrounded by buildings; modern "courtyard developments" are based on the same principle. A courtyard is always regular in shape and often has a central feature. It usually has a hard surface, such as cobblestones or gravel, and is always surrounded by walls.

Formality is the keynote; symmetrical planting schemes, traditional-style containers and ornaments, plant standards, clipped topiary, and regulated color schemes all help to give the right effect. A small pool, fountain, or tree makes an excellent focal point; a sundial, birdbath, striking ornament, or well-planted container would also look good.

This traditional courtyard garden at the centre of a house is complete with trees, classical ornaments, and a stone birdbath.

Enclosed gardens

Basements

An area that lies below the level of its surroundings, a basement is generally found where a house is built on sloping ground: part of the higher side of the slope is dug out to enable full use to be made of the lower floor. The size of the basement area can vary considerably but it is rarely large; it may be big enough for access down a flight of steps, or it may simply allow light through a single window.

Basements are usually a feature of older houses and are traditionally depressing areas, frequently gloomy and sunless. Ironically, it is often the kitchen that looks on to the basement—the room that may form the main living area for the whole family and where a great deal of time is spent. When the house was built, it was probably a servant who was condemned to a view of a plain brick wall; today's householder demands a more cheerful view.

Because a basement is a sunken area, there is bound to be less light than at ground level, and what light there is decreases as the depth of the basement increases. Plants grown in such a position are likely always to be reaching upward for light, and sun-loving plants will probably fail entirely, but there are plenty of attractive shade-tolerant specimens to choose from. The low light levels can often be considerably improved by painting the walls white or a light color; the floor can also be painted with floor paint, covered with light-colored stone chips or gravel, or resurfaced with suitable paving slabs. If there is a brighter outside area, containers of plants can be rotated, giving them a fairly short spell to cheer up the basement before bringing them back up to the daylight to recuperate. Supplementing the natural light with artificial lighting may be a possibility.

Small spreading plants set in holes in the paving give a charming checkerboard effect to this yard. The white-painted fence and cheerful planting have transformed an otherwise dreary area into a bright, airy space.

SHARED GARDENS

Communal open spaces are increasingly becoming a feature of modern housing developments. Attractively planted areas make the houses more desirable, but they can often be frustrating for gardeners. Usually contractors are employed to maintain the gardens, and because the landscape has been carefully planned, owners are often prevented from taking any part in the planting designs. Sometimes they are allowed to tend their immediate "gardens," but with strict limitations on the size and type of plants that may be used or the structures that may be erected.

Before buying such a property, check any limitations on your gardening activities. It is intensely disappointing to discover, too late, that you can play no part in maintaining or improving your surroundings when they may be what attracted you initially.

In a warm climate, a basement area such as this, with creeper-clad walls and overhanging bushes, makes a safe, cool place for children to play.

Water can also be a problem. The proximity of the building will prevent useful amounts of rain from reaching plants, but the basement might receive sufficient run-off to cause flooding, and it can be flooded by over-enthusiastic watering. Efficient drainage is essential to prevent dampness from penetrating the house, and drain holes must not be blocked by dead leaves, soil, or containers full of plants.

On the plus side, basements have ready-made supports for plants in the form of walls, which can be covered in climbers, and they are sheltered from wind, forming true "sunken gardens." But bear in mind that cold air sinks, and it will tend to flow downward and settle in basement areas, making them unsuitable for tender plants in winter.

Utility area

Usually paved and surrounded by walls or fencing, this area is often no more than a place for trash cans. As with a basement, simply painting the walls in light colors and breaking up a concrete floor and, if the area is small, replacing it with paving can be a tremendous improvement. Climbing plants and shrubs in containers can be trained on the walls, plants on trellises can screen sheds and trash cans, and a wooden pergola covered with climbers will provide privacy and a pleasant place to sit.

Conservatories and garden rooms

An increasingly popular feature of homes today is the "conservatory," sunroom, or Florida room, often simply a light, airy, extra room for family use, complete with carpet and soft furnishings. This is a long way from the conservatory's original purpose as a type of ornate greenhouse attached to the home, primarily for growing plants, usually exotic species that required warmth and shelter and a lot of expert care.

A conservatory may be made from plastic, wood, or metal and has glass walls, usually to ground level, and generally a transparent roof as well. Because the conservatory is in frequent use by people, the panels should be made from reinforced glass for safety. In very sunny climates, the roof may be solid. As a general rule, conservatories are "add-ons." Their position is often dictated by exposure—a sunny site is preferable in cold climates, a shaded one where the sun is intense—but they tend to be more common in the back of a house than the front.

Converting an indoor room

If you inherit a conservatory, you may want to convert it from an indoor room to an outdoor room, if climate permits. A suitable floor is essential: paving slabs, stonework, bricks, or gravel will give the strongest garden feel, while quarry or ceramic tiles give a "halfway house" effect. Make sure that the flooring will stand up to being frequently flooded with water and that there is efficient drainage. If there is sufficient depth of soil, planting beds can be made in the floor; otherwise you can build raised beds or rely entirely on groups of containers.

The good light, warmth from the sun, and shelter from wind make a conservatory the perfect place for growing plants. Nearly all plants—not just exotic or tender species—will flourish in such conditions. As in all confined spaces, care must be taken to choose suitable plants and to keep them under control. When choosing plants, don't be too ambitious. Trees and vigorous shrubs are best confined to containers. Small shrubs, perennials, and bedding plants can safely be grown in the borders, but remember that they are likely to make much larger, faster-growing plants than they would in the open garden. Take advantage of the protected position to try some choice, slower-growing, and dwarf varieties. In cold areas it is tempting to use the conservatory to grow tender plants, but you will usually need heat to bring them safely through the winter.

Shade and ventilation

While the warmth of the conservatory will be appreciated in the winter and at each end of the growing season, in summer the problem will be too much heat. Shading is essential; roller roof and wall blinds are the easiest method but can be expensive. Paint-on shading materials are cheap but unattractive. Climbers on trellises can be effective, since as the season progresses they will grow to provide increasing shade when it is needed.

Good ventilation is essential, too. There should be opening vents in the roof as well as in the side walls; have them fitted as extras if necessary. Doors opening to the outside are also useful for ventilation even if there is virtually nowhere to step out to. Fresh air is needed to prevent overheating, and it will maintain the buoyant atmosphere required for healthy plant growth. It will also enable you to feel that you are sitting in a protected garden rather than an exotic hothouse.

Screen houses

A screen house—a treated-wood structure to which wire or plastic screening is stapled—is generally a feature of warmer climates. It is much like a conservatory, with fine mesh netting replacing the glass, and can vary in size from a small porch to a sizable room. The mesh affords minimal protection from the weather, but it does cut down wind and offer shade from strong sun, making a protected spot for growing and enjoying plants—and it will keep out troublesome insects. The floor, which is often made from wood as well, should slope away from the house so that any water will drain away.

The wooden slatted walls and roof in this garden room (right) have been made in removable sections and provide welcome shade in summer, and when removed, sun in winter, creating a haven in which to grow tender plants for cutting, such as these birds-of-paradise, or Strelitzia.

Assessing your own situation

Once you have decided that you are going to make the best of the space you have for growing plants, you need to think carefully about exactly how you are going to do it. No two situations are exactly the same: even if your circumstances are very similar to those of your neighbor, you will probably have quite different ideals and capabilities. It helps to sit down with a notebook and work your way through a list of exactly what you have and what you would like (or feel you are able) to do with it. The smaller the space, the more precious it becomes, and the less tolerant you are likely to be of mistakes and wasted effort.

First, outline the basic facilities you have, then make a note of what you would like to achieve. Go on to make more detailed notes about your own situation—on the following pages we will go through several of the points you need to bear in mind, some of which may not immediately occur to you. After you have done this, go back to your original objectives and see if you need to adjust them or would like to add to them in light of the information you have gathered. It's well worth spending some time on this, since it is often the case that the smaller the space, the more planning is required in using it to full advantage.

What space do you have?

Which of the three main categories we have covered fits your "no-garden" best—no ground space, a small amount of ground space, or slightly larger ground space? Make a note of exactly what it is—terrace, patio garden, roof garden, and so on—and its overall size. If applicable, look into its load-bearing capacity and structural details, getting expert advice where necessary. (It helps to have a good idea of what you would like to do with the area so that you can discuss all the possibilities with an engineer.)

How much time do you have?

You may be able to do "little and often" on a daily basis or have only a few hours on weekends. How much interest do you have in gardening? Do you want to spend a lot of time on challenging plants and designs, or are you more concerned with getting the maximum results for the minimum of effort?

You may lack confidence in your horticultural skills and want to start with something quick and simple, moving on to more "difficult" specimens as your experience increases, or you may already be a skilled gardener who has had to give up a larger garden and wants to make the most of the possibilities now available.

What do you want?

There are many good reasons for growing plants around your home. You may agree with some or all of those that have already been mentioned, or you may have a different set of ideas. It will help to avoid mistakes if you have a clear idea of your aims and your likes and dislikes; to help you think it through, the main points to consider are listed below.

POINTS YOU SHOULD CONSIDER

COLOR In a small space it is usually wiser to decide on a color theme rather than to mix plants at random. If you want somewhere to relax, flowers in soft pastel shades may suit you, or consider the ultimate in calming color schemes, a white garden, where pure white flowers gleam against soft green foliage—particularly effective in the evening light. Hot colors—brilliant scarlets, oranges, and yellows—give a quite different effect from cool blues, purples, greens, and white.

FOLIAGE Flowers are not the only decorative feature of plants. Along with the many shades of green, gray, cream, blue, purple, red, yellow, and orange that exist in foliage, there are the shapes and textures of the leaves to take into account—the large, bold hand-shapes of fatsia; cool, frilly ferns; spiky New Zealand flax; puckered hosta; the delicate filigree of steely blue rue. Some leaves, such as those of soft, velvety lamb's ears, beg to be touched; others, like prickly hollies and tooth-edged agaves, are less than inviting.

FRAGRANCE In a small area this is even more enjoyable than in a large garden. Jasmine, honey-scented petunias, philadelphus, and butterfly-attracting buddleia are some of the scents of summer; shrubby honeysuckles, witch hazel, daphne, violets, viburnum, and wintersweet give off amazingly powerful fragrances on cold winter days. Foliage can be strongly aromatic, especially when

Suit your "no-garden" to your life-style but remember to leave enough space among the plants so that you can sit out and enjoy it.

bruised or rubbed; Mexican orange, Russian sage, myrtle, rosemary, wormwood, and many others have fascinating spicy scents.

TIME OF DAY When your "no-garden" is most often used may influence you; perhaps bright morning sun makes it the ideal place to have breakfast, or maybe you want a place to sit out in the evening, when you come home from work. If evenings are important, fragrant, night-opening flowers, such as flowering tobacco (nicotiana), are more appropriate than those that fold their petals as soon as the sun sets, and some form of soft artificial lighting will greatly extend your use of the area.

SEASONAL INTEREST Although summer is the most obvious time to enjoy plants, you may also want to plan your design so that it is pleasing year-round. Once the summer bedding plants have faded, do you put the gardening tools away until next spring? Or do you extend your gardening into fall and winter, with containers of shrubs for fall color, fall-blooming plants, evergreens with bold foliage for interest throughout the year, and winter-flowering bulbs?

SCREENING Protection from neighbors or nearby windows may be valuable to you, and the positioning of tall plants and climbers can help greatly. If your "no-garden" area is in full sun, plants or a pergola or arbor to provide shade in warm weather will be important. And will your plants be viewed mainly from inside or outside the house? It will make all the difference in the way you arrange them.

Assessing your own situation

In a narrow passageway, set flowering plants where they will benefit from whatever sun shines on the area. Climbing plants will reach upward for the light they need to thrive.

Exposure and light

All plants need light to grow. If deprived of light entirely, the plant will lose its chlorophyll and the leaves and stems will become white instead of green. More importantly, this will prevent the plant from manufacturing food, and it will eventually die.

Few plants are faced with complete darkness, but the amount, duration, and quality of light varies greatly from one location to another, and the growth of plants will suffer progressively if the light they receive is not adequate. Small areas are more often likely to suffer from lack of light than larger gardens, because the surrounding objects that block out light remain the same height and cast the same amount of shade regardless of the size of the plot. So the smaller plot receives a far greater proportion of shade than a large plot in a similar situation.

If your "no-garden" is shaded or partially shaded, you will need to know the extent of the problem. Draw a rough scale diagram and note the direction in which the plot faces. Sketch the position and extent of the shade at different times of the day, say 9AM, noon, 3PM and 6PM. (If possible, carry this out in all four seasons, but the main growing season is obviously the most important time.) You may find that some areas are in constant shadow, whereas others receive several hours of sun at different times of the day.

Density of shade

Even in an area that receives no direct sun, the type of shade can be quite variable. Density of shade is difficult for the human eye to judge accurately, and a photographic light meter is useful for determining just how gloomy the different parts of your growing space are. A plot that appears to be

An area that gets too much sun can be turned into a cool green retreat during hot weather by a slatted roof built over part of it and a large tilting garden umbrella to provide shade all day.

more or less evenly shady can, in fact, have much lighter and darker areas within it, and this can be important when it comes to positioning the plants.

Shade can be cast by surrounding buildings, fences and walls, shrubs, hedges, and trees. It may be possible to remove some obstacles to allow more light through; even if they don't belong to you, you may find the owners happy to cooperate if approached in the right way. Trees can be lopped or thinned; hedges and fences can be lowered. Buildings and high walls are obviously permanent features, but painting walls white or in light colors, or even siting a mirror in a suitable location, can improve the overall brightness.

Plants vary considerably in the amount of light they need to remain healthy; as a general rule, those with silver, blue, or variegated foliage need bright, sunny conditions and will not thrive in a gloomy situation. Silver plants tend to be covered in fine hairs that are meant to protect them from too much sun in their native climates; variegated plants may grow satisfactorily in shade, but they tend to lose their leaf markings and become plain green. Other plants are well adapted to low light levels, and these are the ones to choose *(see p.162)*.

Light from one side

Many small areas, and terraces in particular, suffer from a one-sided light source. Plants grow toward the light, and you will soon find your plants leaning in that direction. This spoils their appearance and makes plants in containers more likely to topple over. To keep the plants upright and bushy, turn the containers a quarter-turn every few days. Those plants that are in the ground or in raised beds can sometimes be evened-up by careful pruning, but a strongly one-sided light source will always produce plants that grow toward it.

Too much sun

The sun-trap patio or balcony can be an inhospitable place. Constant, bright sun can be almost as much of a problem as excessive shade, causing delicate foliage to become scorched and soil mixes and plants to dry out rapidly. Fortunately, the problem is usually more easily solved than that of too much shade and it may only be temporary—to protect seedlings at the beginning of the season, for example.

Once again, note the direction the area faces and the times when it receives the strongest, hottest sun. You can then provide shading to give some relief when the plants most need it. A trellis covered by climbers, bamboo fencing, awnings, and plastic shade netting could all be used.

As with shady areas, choice of plants is important *(see p.163)*. In a sun-baked plot you can grow sun-lovers that are drought tolerant and often have the bonus of brilliantly colored flowers. But don't be misled into thinking that you can necessarily grow exotic, tender specimens; you may have sufficient sun, but bear in mind the plants' minimum temperature requirements as well. Because the area is hot on sunny summer days doesn't mean it is mild enough for tender plants in the colder seasons.

Assessing your own situation

The brilliant scarlet berries of evergreen skimmia persist throughout the winter, and even the white spring flowers will survive some frost.

Climate

There are two ways in which to consider the climate of your gardening space—the macroclimate, or the prevailing weather conditions in the part of the world in which you live, and the microclimate, the climate of your immediate surroundings.

The big picture

When you are growing plants in a very small space, a lot of human intervention is needed to ensure that they survive, and this reduces the effect that the natural climate has upon their growth. For example, few small-space gardeners would rely on rainfall to supply all their plants' water requirements. However, one natural condition that retains its importance is temperature, particularly the likelihood of the plants being exposed to subfreezing temperatures. Each plant species has its own optimum temperature range for growth; outside this range growth will slow down or even stop, although the plant may remain alive. There are degrees of susceptibility to frost damage.

Plants that would usually be grown as houseplants, such as Swiss cheese plant, **Monstera deliciosa,** *and* **Fatsia japonica** *may flourish in a small sheltered patio, which can be several degrees warmer than an adjoining open garden.*

HARDY PLANTS These will survive frost, generally in a dormant state. Some plants have branches, and even foliage, with natural protection against cold weather. Others may have their top growth killed, but the roots will survive underground to produce new shoots the following spring. Some species will survive short spells of temperatures just below freezing but may be killed by repeated or prolonged frosts or temperatures that dip more sharply. You will occasionally see plants described as "marginally hardy," meaning that sometimes they survive low temperatures, sometimes they don't—it's a matter of luck.

There are hardy plants that will not themselves be harmed by frosts but their beauty may nevertheless be spoiled. The waxy, pink-white chalices of magnolia blossoms are reduced to unappealing brown mush by late spring frost, and if one cold night turns the centers of strawberry blossoms black, you can wave good-bye to fruit in summer.

TENDER PLANTS For certain plants, temperatures that drop to freezing or below spell death; water in the cells expands as it freezes, ruptures the cell walls, and the plant tissue collapses. Such plants are known as tender, frost-tender, or nonhardy. In an area subject to frost, tender plants can be grown only in warm weather, once the risk of frost is over. The average date of the last frost for your area can usually be obtained from the local Environment office, but this may vary from one year to another, and you should allow plenty of leeway before putting tender plants outdoors. Most tender plants you buy will have been raised in a greenhouse, where conditions are warmer and more protected than those outside. Putting them outdoors right away can hinder their growth or even kill them, and they must be gradually acclimatized. This usually means putting them, in their containers, first in a sheltered spot outside, then bringing

A narrow basement area, filled with plants in hanging baskets, shows how an unpromising space can be clothed in green. The large mirror in the bathroom cleverly doubles the impact.

them indoors at night, then leaving them out night and day, and finally moving them to their final growing positions. This process is called hardening-off, and usually takes about a week to 10 days.

In temperate zones, some warmth-loving plants will survive the summer outdoors but never achieve their full potential because the temperatures are not high enough or the season is too short. Usually they fail to flower or fruit, but this may not be important if their foliage or growth pattern is reason enough to grow them.

Your own microclimate

There is no substitute for personal experience when it comes to microclimates, and it is worth buying a maximum/minimum thermometer and keeping a year-round record of temperatures, weather conditions, and other information on plant performance in your plot.

SMALL YARDS AND PATIOS Especially in urban areas, these often have a distinct microclimate. Cities tend to be several degrees warmer than the surrounding suburbs for several reasons: industrial and commercial processes release waste heat into the atmosphere; artificial heat leaks even from well-insulated buildings during winter; streets and buildings absorb the sun's warmth during the day and release it at night like giant storage heaters. City gardens tend to be surrounded by walls and buildings that protect them from wind and give them shelter. This may well extend the growing season at both ends and, if you have a particularly sheltered location, allow you to cultivate some of the more exotic plants for fun; your microclimate may be sufficiently different to coax them into a good display.

TERRACES, ROOF GARDENS, AND HANGING BASKETS On upper floors these can be very exposed; temperatures may be lower overall, and the wind can dry plants out and damage foliage and flowers. A basement or patio that is in constant shade will also be much cooler than one receiving at least some direct sun. Ironically, the most sheltered gardens are also sometimes the most prone to frost damage. Cold air behaves like water, flowing downhill and sinking to lower levels. If it cannot escape from the area—say, if it is stopped on its downhill run by a brick wall—the cold air is trapped and the site becomes a frost pocket, making plants within it more prone to damage than in neighboring spaces.

The spring-flowering Japanese quince,* Chaenomeles japonica, *and Dutch hyacinths thrive here in the protected microclimate provided by the wall, which shelters plants from wind and radiates warmth.

Assessing your own situation

The water supply

All plants need water to grow. In the wild, this is supplied by rain, but in "no-garden" gardens natural rainfall is unlikely to be sufficient. Plants grown in small areas or against walls are usually sheltered from rain, and the water doesn't reach their roots. Plants are also more likely to be in containers, which hold only a small volume of soil and so have a limited capacity for water storage. Vigorously growing plants soon fill their containers with roots, decreasing the space for water, while at the same time increasing the demand.

Hand in hand with water goes humidity—the amount of water vapor in the air. Most plants grow better in relatively humid conditions than in dry air, and even when sufficient water is available to the roots through the soil mix, the atmosphere can remain uncomfortably dry for them.

When to water

Water is becoming an increasingly valuable resource and you should try not to waste it. The best time to water is in the early morning. Watering plants in full sun can lead to leaf scorch, since water droplets on foliage act like magnifying lenses to intensify the sun's rays; the water will also evaporate more quickly and be wasted. But if plants show signs of severe wilting, they should be watered as quickly as possible, even if they are in the sunshine.

Many containers will need watering three times a day in hot, sunny weather. The "no-garden" gardener will, therefore, find watering a constant task, and the easier it can be made, the better. If daily watering entails constant trips from the plants through the living room to the kitchen in order to refill watering cans, it will soon become a hated chore. And many kitchen and bathroom faucets are simply not designed for filling large containers. So wherever possible, a faucet should be installed close to the plants; this is particularly relevant for roof gardens, where the water must be carried up stairs.

Watering can be carried out by means of cans, hoses, or a permanent watering system. For a fairly small number of plants, a watering can is sufficient. Choose one that is well balanced and not too heavy when full. Check that it will fit easily under your faucet. A long curved spout makes it simpler to get the water where you want it and a rose, or sprinkler head, will be useful for watering some plants. Hoses make watering quicker and easier, but it can be difficult to control the supply. Attaching a watering wand that allows you to switch off the supply will help, but make sure you buy good-quality hose and use tight-fitting connectors between the hose and the faucet and wand; otherwise, the water pressure could burst the hose or blow it off the faucet.

Growing plants that need little water, such as hardy daisies, geraniums, and echeveria (right), and mixing water-retaining granules with the soil mix help minimize water use.

The ultimate in labor-saving devices is an automated watering system. Computer-controlled systems are available to carry out watering in your absence, which can be a boon for vacations or if you are away often. Simpler soaker hoses or sprinkler systems can be set up permanently among the plants, ready to attach to a faucet and turn on as required; there are also plenty of "self-watering" containers, which generally incorporate a reservoir of water plus a wick system to keep the soil mix moist.

Drainage

Although drying out is a major problem with plants in containers, the soil mix must not remain saturated—efficient drainage is essential to enable air to penetrate to the roots. Moisten the soil mix thoroughly, right to the base of the pot, then allow the excess water to drain away. Think about where this water will go and whether it is likely to cause inconvenience or damage to your own or neighboring properties: drips from hanging baskets and wall pots can be particularly troublesome. You may need to consider some form of drainage system.

Subsidence

Plants growing too close to buildings can cause all sorts of problems in small gardens, but the main ones occur where trees are grown direct in garden soil. In certain types of clay soil, the large volume of moisture removed from it by a tree or large shrub can cause the soil to shrink, leading to subsidence and cracking of nearby buildings. Removing the offending tree does not necessarily help: the sudden increase in the amount of soil water can cause the soil to heave, leading to more or less the same effect on the buildings.

Plants grown in containers are safe unless the roots penetrate the soil beneath the container; raising containers off the ground slightly makes this less likely and also improves drainage. Wall plants and climbers set into soil at the base of walls are unlikely to cause damage because neither their root systems nor leaf area are extensive enough to make sufficient difference to the soil moisture levels.

Urban situations

Many "no-gardens" are likely to be in densely populated areas, and this brings its own problems. Our territorial instinct becomes intensified when we don't have all that much space of our own, and our defense of it often leads to surprisingly aggressive behavior. Trouble arises both when we feel our territory is being encroached upon, and when our neighbors feel that we are encroaching upon them.

A flourishing vine makes a "ceiling" for an outdoor room—neighbors are unlikely to protest a situation that simultaneously guards the owner's privacy and enhances their own view.

Avoiding trouble

Boundaries are a common cause of contention. Where possible, check the legal ownership of boundary walls and fences; this should appear on your property deed. If ownership is not clear, it is a good idea to ask neighbors whether they object to your attaching plant supports or similar to your side of a common wall. Remember that if your plants cause damage to property that is not your own, you could be liable to pay compensation; climbing plants have been known to damage woodwork, stucco, and mortar.

Always check that your homeowner's insurance covers you and third parties against accidents that could occur because of your plants. A hose left running could flood your own and neighboring premises, badly positioned and overweight containers may cause the collapse of a roof; an insecure pot or window box falling from an upper level may damage cars parked below or injure passersby. It is up to you to take all possible steps to ensure that accidents don't happen, but there is a limit to the number of problems you are able to anticipate.

There is plenty of potential for more minor annoyances, too. Your lush screen of climbing plants may provide you with privacy but deprive the adjoining property of sunlight. Leaves and petals fall not just on your own plot but may cause a nuisance to neighbors. Plants have no regard for boundaries, and branches, roots, and suckers can spread well beyond their own territory. In most instances, owners are within their rights to remove any part of a plant that trespasses on their property, even if their actions damage or kill the plant; it is up to gardeners to make sure they keep their plants within bounds.

Wooden trellises, lightly covered in creeper, and tall tripods with sweet peas and runner beans help to provide some privacy on this roof garden and to disguise the bleak surrounding walls.

Many disputes end up unnecessarily as costly, protracted legal cases; the only ones who gain from these are the lawyers. Common sense, thoughtfulness, and good communication should prevent things from going as far as this. Consider what impact your activities may have on other people at the planning stage and try to forestall possible difficulties by talking to the people concerned at the start.

Protecting yourself

In some situations you are far more likely to find yourself on the receiving end of a nuisance than being the cause of it. If your plot, or parts of it, are accessible to the public, it is a sad fact that you may find it subject to theft, vandalism, or simple carelessness that causes a great deal of damage.

Theft of plants, ornaments, and garden equipment is becoming increasingly common. Plants in containers are prime targets because they are relatively quick and easy to move; it has been known for the hanging baskets and window boxes of an entire street to be removed overnight, presumably to reappear within a few days at a tag sale or at a flea market. Several antitheft devices are available—hanging basket brackets that incorporate padlocks, chains, and locks to secure ornaments or tubs to brackets set in concrete, intruder alarms, and so on. Outdoor lighting is also a useful deterrent, but the types that are operated by sensing body heat or movement are not appropriate where legitimate passersby would trigger them frequently. Permanent, low-level lighting in such a situation is less irritating than the continual "on-off" operation of high-intensity security lights. Vandalism is another common concern and is often particularly prevalent where a house with an attractive display of plants is unusual. Whether it is through boredom, jealousy, resentment, or simply the distrust of anything that does not conform to the norm, such plant displays are often the target of destructive attacks, which can be heartbreaking as well as costly. Taking the same precautions as you would against theft can help prevent damage, but vandalism is more difficult to guard against. Special insurance policies for garden plants and equipment are available if such items are not covered by your homeowner's policy.

An airy trellis supporting shrubby foliage provides seclusion for this al fresco sitting and dining space but is unlikely to rob neighboring apartments of light.

If your plants are along a public walkway, they may be damaged unintentionally by people walking past them or taking a short cut across a corner of your yard. The remedy lies in planting those species, such as prickly hollies, that offer natural resistance to both theft and damage.

Special needs gardening

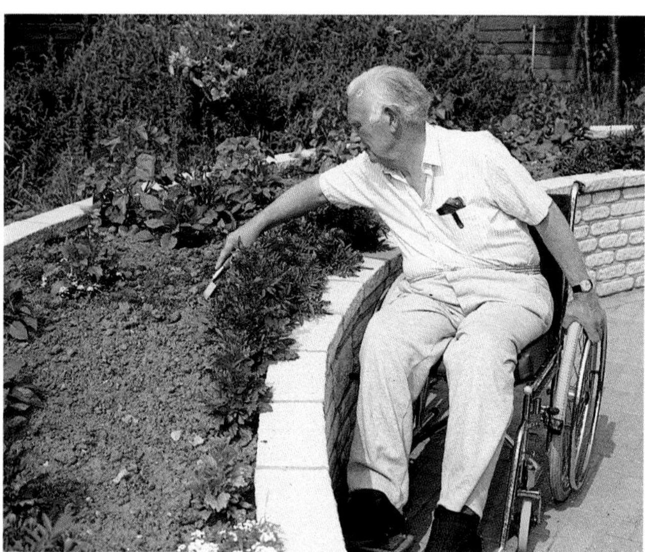

A gardener confined to a wheelchair can enjoy preparing the soil and tending plants in a raised bed without assistance.

There are many groups of people who require something a little different from their plants and gardening activities. They may be physically challenged in a number of ways, limiting the tasks they can do or the stimuli they can enjoy; they may have emotional or mental needs that can be at least partly fulfilled or helped by growing and appreciating plants. Among gardeners who could be classed as having special needs are those with chronic back trouble, blind people, those with arthritis, wheelchair users, and people with learning difficulties.

"No-garden" situations are often particularly appropriate for special-needs gardeners. The areas involved are small, requiring less work to keep them looking good, and making it easier to plan the entire space around the requirements of the gardener. Close contact with the plants is possible—indeed, often unavoidable—so their finer details can be appreciated and their needs and problems more easily and quickly noticed.

The requirements and capabilities of different people are so variable that individual planning is necessary and should always closely involve the gardeners themselves, or at least those who have a good knowledge of their condition and limitations. Don't forget that in some instances the person involved may become increasingly less able with time. If this is the case—when planning for an elderly person, for example—build in features that can easily be adapted to something less labor intensive at a later stage. A raised bed could be used initially for growing vegetables from seed; if this becomes too difficult, it is simple to replant it with permanent ground-cover specimens. But bear in mind that most gardeners find it more rewarding to work to the limit of their capabilities. If people are ambitious and reasonably able gardeners, a totally labor-free plot will be frustrating and disappointing, no matter how attractive it might look. To provide a sense of achievement, gardening needs to present some sort of challenge, no matter how small, and overcoming obstacles and difficulties gives the grower a real sense of pride; so don't underestimate the capabilities of the gardener.

Many accidents and injuries involve gardening activities, and special-needs gardeners are likely to be particularly at risk. Safety is of primary importance, and while many aspects of safety are common sense, different groups may have their own particular problems that would never occur to someone else and help and guidance can often be obtained from specialist associations.

Independence is valuable to all of us, and it becomes particularly precious when threatened. Maintaining or increasing the independence and self-confidence of those with special needs through plants and gardening is important, and it is certainly worth spending time and thought on it in the initial planning stages.

Infirm and elderly gardeners

Into this "catch-all" category come those who lack strength and dexterity to a degree that interferes with normal gardening activities. This may be due to one or more reasons, from a simple "bad back" to old age or severe physical disablement, requiring the use of a wheelchair. Lifting, bending, and stretching are all likely to be restricted, and some people may lack the stamina to continue working for more than a short spell at a time.

Plots for such gardeners need to be safe and plants easily accessible.

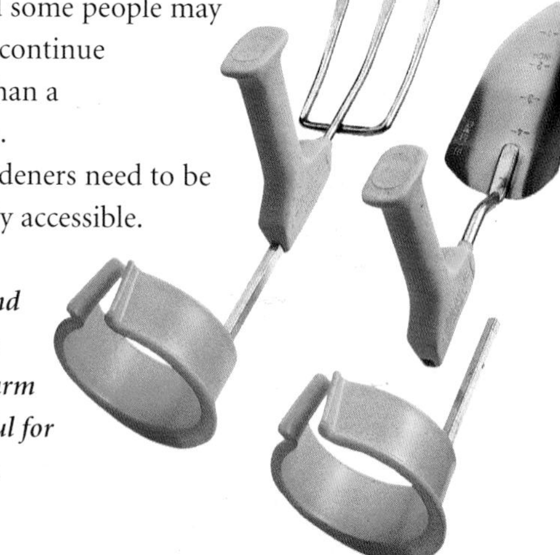

Special easy-grip hand tools with extensions that fit over the forearm are particularly useful for people with arthritis.

The visual liveliness, the subtle and attractive water features, and the broad, paved path in this professionally planned area for both gardeners and garden users with special needs could all be adapted for use in a smaller space.

Paving should be firm and level, without the hazards of creeping plants, slippery leaves, moss, or algae growth. Clear areas about 3ft (1m) wide so that wheelchair users or people with walkers or canes are able to move about comfortably; changes in level should be dealt with by ramps or very wide, shallow steps. Hand rails will also be useful.

Raised beds are an excellent way of bringing plants up to an easy working level. They are not only good for wheelchair users and those who have problems bending but also make gardening far less tiring for anyone who is not physically strong. The ideal height is usually about 24 in (60 cm); top the walls with broad, flat coping stones to make them suitable for sitting on while working with the plants. The width of the bed should be limited to suit the reach of the gardener—about 4ft (1.2m) if it is accessible from all sides.

If space allows, a potting bench, with soil mixes stored in a raised bin below, will make it easier for those in a chair or wheelchair to work with seedlings or young plants or plant up small containers. Larger plant containers can be moved about more easily if they are placed on dollies, or small wooden stands on wheels, and hanging baskets with a pulley

Special-needs gardening

system allow the basket to be lowered for watering and maintenance. Watering is often a problem, since water is heavy to carry and cans may be difficult to control.

The best method of watering is with a hose, preferably on a reel that permits water to flow through the hose when it is not fully unwound from the reel. Attach a trigger nozzle so that the water flow can be turned on and off at the end farthest from the faucet. Sprinkler or drip systems will automate watering to a large extent, or a computerized system can be set up to automate it completely. This is easier and less expensive to install in a small growing space than in a larger garden.

Garden tools can often be adapted to make them easier to use, and specialized tools are also available. Fitting a hand grip half-way up the shaft of a normal spade or fork gives better control, and attaching a long handle to hand tools such as trowels and forks means they can be used without bending. Long-handled cultivators, seed sowers, and bulb planters are also available, and ratchet-action hand pruners help those who have a weak grip.

Japanese bamboo pipes operated by water make a regular, pleasant hollow ring as they knock rhythmically against stones placed in a pool beneath them.

Blind and partially sighted gardeners

It is unfortunate that sight is often the most important sense as far as many gardeners are concerned. If we considered our other senses a little more when growing plants, we would all find the end result so much more rewarding.

Those people who have some limited vision may be able to appreciate strong colors and distinctive shapes. Blocks of single colors, rather than mixed plantings, stand out best, and bold, repeated color patterns work well. Choose plants whose flowers provide a sharp contrast to their leaves: white flowers, for example, show up better against dark green or red foliage than they do against pale or variegated leaves. Keep backgrounds such as paving, walls, and fences simple and unpatterned to avoid confusing images.

For those without sight, the senses of smell, touch, and hearing take over, but these senses can be stimulated in all gardeners, not merely those who are blind. Scent is provided not only by flowers but also by foliage and can range from the sweetly fragrant to the unexpectedly pungent. Position scented plants with care.

The leaves of many of the common herbs, such as sage, have a pleasing texture as well as a pungent aroma.

Low-growing flowers such as hyacinths should be planted in raised beds or tall containers, where their fragrance may be enjoyed; flowers that give off their perfume in the evening, such as night-scented stock and nicotiana, are best placed by a door or window, so the scent will drift into the house. Foliage often needs to be bruised before it will release its fragrance, so place aromatic plants where they will be brushed against or stepped on or where their branches can be easily stroked or squeezed.

Don't stick to flowers with sweet perfumes, such as lilies and jasmine; also try the sharp citrus aromas offered by lemon verbena or lemon-scented geranium, the pineapple smell of pineapple sage, or the spicy aroma of the curry plant. Some plants have surprising scents—the strong, musky odor of crown imperials or the pungent rancid-coconut of rue—which add an element of fun and variety.

Textures of plants are fascinatingly diverse, too. The smooth, velvet plush of lamb's ears *(Stachys byzantina)* just asks to be stroked, while the softly prickly needles of spreading junipers form a resilient spiky mat. Beware of planting sharply thorned or very spiky-leaved plants such as yuccas, which could cause injury. The blue grass *Festuca glauca* makes rounded hummocks of fluffy spikes, and the small globe thistle *(Echinops ritro)* forms perfectly round, lightly prickly globes.

Adding sound

One of the most pleasant sounds is that of water, and a splashing fountain always has a soothing effect. It is not necessary to have a pond, but there must be some standing water to provide the splash—a fountain or wall spout falling on pebbles is virtually silent. Some other garden ornaments, such as wind chimes, make a pleasant sound. They may be made of metal, wood, ceramic, or seashells, and each produces a completely different sound.

Differing textures can be provided by ornaments and surfaces as well as plants. A change in the surface texture underfoot helps blind people to know where they are or if they are approaching a possible hazard such as steps, while pebbles, stonework, and smooth wooden sculptures are all pleasant or interesting to touch.

Gardeners with learning difficulties

These are usually, though not always, young people, and as with other forms of disability, their difficulty can be mild or severe. For far too long, people with learning difficulties were guided towards an occupation in horticulture for all the wrong reasons—mainly that it was felt not to be too intellectually demanding. Growing and caring for plants is certainly a suitable occupation, but because it is enjoyable, rewarding, stimulating, and encourages improved self-esteem and independence.

It is impossible to generalize about the conditions that are described as "learning difficulties" because they are so diverse, but the skills that are involved in growing plants are valuable for many young people, and adults, too. Simple tasks such as pricking out seedlings improve dexterity, watering encourages estimating skills, planting in regular formations helps the appreciation of pattern and number skills. Simply taking responsibility for plants and watching them develop and grow builds up confidence and can be a source of pleasure and pride.

Many people with learning difficulties require a great deal of stimulation, and the ideas discussed already in gardening for the visually handicapped can be put to good use for them. Plants and garden features should be touched, stroked, and sniffed and offer different textures, smells and sounds. Another sense that should not be forgotten is taste; all children like to grow something they can eat, especially if it is quick to develop. Fragrant herbs, cherry tomatoes, sweet peppers, different varieties of lettuce with a range of leaf shapes and colors, radishes, scallions, carrots—they are simple to grow and can be fitted easily into small space gardens, window boxes, or hanging baskets.

Make sure that poisonous or potentially damaging plants are excluded and that water features are safely constructed. There is not only the danger of children drowning in a few inches of water but of electrocution if pumps are installed.

Laburnum seeds

Yew berries

SOME COMMON POISONOUS GARDEN PLANTS

BOTANICAL NAME	COMMON NAME	POISONOUS PART
Aconitum napellus	monkshood	leaves and seeds
Colchicum autumnale	autumn crocus	corms
Convallara majalis	lily-of-the-valley	red berries
Daphne mezereum	February daphne	yellow or red berries
Ilex aquifolium	English holly	red or yellow berries
Iris foetidissima	Gladwyn iris	orange berries
Laburnum anagyroides	golden chain	seeds in beanlike pods
Ligustrum vulgare	common privet	black berries
Lupinus spp.	lupine	seeds in beanlike pods
Phytolacca decandra	pokeweed	purple-black berries
Prunus laurocerasus	cherry laurel	black berries
Taxus baccata	English yew	seeds contained in fleshy, red, berrylike capsules

 Chapter Two

Design and planning

The smaller your plot, the more important good design becomes—it is an essential factor in making the most of very little. In the following chapter we look at some of the basic points to consider when planning your planting, so helping to ensure that you get the maximum pleasure and satisfaction from your growing space, however limited it may be.

As well as general design considerations, we look at a wide range of special features that will give your "no-garden" the extra something that will turn it into a special place. Being limited in space doesn't mean being limited in imagination, and it is surprising what can be achieved in even the smallest area.

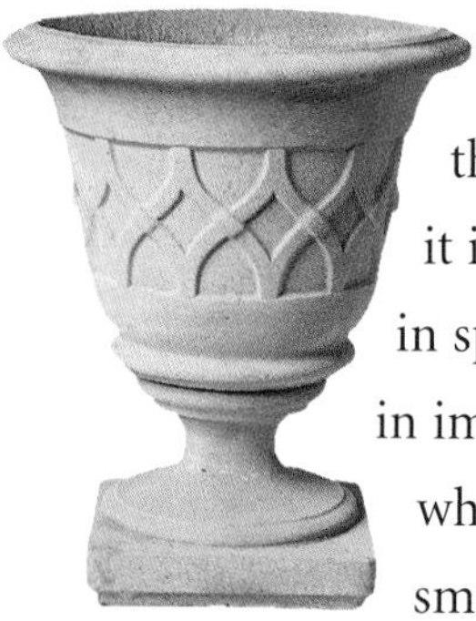

A limited range of plants and colors—grasses shading from yellow-green to almost blue, natural wood decking and chair, and russet-leafed Japanese maple and terra-cotta pots—are used here to create a feeling of space and unity in a small area.

The importance of design

The matching pairs of upright plants marching up the broad, straight steps to the twin conifers, and the restricted colors, are all in keeping with the formal lines of this patio garden.

Garden design is a grand-sounding term perhaps more readily associated with rolling landscapes than with our tiny plots. But as soon as you have a group of plants, you have the potential to increase or decrease their aesthetic appeal by the way the plants are arranged, both in relation to each other and to their surroundings. That arrangement is what design is about.

If you have followed the steps in assessing your situation on pp.34–43, you have already begun the process of design. You know what you have and what you want from it, and the practical aspects of whether it is possible to achieve your goal, or whether you must compromise and adapt. You have the basic outline; now it's time to put some detail on the plan.

Choosing the materials

Materials for paving, walls, ornaments, containers, and so on should be chosen to complement each other and the surroundings. Terra-cotta pots, for example, fit in more comfortably with a red-brick house than they would with one of grey stone. And a wall decorated with hanging baskets and window boxes is more pleasing if the boxes and baskets are all constructed from a similar material, such as black wrought iron, than if a mixture of plastic, wood, and metal containers is used.

If you have a collection of ornaments and containers in different materials and colors, you can often unify them by painting them with ordinary emulsion paint. A subtle variety of tones of the same color may be more successful than painting each pot exactly the same shade. You can also paint patterns, either by eye or using stencils, or carry out special paint effects to give a "distressed" appearance—the technique is much the same as that used for home decorating.

Warm, earthy tones of greens and reddish browns give a natural-looking result, but bright, bold, primary colors can

Informality is the keynote of this natural-looking planting, while the soft yellow-orange flowers make a pleasing contrast with the blue front door.

Pots that coordinate with the bricks and tiles and flowers with a linking colour theme give this group unity.

GARDEN STYLES:

Most planned gardens are based on a definite style, whether it is an informal cottage garden or a modern garden with stark landscaping and striking planting. Our "no-garden" areas don't have as much scope, but you should still plan them with a particular style in mind to ensure that the end product is harmonious and not simply a jumble of assorted plants and containers. Here are a few suggestions to help you.

FORMAL Straight lines, evenly spaced plantings, planned colour schemes. Regular shapes for beds or arrangements of containers. Matched plants and containers, often in pairs or rows. Clipped shrubs.

INFORMAL Flowing lines, plants allowed to make their own shapes. A mixture of colors and textures; planting in groups of odd numbers. Rural, cottage-style gardens.

RELAXING Muted tones, white and pastel colors; soft outlines; silver and gray foliage; gentle sounds. Somewhere to sit a priority.

EYE CATCHING Bright colors; architectural plants; exotic flowers; a striking sculpture or ornament.

PRODUCTIVE Featuring fruit, vegetables, and herbs, planned to match or contrast their forms and colors so that they are appealing to the eye as well as useful.

OUTSIDE ROOM A continuation of the color scheme of an interior room; somewhere to sit, with awnings and trellises for shelter. Containers and ornaments, such as large glazed pots, which would be equally at home indoors or outside.

also be very effective if the right plants are chosen to complement them. But you must beware of making the containers more eye-catching than the plants you intend to put into them.

Designing with plants

The design of larger gardens is often based on overall shapes, with plants simply providing blocks of color and variations in height. In "no-garden" situations, individual plants play a much more significant role. A limited color range is usually the most effective. Colors can be chosen either to harmonize or to contrast: on a color wheel, those adjacent to each other harmonize, while those opposite contrast. Brilliant red blooms standing out against a background of green foliage are an obvious example of the power of contrasting colors, while a mixture of silvery blue leaves, pale blue, lilac, and pink flowers forms a restful combination. Colors are often divided into "hot" (yellow, orange, red) and "cool" (green, blue) shades, but the depth of color must also be taken into account—a pale, creamy yellow has a quite different effect from that of an intense golden yellow. If you use the full range of colors, place the strongest ones furthest away, graduating to pastels and white at the front of the display.

The shape, size, and texture of flowers and foliage must also be considered: small blooms and delicate foliage are easily overpowered by robust specimens, which need careful siting.

Creating the illusion of space

Even simple ploys can trick the eye. This garden is made to seem bigger by the winding path, part of which is hidden from view, and the line of pots that are smaller the further away they are.

Every garden needs storage space, and as this amusing picture shows, even the most mundane shed can be turned into an unusual and attractive feature that adds another dimension to the garden.

A small space can be made to look and feel bigger than it really is by the careful use of plants and features. Even on a balcony or terrace, where the boundaries are obvious, a feeling of openness can make it a much more pleasant place. In order to achieve the desired effect, we must deceive the eye in one or more of a number of ways, manipulating perspective, proportion, and scale, and color.

Using perspective

As children, we learn about perspective with the example of parallel train tracks, which appear to come closer to each other as they recede until they finally meet at the horizon. A false perspective can be created by deliberately narrowing the width of a path, for example, as it extends away from the viewing point, making the end seem further away than it really is. But the eye will not be deceived by this unless the proportions of the surrounding plants and objects are in scale.

Objects in the distance appear smaller, so shrubs, plants, and ornaments should decrease in size the further away from the viewing point they are. In a very small plot the effect can be achieved by using just two objects, such as plant pots which are identical in all but size. Place the larger one in the foreground and the smaller at the furthest point, and the distance between them will be exaggerated. If the plot is surrounded by walls, fences, or hedges, the tops can be sloped so that their height decreases towards the far end of the plot.

This manipulation of perspective will, of course, work from one viewpoint only. Generally the main viewpoint is near the entrance to the house, but it may be advisable to create a slightly different sitting and "viewing" area to fit in with the shape of the plot.

On a terrace, for example, the doors are likely to open midway down the long axis, and while a sitting area just outside the doors may be practical, it cuts the terrace in two, making it appear even smaller than it really is. Move the sitting area to one end of the terrace, and you can extend the view and have more scope for imaginative design.

Specially constructed trellis panels can be bought that give an altered sense of perspective, appearing as a receding tunnel around a doorway or a focal point.

A mirror, placed some distance behind the gate and fence, creates the illusion of a path bordered by flowers running between a pair of gates and greatly increases the feeling of space in this garden.

In this tiny enclosed space, the clever siting of a mirror deceives the eye and makes the garden appear much larger than it is by allowing you to see the sculpture in the round.

Unity of style

Use either curves, circles, and flowing lines, or straight lines and sharp angles—don't mix the two. Unity is important to give an impression of space. A mish-mash of different styles is busy and makes an area seem smaller than it is because the eye constantly tends to be moving from one object to another, rather than following a continuous line without unnecessary interruptions. Keep to one style of container and ornament, rather than using several different types.

Using color

The eye can also be tricked by color. The "hot" colors of the spectrum stand out more and appear closer than the "cool" colors, which tend to recede. So colors are often arranged with the hot shades farthest away and the cool ones in the foreground, an arrangement which is intended to even out this tendency and give the colors equal prominence.

But if you want to make an area appear larger, this can be achieved by placing the hot colors in the foreground, with the cool shades receding into the distance. This mimics the natural landscape, where distant objects appear as soft gray or blue shapes on the horizon. Misty pastel shades blur the edges of boundaries, giving the impression that the "garden" extends beyond the line of sight.

Trompe l'oeil

This is deception of the eye carried to extremes. Whereas the manipulation of perspective and color is relatively subtle, a *trompe l'oeil* is a straightforward trick, creating an illusion of something that is not there at all. Some effects are simple to achieve, while others require considerable skill. Generally a blank wall is necessary on which to create the illusion.

A gateway on a wall suggests a garden beyond it, although the gate may be entirely false. An archway of artificial brick facings or trelliswork framing a wrought-iron gate on a solid wall is both effective and easy to construct. For extra realism, a mirror behind the wrought iron gate will reflect the existing planting, while the wrought iron "screen" of the gate helps to conceal the fact that it is just a reflection. Carefully placed mirrors are invaluable for giving an impression of a larger plot or increasing the impact of a special feature, but they should be positioned so that they do not immediately reflect the viewer, thus giving the game away.

If you are skilled with a paintbrush, you could paint a scene to enlarge your "garden," using a knowledge of perspective to give a realistic effect—an open gate with a glimpse of flowers and lawns beyond, pathways, climbing plants and flowers, trees, or simply blue skies and white clouds to give an impression of fresh air and open spaces.

Maintaining year-round interest

Although it is relatively easy to achieve an attractive blaze of colour from plants during the summer, it is less simple to make sure that there is something of interest for the rest of the year as well. In most "no-garden" situations, all the plants are on display all the time; there is rarely room to bring plants on in the background and set them out only when they have started flowering. So good planning is essential to get the most from your plants throughout the year.

If you have no ground space or only a small amount of ground space, you need to rely entirely on the plants to provide interest. There are two ways to approach the problem: either to use evergreens as the main plants, changing the flowering plants around them with the seasons, or to replace all the plants two or three times a year.

Establishing a basic framework of evergreens

Most of the plants grown in these situations are likely to be in containers. If you want to maintain a basic framework of evergreens all year round, use as large a container as is practical, preferably filled with soil-based compost, since this will keep the plants growing healthily for longer. Among the evergreens could be dwarf conifers, cordyline, euonymus, camellia or bay, planted either as single specimens or in groups, depending on the size of both the plants and the container. Fill in with trailing ivies and hebes, which remain attractive all year, leaving space for seasonal flowering plants to be added. The temporary residents should be planted in pots, sunk into the main container and covered with a thin layer of compost; this makes it easy to remove them as they pass their best.

Replacing the entire planting can pose difficulties when you are short of space. If you want winter-interest plants to become well established, you have to take out summer-flowering ones while they are still looking good in early to mid-autumn. There may be several dull weeks before the winter plants come into their own.

It is useful to have two containers, planting up one with the next season's plants in advance of the end of the current season's display, and keeping it out of the way until it is time to change them over – but this depends on your having a suitable "out of the way" place to grow them on.

If you have space to grow plants in the ground, the choice is the same as for containers – to have some permanent specimens, or replant regularly with seasonal plants?

Hanging baskets are a problem in cold winters. However, in a sheltered position you could try a basket planted entirely with hardy trailing plants such as variegated ivies. Line the basket in the usual way, then, to give extra insulation to the roots, place a piece of bubble polythene (perforated for drainage) inside the lining before filling it with compost.

Using hard landscaping

In the larger ground space provided by a patio or roof garden, you can provide year-round interest with ornaments, statues and sculptures, and even the materials for walls and paving can combine to form a pleasing scene when some plants have died back. It is important to keep an out-of-season garden area tidy. Remove dead and dying foliage, prune plants that require it, and keep the ground swept and clean.

Plants for year-round interest

Some strongly architectural shrubs such as *Cordyline australis* and *Yucca gloriosa*, or the fantastic corkscrew branches of the twisted hazel, *Corylus avellana* 'Contorta', show up even better in winter. The bright red stems of the dogwood, *Cornus alba* 'Sibirica' make a showy display in winter, camellias flower, and a wall plant such as pyracantha provides interest both in early summer, with its creamy flowers, and in winter, with bright evergreen leaves and long-lasting scarlet or orange berries. Spring can begin early and continue into summer with bulbs, daisies, forget-me-nots and polyanthus. There is no shortage of plants for summer, some flowering well into autumn, when bulbs such as colchicums and nerines take over. Japanese acers provide splendid autumn leaf colour, while winter-flowering heathers and pansies, and many conifers and evergreen shrubs with variegated and coloured leaves, will give winter colour. More ideas for year-round plantings are given on page 165.

Ornamental cabbages are unusual and hardy plants that will thrive in a pot and provide colour on bleak winter days.

Pyracantha will survive severe winter conditions, rewarding you with a glimpse of its bright berries even under a blanket of snow.

Grouping containers

When planting a flower border, it is advisable to follow a planting scheme, bearing in mind how the plants relate to each other and considering the border as a whole. When planting a number of containers, this may not be the case. Each container tends to be regarded as a separate entity and is not considered in relation to the others. This is a pity, since in a small area especially, the various containers look best when they are grouped together to form a pleasing and harmonious whole, giving a sense of unity and making a "garden"—rather than a jumbled collection of pots—out of the smallest space.

You will need something of a designer's eye to arrange your containers in the most pleasing manner. An arrangement works best if there is some theme to link all the parts: using all terra-cotta pots in varying styles, perhaps, or a variety of tubs and troughs made from wood. If the containers are in a mixture of styles they can be linked by their color, or the planting can form the linking theme, with some of the same plants appearing in each of the different pots, or a similar color scheme can be replaced in all the containers.

Creating a satisfying composition

Your container grouping may be viewed from one direction only or from several different sides—you will need to take this into account when planting it. A roughly triangular outline is often the most successful composition. The apex of the triangle can be central or to one side, formed by a tall plant in a tall container. (Try to achieve a balance between the size and shape of the container and the plant it holds. Not only does a tall specimen in a low container look uncomfortable, it is at risk of being blown over.) If you don't have a container of a suitable height, you can stand it on a brick or an upturned pot, which will eventually be hidden by the plants around it.

Other containers and their plants of varying shapes and sizes should be arranged to fill in the triangle. You will need to assess whether it is the pot or the plant it contains that is the more eye-catching and position it accordingly. Sometimes a decorative empty container, perhaps lying on its side, makes a perfect addition to the compositions.

Making an impact

Groups of odd numbers of containers are always the most satisfying—one large pot and two medium-sized ones, for example, or one large, one medium, and three small. Avoid placing the pots in straight rows; a slightly staggered outline works best. If you have raised beds, low walls or steps, use them to vary the levels of the containers. You can also add height with hanging baskets in relatively low positions on walls or fences so that they form part of the group. Make a link between them and the containers at ground level by using similar plantings or by carrying the color scheme upward.

The basic rules of using odd numbers and different heights of containers are successfully demonstrated by this grouping. The link between the colors of both pots and plants helps to give the arrangement cohesion.

In this more complex grouping (above), the symmetrical placing of the pots, the similar planting, and the triangular shapes formed by the canes all draw the eye upward to the wall fountain.

It is not immediately obvious that the arrangement (left) is based on a triangle. The planting and colors are varied, but a feeling of unity is achieved by using the same material—gravel, pebbles, and rocks—and, dominating the group, a fine raised stone trough.

Rock gardens

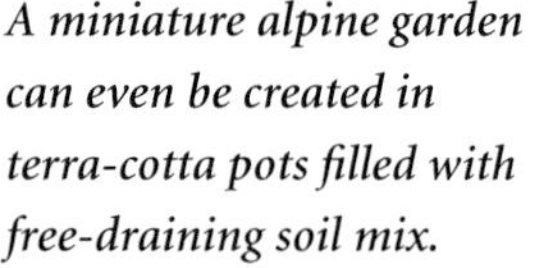

A miniature alpine garden can even be created in terra-cotta pots filled with free-draining soil mix.

The neat forms, low growth, and small, jewel-bright flowers of alpine plants need to be appreciated at close quarters, and they are perfectly in scale in confined spaces. They do, however, generally need a degree of specialized care, and there are several ways in which they can be grown. Alpines are defined as plants that in the wild are found growing above the tree line. As far as most gardeners are concerned, that definition is not too strictly adhered to, and the term tends to include a fairly wide variety of similar, low-growing subjects, which will happily grow at lower altitudes and are sometimes loosely known as rock garden plants.

In the mountains, alpines are subjected to dry, cold, windy conditions and grow in thin, stony soil or in crevices in rocks. Their low habit of growth helps them to resist the wind, and spreading root systems enable them to extract the maximum moisture and nutrients from the poor soil. They have adaptations to help them cope with high water loss, and this is possibly the most important point to bear in mind when growing them away from their natural habitat—they demand very free-draining conditions, and waterlogging, or moisture remaining in the crowns of the plants, will quickly cause them to rot and die.

Scree gardens

Natural weathering of the rocks in mountain areas produces slopes consisting of small rocky fragments and stones known as scree, which is colonized by a variety of attractive plants. In a small area, a scree garden can sometimes be more successful than a rock garden, which uses rocks and boulders on a larger scale. As for all alpine and rock garden plants, an open, sunny site is necessary.

Such a garden must be very well drained, and constructing a scree bed on a slight slope improves drainage and helps to display the flowers well. If the bed is to be at ground level, the soil beneath it should be dug out and replaced by a layer of free-draining builders rubble before being topped with scree material; a raised bed is often more practical

(see pp.78–81), provided you pay particular attention to good drainage.

Scree material is seldom available even from larger garden centers, but if you live in a suitable area, a visit to a stone quarry is the ideal way to obtain it. The main area of the bed should consist of scree mix, made from one part of good-quality topsoil or soil-based potting mix, one part of peat moss or peat substitute, and three parts of gravel and rock fragments. Once planting is complete, the area is topped with a layer of scree material.

When planting in scree mix, shake or gently wash off much of the existing soil around the roots of the plants, and spread the roots out well in the scree bed. Firm plants in lightly, taking care not to damage the roots or crown, and finish with a 10in (25cm) layer of rock chips spread over the surface and tucked around the crown of the plants. They will need careful and regular watering for a little while after planting, but once they are established they will require

Colorful, low-growing alpine plants are most at home in an open, sunny bed that has been built up with rocks and the surface covered in rock chips and gravel to ensure good drainage.

watering only occasionally, if at all, depending on how much rain they receive. In wet weather, individual plants may have to be protected from excess rain to prevent the crowns from rotting. The easiest way to do this is to erect a pane of glass supported on sticks over the top of the plant; this protects it from the wet while allowing the free flow of air.

Rock gardens

Building a natural-looking rock garden is an art. Take your time when selecting stones, ensuring that they will fit together well. Although stone is expensive, buy reasonably large pieces, remembering that about one-third of each rock will be buried in the soil—but make sure that the pieces are not so large and heavy that you will not be able to maneuver them into position. To cut down on the number of stones, plan the rock garden as two or three rocky outcrops of larger stones surrounded by scree.

The "polka dot" style of rock garden is all too often seen—a large mound of soil with stones pushed onto the outside like decorations on a cake. Use stones and soil together to build up the slope as you go. Make a base of rubble for good drainage and cover this with good-quality topsoil. Form outcrops of rock from small groups of suitable stones, setting each one on a ledge of soil that slopes slightly backward and building up well-trodden topsoil around and behind it to hold it firmly in place. For a natural look, the strata lines must run in the same direction on each piece of rock. Try to use the larger stones at the highest point of the rock garden.

Once all the stones are in place, plant your chosen plants in pockets at the base of the rocks, in fissures within the rock, and in scree areas between the stones. Then top-dress with gravel or rock chips to improve the drainage around the plants and overall appearance of the garden.

MAKING A TUFA ROCK GARDEN

Tufa is a soft, porous limestone that plant roots will penetrate readily, and a piece of tufa planted with alpines makes an unusual feature that will take up little space; it can either stand alone or form part of a rock garden.

Choose an attractively shaped piece of rock and set it in position. Use a cold chisel to form or enlarge suitable, downward-sloping planting holes. Wash most of the soil from the roots of the plants, then set them in the holes. Firm the plants into place with an alpine planting mix made from one part topsoil or soil-based mix, one part peat moss or peat substitute, and one part coarse grit. Water regularly until the plants are established, and then only when necessary—the porous rock will soak up moisture and make it available to the plants.

Alpines root quickly in holes in tufa rock.

Vertical gardening

When space is limited, it is often possible to make use of house and garden walls, fences, and trellises to support climbing, trailing, or wall-trained or espaliered plants. If you can't spread out—spread upward.

Climbing plants are those that have a natural tendency to scramble upward and outward. They may be self-clinging or may need to be tied in to supports. Trailers produce long, lax stems, which hang down rather than growing up—although a climber with no suitable support is likely to turn into a trailer. Wall plants are those shrubs that are easy to train against a wall or similar support, but which do not produce long, questing stems and are not self-clinging. Climbers include honeysuckle and Virginia creeper; trailers, moneywort and creeping Charlie; wall plants, firethorn and cotoneaster.

How plants climb

In nature, the shoots of climbing plants extend until they find something up which to travel. They make their upward journey in a number of ways. Truly self-clinging types produce pads of aerial roots, or tendrils that cling tightly to rough surfaces—ivy and Virginia creeper are among them. Other climbers, such as scarlet runner beans and honeysuckle, have twining stems that coil clockwise or counterclockwise according to species. Sometimes they need a little help to start them climbing, so it is important to know in which direction they twine. Start them off the wrong way and they will simply unravel themselves. Plants such as clematis have twining leaf stems; some, like passionflower, have slender tendrils that coil tightly as soon as they touch a suitable object. The exotic glory lily, *Gloriosa superba*, has leaves that are modified into twining tendrils at their tips. Some plants grown as climbers have long, supple, arching stems that, left to their own devices, would tend simply to sprawl over other plants and need training and tying in if they are to climb.

Fragrant honeysuckle (above), with its trumpet-shaped blooms, is one of the most rewarding climbers to grow in a small garden area.

Self-clinging climbers have a bad reputation. While they are not likely to do serious harm to walls in good condition, they can dislodge loose mortar and stucco; their growth may block gutters and they can lift shingles if allowed to scramble over roofs. Keeping the plants trimmed and growing them up a suitable support will avoid these problems *(see pp.128–129)*.

Growing climbers in containers

Most climbing plants can be grown in containers, although this may limit the height they will reach. Generally, the larger the container, the better, particularly for perennial and shrubby species. Care is needed to ensure that the top growth does not overbalance the container; use sturdy terra-cotta or ceramic pots rather than lightweight plastic ones and loam-based rather than soilless growing mix. Planting climbers in the ground at the base of walls cuts down the amount of watering needed, allows the plants a free root run, and keeps the root area cool for those species, like clematis, that prefer to have their roots in the shade.

Choosing the plants

Careful pruning is necessary to prevent climbing plants from developing unattractive bare stems at the base. This can also be overcome by planting climbers in association with each other or with plants that have bushy growth low down. Careful selection of the companion plants can also provide flowers, fruit, or leaf color when the climber is not at its best. The flowers of spring-blooming *Clematis alpina*, for example, may be followed by those of a climbing rose in midsummer, while a variegated or plain-leafed ivy will provide a pleasing backdrop at all times.

The aspect of a wall or fence can be important. Most prefer a sunny location, but ivies, some honeysuckles, and some species of Virginia creeper and Boston ivy will tolerate a sunless position.

Many climbing plants are perennial, but there are several useful annuals that are easy to control and allow access to walls and fences for maintenance during the winter. Species such as morning glory, sweet pea, nasturtiums, and black-eyed Susan, are easy to raise from seed and make rapid growth when planted out.

Growing plants on vertical supports means you can enjoy some you would not otherwise have room for in a shady narrow town plot, and it allows the plants to reach upward for light and air.

Vertical gardening

Walls and fences

Always make certain that any wall or fence that is to support a climbing plant is in a good state of repair before planting against it. Loose, crumbling mortar or stucco, unstable bricks, siding, or shingles that can be dislodged will only be made worse by attaching plant supports or training self-clinging climbers against them. Carry out any necessary repair work before planting.

The wall in question may be the wall of your own house, a neighboring house, a boundary wall in a garden, or that of a shed or other outbuilding. Walls of houses are there primarily to provide insulation and protection against the weather for the house occupants and are constructed to maximize that protection, with moisture barriers and hollow, or dry, walls. Uncontrolled growth of plants can compromise this function, bridging air gaps, holding moisture against the wall, harboring vermin, and penetrating the brickwork, to say nothing of blocking gutters and causing damage to roofs and downspouts.

Controlling climbers

Before planting a vigorous climber, ensure that you will be able to keep its growth under control; this may be even more important if the wall is that of a neighboring home, since you could find yourself liable for any damage caused. A ladder, pole pruners, or pruning saws may be required; sometimes the necessary pruning can be carried out—with care—from an upstairs window to prevent growth extending into gutters or onto the roof. If you own only part of the wall, you will need to be able to prevent the climber from extending to the parts of the wall that do not belong to you.

Similar care should be taken to prevent damage to the walls of outbuildings, although these are usually less important, and to garden walls. They are generally all there for a purpose other than providing a home for climbing plants and are likely to be troublesome and expensive to rebuild or repair.

While a wall is often simply a convenient surface on which to extend your plant display, sometimes you will want to grow plants over it specifically to disguise it; not all walls and buildings are things of beauty. You may also wish to extend the height of a wall or fence with trelliswork in order to screen off an unappealing view or to provide extra privacy. In addition, a house wall is often a particularly good place to grow a scented climber, such as honeysuckle, jasmine, sweet peas, and wisteria, since the fragrance will drift in through open windows.

Besides providing privacy, the high white wall, topped by a classical bust, and the rose-covered trellis, coupled with the lush flowering plants, give this city roof garden an almost tropical feel.

If the wall is to be left partly exposed, choose a plant that will blend well with the texture and color of the materials from which the wall is made. It may be made of brick, concrete, stone, or stucco—each provides a completely different

background for the plants. Fences, too, come in a variety of colors and styles, and you may find that it is desirable to repaint or stain them to give a more pleasing foil for your chosen plants.

Garden walls are sometimes constructed with a hollow top section that can be filled with soil in which trailing plants can be set. It may be possible to add such a planting area to an existing wall by building up a few courses of bricks. The

A vigorous climber, such as Virginia creeper, will thrive in the small amount of soil at the base of a wall.

hollow area should be as deep as possible, since it will dry out quickly, and it should be filled with good-quality, fertile topsoil. The construction of dry-stone walls means that plants can be set in pockets of soil mix between the stones; use compact plants that will thrive in these free-draining conditions and avoid vigorous growers with strong, penetrating roots, since they could undermine the stones and cause the wall to collapse.

Terraces and roof gardens

Climbers and trailers are especially suitable for terraces and roof gardens. They help to make the garden area three-dimensional, provide privacy, and give protection from strong winds, which can be a problem in any area raised off the ground. At the same time, trailing plants tumbling over the boundaries disguise the edges of the area and help it to merge with the more distant scenery.

In these situations, climbers and trailers will of necessity have to be grown in containers. Vigorous climbers that are to help provide a weather screen will be particularly prone to being blown over and damaged by wind. Make sure that all containers and plant supports are firmly secured; once the supports are covered by stems in full leaf they will provide a considerable amount of resistance to the wind and may easily be damaged. In exposed positions, it is probably best to grow annual or deciduous climbers or species that may be cut down in autumn to regrow the following spring. This reduces wind resistance during the winter, when the weather is likely to be at its worst, and may prevent a great deal of damage.

Vertical gardening

A pergola covered in wisteria gives this patio the air of a much larger garden and provides a welcome sitting place in summer.

Pergolas, arches and pillars

As well as walls and fences, there are several other means of supporting plants to make use of vertical growing space.

A pergola consists of wooden uprights supporting an open arrangement of crossbeams. It is often rectangular, but a round or octagonal pergola can be both attractive and practical in a small area. Any pergola gives at least an impression of providing some shelter; once clothed in plants, this impression can become reality, with more vigorous varieties allowed to grow over the top of the pergola to provide shade and a little protection from rain. Hanging baskets can be suspended from the crossbeams, but make sure that they hang sufficiently high to allow you to walk underneath them or trailing plants. Pergolas are often used over walkways to link two different areas, as are arches, which can also frame a gateway or entrance.

A traditional arch has a rounded top, but rectangular, flat-topped frameworks are also known as arches. They may be made from wood, metal, or wirework and may be two-dimensional or extended to form a short tunnel. A slightly elongated archway with a seat under it becomes an arbor, a pleasant, intimate place to sit and enjoy the view. As with a pergola, plants may be grown up the uprights and over the top of an arch.

Pillars are simply uprights that can be covered with plants. They may be single or grouped in rows or patterns and are most frequently sturdy wooden posts driven firmly into the ground to hold them upright. In most "no-gardens," where a hard surface makes it impossible to drive a pillar into the ground, it can be supported on a crosspiece of wood at the base, with climbing plants in containers around it.

Tripods, consisting of three pieces of wood lashed firmly together at the top to form a tepee, give a similar impression to pillars. Plants may be set either in soil at the base of each upright or in a large container in the centre of the tripod, the shoots being trained around the uprights and eventually forming a complete screen. A sturdy tripod may be free-standing on a hard surface as long as it is firmly secured at the top and is strong enough to support the plants' weight.

Outbuildings and porches

Garden sheds, garages, and porches also provide an opportunity for growing plants; indeed, sometimes climbers may be necessary to disguise an unattractive outbuilding. Very vigorous growers, such as silver lace vine, *Fallopia baldschuanica*, will rapidly cover an entire building but can be invasive and difficult to control, and the heavy growth can easily cause the roof of a decrepit or old building to collapse, so take care.

Ivy is another rapid grower, but when it reaches the top of its climb it produces shrubby and woody shoots. These bear differently shaped leaves and panicles of flowers and fruits, and their growth is very dense.

A porch may provide both uprights and a roof for plants to grow over, but a porch roof that is attached directly to the house wall, rather than being supported by uprights, is not likely to be able to bear much weight. Where the structure is sturdy enough to support dense plant growth, this can form a welcome screen and weather protection by a door.

Plants as supports

Climbing and scrambling plants can also be grown through other plants, in imitation of their natural conditions of growth. Take care that the climber does not overpower or damage the supporting plant, which may be a tree, shrub, or another climber. Choose plants that complement each other or extend the season of interest of the partner plant. A large-flowered hybrid clematis twining through a spring-flowering shrub, for example, will produce flowers ready to take over for the summer once those of the shrub have faded.

Climbers around the door to a courtyard garden emphasize its rustic nature and soften the starkness of the high walls.

Water gardens

There is something intrinsically fascinating about water, and certainly it adds a new dimension to a garden. Fountains and waterfalls add life to a still garden scene; their gentle splashing sounds are soothing and relaxing and provide a welcome touch of coolness on a hot summer day. Many types of wildlife are attracted to water, even in inner cities, and birds, insects, and amphibians may become regular visitors.

Will a water feature work?

A pond or water feature is often considered suitable only for a large garden—something that demands plenty of space and is time-consuming and difficult both to construct and maintain. This is far from the case: if you have sufficient ground space to stand a large tub, you have enough room for a minipond, and setting it up is hardly more difficult than planting up the tub in the normal way.

Points to consider

If your garden space is a roof garden or balcony, the weight of the water must be taken into account; it is remarkably heavy, and you must be certain that the structure will be able to support the volume of water that you have in mind. You must also be quite sure that your feature is watertight and not likely to spring a leak.

A pond of any sort needs full sun to thrive; a shady position is not ideal for water plants, and overhanging trees or shrubs should be avoided, since their falling leaves will pollute the water. However, do not be discouraged if your garden space is in the shade, for a water feature that does not involve water plants is still a possibility.

Any water feature requires a convenient supply of water. Pools need regular topping off and occasionally a complete change of water (although this should be avoided if possible). However, it is unavoidable that some water will be lost through evaporation, and this will need to be replaced. And if your aim is to have moving water, there must be a convenient supply of electricity to operate a pump to recirculate the water from a reservoir.

Fish not only add to the attraction and interest of a pool, they make short work of mosquito and other troublesome insect larvae that hatch in still, open water. In small pools in cold climates, fish may be a problem to care for during the winter, and they are likely to need feeding during the spring and summer, too. If you don't want the responsibility of fish, you will need to control breeding mosquitoes otherwise.

Young children are fascinated by water even more than adults, and even a small pond can be a dangerous place for a toddler. A child can drown in water that is less than 6in (15cm) deep. However, the very small garden spaces we are considering are likely to be safer than larger gardens, simply because it should be easier to keep a young child in sight.

The amount of space you have will dictate whether you opt for a minipond in a container, a larger pool, either raised or at ground level, or a water feature, which can make better use of vertical space. Then you must choose between formal and informal styles, giving regard to your surroundings: formal styles usually integrate better into small spaces.

You do not need much specialized equipment to construct a water garden, and most large garden centers stock a sufficient range of items. For a wider choice, it is worth visiting a specialist aquatic garden center, many of which also operate a mail order business and have useful catalogs.

An informal pond, with water spilling from a terra-cotta urn over stones, provides ideal conditions for moisture-loving plants and will add interest to your garden by attracting birds, dragonflies, and even, if you are lucky, a frog or two.

Ponds

Where there is space for something a little larger than a minipond, you must choose between a sunken pond, where the surface of the water is level with the surrounding ground, or a pool constructed above ground level. In many "no-garden" situations, the excavation necessary for a sunken pond may be impossible, or you may be able to compromise with a shallow excavation and low retaining wall so that part of the pool is below ground level and part above.

The most popular materials for pools are fiberglass or a liner of laminated PVC or butyl rubber. Fiberglass is inflexible and available in only a limited range of preformed shapes and sizes. It must be installed below ground or only partially above ground, the above-ground portion being surrounded by packed soil and a retaining wall, since it is not strong enough to support the weight of the water by itself.

Liners are much more flexible and can be cut to suit whatever shape is desired; they are particularly useful for raised ponds. Butyl is more expensive than

Water gardens

PVC but longer lasting. It is also less easily punctured, but both PVC and butyl can be repaired if necessary. To calculate the size of the liner, measure the pond's maximum width and add twice its maximum depth plus 6in (15cm) for overlap, then measure the maximum length plus twice the maximum depth plus 6in (15cm).

Raised ponds

Raised ponds can be constructed of stone, brick, or concrete; the construction must be sufficiently strong to support the pressure of the water inside it. A double-skinned hollow wall is preferable—the two skins are linked with wall ties and the inside lined with butyl or laminated PVC before filling. The walls should be high enough to allow a minimum depth of water of 18–24in (24–60cm). It is most important that the top of the pond is dead level, since the water will show up the slightest slope and this will be a constant source of irritation. For a neat finish to the inside of the pond, put the liner in position before laying the top two courses of bricks on the interior wall. A layer of builders' sand on the base of the liner will protect it from sharp stones, which could cause punctures or uneven wear. Lay the liner fairly loosely over the pool, weighting the edges with bricks. Run water in slowly through a hose, lifting the bricks as necessary to allow the liner bit by bit into the pond; it will stretch to form a tight, almost wrinkle-free fit. When the pool is almost full, lay the remaining two courses of bricks on the interior wall, over the liner, to hold it in place. Then fold up the edge of the liner over the final two courses toward the interior of the pond and top it off with coping stones, trimming the liner so that it does not show. Be careful not to drop mortar into the water and allow the mortar to dry thoroughly before filling the pond to the top.

Sunken ponds

You need to excavate a sunken pond reasonably accurately. If you are using a preformed fiberglass mold, turn the mold upside down on the site and run a stick around the edge to mark its shape in the soil before starting to dig. Excavate the hole slightly wider and deeper than the size of the mold, allowing for any marginal shelves. Line the base of the hole with sand to bring it up to the correct depth and check the level of both the base and top of the excavation with a spirit level. Lower the mold into place, check the level again, and begin slowly to fill it with water through a hose. As the pond fills up, backfill the excavation with soil or sand, firming it thoroughly, and continue to check the level of the pond at intervals. When the pool is full, lay paving stones around the edge, so that they slightly overlap the top of

MAKING A MINIPOND

1 Assemble the equipment you need to prepare your minipond: wooden half-barrel, black plastic liner, hammer, nails, your chosen plants, planting baskets, soil mix, and some coarse gravel.

2 Cut a circular piece of plastic considerably large than the size of the barrel. Position it centrally over the top of the barrel and push it in so that it fits loosely. Fold the edge under, then nail it to the barrel with galvanized nails.

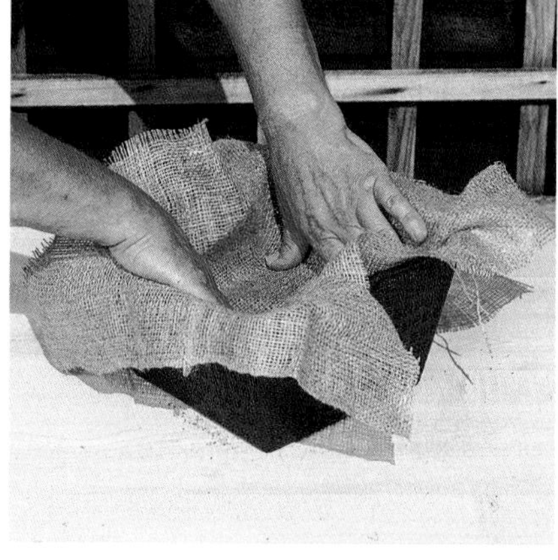

3 Half-fill the barrel with water. Line the planting baskets with burlap, which will help keep the soil from being washed out. Fill the baskets two-thirds full with soil mix, then cut away the excess burlap level with the top of the baskets.

the mold to disguise it. If you are using a flexible liner for a sunken pond, excavate the pond accurately, smooth the sides (which should slope outward slightly) and put a layer of sand in the base, then lay the liner loosely over the hole and fill it in the same way as for a raised pond.

Miniponds

The most popular container for a minipond is a wooden half-barrel. These are usually waterproof (they were originally used for holding liquid, after all), but once they have been allowed to dry out, the wood shrinks slightly, opening up gaps between the staves. If the barrel can be submerged in water, or filled and refilled several times, the wood should swell sufficiently to stop leaks. The inside can be lined with heavy duty plastic (preferably black) or painted with bitumen paint to ensure that it remains watertight. Before beginning to plant the barrel after painting, empty and refill it several times to wash away any residue from the paint.

Other containers can also be used for miniponds, but they should be at least 15in (38cm) deep: algae will be difficult to control in anything shallower. A container the volume of a half-barrel can support a basket of oxygenators, a couple of submerged aquatic plants, a marginal plant, and a goldfish or two. Compact types of plant should be chosen—a miniature water lily and the dwarf cattail, *Typha minima*, for instance—and ordinary goldfish rather than the active golden orfe, which would find the confines of a barrel too restricting.

The question of balance

A well-maintained pool will contain sparklingly clear water in which fish and water plants can easily be seen and enjoyed. Often, however, particularly in new pools, the water is a thick murky green or sometimes reddish brown. This is caused by a sudden explosion in the growth of algae. In a newly filled pond, the algae feed on the abundance of mineral salts present in tap water and make use of the sunlight that at this stage can enter the water unimpeded by plant growth.

Although this "pea soup" stage does not look attractive, resist the temptatation to interfere. As plants become established, they (and the algae themselves) will use up the excess minerals; the leaves of floating plants will cut down the amount of sunlight entering the water, and the algae will die out. This often happens literally overnight, but it may take a few days or weeks. Emptying the pool and refilling it will simply introduce a new supply of mineral-rich water and delay the clearing process; commercial algicides may kill existing growth, but until a good balance is achieved naturally, the problem will only recur.

To keep the water clear you need oxygenating plants. Plants with floating leaves that cover part of the water surface will also help to control algal growth—water lilies are the favorites. Both of these types should be planted at the bottom of the pond. Floating plants, such as mosquito plant, or fairy floating moss, *Azolla caroliniana*, can also help to reduce algae by shading the water.

4 *Set the plants in the soil and add a layer of gravel to hold the sand. You will need oxygenators: a miniature water lily and perhaps a marginal plant, such as dwarf cattail or marsh marigold.*

5 *Lower the baskets gently into the barrel. Set the basket containing the marginal plant on submerged bricks to raise it to the right height. In a short time the water will clear, and your minipond will begin to flourish.*

Water features

The sound and movement of water can be enjoyed without having a pool: a recirculating pump will enable you to have an attractive water feature in a very small space. However, a header pool of some sort is needed to supply sufficient water for the pump to circulate; this can either be a part of the feature or can be hidden behind or below it.

A wall fountain, with the water falling into a basin or into a small pond, makes a charming focal point in a small area.

Water pumps

There are two main types of pumps—surface or submersible. Surface pumps run off mains voltage and are useful for moving large volumes of water. They must be housed in a waterproof, ventilated pump chamber near the water feature and should be installed by a licensed professional electrician. For small water features, submersible pumps are much easier. They require a transformer to step down the mains voltage (transformers are usually included as part of a kit) and are simply lowered into the water they are required to pump. They must remain covered while they are working.

Decorative water features generally make use of falling water, as in waterfalls and cascades. Here the pump is sited in a small pool or container, and the water is pumped upward through a hidden hose to the top of the feature, where it is allowed to spill out. A fountain is slightly different, where both the upward movement and fall of the water provide the decorative effect.

Fountains

A fountain is often part of a formal rather than an informal feature, although it can be used in both. It is easy to install, since the fountain jet generally fits directly on to the pump, so no pipework is required. For most effects, the top of the jet should be just above the water surface; the pump can be raised on bricks to reach the correct level. Many different types of jets are available, to give a variety of water patterns, some complex, others quite simple; most can also be adjusted to raise or lower the height of the water. Merely lowering the pump so that the fountain jet lies just below the water surface also gives a different effect—like that of a spring bubbling up. Fountain ornaments can be situated in the center or at the side of a pool or they can be free-standing, when the falling water is collected in a chamber beneath the ornament to be recirculated.

A word of warning. In very windy locations, water will be blown away from the pool, making the surroundings wet, and the pool can empty and the pump burn out.

Cascades

Like a fountain, a cascade may be part of a pool or form a feature on its own. It consists of a step or series of steps over which water falls to provide a splash. The abrupt fall of water from one level to another is critical, so it is important that the water does not simply run down a sloping course, since this provides little sound or noticeable movement.

Plastic or fiberglass waterfall sections are available in many garden centers, but they are not really successful, being a poor imitation of stone. It is better to use a flexible liner to cover steps that have been cut into well-firmed dirt, topping the liner with an overhanging stone on each step to form a lip from which the water will fall cleanly. A submersible pump sited in the bottom pool pumps the water back up to the top through a hose buried in the soil behind the steps. With a little imagination, a variety of attractive individual features can be constructed using the principles of the fountain or cascade.

Other features

A large, waterproof, decorative pot filled with water can froth with a bubbling jet at its surface, or water can spill out continuously from a tilted urn or through an old-fashioned hand pump. A foaming water spout emerging through a circle of cobblestones or the center of a millstone has become a popular feature, and there are many different types of masks or gargoyles that will spout water from a wall or poolside. Some ingenuity will often be needed to ensure that the working parts (the electricity cable and hoses) are concealed, but this need not be a major problem.

A simple fountain bubbling up over pebbles in a small container, set within a larger stone circle, makes an imaginative water feature and provides perfect conditions for marginal plants.

Algae are likely to be more of a nuisance where oxygenating plants cannot be used to keep the water clear. Several chemical algicides will do the trick, but the treatment needs to be repeated at intervals. Algal growth is also a problem with millstones or pebble fountains, since a film of algae will soon form on stone that is constantly wet. Regularly switching off the pump to let the stones dry out completely will help delay its formation, but an algicide is also likely to be needed—plus occasional scrubbing, or even replacement, of the affected stones.

Chemical algicides are fairly efficient, but they are not normally recommended for use in ponds—they are never a substitute for the correct balance of plants—but with a very small or shallow area of water, you may sometimes need to use them. Remember, though, that treating heavy algal growth can pollute the water when the algae die and decompose.

Food from small areas

Many gardeners feel that home-grown vegetables and fruit are too much to expect from a tiny garden, but it is surprising just what can be achieved. Selecting the right crops is of paramount importance. There is no point in trying to grow varieties that need a deep root run, wide spacings, and a long growing season, nor those that produce a small crop in relation to the amount of space they take up. Nor is there generally any point in growing fruit or vegetables that can be bought cheaply and easily in the supermarket.

The types to go for are those unusual varieties that are difficult or very expensive to buy, crops that give a heavy harvest from a small area, varieties that are especially noted for their superior flavor, and those where absolute freshness is of vital importance to the quality. They should be compact, quick-maturing, and easy-going. Most importantly, they should be crops that you enjoy eating: there's no point in producing a bumper harvest if your family doesn't like them.

Cherry trees are best grown trained as a fan on a warm wall or fence. This has the added advantage of making them easier to protect from raiding birds.

Growing in containers

It is quite possible to grow a reasonable selection of vegetables in a hanging basket or window box, so no one need feel that their "no-garden" is too small. As with most plants, the more space you can provide, the better the plants will grow and the wider the choice of suitable subjects you will have.

Special growing bags are sometimes sold, largely for growing tomatoes, but they are suitable for many other crops as well, such as lettuce, beans, eggplant, and sweet peppers. They can quite comfortably be positioned on terraces or balconies, patios, and on low walls. Ordinary plant pots can also be used: 15–18in (38–45cm) pots will support most fruit trees and bushes and a reasonable number of vegetables, depending on the variety. Nearly all fruits and vegetables prefer an open, sunny location, and growing in containers enables you to select the best spot for them.

A miniature potager, including Swiss chard, beets, and lettuce, forms the centerpiece in this small paved plot.

Growing in the ground

Growing plants in beds in the open ground increases the number of types and varieties you are able to try. In many "no-gardens" these beds will be raised beds, which can be excellent for edible crops as long as you remember that they are free-draining, so frequent watering will be necessary. The depth of soil or soil mix is also limited, so plants require regular feeding.

All plants in tiny garden areas have to work hard to earn their place, and fruit and vegetables are no exception—they should be attractive to look at as well as to eat. Select varieties with striking, bright colors, frilly leaves, or fruits with interesting shapes. Grow them in a decorated pattern—not necessarily in straight rows—and edge the beds or pots with plants such as curly-leaved parsley or edible flowers such as pinks. Beds of edible plants grown in this way become potagers and can be easily as ornamental as any beds of flowering plants.

Herbs for containers

The fragrant foliage, attractive appearance, and fascinating history of herbs make them popular plants with most gardeners. Most varieties form compact plants that are perfect for small areas; many grow well in containers and some, such as mint, are actually more manageable when their natural exuberance is restrained by containing their roots.

The most useful herbs are those we rely on in the kitchen to add spice to meals, and these are the ones that are best grown close at hand—perhaps in pots near the back door or in a window box outside the kitchen window. Herbs also lend themselves to being planted in raised beds, cracks in paving, and crevices in walls, as well as in small, formal beds in courtyard gardens and patios. Chamomile and thyme can even be grown as aromatic lawns or fragrant "seats," and some herbs, such as lavender and rosemary, perform well as low hedges in mild climates.

Most herbs need light, free-draining soil—they will not tolerate being waterlogged—and a sunny, open, but protected location. Containers must have sufficient drainage holes and a good layer of gravel or stones on top of the soil to serve as a mulch. For the best flavor and aroma, fertilize sparingly.

Recommended culinary herbs

BASIL An excellent culinary herb, with a strong, warm, clove scent. It forms a small bush with pointed, tender, light green leaves; there are many different varieties with subtly different scents, leaf sizes, and shapes. 'Dark Opal' is an attractive purple type. Basil likes warmth and will grow well in small pots.

SAGE A bushy, wide-spreading perennial with gray-green leaves and blue or pink flowers; there are also gold- and red-leafed varieties. Given plenty of sun, sage will grow well in pots, window boxes, or hanging baskets.

PARSLEY Perhaps the best-known herb. The deep green, tightly curled leaves make a good ruffled edging for decorative beds. The plain-leafed form is less attractive but has a more pungent flavor. Excellent for pots.

MINT A vigorous, spreading plant with underground runners that should be contained in a pot or tub. There are many different types including spearmint, eau-de-cologne mint, and golden variegated ginger mint. Likes moist soil and will grow well in light shade.

THYME A short upright bush or low-growing, spreading plant, depending on variety, which include gold- and silver-variegated types. Small leaves on wiry stems have a warm, spicy scent, and the pretty pale pink or white flowers are very attractive to bees. Will grow in tubs, window boxes or borders; makes a good edging plant.

A pot of fresh herbs for cooking, such as this one containing sage, chives, and parsley, can easily be grown on a sunny kitchen windowsill.

MARJORAM Sweet marjoram is a low, spreading herb that does well in gaps in paving. The golden-leafed form is especially attractive. Trim the plants back after flowering to keep them neat.

CHIVES Round, pink, papery flower heads make this a decorative plant. Its clumps of slender, grassy leaves have a mild onion flavor and are useful in cooked dishes and salads. Chives prefer slightly moister soil than most other herbs.

ROSEMARY The spiky, silvery leaves are strongly aromatic, and plentiful hooded blue flowers enliven the plant's appearance in summer. Grows best in a large container or raised bed. Can be clipped to form a low hedge.

BAY Unusual in that it forms a tree when allowed to do so, but amenable to clipping and growing in pots as standards, pyramids, globes, and other decorative shapes. It is slow-growing, so trained plants are usually expensive. The dark green, lance-shaped leaves have a characteristic aroma. Tender, it needs a protected location in cool areas.

Vegetables for containers

Most vegetables are annuals that are fairly easy and cheap to raise each year. If the crop is a failure, it's disappointing, but it has not usually cost you too much; you can try again, or try something different, next year.

You can buy popular varieties of vegetable seeds at any garden center or store, but a far more comprehensive range can be provided by mail order specialists. Their catalogs give much more detailed information than that found on the back of the seed packets, and many catalogs have a section devoted to varieties suitable for smaller spaces or container growing. It is also often possible to order young vegetable plants for home delivery if you don't have the facilities for raising seed at home.

Many modern varieties are F1 hybrids, which are often the best option where space is limited. The seed is much more expensive than open-pollinated types, but the resulting plants are more consistent in size, growth habit, season, and cropping. The varieties specified here are particularly suitable for gardening in a small space, but every year the catalogs are filled with introductions and improvements. Don't be afraid to experiment; it's part of the fun.

Besides being delicious when home-grown and picked as they ripen in the sun, tomatoes are extremely decorative, and some varieties, such as 'Sweet 100' and 'Garden Pearl' can be trained on a support to form a tower of small red fruits.

Recommended vegetables for container growing

POTATO Try the "gourmet" varieties. Sprout the tubers in a light, cool room, set them on a 4in (10cm) layer of soil mix in a deep tub or barrel and cover them with 4in (10cm) of soil mix. Keep adding mix almost to cover the shoots as they grow through until the tub is full.

BEETS Use globe varieties for baby beets. Sow the seed clusters in spring and thin the seedlings to one plant per station. Harvest at golf-ball size. 'Little Ball' is a good, uniform shape, while 'Burpee's Golden' is a dual-purpose variety with attractive, deep yellow roots and leaves that can be eaten like spinach.

KOHLRABI Produces turnip-like swollen stems that should be harvested at golf-ball to tennis-ball size: the smaller, the sweeter and less woody they are. 'Express Forcer' is a compact, fast-maturing variety; 'Purple Danube' is an attractive deep violet color. Sow seed in spring.

CARROT Sow very thinly in spring and pull as soon as they are large enough to eat. Choose short-rooted types for limited soil depth. 'Suko' is a fast-maturing variety suitable for a window box; 'Parmex' is almost round, like a radish.

TOMATO Always popular and not difficult to grow in a sunny spot. Start seeds indoors and plant out after frosts or buy plants. Does well in growing bags, tubs, pots, or even window boxes and hanging baskets when the right varieties are chosen. 'Tumbler' is specially bred for hanging baskets, while 'Patio' is recommended for containers, and 'Tiny Tim' can be grown in windowsill pots or window boxes. Liquid feed every 10 days once the first flowers are setting.

EGGPLANT (AUBERGINE) Grown like a tomato, eggplant need a warm, sunny location. Raise seed on a windowsill or buy plants, setting two plants in a 15in (38cm) pot once frost is past. Stake them as they grow if necessary. Pinch out the growing tips at 12in (30cm) tall to encourage bushy growth. Keep the soil moist and liquid feed every 14 days.

PEPPER Sweet peppers, grown like tomatoes, carry lantern-shaped, mild-flavored fruits that can be eaten green or allowed to ripen to yellow, red, orange, or chocolate. 'Jingle Bells' and 'Baby Belle' are ideal for small spaces, carrying plenty of miniature red peppers. Chili peppers are much more fiery in flavor: 'Super Cayenne' bears long red fruits in great profusion on a compact plant. They are very decorative and good for pots.

Nothing tastes better than freshly picked vegetables—plump small beets, crisp lettuce, succulent tomatoes, green or red peppers, and zucchini and their flowers, which are perfect for stuffing to make an unusual savory dish.

ZUCCHINI (COURGETTE) Set plants out after the risk of frost is past. Keep the soil mix moist and liquid feed every 10–14 days. Cut the fruits young and regularly for continued cropping.

BEANS Bush (snap) beans carry heavy crops on compact plants. Yellow and purple varieties add interest to plain green types. Pole (runner) beans can be trained up a tripod of canes and are very productive. Sow beans outside in late spring in tubs, as well as in raised beds. Keep all beans well watered while flowering and pick them regularly.

LETTUCE Particularly good when eaten super-fresh—within a few minutes of picking. Sow through spring and early summer for a succession of crops. 'Italian Red Parella' is a baby bibb, tinged with red and ready at tennis-ball size.

CHARD A decorative spinach-like vegetable with crinkly leaves and broad leaf stems—white in silver chard and red in ruby chard—excellent for planting among flowers in an ornamental bed. Grows better in beds than in pots; sow in early spring and thin to 8in (20cm) between plants.

SCALLIONS Sow from early spring onward and pull when pencil-size. Keep moist for a mild flavor. Good for growing bags and window boxes. 'White Lisbon' is an old standby; the stems of 'Santa Claus' are rosy pink toward the base.

RADISH One of the fastest and easiest crops. Sow in spring, in pots, beds, window boxes, or growing bags; keep moist and harvest while they are small and crisp. Many varieties are available, in varying shapes and sizes. 'French Breakfast' is red, tipped white, and cylindrical; 'Roodbol' is a cherry globe. Mixtures are also popular, with red, pink, white, purple, and bicolors.

SALAD MIXTURES (MESCLUN) There are several varieties of "cut-and-come-again" salad leaves that can be harvested while they are young and tender. Sow throughout spring and summer. Mixtures may contain various types of lettuces, herbs, purslane, rocket, cress, chicory, and cress. Colorful and very useful for small spaces.

Fruit for containers

There is space for at least a few types of fruit even in very small areas. Crops are grown on trees, bushes, climbing stems and canes, and ground-hugging plants. Use as large a pot as possible, filled with soil-based mix, and be careful about watering and feeding.

Tree fruits obviously present most problems in a limited space, but their size can be controlled by using the right rootstock and training the trees correctly. Most tree fruits consist of a rootstock, which determines the size and rate of growth of the tree, on to which is grafted the variety chosen for its fruit quality. For fruit trees grown in small areas, a dwarfing rootstock is required. Several types of tree fruits can also be grown as restricted forms against a support; cordons, espaliers, and fans are the most common *(see pp.130–131 for further information)*. You can use existing walls and fences against which to grow the trees or erect simple post and wire supports. "Step-overs" are low, single-tier espaliers and are used to edge beds and borders—novel and attractive, but don't expect a lot of fruit. The trees are kept to shape by regular summer and winter pruning.

Apples and plums are among the tree fruits suitable for growing in containers as miniatures, and it is possible to have several heavily fruiting trees in a very restricted space.

Recommended fruit for container growing

APPLE Compact, columnar forms of apple known as Colonnade and Miniature trees have been developed especially for small areas and pot culture; they are like an upright cordon. Best rootstocks are the very dwarfing M27, which produces trees up to about 6ft (2m) tall, and M9, which allows them to grow slightly taller. Trees need to be staked firmly throughout their life and must be fed and watered regularly. They will begin cropping at two to four years old. There are dozens of varieties available. Since nearly all require pollinating by a different variety in order to set fruit, grow two or three different trees, making sure that they are compatible and flower at the same time; the supplier will advise you. A "family tree" has three or four different, compatible varieties grafted on to the same rootstock—a neat way to ensure pollination and give you a selection of fruits.

CRAB APPLE Several varieties of crab apple are available on dwarfing rootstocks. Besides being decorative and useful in their own right, they also act as pollinators for eating apples. 'Donald Wyman' has white spring blossoms and small red fruit that birds enjoy; 'Madonna' has white double flowers and cherry-sized yellow fruit.

PEAR Pears are rather more difficult to grow than apples, particularly in containers. Quince C is the most dwarfing rootstock, but trees will still grow to around 8ft (2.5m) or more. Pears can also be grown as fans, cordons, and espaliers. As with apples, pollinating varieties are required. 'Moonglow' and 'Honeysuckle' are two comparatively new varieties that can be relied on to carry heavy crops.

What could be more satisfying than a bowl of currants, strawberries, and blueberries grown in your own "no-garden"? The plants take up little room, and the freshly picked fruit is likely to be far better than the bought variety in terms of flavor and color. It is also easy to protect the fruit from birds, and standing the pots on trays of gravel will keep them away from slugs and snails.

PEACH Fan-trained trees against warm, sunny walls usually give the best results. The flowers open in early spring and may require hand-pollination in cooler areas. Peaches fruit on one-year-old wood, so pruning to remove fruited wood and encourage its replacement is necessary. Peach leaf curl disease can be a problem. You may be able to find trees grafted on dwarfing rootstock or as a natural, or genetic, dwarf. 'Reliance' is perhaps the least demanding variety to grow, while 'Rio Osa Gem' has a very good flavor. 'Redgold' is a nectarine—a smooth-skinned form.

PLUM Plums grow well as fans on warm walls; they can be grown as cordons but tend not to crop heavily. Like peaches, they flower early in spring. Do not prune trees in winter, since this may encourage infection by bacterial canker. Choose a dwarf, self-fertile variety if you have room for only one tree. 'Superior' is dark red with yellow flesh; 'Early Golden' has an especially good flavor.

CHERRY Dwarfing rootstocks Inmil and Damil are now available to keep cherries to around 6ft (2m) or so; trees on Colt grow up to twice that size. The acid cooking cherry 'Morello' is self-fertile and will do well as a fan against a wall or fence, even a north-facing one. Several self-fertile sweet varieties are also being introduced. 'Stella' was the first, and it has been joined by others, such as 'Lapins' and 'Sunburst'.

GRAPE Grape vines can be grown over pergolas, against walls and fences, or on post and wire supports. They need training and pruning routinely. Select a variety suitable for your climate.

BLUEBERRY An attractive bush that grows well in a container but needs lime-free (acid) soil. Creamy, urn-shaped spring flowers are followed by round, sweet fruits, which are deep purple with a blue "bloom." The foliage has excellent autumn color. Pollinating varieties are not essential, but growing two or more different varieties may improve the yield. The fruits will need protection from birds as they start to ripen. 'Bluecrop' is one of the most popular and reliable varieties.

CURRANTS Black, red, and white currants are available; red and white are more suitable for growing in pots. Red and white currants produce fruits on spurs on older branches, allowing them to be trained as cordons. 'Perfection' and 'Red Lake' are good red varieties; 'White Pearl' is the most commonly found white one. Black currants produce the best fruit on one-year old branches; an easy way to prune them is to cut out the whole branch bearing fruit at picking time, encouraging strong growths to be produced for cropping next year. 'Ben Sarek' is a good compact variety.

STRAWBERRY This is the fruit that everyone can find room for. Strawberries can be grown in pots, as edgings to borders, even in window boxes and hanging baskets. Plant in mid- to late summer for cropping the following year. Some varieties can be raised from seed sown indoors in early spring and planted out to crop the same summer; the tiny-fruited alpines can be grown like this, but seed of large-fruited varieties is now also available. Most strawberries fruit for a short season in summer, but the season can be extended with perpetual or fall-bearing varieties that bear a smaller flush in late summer or early fall.

Raised beds

Brick is one of the most long-lasting and attractive materials for raised beds and paving. Its warm tones are a perfect foil for plants, and by setting low-growing types in pockets in the brick, the hard outline of the bed can be softened.

A raised bed is really just an extra-large, permanent container for your plants. Where you have no soil, but concrete or a similar hard surface, a raised bed allows you to achieve a better approximation of natural growing conditions than pots and tubs do. Even if you have a soil base, it can be useful to make a raised bed that is isolated from the existing soil so that a different range of plants can be grown.

Why build a raised bed?

There are many advantages in building a raised bed. It can be filled with a specific type of soil enabling you to grow special plants. It will also bring the plants up closer to you. This is of special benefit with low-growing fragrant plants, whose scent may otherwise go unnoticed, and with small, delicate plants, such as alpines and rock-garden plants, which often repay closer inspection. If a suitable coping is used on the top of the walls, they double up as seating areas, making efficient use of space. Changes of level provided by the beds improve the garden's appearance and can make a small area look larger.

Physically challenged gardeners often find raised beds particularly handy. When constructed at a suitable height, they can be worked on from a wheelchair or simply from a garden seat for those who find it difficult to bend or stand for a long time. As long as they are no wider than an arm's length—or two, if there is access from both sides—planting, weeding, and general maintenance is easier and less tiring. Gardeners with poor eyesight will appreciate the increased visibility of plants, and everybody will be encouraged to touch textured and tactile plants when they are within easy reach.

Use imagination when designing your raised beds. They do not have to be built singly—ascending tiers can be very successful; neither do they have to be formal shapes, flowing curves can look most attractive. In a small space, simplicity is usually far more effective than an intricate design, but that does not mean you have to limit yourself to a rectangular box.

Because a raised bed is a type of container, it shares some of

In the greater depth of soil in a raised bed like this one, small trees and shrubs will thrive, giving a patio or balcony the appearance and feel of a much larger garden.

the same problems of cultivation. The depth to which the roots can penetrate is limited (unless there is soil beneath the bed), which will in turn limit the size of the plants to some extent. Drainage tends to be free, so plants can suffer from drought unless watered regularly. Roots are not as well insulated as they would be in the ground, and in colder areas tender plants may be damaged or killed by cold.

The main advantage of a raised bed over other types of container is its greater size, but this can also be a drawback when it comes to finding suitable soil with which to fill it. Topsoil can be delivered by the truckload, but access is often a problem in many "no-garden" situations. The quality of topsoil is also variable and it is likely to contain a lot of weed seeds. Bagged soil mix is expensive, and buying sufficient to fill a large bed may be uneconomic, so estimate the amount required before starting on the building work.

Soil mix is generally packed in cubic feet (or liters), so you will need to find out the volume of the bed by multiplying together its height, breadth, and length in inches (centimeters). Divide the answer by 1728 (1000); this will give the number of cubic feet (liters) of compost required. For example, a bed 60cm high, 150cm long and 100cm wide would require 60x150x100=900,000/1000 = 900 litres of compost. You can then find out the cost of the compost you require and adjust the dimensions of the bed accordingly.

Plants for a raised bed

There are few limits on the types of plant that can be grown in a raised bed, but some are more suitable than others. Avoid very deep-rooted and invasive types. Trees, shrubs, and perennials can be left in the bed permanently, so plants that spread rapidly by underground runners or suckers are soon going to become a nuisance.

Among the acid-loving plants are many choice specimens that you will be able to enjoy if you fill the raised bed with acidic (ericaceous) soil mix: azalea, rhododendron and lily-of-the-valley bush among them. Free-draining soil with plenty of coarse grit mixed in provides ideal conditions for alpine plants. A lightly shaded bed filled with moisture-retentive soil mix will provide a home for plants that like cool, moist, woodland conditions. Lining the bed with plastic—with holes made in it for drainage—will even enable you to turn the bed

Raised beds

into a bog garden, in which you can grow plants such as primulas, marsh marigold, and moisture-loving irises.

Raised beds can be constructed from a variety of materials, so choose one that complements your house and surroundings. Brick is one of the most common materials and is fairly easy to build with; use frost-proof bricks. Dry (unmortared) brick beds are often seen, but for all except very low walls it is more satisfactory to bond the bricks properly and mortar them together. Most beds will use single bricks laid lengthways, known as a half-brick wall: for this a simple running bond, where the joints are staggered on each course, can be used. More decorative effects can be provided by full-brick walls, which are two bricks thick. Leave unmortared gaps between the bricks on the lowest course to act as weep holes, which will allow excess water to drain away.

Concrete and stone

Cinder blocks can be used in a similar way to bricks and are available in a range of finishes. Stone-effect blocks, with textured finishes in various colors, are popular; sometimes these come in "units" constructed to give the appearance of several stones already mortared together, which makes laying the blocks quick and easy. Natural stone is more expensive, but the variation in its shades, textures, and shapes gives it a more aesthetically pleasing appearance.

Dry-stone walls form an ideal bed for rock plants, but are not easy to build; the stones can be mortared in place for extra security.

Logs and peat

Whole or half logs make a pleasant, informal-looking raised bed; the height of the logs can be varied to give it a flowing outline. Kits are available consisting of sections of log bound together with wire, which simply need rolling out. However, they must be partly buried in soil for stability. Acid-loving plants were at one time grown in beds with the retaining walls made from blocks of peat. These were soaked and allowed to drain before being used to build walls one or two courses high. The beds were filled with soil mix made from peat mixed with acid topsoil and a small amount of grit, but the peat blocks tended to dry out and shrink. Because of the need to conserve natural peat supplies, beds formed from logs, filled with soil mix based on a peat substitute, are a more ecologically sound (and easier to manage) alternative.

How to build beds from brick and stone

The weight of damp soil within a raised bed will exert considerable outward pressure on the walls—the amount of pressure depends on the height of the walls. Most raised beds are at least 1ft (30cm) high, and to raise them to an easy working height means making them 2–3ft (60–100cm) high.

MAKING A RAISED PEAT-TYPE BED FROM LUMBER

1 *Lumber is particularly appropriate for peat-type beds for acid-loving plants. Lengths of 4 x 5in (10 x 12.5cm) lumber, bought from a lumber yard and treated with non-toxic preservative, are the easiest to use.*

2 *Choose a place that provides a firm base on which to build, and one that will suit the plants—the petals of camellias will turn brown if they receive morning sun when they are frosted. Bond the ties in staggered rows, like bricks.*

3 *For extra security, drill holes through the lumber and insert steel rods to pin them together. Use a hammer with a heavy metal head and, where possible, drive the rods through the wood and into the ground for several inches.*

A raised bed made from logs with an integral seat provides a resting place from which to contemplate your handiwork. Logs are particularly suitable for informal beds and woodland plants.

For walls over 1ft (30cm) high, a proper foundation is recommended, except where you are building on a level concrete surface in good condition. Where foundations are to be used, mark out strips at least twice the width of the wall with pegs and string and dig a trench 8–12in (20–30cm) deep. Consolidate the soil base well and drive in pegs to show where the top of the concrete should be. Make sure the tops of the pegs are level; half-fill the trench with concrete, tamping it down and leveling the surface. Allow it to harden for a few days before starting to build the wall.

The first course or so of bricks, stones, or cinder blocks will be below ground level where this type of foundation has been used. When building the wall, check both vertical and horizontal levels frequently, using a spirit level. Use posts and taut string stretched between them as a horizontal guide for each course of bricks or stones. Leave some unmortared joints between the building blocks on the course at ground level, to act as weep holes. Topping the walls with coping stones gives a finished appearance and the overlap affords the wall some protection from the weather.

It helps to conserve moisture if you line the base of the interior with heavy-duty plastic, but you need to make sufficient holes in it with a garden fork to enable water to drain freely. On a concrete surface, a layer of hardcore will ensure sufficient drainage. If you want to grow acid-loving plants in a bed with a mortared wall, paint the inside of the wall with asphalt or other waterproof paint to prevent lime from leaching into the soil from the mortar.

If you are not sufficiently skilled to build your own beds, you can pay a professional to do the work—but make sure he knows your requirements and uses appropriate materials.

4 *To suit plants such as rhododendrons, heathers, and azaleas, the soil mix must be acidic, so fill the bed with moist peat-based soil mix or one based on a peat substitute. Water the bed well before starting to plant.*

5 *Remember that even if you choose smaller varieties, the rhododendron, camellia, and azalea will grow into quite large plants, so do not overcrowd them.*

6 *Finish the planting by adding some heathers and primulas that are already in flower to complement the shrubs and to provide extra instant color.*

Choosing containers

Visit any garden center in order to pick a container for your plants, and you are likely to be spoiled for choice. While appearance is important—the container is often just as much on show as the plant in it—the style of the container must also be practical and suitable for the purpose you have in mind. What plants need from a container is an adequate volume and depth of soil and an efficient method of drainage to prevent waterlogging. Choose the size and shape of the container to suit the plant: a shallow pan is fine for alpines but hopeless for a vigorous, deep-rooted shrub. Check that the drainage holes are sufficient; sometimes, particularly with plastic pots, you can add extra holes yourself, but this is not always possible. Having catered for the plants' requirements, you then need to concentrate on picking a container of a material, shape, and design that you find pleasing to look at and that will blend comfortably with its surroundings.

1 Blue earthernware pot with a shiny blue-glazed exterior and a cream interior. Best planted with an architectural plant, such as yucca, or a shrub or tree. 2 *Terra-cotta strawberry jar pot with lipped holes for growing strawberries, herbs, or alpines.* 3 *Traditional terra-cotta, or clay, pots, one plain and one embossed with a design of swags of leaves and flowers. Terra-cotta is an excellent material for plant pots, since it is porous and breathes and also looks good, especially when it has weathered; it is, however, brittle, prone to frost damage, and will dry out quickly in hot weather.* 4 *Novelty basket made from cement, then painted. Cement containers should be allowed to weather before being planted.*

5 *Terra-cotta pot with a decorative wrought iron stand, which would be attractive standing on a patio or in a sunroom.* 6 *Large container made from reconstituted stone, a mixture of crushed stone and concrete. This is much cheaper than real stone, although the appearance of good-quality pots is similar.* 7 *Stoneware pot—when weathered, stone is probably the most attractive of all materials for containers, but it is also the most expensive.* 8 *Terra-cotta feet, useful for raising pots off the ground to ensure good drainage.* 9 *Partially glazed earthernware pot, with a checkered pattern. A good sturdy pot for a larger specimen plant.*

10 *Traditional square terra-cotta planter; planted with bay trees or clipped boxwood, a pair of these planters would add a formal note to an entrance porch.* 11 *Shallow terra-cotta bowl, ideal for alpines and low-growing plants, such as pansies or miniature daffodils.* 12 *Terra-cotta stand with a shallow bowl—useful for adding height to an arrangement of containers.* 13 *A deep urn made from reconstituted stone, which would make an eye-catching feature in a small plot, especially if raised on a pedestal.* 14 *Low glazed pot, which is large and deep enough to accommodate some summer salad crops or decorative winter cabbages.*

Choosing containers

The typical round, sloping-sided plant pot has proved itself a practical and efficient shape for growing and working with plants, but other shapes can often be particularly useful for small spaces. Rectangular troughs fit on or under windowsills or close up against a wall; half-round pots can be hung on walls or fitted on narrow ledges.

Hanging baskets, which are perhaps the ultimate in space-saving plant growing, come in a range of styles, some of which are much easier to keep watered than others. When considering less traditional types of plant containers, avoid those with narrow necks or waists, such as Ali-baba jars. They may look attractive, but when it is time for the plant to be repotted, it is virtually impossible to remove it with its roots intact without breaking the container. If a container has sufficient style, it can be used as a garden ornament in its own right and does not need to be planted.

Hanging baskets

SOLID-WALL BASKET

This type of container, made from plastic or terra-cotta, is really a flowerpot suspended on chains, rather than a basket. The bare wall can look unattractive, and you need to set trailing plants all around the edge of the pot so that the outside is quickly covered up. The great advantage of such solid-wall baskets is that they often have a drip tray built in or one that can be clipped on. This is particularly useful in places where people either sit or walk underneath the hanging basket.

Tubs and troughs

1 *Deep blue-glazed trough, excellent for use on a patio or on the top of a wall.* 2 *Small terra-cotta window box, with a molded pattern of acanthus leaves. This type of container is suited to more formal planting, perhaps with evergreens and other foliage plants.* 3 *This plastic window box with two built-in reservoirs for water would be a good choice for anyone with little time for watering.* 4 *A wooden half-barrel makes a good container for large plants needing special treatment, such as acid-loving camellias or rhododendrons, which must have acid soil to thrive.* 5 *A large and substantial tub, such as this treated wooden one, is essential if you plan to grow trees in your "no-garden."*

Wall pots

Pots that can be mounted on the wall usually have flat backs with a hole or two in them so that they can be screwed to the wall or a batten or hung on hooks. Shapes vary from round to half-round, to the novelty "swallow's nest" pot with a high back, which holds so little compost that it is suitable only for succulents and cacti.

SELF-WATERING BASKET

Several versions of this type of solid-wall hanging basket are available. However, the general principle is the same: a reservoir for water is built in at the base, and capillary matting is laid above this and below the compost. The matting is kept damp by water from the reservoir, which means that the basket needs to be watered only once every week or so.

TRADITIONAL BASKET

The hanging basket made from plastic-coated wire is the most popular type. Originally such baskets were lined with sphagnum moss, which is still used today, usually in combination with plastic to prevent its drying out so rapidly. Other types of liner include those made from coir, or coconut fiber, and preformed compressed fiber. The great advantage of the wire basket is that plants can be inserted through the holes in the sides.

Hayrack

Also known as a manger, the hayrack is another, generally larger, type of wall-mounted container. It is made from flat strips of metal, usually coated with black, green, or white plastic to prevent it from rusting. The container must be lined with plastic and sphagnum moss before filling it with compost and plants.

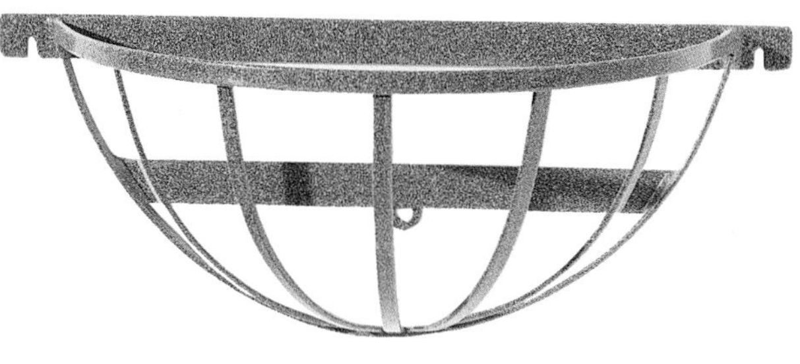

Window boxes

Window boxes are the nearest many city dwellers come to having somewhere to grow plants. They need to be about 8in (20cm) wide and deep so that they will hold sufficient soil mix to sustain plants during the season, although if plants are set in the window box in their own individual pots, they can be replaced as they fade. In addition to the usual unlined plastic window box, it is possible to find wooden containers that contain plastic liners (above), which can be planted and put into the box when they are at their best. Watering can be a problem, but plastic window boxes are now available with a built-in water reservoir (below).

Plant partners

The pleasing combination of different types of plants is one of the joys of garden planning. Often you will discover a particularly attractive combination accidentally, but careful consideration before planting will usually pay dividends. Take into account the contrasts and similarities of shapes, colors, textures, and sizes of the various members of groups of plants, remembering the effect of the different seasons of the year, and you will be able to create a garden where the whole really does seem to be greater than the sum of its parts.

Size and scale: The intense blue of grape hyacinths is offset perfectly by the cool lemon yellow of dwarf narcissus. Relative sizes of the flowers are important; in this situation large-flowered narcissus would tend to overpower the grape hyacinths so that a major part of the effect would be lost.

Winter planting: Winter is often a difficult time of year in a small garden, but this terra-cotta container will be a season-long delight. The creamy white of the frilly-edged ornamental kale plants dominates the arrangement, but bright spots of color are provided by the red skimmia berries, while trails of ivy soften the overall outline. The branching central brachyglottis provides height and structure in mild winter climates.

Color and contrast: Acid-yellow euphorbias and bright primroses make an effective color contrast with deep blue Myosotis *(forget-me-nots), but what gives this plant grouping its real impact is the brilliant scarlet of the lily-flowered tulips, which rise above the low-growing plants.*

Cool shade: Perfect partners for a cool, shady spot, the lush, bold leaves of hostas form an effective contrast with lacy fern foliage. A variety of shades of green can be just as effective as brighter color combinations.

Texture and foliage: The texture of flowers and foliage is an aspect that is often overlooked when planning plant combinations. The blue and white heads of love-in-a-mist rise from a feathery mist of foliage and bracts, complemented by the acid-green, foamy flowers of lady's mantle in the background. A ribbon of rosy red wallflowers brings solidity to the combination.

Containers for all situations

Few plant lovers are lucky enough to have perfect growing conditions, but usually plants can be found to suit even the most difficult situations. A cold, exposed, windy spot demands particularly tough plants that are adapted to water loss as well as cold conditions.

In many ways, a sunny position is one of the easiest to plan for as far as plants are concerned. There are many that revel in full sun, although frequent watering will be needed to keep the compost moist. Plants with delicate flowers and foliage are also more likely to be scorched in a sunny situation, particularly if water droplets remain on the plant tissue to act as a magnifying lens for the sun's rays.

In the hottest, brightest areas, unrelieved sun can be difficult for most plants to cope with, particularly in an enclosed courtyard or patio garden, where the heat is reflected off stone or tile floors and walls. In these situations, opt for succulents or desert plants that are well adapted to bright, hot, dry conditions.

Many "no-garden" areas may have the opposite problem—little or no direct sun and generally low light levels. But there are also plenty of plants, whose natural habitat is under the shady canopy of trees, that are perfectly adapted to these conditions. They may not be as brilliantly colored as sun lovers, but their subtle shades are still very attractive.

The plans shown here offer suggestions for planting, but it is easy to design containers to suit your own situation.

Plants for a cold, exposed position

Plants with leathery, waxy or needlelike leaves are well adapted to cold, drying winds. By choosing varieties with variegated and colored leaves, you can make sure that such robust and sturdy plants will not look dull.

The roots of plants in containers are more susceptible to damage in extremely cold conditions, but by insulating the containers you can help to protect your plants.

THE PLANTS

1 *Aucuba japonica* 'Gold Dust'
2 *Euonymus fortunei* 'Emerald 'n' Gold'
3 *Hedera helix* 'Goldheart'
4 *Juniperus communis* 'Compressa'

Sun-lover's trough

This is a trough for a really hot spot, which uses just three succulent plants well able to cope with the conditions. The contrast of form and size makes this a very effective combination.

THE PLANTS

1 *Agave americana* 'Striata'

2 *Sedum spathulifolium*

3 *Sempervivum tectorum*

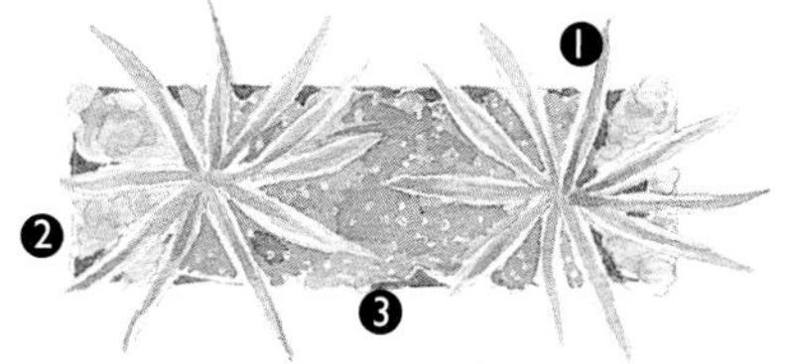

A tub for shade

Hostas are among the best plants for shade, with their heart-shaped leaves in a wide variety of sizes, textures and colors. In contrast to the fleshy-leafed hosta, Alchemilla mollis *has delicate lobed leaves and frothy heads of lime green flowers, while trailing* Vinca minor *is a vigorous grower with bright blue flowers.*

THE PLANTS

1 ***Alchemilla mollis***

2 ***Hosta* 'Shade Fanfare'** or other variety

3 ***Vinca minor***

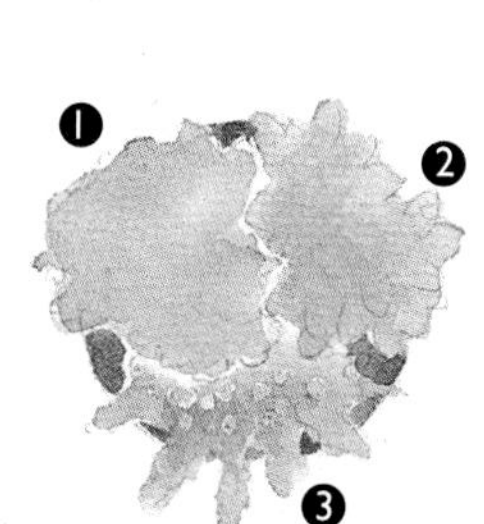

Plants to catch the eye

Planting for visual impact involves not only the considered use of color, but also of plant form and texture. Frequently a container is required to make a dramatic statement, particularly in a confined area where there is no room for a lot of other plants. Here, a simple arrangement is often most effective, relying on the individual plants themselves to provide the punch, and so-called "architectural" plants, with their bold shapes and plant forms, come into their own. A simple but striking container will reinforce the effect.

A traditional "riot of color" from a window box or hanging basket is the aim of many a gardener, but color theming of containers usually gives a far more pleasing effect than the random mixing of shades, though it need not be unduly restrictive. Boldest, brightest shades are the "hot" colors of the color wheel—reds, oranges, yellows. "Cool" colors are blue, green, and purple, which have a more restful effect.

Pastel tones can come from any part of the spectrum and are simply much paler tints of a particular color; like cool colors, they are quiet and restful. Pastel colors are often particularly successful in slightly shaded situations, where their delicate colors will not be bleached out by brilliant sunshine.

Dramatic urn

Cordylines can be relied upon to provide a strong, dramatic shape—like an exploding firework. Both variegated and plain-leafed forms are successful, and in mild areas will continue to provide winter interest. The silvery cascades of **Lotus berthelotii**, *parrot's beak, with its red and yellow flowers do not detract from the bold shape of the cordyline, but they do help to disguise the bare stem that this plant tends to develop.*

THE PLANTS

1 *Cordyline australis* 'Torbay Red'
2 *Lotus berthelotii*

Hanging basket in pastel colors

Subdued pastel tones have a quiet, relaxing effect. Here, pale blues, pinks, and whites are complemented by silvery foliage plants for a cool summer basket. Don't position containers of pastel-colored plants too close to plantings in bright colors or the paler tones may be overwhelmed.

THE PLANTS

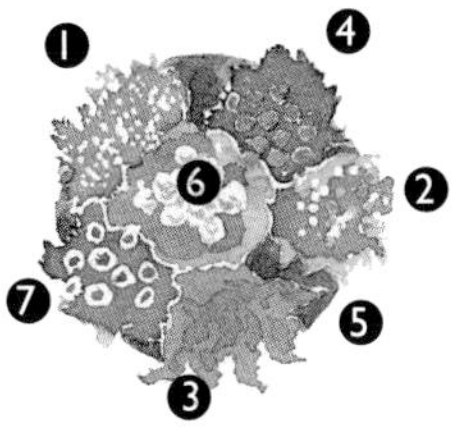

1 ***Bacopa*** **'Snowflake'**
2 ***Felicia amelloides***
3 ***Helichrysum petiolare***
4 ***Impatiens***
(pale pink variety)
5 ***Lobelia*** **'Fountain'**
(mixed blue and white shades)
6 ***Geranium*** (white variety)
7 ***Petunia*** **Surfinia Series 'Blue Vein'**

Trough in "hot" shades

This is a well-packed trough with plenty of contrast in flower shapes and plant forms to add to the liveliness of the brilliant colors. The trough uses colors from the "hot" range of the spectrum—intense reds, yellows, and oranges. Take care to use the compact forms of rudbeckia and bidens; some varieties are too vigorous for container use.

THE PLANTS

1 ***Begonia*** (scarlet tuberous variety)
2 ***Bidens ferulifolia***
3 ***Fuchsia*** **'Thalia'**
4 ***Lysimachia nummularia***
'Aurea'
5 ***Geranium*** **'Balcon Red'**
6 ***Petunia*** (creamy yellow
variety)
7 ***Rudbeckia*** **'Toto'**

The value of foliage

Flowers are often the most colorful and eye-catching parts of a plant, but the value of foliage should not be underestimated. Apart from providing a useful foil to the flowers, the leaves can be a striking feature in their own right. They may be large and showy, with bold, dramatic shapes, or tiny and numerous, forming an overall cloudy haze of green. Their arrangement on the stalk can provide distinctive and attractive plant outlines; they can be colored, variegated, spiky, leathery, hairy, or fragrant.

Sometimes a foliage plant on its own makes a perfect container specimen, its simplicity being the key to its effectiveness. A container of mixed foliage plants enables textures, colors, and forms to be complemented or contrasted, making an arrangement of long-season interest.

Single variety planting

Depending upon the type of plant, a single specimen or a small group of one variety—even a simple grass or bamboo—can make a striking display. This variegated hakonechloa makes a spectacular fountain of colorful foliage.

THE PLANT

Hakonechloa macra 'Alboaurea'

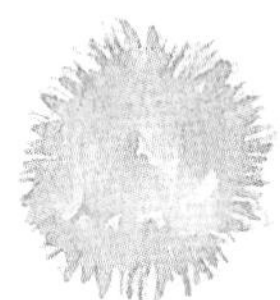

Color from foliage

Leaves sometimes have surprisingly intense and unusual colors. In this planting, plum purple and red shades of euphorbia and grey-mottled heuchera are highlighted by the silver filigree foliage of artemisia and the almost black, strap-like leaves of ophiopogon.

THE PLANTS

1 ***Artemisia*** 'Powis Castle'
2 ***Euphorbia amygdaloides*** 'Rubra'
3 ***Heuchera*** 'Pewter Moon' or 'Palace Purple'
4 ***Ophiopogon planiscapus*** 'Nigrescens'

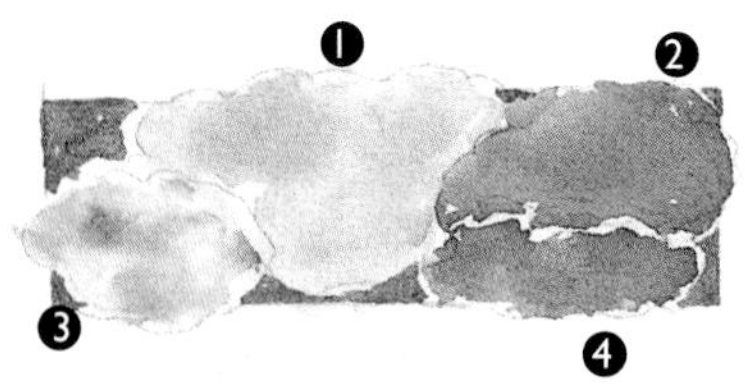

Scented and aromatic plants

The smaller your growing space, the more important it is that plants should earn their keep. As well as looking good, they can please some of the other senses too.

Selecting strongly scented flowering plants gives you an opportunity to gain immense pleasure from a container that is situated near a sitting area, where the plants' fragrance can be enjoyed in moments of relaxation. But it is not only flowers that are aromatic—foliage can be scented too. A trough of herbs is attractive, fragrant, and practical, since many of the herbs can be used in the kitchen.

Herb trough

Herbs are perfect for container growing, and, if picked reasonably sparingly, will provide sprigs for use in the kitchen over an extended season. There are plenty of contrasting forms and foliage colors to give visual interest to the trough.

THE PLANTS

1 ***Origanum vulgare*** (oregano, marjoram)
2 ***Petroselinum crispum*** 'Curlina' or similar compact, curled variety (parsley)
3 ***Salvia officinalis*** 'Tricolor' (variegated sage)
4 ***Satureja hortensis*** (summer savory)
5 ***Thymus* × *citriodorus*** 'Aureus' (golden lemon thyme)

Tub with scented plants

Many flowers are most strongly scented in the evening, but this tub contains sufficient variety of plants to be fragrant throughout the day. The color scheme has been kept simple, with purple, pink, and the pure white of the lily.

THE PLANTS

1 ***Glechoma hederacea*** 'Variegata'
2 ***Heliotropium*** (heliotrope)
3 ***Lilium regale***
4 ***Nicotiana*** 'Havana Apple Blossom'
5 ***Petunia*** (purple-pink variety)

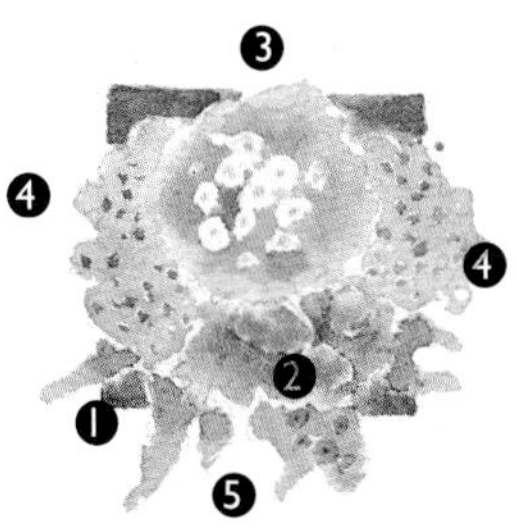

Chapter Three

Basic gardening

Green plants have a major advantage over many other types of organism—they can manufacture food from sunlight, converting the sun's energy directly into energy for their own maintenance and growth. To do this, they need certain chemicals, water, moderately warm temperatures, and physical support.

In the natural world, soil provides a reservoir of rainwater and suitable chemicals for the plants' needs. It also forms a support system for the roots, enabling them to anchor plants firmly in place while they grow outward and upward above the soil surface. In the growing conditions of a "no-garden" space, a good depth and expanse of soil is exactly what is missing. So the plant-grower must provide the necessary pieces of the puzzle to enable the plants to thrive in unnatural conditions.

This tiny, lavishly planted space is deceptively casual: it features dozens of different ways of growing plants. To achieve such a rich effect in a small corner needs a sensitive and creative understanding of the way plants work.

How plants grow

Plants that grow in a garden usually benefit from receiving much more light than houseplants do, but light can still prove a problem in our "no-garden" growing areas. Small plots may be bounded by high walls or fences or overhung by neighboring trees; basement areas become increasingly dull the deeper they are; walls may never receive direct sunlight.

Light

All green plants need light in order to grow, but plants need a particular quality of light in order to photosynthesize, or manufacture carbohydrates. The different parts of the spectrum are split into wavelengths, and the varying wavelengths of the visible spectrum consist of light of different colors. The portion of the light spectrum that is useful to the plant is absorbed by it, while the light that is of no value is reflected. The fact that plants are green shows that green light is of little use to them and is being reflected—the most valuable light for photosynthesis is an orange-red shade.

As far as gardeners are concerned, the practical application of this is to ensure that plants receive an adequate amount of ordinary daylight, a large proportion of which is useful to them. Artificial lighting, while it is valuable for adding to the visual appeal of a plot, is unlikely to be of any benefit for plant growth unless special growth-promoting light bulbs are used, and these are only really practical for use with indoor plants.

For the most part, plants try to maximize the amount of light they can absorb. This is why leaves are usually flat and thin and are arranged on the branches in such a way as to present the maximum surface area to the sun. The basic outline of many plants is a conical shape, which ensures that the lower leaves are not overshadowed by the upper branches. Plants may also be able to turn the surface of their leaves to follow the sun during its daily journey across the sky or to adjust them to variations in light intensity due to cloud cover.

Plant species vary in the intensity of light they require. Some thrive only in full sun, while others are well adapted to low light conditions—those plants that form the understory of a forest or woodland, for example, where little light penetrates the dense tree canopy. Such shade-loving plants are adapted to absorb what little light there is and would soon be scorched and damaged by a location in strong, bright sunlight. Plants that in nature grow in open locations in full sun have a variety of mechanisms to protect their leaves from excess exposure, including dense silvery hairs and shiny reflective surfaces. These impede light absorption, so the plant is unable to cope with shaded conditions. Choosing the right varieties of plant for the quality of light in any given situation is, therefore, the first important step to growing them successfully.

The effect of varying light intensity is most easily observed on variegated plants. In bright conditions, there is ample light for the leaves to absorb, and the active, green portions of the leaves can afford to be relatively small, with large, well-defined colored areas (usually yellow or white), which do not photosynthesize. Where light levels are lower, however, the amount of variegation decreases as the green areas increase, in an attempt by the plant to improve the overall absorption of light. Frequently, a plant in shady conditions will lose its variegation altogether, and revert to an all-green form.

Air

Air is vitally important to plants because the carbon dioxide it contains forms part of the equation for photosynthesis (in a simplified form, $CO_2 + H_2O \rightarrow CH_2O + O_2$, or carbon dioxide plus water gives carbohydrate plus oxygen). Air is also necessary for respiration, another process carried out by plants. This is almost the reverse of photosynthesis,whereby oxygen is taken in and carbon dioxide is released while carbohydrates are broken down for use by the plant.

There is no need to worry about enough air being available for these functions to take place in plants, but sufficient fresh air can be vital in preventing fungal diseases. These tend to thrive in humid conditions with little air movement, such as those found in overcrowded plantings. When gardening in small spaces there is a great temptation to cram in as many plants as possible, but being a little more generous with plant spacing can often prevent a display being ruined through damping off, gray mold, or other, similar diseases.

THE PARTS OF A TYPICAL PLANT

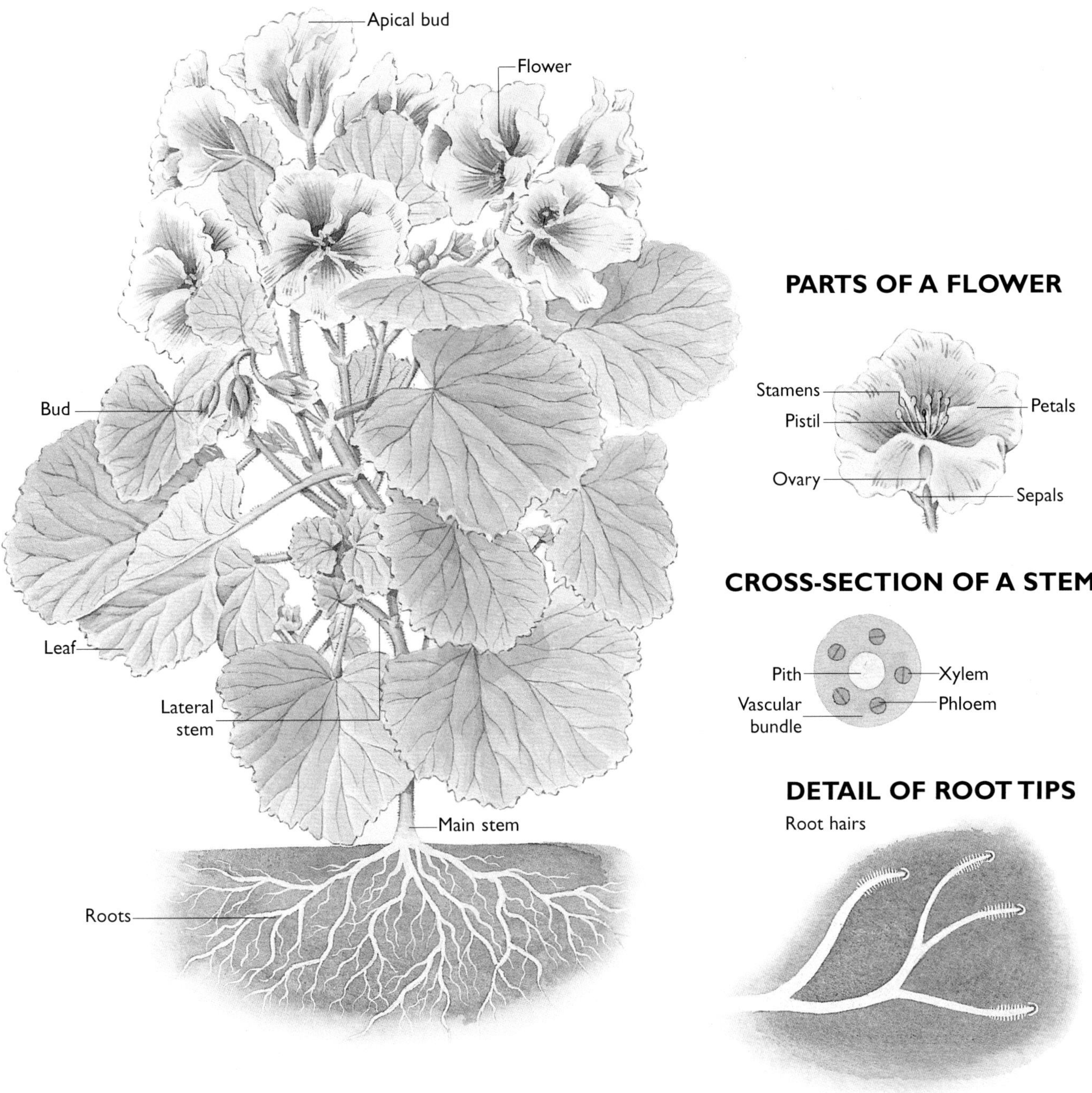

Plants vary greatly in form, but the main parts are evident on almost every type of plant. The plant's food is made in the leaves, while the flowers carry the reproductive organs. The female reproductive organs, known collectively as the pistil, are the ovary (usually hidden by the petals); the style or stalk; and the stigma, which receives pollen grains from another flower. The male reproductive organs are the stamens, made up of filaments, topped by pollen-bearing anthers.

The stems, shoots, and roots contain vascular bundles, which act like veins and arteries, carrying food to all parts of the plant. Xylem carries water from the roots, phloem transports nutrients, and the pith provides support. Apical buds are the growth buds at the tips of shoots.

Fine hairs on the roots absorb water and nutrients from the soil. The root system, which may be extensive and fibrous or a tap root, also anchors and supports the plant.

How plants grow

Water

Another essential element of photosynthesis is water, but it also performs other important functions. The various chemicals needed and used by the plant are dissolved in water, enabling them to be transported in solution to different parts of the plant so that the correct chemical reactions can take place. The pressure of water within each cell also keeps the whole plant turgid, or swollen, and erect. If a plant has insufficient water, the leaves and stems lose their turgor and begin to go limp—in other words, the plant wilts.

The natural water supply for plants is rain that is held in the soil in spaces between the soil particles. The plant's tiny rootlets and root hairs penetrate these spaces and absorb water as part of a process known as transpiration. The wide, flat leaf surfaces that are such a good shape for absorbing sunlight are also a good shape for the evaporation of water to take place, so a plant is constantly losing large amounts of water from its foliage. Water is carried through the plant in a continuous pipework of cells called xylem; as water evaporates from the cells of the leaf, more water is automatically sucked up through the pipework from the soil. This system works well until the reservoir of soil water is empty; moisture continues to evaporate from the leaves but cannot be replaced, leading to the wilting and eventual collapse of the plant.

Even in natural conditions, and in areas with relatively high rainfall, the death or stunting of plants due to drought is common; in "no-garden" situations, the problem is particularly acute. Soil depth is shallow; the soil in containers drains freely and is exposed to all-round evaporation. Dense plantings lead to heavy competition for water as the soil becomes filled with roots and profuse leaf cover prevents rain from reaching the soil; little rain may penetrate to the sheltered locations in which we try to grow our plants in any event. As a result, frequent watering is likely to be necessary throughout the growing season. Hot sun obviously increases the rate of evaporation from plants, but windy conditions can be just as damaging, whipping away moisture from the leaf surface. Increased watering is likely to be necessary in both sets of conditions.

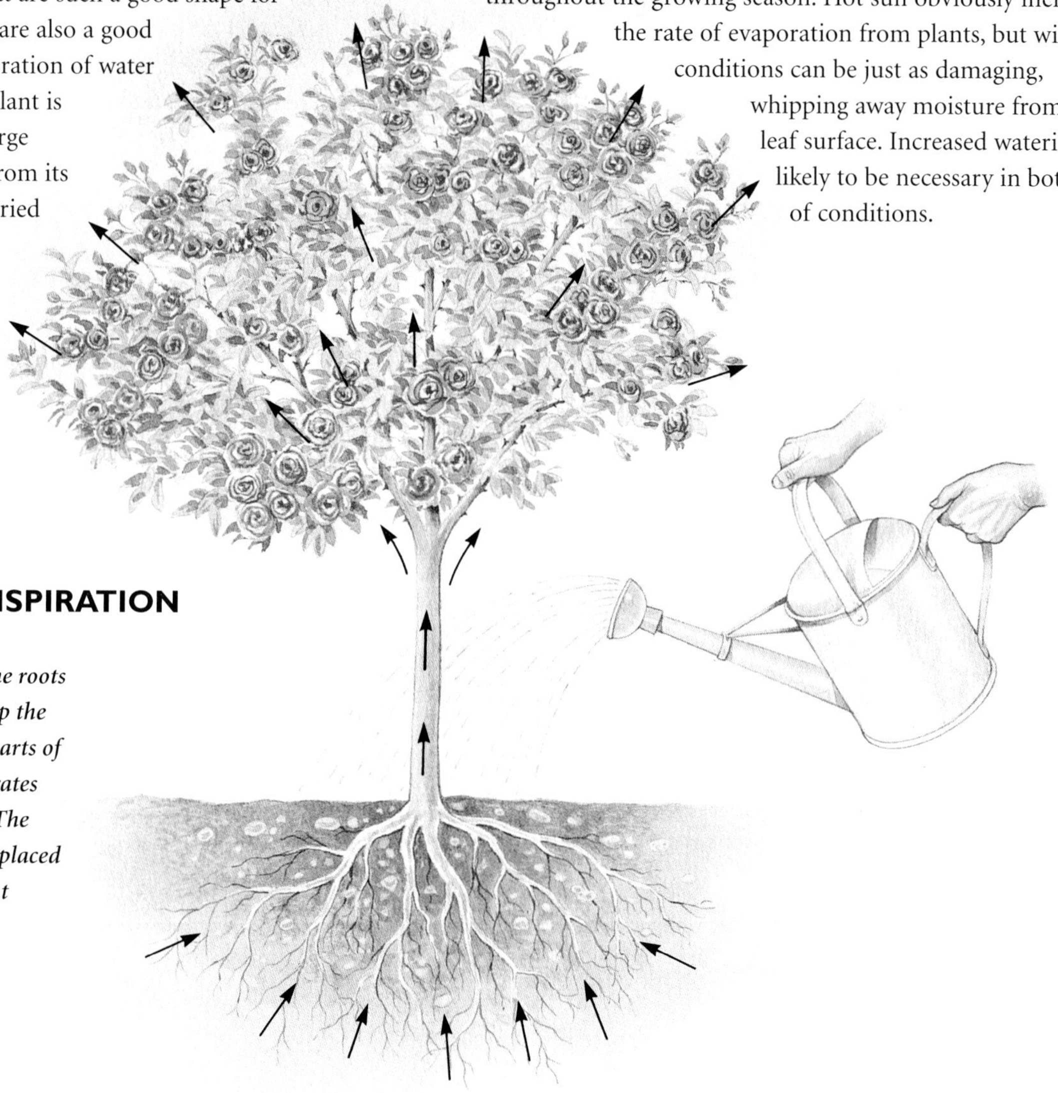

EVAPOTRANSPIRATION

Water taken up by the roots of the plant travels up the xylem system to all parts of the plant and evaporates through the foliage. The water in the soil is replaced by rain or by frequent watering.

Nutrients

Plants cannot survive solely on the energy they derive from sunlight, and a variety of chemicals is also needed to carry out a wide range of functions within the plant. These chemicals are usually referred to as plant nutrients. They are normally present naturally in the soil, but where artificial composts and only small amounts of soil are used, many of the chemicals will have to be provided or supplemented by the gardener.

Three major plant nutrients are required in relatively large quantities—nitrogen, phosphorus and potassium—and they are commonly in short supply in heavily cropped soils. The role of these chemicals is quite complex and they play a part in many aspects of the plant's growth. In broad terms:

NITROGEN is responsible for the leafy growth of plants.

PHOSPHORUS is needed for good seed germination and healthy root development.

POTASSIUM is required for flower and fruit formation and general hardiness. Calcium, magnesium, sulfur, and iron are also required but in lower doses.

CALCIUM is an important constituent of the cell and has a particular role to play in the development of shoot tips (for example, the death of the tips of developing tomato fruits, known as blossom end rot, is due in part to calcium shortage). But for most gardeners, the main importance of calcium is the way in which it interacts with other essential nutrients, making some of them unavailable to the plant. Some plants are particularly sensitive to this and will not grow satisfactorily in soil in which calcium (in the form of lime) is present—they are called calcifuges, or lime-haters, and include rhododendron, pieris, and camellia.

MAGNESIUM is essential for photosynthesis to take place, and a shortage leads to yellowing of the leaves (especially the older ones) between the veins.

SULFUR plays a part in cell division and protein structure, but it is rare for it to be in short supply in the soil.

IRON is also rarely in short supply, but plants often show signs of iron shortage because they cannot use what is available, generally because of the presence of calcium. The characteristic yellowing between bright green veins that results is known as lime-induced chlorosis. Like magnesium, iron is necessary to enable photosynthesis to take place.

TRACE ELEMENTS (micronutrients) are also required in tiny amounts. They are, nevertheless, essential to the plant and will cause symptoms of distress if not available. They include elements such as molybdenum, boron, manganese, copper, and zinc, but any one trace element deficiency is normally dealt with by using a fertilizer containing the complete range. Because deficiencies are frequently caused by calcium rendering minerals in the soil unavailable to the plant, these fertilizers are often formulated as foliar sprays, to be taken up directly by the leaves.

Warmth

The climate around the world produces widely varying temperatures, but most of the plants we grow do best within the range of 41–77°F (5–25°C). Above and below these temperatures, growth will be much slower. For most plants, 50–68°F (10–20°C) provides the optimum temperature range for growth.

In what we think of as the "warmer" areas of the world, it is not the temperature peaks that promote lusher, faster growth, but the fact that the temperature range stays within the plant's optimum growth range for a larger proportion of the year. In temperate climates, growth is virtually halted for several months when the temperature drops in winter; similarly in hot, desert regions, plants grow much more slowly as temperatures rise.

Ferns such as Nephrolepis *can tolerate widely fluctuating temperatures.*

Because high temperatures cause greater evaporation of water, plants tend to suffer from water stress as well. In "no-garden" situations, plants growing in enclosed areas, on balconies in full sun, and against sunny walls can become much hotter than in larger, more open gardens. As long as plants have sufficient soil moisture and humidity, high temperatures on their own are not likely to cause too much damage, although sun scorch may be a problem.

In temperate regions, the onset of cold weather must be dealt with. Some particularly tender plants will die when the temperature drops to a certain level above freezing, but usually it is frost that sounds the death knell. As the plant's tissues freeze, the cell membranes rupture and the soft growth collapses and turns black. Firmer growth, such as older stems, can withstand the effects of freezing to a certain extent, but hard frosts may eventually kill this too.

Shrubs and trees, which have woody stems and branches, are more resistant to the effects of frost, and although leafy growth may be killed, the framework of branches may sprout again from dormant buds the following spring. Roots are also protected from cold by the soil, and some plants survive freezing weather as dormant rootstocks, even when the top growth has been killed. Different species of plant have different degrees of cold tolerance, or hardiness.

How plants grow

Tender plants, with little cold tolerance, can often be grown in cooler climates in summer, being discarded at the end of the season. Half-hardy plants will not withstand long periods of cold but are more tolerant than tender plants, while hardy plants should survive spells of freezing temperatures.

The role of the roots

A plant's roots have two functions. They take up moisture and nutrients, and they also anchor the plant. In nature, plants usually grow in soil, but they can grow on other plants, like some orchids in tropical jungles; in water, like aquatic plants; and in gravel, shingle, or fissures in rocks, like alpines. But if they are going to photosynthesize, they usually need to be able to stay in one place and to spread their top growth to maximize its exposure to sunlight. If its roots are not firmly anchored, the plant runs the risk of falling over.

The qualities of soil

Soil varies widely from place to place, but it has usually developed from weathered rock, which has gradually been eroded down to fine grains. Most soil also contains organic matter in the form of dead animal and plant remains, which are broken down by bacteria and soil organisms to form humus.

The type of rock from which soils have developed, and the amount of humus they contain, give them different qualities. The size of the soil grains, and therefore the spaces between the grains, are all-important; large grains, as in sandy soil, have large spaces between them, so water and dissolved nutrients drain away rapidly.

Small grains, as in clay and silt soils, have only small spaces between them, which trap water and nutrients. Plants in sandy soil often suffer from drought and nutrient deficiencies; plants in clay soil may suffer from waterlogging of the roots. Humus—decayed organic matter—improves both types of soil, acting as a sponge to soak up moisture and make it available to the plants.

Since "no-garden" gardens contain no (or very little) natural soil, the growing medium has to be imported in the form of prepacked soil mix or potting soil of different types.

A colorful summer display of pansies and lobelia in a hanging basket will do best in a lightweight soil mix with perlite or other water-retaining granules added.

TYPES OF SOIL MIX

Most soil mixes are generally of a reliable standard if a reputable brand is bought. Soil-based mixes are very like garden soil; soilless mixes are based on peat moss or a peat substitute. For larger areas, such as raised beds, topsoil can be bought, but the quality is often variable and it is difficult to check it before buying. Special soil mixes are also available.

Because varying amounts of fertilizers are added to prepacked soil mixes, check the package to see when you need to start feeding plants with extra fertilizer. Soil-based mixes generally have the longest-lasting nutrient reserve.

Different ingredients give different amounts of support to a plant's roots, with the heavier, soil-based mixes offering the most stability. You can also provide root support with pebbles, stone chippings, sand, tree bark, rock, and clay granules. But few of these offer nutrients as well, so you will have to adapt your fertilizer schedule accordingly.

Soil-based mix

This is similar to garden soil. It contains a higher level of nutrients than other mixes and retains water well. Use it for trees and shrubs, such as butterfly bush.

Peat-based soil mix

Lighter and cleaner to handle, a peat-based soil mix runs out of nutrients quickly and dries out easily. Use it for annuals, bulbs, and tubers.

Peat-substitute soil mix

Made from substances such as tree bark or coir, with added nutrients, this can be used instead of peat for plants such as florist's chrysanthemums.

Ericaceous soil mix

This is a soil mix without free lime, which acid-loving plants such as azaleas, pieris, heaths, and heathers, need in order to grow well.

Perlite and peat mix

Lightweight mix with water-retaining granules, such as perlite, mixed in is ideal for hanging baskets and window boxes, where weight is critical.

Types of plant

Plants are divided into a number of general categories according to their physical characteristics and the way in which they grow. Knowing which category a plant belongs to will help you to care for it correctly and enable you to plan for future years. The different categories are not always straightforward—there is often some overlap between them.

Annuals

These are plants that germinate, flower, set seed, and die within one year. Some hardy annual plants, such as candytuft and bachelor's buttons, can be sown in fall and overwinter to flower and die the following season; although they seem to span two growing seasons, they still complete their life cycle within 12 months. Plants sown in fall will flower earlier and give a longer display than those sown outdoors in spring.

Hardy annuals will tolerate frost; half-hardy annuals will not. In cold areas, half-hardy annuals are often sown indoors and transplanted to their flowering positions once the likelihood of frost has passed. They may be raised at home in a greenhouse or conservatory, or on a sunny windowsill, or they can be produced commercially and bought as young plants from garden centers in spring. Some half-hardy annuals can be sown outdoors where they are to flower once the danger of hard frost is over.

Many plants appearing in seed catalogs as annuals are, in fact, perennials—if left to do so, they would survive for a number of years. However, because the display they give is much less attractive after the first year, they are treated as annuals and replaced at the end of the season.

Biennials

Plants that produce only leafy growth in their first season, then overwinter to flower the following spring or summer, are known as biennials; they need two seasons to complete their life cycle. They are sown in fall or spring to early summer, depending on climate and germination temperature, and transplanted later. Where space does not allow them to be raised at home they can be bought from garden centers. Popular examples include wallflower, English daisy, and forget-me-not. As with annuals, some plants treated as biennials are actually perennials that are discarded after their first flowering season.

Two commonly grown biennials are the stately summer-flowering hollyhock (above left) and the cheerful honey-scented spring-flowering wallflower.

Lupines, with their close-packed heads of pea-like flowers and handsome foliage, are among the most rewarding perennials.

Bedding plants

This is a loose term for young plants that are set out in beds and borders in spring and discarded at the end of the flowering season. Many of them are annuals and biennials, but plants from other groups may also be included. They are always temporary residents.

Perennials

Unlike annuals and biennials, these plants do not die once they have flowered, but live for a number of years, given appropriate conditions. Many perennials are herbaceous—they die down in winter in cool climates, reappearing from the rootstock again in spring. However, some perennials, such as bergenia and some species of hellebore, are evergreen.

An increasingly popular bedding plant is the vivid annual zinnia (right), which is also an excellent flower for cutting.

Types of plant

Shrubs

These plants maintain a woody framework of branches above ground year-round, although some species may be killed-back by frost in colder climates. The distinction between shrubs and trees is not clear cut, and there is some overlap; there are also some small, low-growing shrubs, such as garden thyme and lavender, which are generally known as subshrubs, or sometimes as shrubby perennials.

Shrubs may be deciduous or evergreen and have a wide variety of attractive features, being grown for their foliage, flowers, berries, or attractive stems, as well as their general shape and form. Foliage can be variegated or plain or have spectacular fall color; flowers can be carried at every season of the year.

Even in small spaces, shrubs are valuable to create a basic framework for the overall garden design. And where there is no space for a tree, a large or medium-size shrub can act as an eye-catching feature. The secret is to find the right shrub for the purpose you have in mind.

Consider the shape and the eventual height and spread of the plant. Do you want an evergreen that will contribute to the form of the garden year-round? Do you want spring flowers or fall color, or both? In a small "no-garden" area, it will pay to take time in selecting the perfect shrub for what may be the only spot in which you can plant one.

There is an enormous range of shrubs available, so try to choose one that offers more than one attractive feature—flowers, fruits, fall coloration, beautiful bark—so that it will earn its place in your garden all through the year.

The mophead hydrangea, with its great heavy heads in pink, blue, or white, is an accommodating shrub, which will grow well in a container and in almost any type of soil.

The Japanese maple Acer palmatum *'Osakazuki', with its dazzling display of fall color, welcomes the shelter of a wall.*

Trees

The main distinction between a tree and a shrub is the tree's larger size and its single stem, which forms a trunk, but this does not always hold true. Some vigorous shrubs grow far larger than some small species of tree, and a tree may grow several stems while a shrub sometimes develops (or is trained as) a single stem. Plants that would form large trees in their native habitat remain small and shrubby when grown in different climates, and some trees are regularly pruned back to keep them bushy—eucalyptus, for example, when it is grown for its juvenile foliage.

Large, spreading trees are obviously unsuitable for "no-garden" areas, but that does not mean all trees are out of bounds. Some smaller species adapt quite easily to growing in containers and provide useful height and vertical emphasis. Maples (*Acer* spp.), some birches, bay (*Laurus nobilis*), and conifers, such as yew (*Taxus baccata*) or arborvitae (*Thuja occidentalis*), make ideal trees for small spaces.

Bulbs, corms, tubers, and rhizomes

All of these plants have underground storage organs that enable the dormant plant to survive. There are subtle differences between them, although they are often lumped together as "bulbous plants." Bulbs consist of fleshy leaves wrapped around an embryo flower bud, all usually covered by a dry, papery, protective skin; narcissus and tulips are well-known examples.

Corms are swollen stem bases that are renewed each year and include plants such as crocus and gladiolus. Tubers are either swollen stems, as in begonias and cyclamen, or tuberous roots, such as dahlias. Rhizomes look like roots but are swollen underground stems, generally growing horizontally, so they tend to move forward through the soil. Bearded irises are probably the best-known rhizomatous plants.

Tuber

Anemone blanda *grows from a tuber.*

Bulb

Bulbous tulips enliven late spring days.

Corm

Crocuses grow from corms.

Rhizome

The beardless Iris versicolor *has a rhizome.*

Choosing plants

There are many different ways to obtain plants, and your choice will depend, among other things, on how much money you want to spend, what facilities you have, and how much work you want to do. Your first choice is between raising your own stock from seed or cuttings and buying ready-to-plant specimens.

Raising your own plants is satisfying, usually cheaper, and often gives you a greater selection of varieties and flower colors. However, you do need to be able to provide the right facilities for germination or rooting and transplanting. Some seeds will germinate quite easily in a dark, warm place; for others you will need a heated propagator. If you are to be successful, you also need to have sufficient space and time to allow the plants to develop and be reasonably skilled in the propagation and care of young plants *(see pp.142–149 for details of propagation techniques)*.

Sowing seeds

If you want only one or two packets of seed, a reduced selection of varieties from seed companies is available at garden centers and stores. From them you can also obtain seed which has been treated in various ways to make it easier to sow and germinate.

PELLETED SEED is covered in a clay mixture that separates the seeds and makes them a more suitable size for easy handling and space sowing. It is useful for plants that have very small seeds, such as petunias.

SEED TAPES have the seeds evenly spaced along a length of paper tape, which is laid where you want the plants to grow and then buried.

SAVING SEED The cheapest way to obtain seed is to save it from flowers grown by yourself or by friends, but not all varieties will give good results. Hybrid varieties do not breed true from seed, so if you save seed from them you will end up with something quite different from what you were expecting.

Seed gathered straight from flowers often needs to be sown immediately to give a good germination rate—commercially collected seed is specially treated and kept in carefully controlled conditions to preserve its viability.

BUYING SEED BY MAIL ORDER

Mail order seed catalogs provide a wealth of ideas and information about plants, as well as offering a good selection of varieties—some old favorites, some new introductions. Flowers are generally available in single color selections, making it easier to plan themed plantings; plants offered at garden centers are often available only as mixed colors, so you have to take pot luck. There is usually an excellent selection of annuals, biennials, and vegetables, letting you choose varieties according to size, habit of growth, foliage color, and so on. Most catalogs also offer seeds of perennials, although not in the same abundance as annuals, and some seeds of shrubs and trees.

mix, increase the heat and amount of water they are given to start them into growth, and take cuttings from the new shoots as they develop. Geraniums, begonias, fuchsias, and many other plants can be propagated in this way. Besides using your own plants, you can also ask for cuttings from the plants of friends and neighbors.

Buying in plants

Plants can be bought at various sizes and stages of growth, either by mail order or from nurseries and garden centres. Generally, the smaller the plants supplied, the cheaper they will be, but the more difficult to raise to flowering size. Plants for transplanting are usually sold as seedlings or "plug plants."

Quite large specimens of popular plants such as fuchsias and geraniums (above left) are usually potted up individually. Small seedlings for transplanting (above right) are usually sold in trays. Plug plants (right) can be bought in different sizes in lightweight plastic or foam trays. Seedlings of annuals ready for planting out (below) are also sold in trays or strips.

SEEDLINGS have been germinated under the correct light and temperature conditions, and they are supplied to you at a time of year when it is easy to provide the necessary warmth and light for their continuing development. They are normally available in small trays of soil mix that contain different numbers of plants according to variety. Within a short time of their arrival, the seedlings will need pricking out (replanting into seed trays so as to give them more room to grow), and you will need to have sufficient well-lit space to grow them unless they are large enough to plant in the desired location. You will also need soil mix and small pots or trays into which to prick out the plants.

"PLUG PLANTS" do not need pricking out—they have been raised in individual cells containing a small "plug" of soil. They will need to be repotted into larger containers, but there is not the same urgency as with other seedlings, and the individual plants are much easier to handle. Plugs are usually available in a range of different sizes.

READY-TO-USE PLANTS are large enough to plant out into beds or containers—ideal if you don't have the facilities for transplanting. Some mail order suppliers offer larger-than-normal plug plants for setting out immediately and will deliver them at a time when you can do this without worrying about frost. There are many ready-to-use plants at nurseries and garden centers, including herbs, advanced seedlings, climbers, and rock-garden plants. A large range of perennials, shrubs, and trees are sold in individual pots. The larger the plant, and its pot size, the more expensive it tends to be. Such plants, which have been raised in containers, can be planted out at virtually any time of year.

Taking cuttings

Many plants are easy to root from cuttings and will give you a good stock of young plants for little cost. Plants that have performed particularly well can be propagated in summer, and the young plants overwintered in frost-free conditions for setting out the following spring. If space for overwintering is a problem, retain just one or two of the best original specimens, keeping them frost-free and just moist during the winter. In early spring, repot them in fresh soil

Choosing plants

BARE-ROOT PLANTS This used to be the only form in which most plants were available, and they are still obtainable from various nurseries and may sometimes be supplied by mail order. Bare-root plants can be planted only in the dormant season. They are often "lined out" in nursery rows, and when the dormant season arrives they are lifted and transplanted as required. It is a cheaper way of buying relatively large quantities of plants. When a plant has been lifted, efforts should be made to prevent the roots from drying out (in the dormant season, wind is the major drying factor). Wrap the roots in plastic or in a paper sack for the journey home, then set the plant in its permanent position as soon as you arrive there. If it is not possible to plant it immediately, cover the roots with moist soil or potting mix and keep the plant in a sheltered, frost-free place until you can.

BALLED-AND-BURLAPPED PLANTS Balled-and-burlapped shrubs and trees are similar to bare-root specimens, but the plants have been undercut while growing in the nursery bed to encourage them to form a compact ball of fibrous roots. They are then lifted with as much soil as possible around the intact root ball, which is generally wrapped in burlap or netting to hold it together. This method of growing plants helps to avoid root damage when the plants are lifted and so permits plants to be established more easily.

Where to buy plants

The main options for buying plants are mail order, garden centers, or specialist nurseries.

MAIL ORDER is convenient; you can choose plants from a catalog at home and they are delivered to your door, saving you the trouble of making a special journey and possible problems in transporting the plants. For rare or speciality plants, mail order may be the only option, since unusual plants may not be available at any outlet within traveling distance. The drawbacks of mail order are that you have to rely on catalog descriptions and you cannot see the size or quality of the plants you are ordering. You usually have no control over the date they will arrive (although some catalogs allow you to specify delivery dates). Plants may be damaged in transit, and though you can usually obtain replacements or refunds, this involves extra trouble and loses valuable growing time. You also have to pay for the shipping of the plants, which can be fairly expensive.

GARDEN CENTERS are popular, since most have a good range of competitively priced plants and also stock many of the sundries you are likely to need, making "one-stop shopping" possible. However, they are unlikely to stock unusual species or varieties, and they can quickly sell out of seasonal items. The quality of the plants is also sometimes indifferent at poorly run outlets, but you can at least select them yourself.

SMALLER NURSERIES where plants are raised on the premises are dwindling in number, but here you can usually buy from a knowledgeable seller who gives advice freely. This type of nursery often specializes in specific groups or species of plants (clematis or hostas, for example) and you are likely to find a much better selection of those particular plants than you would at garden centers.

The range of types of seedlings in a garden center is often rather limited, but you can check them over and choose strong, healthy plants.

WHAT TO LOOK FOR

GOOD SIGNS

BAD SIGNS

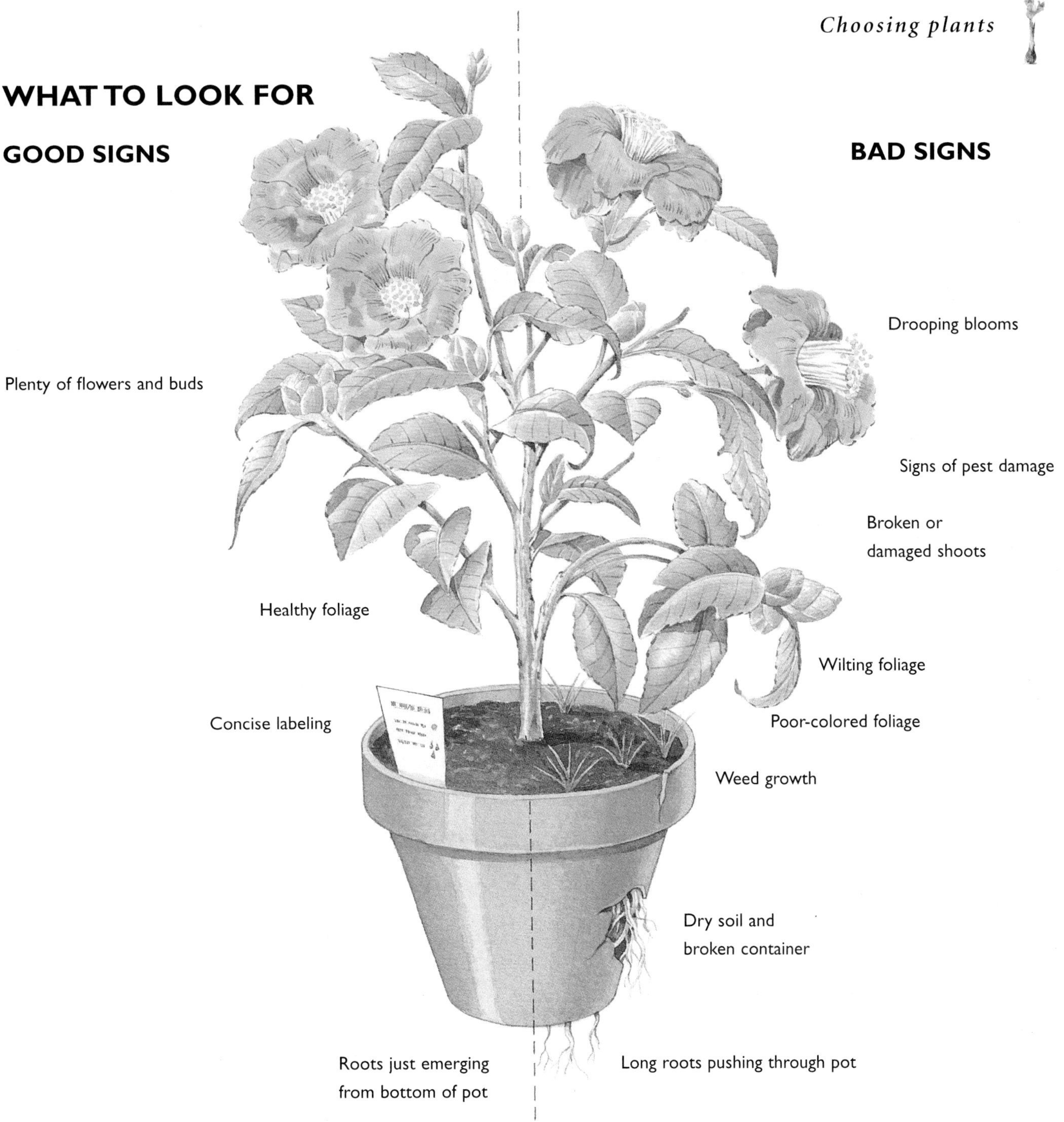

Look for a plant that appears healthy, with good-sized, evenly green leaves (poor-colored leaves indicate that the plant has been starved). Select a well-balanced, sturdy specimen with stocky stems, avoiding those that are one-sided or have soft, elongated stems. Bigger is not necessarily better; smaller, sturdier plants grow more quickly and can often overtake initially larger specimens after a short time in their permanent locations.

With container-grown plants, check the base of the pot; root tips should be just emerging from the drainage holes. If long, matted roots are protruding, the pot is too small, and the plant's growth will have been checked. If there is no sign of roots, try gently tipping the root ball from the pot—after one or two taps the whole root ball should slide out cleanly. If it does not, it could indicate that the plant has only recently been potted and should be left a little longer to establish itself. The surface of the soil should be free from weeds, which will have been competing with the plant and that could be a nuisance if they get established among your plants at home. The soil should also be evenly moist; do not buy plants where the soil is dry and has shrunk away from the sides of the pot.

Check the undersides of the leaves for any telltale signs of pests and diseases and reject any plants that are damaged or infested.

Tools and equipment

Only a few tools are essential for "no-gardens," which is just as well, since tool storage can be a problem where space is limited. Tools can be expensive, but it's worth buying the best quality you can afford—buying cheap brands often proves to be a false economy.

Caring for the tools properly will extend their life and improve their performance. Small hand tools can usually be kept somewhere in the home, or you can keep them outside in waterproof wooden or plastic storage bins and boxes. A useful way to keep long-handled tools tidy is to hang them on a wall rack with hooks. Some manufacturers supply sets of tools with one handle and a number of interchangeable heads (hoes, brushes, and forks for instance), and these are particularly useful where storage space is limited.

Always clean your tools properly after use. Remove all soil and mud, wipe the tools over with a damp cloth, then dry them and rub the bright parts over with a little oil to prevent rust. Stainless steel blades are expensive but long-lasting, and there are various other metal finishes that are claimed to improve performance and prolong the life of the tools.

What you will need

What tools you will need depends on the space you have and the type of gardening you are going to do; if your plant-growing is limited to containers, you will need fewer tools than if you have larger areas of raised beds to cultivate.

TROWEL AND HAND FORK A trowel is not essential for planting in containers, but it does make life easier and is useful for planting in beds or in the ground. It is is probably the tool that is going to get the most use in a "no-garden" situation. Besides digging holes for planting, it can be used for digging out weeds, mixing compost, and incorporating fertilizer. A hand fork is useful for aerating soil in containers. Make sure you buy sturdy tools that will not bend when pressure is applied.

HAND PRUNERS These are necessary to keep plants within bounds in limited spaces, to do general pruning work, and to help with cleaning up at the end of the season. There are two basic types of pruners: bypass (parrot-billed), where the two parts of the blade pass each other like scissors; and anvil, where the blade meets a flat surface when cutting. It is usually easier to obtain a clean cut with the bypass type. Test out the feel of pruners when buying them, since it is important that they fit your hand comfortably and are easy to use. Check that the handles are not likely to pinch the fleshy part of your hand. Brands with a rolling handle may be worth considering if you find constant squeezing tiring, although they are really intended for people who are likely to be pruning for hours at a time. If you have a weak grip, ratchet-action pruners make tough cuts with the minimum of effort.

Along with your hand pruners you may like to use a knife occasionally, but in small spaces it is not an essential gardening tool. For most functions, hand pruners, a pair of scissors, or a single-sided razor blade are just as satisfactory. If you are planning to use a knife to take cuttings or do pruning, it must be really sharp.

BORDER FORK AND SPADE In most small-space gardens these are not needed, but if you have a raised bed you may find a fork useful for turning over the soil, and the spade for shoveling soil into containers, and cleaning up debris. Choose "border" or "lady's" models, rather than "digging" tools, since they have smaller blades and are easier to manage.

WATERING CAN Choose a can that is well balanced and easy to carry when full, with a long spout that lets you reach awkward spots. Brass cans are expensive; galvanized cans last longer than plastic but are heavier and noisier.

SPRAYER A hand mister can be used for applying foliar fertilizer, pesticide sprays, and water. Have several misters and keep those used for pesticides and herbicides separate. For small areas, pesticides and herbicides are best bought as ready-to-use sprays, since it is often difficult to mix up small amounts of concentrate for a hand sprayer.

RAKE This is sometimes useful for leveling and crumbling soil in larger beds, as well as refreshing and aerating the surface soil and removing plant debris such as fallen leaves. For crumbling the soil, a type of small hand rake is available, which can also be used for stirring up the surface of the soil in larger containers.

SUPPORTS You will need various types of trellis for climbing plants, as well as link supports and stakes to hold up the stems of heavy-headed plants. Soft twine or raffia are the best choices for tying most plants to their supports, but soft garden wire is good for more robust plants and for thick-stemmed climbers.

This hand-weeder is one of many tools that can be slotted into the same handle, saving storage space.

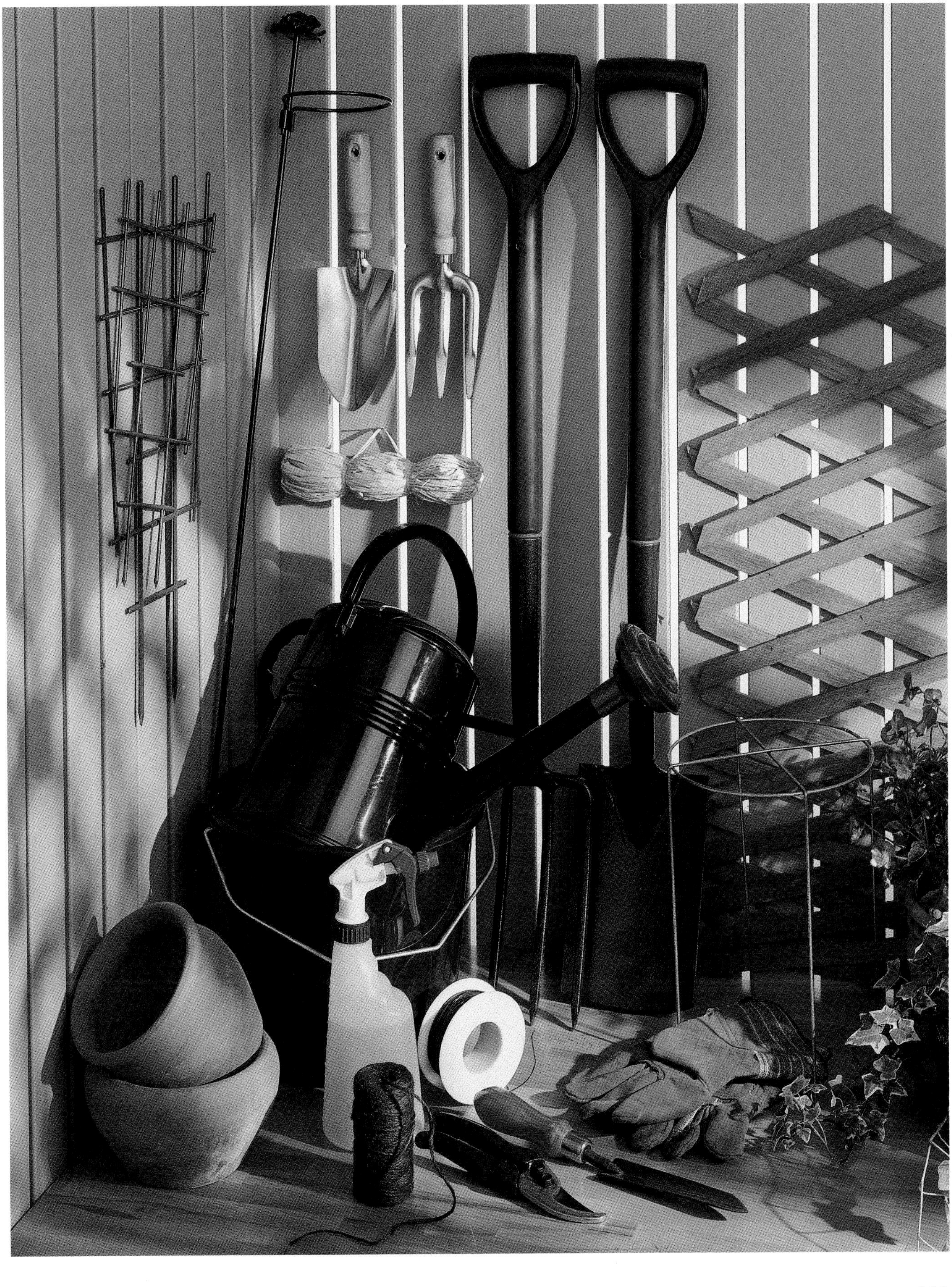

Growing in the ground

To be able to grow plants in the ground in the "no-garden" garden is something of a luxury. By our definition, the ground space available will be small, and there could be problems with the planting itself and with getting the plants established. The quality of the soil present could also leave something to be desired. Builders' rubble or infertile subsoil are common, any good-quality topsoil having been taken away and sold when building work started.

Soil containing a lot of clay will form a ball if you roll a small amount of it in your hand.

If you have some ground space in which you may be able to grow plants, your first step should be to take a closer look at the soil. If possible, excavate a deep hole to expose the soil strata; usually several distinct layers can be identified. You may be able to see the depth of topsoil; how stony it is; whether there is a chalk layer, making the soil alkaline; or a bed of clay, making drainage slow and poor. The topsoil is the most important layer, for it is here where the plant roots develop and obtain their nutrients and moisture. You can carry out several simple tests to learn a little more about the nature of your soil.

Testing the soil

Take a sample of soil from just below the surface, using a trowel. As we have already noted, there are several different types of soil. It may be predominantly clay, sand, or silt, or a mixed loam, and contain varying amounts of humus, or organic matter. Rub a small quantity of wet soil between your thumb and forefinger; does it feel gritty to the touch, or sticky, or slippery? Sandy, free-draining soils feel gritty, while heavier clays and silts feel sticky or slippery.

Take a small handful of moist soil and squeeze it tightly in your palm. When you open your hand, does the soil crumble and fall apart or does it hold together? If it crumbles, it is sandy soil; if it holds together it contains a quantity of clay. Try to roll the handful into a ball, then rub the ball with your thumb to see if it will take a polish. Roll the ball into a long snake, then try to join the ends together. The more of these steps you can achieve, the higher the quantity of clay the soil contains.

CHECKING THE pH CONTENT OF YOUR SOIL

1 The most common type of soil-testing kit consists of a container in which to place the soil sample, a dropper, capsules of chemicals, and a chart against which to compare the results of your test.

2 Take a soil sample 2–3in (5–7.5cm) below the surface. Put the contents of a capsule into the test chamber and add two capsules of dry soil. Fill the chamber with distilled water.

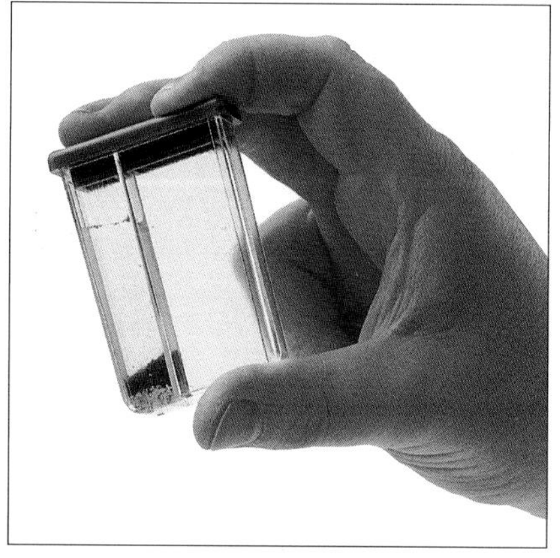

3 Make sure the water comes up to the level of the dotted line. Then fit the cap securely on the tester and shake it until the powder and soil are thoroughly mixed in the water.

Soils are hardly ever pure sand or pure clay, but a mixture. Put another trowelful of soil into a glass jar with a screw lid and half-fill the jar with water. Shake it up well, then leave the jar on a level surface for several hours or overnight so that the contents settle. The soil will separate into layers, with the largest particles (stones, grit, and sand) on the bottom, and fine particles of silt and clay at the top. This is a particularly useful test because it shows you at a glance the different proportions of the various soil constituents. The organic matter the soil contains will float on the surface of the water.

These tests will tell you about the physical makeup of the soil. Sandy soils are light, easy to work, warm up early in spring, and drain freely. Clay soils are heavy, slow to warm up, and prone to waterlogging. Extremes of both types of soil can be improved by the addition of well-rotted organic matter (such as garden compost), which will open up clay soil and improve its drainage and, with its absorbent, spongy texture, will help sandy soil to retain more moisture.

Checking the soil's chemical content

The chemical constituents of the soil are also important, for it is these that provide plants with their nutrients and determine how fertile the soil is. The quantities of these chemicals are not so easy to establish, but already you will have an idea of the fertility from the physical structure tests; free-draining, sandy soils tend to contain fewer nutrients than clays, because the soluble chemicals are washed away. Kits for testing the soil are widely available, and these give an idea of the proportions of the major plant nutrients—nitrogen, phosphorus, and potassium *(see also pp.98–99)*—but the results of the tests should be viewed only as a rough guide. Truly accurate results depend on more sophisticated and rigorous sampling and testing procedures than are possible at home.

One chemical test that it is worth your while to perform is that for soil acidity, or pH. This measures the amount of calcium in the soil and will tell you whether your soil is acid or alkaline, indicating the type of plants you may be able to grow. Neutral or alkaline soils rule out the possibility of growing acid-loving plants such as rhododendrons and camellias. Although electronic meters for measuring the pH are available, a more accurate result can generally be obtained by using a solution that will change color according to the degree of acidity or alkalinity of the soil.

Sandy soil will separate and remain crumbly if you squeeze a small amount of it tightly in your hand.

4 *Let the tester stand for a few minutes to allow the color to develop fully in your sample.*

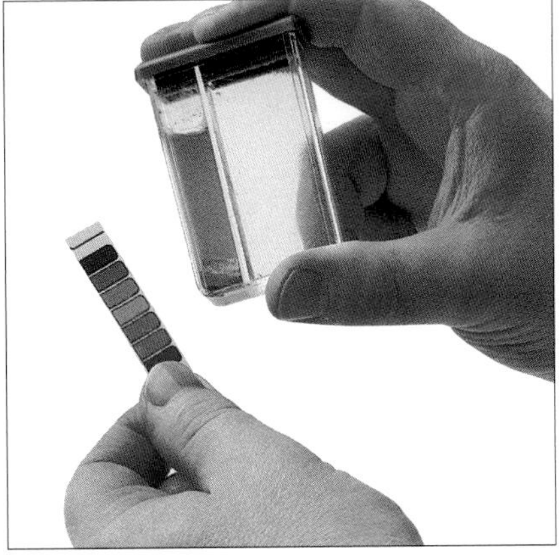

5 *Against a white background and using natural daylight, but not direct sunlight, compare the colored solution in the test chamber with the colors on the chart. This will tell you whether your soil is alkaline or acid.*

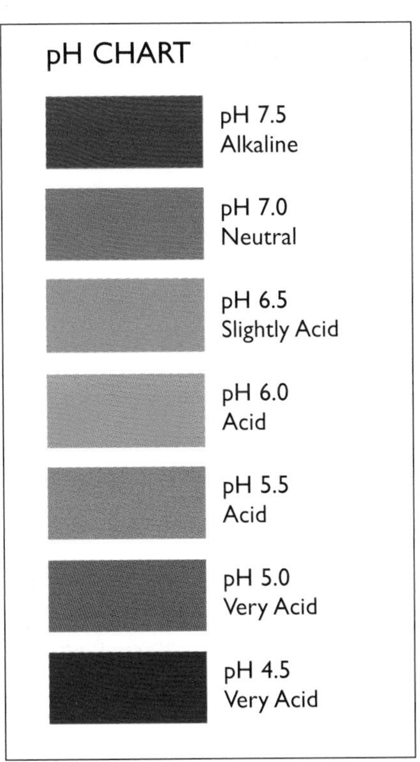

Planting techniques

You may be lucky and have a narrow strip of soil in your "no-garden," but generally you will be faced with a hard surface. If the surface is paving slabs or bricks, it is usually possible to pry up one or two of them and to plant in the gap that is created. If the slab has been cemented into place you may need to break it up with a sledge hammer so that you can extract it piece by piece. If the surface is solid concrete, use a cold chisel and hammer to chase out the area you want to expose, then break up the inside of the area with hard blows on the chisel and remove the bits of broken concrete. Wear protective goggles and gloves when carrying out either of these processes.

Cracks between slabs can often be widened sufficiently to take a small plant by chiseling away one edge, but lifting an entire slab allows you to do a much better job of improving the soil and planting than simply chipping off one corner and squeezing the plant in there. In the same way, when breaking up concrete, be sure to make a hole larger than is needed to allow for the existing plant roots. Once you have cleared a large enough area for planting, dig out as big a hole as is practical and fill it with fertile soil or potting mix. Add some slow-release fertilizer and water-retaining granules, whether you are using existing soil or replacing it. Set the plant in the hole and firm it in, then water it.

You can top-dress around the plant with pebbles or gravel to avoid moisture loss and improve its appearance, or you may want to replace a lifted slab, having reduced its size to allow for the plant's stem. All plants growing in holes in paved areas are likely to be in shallow, fairly infertile soil (apart from the improved soil in the immediate planting area), so they will benefit from liquid feeding during the growing season.

Planting against walls

Several climbing plants are suitable for setting in relatively small holes in paved areas; clematis, in particular, thrives with its roots in cool shade and its head in the sun. When planting a climber, insert a stake at an angle to lead the growth up to the wall you want it to grow on. In such locations plants need regular watering, since sufficient rain is unlikely to reach them. By sinking a length of plastic piping or a small plant pot in the soil near the plant and running the water into it, you will ensure that water gets to the plant roots, especially in the early days. Later, the roots will penetrate the soil farther away and extract some additional nutrients and moisture from that.

PLANTING AMONG BRICKS

1 *When you have decided where you want to place your plants in the paved area, work a brick loose, pry it up, and remove it.*

2 *The soil immediately beneath the brick is likely to be poor quality, usually sandy or stony, so dig the hole out to a depth of at least 4–6in (10–15cm).*

3 *Make sure that the drainage at the base of the hole is adequate. Mix some slow-release fertilizer and water-retaining granules into fertile soil or good-quality soil mix and fill the hole with it.*

Precautions

Take care when planting larger plants in slabs, concrete, or asphalt, since the plants could become a hazard if badly sited, and their root growth could also cause problems, lifting slabs unevenly and raising or breaking through blacktop and concrete. Don't plant anything that has very strong, vigorous growth, and check slabs regularly to ensure that they are level, re-laying them if necessary.

Always be particularly careful what specimens you plant against a house wall, especially in clay soil. Roots can undermine foundations, and vigorous growth can cause structural damage by altering the moisture content of the soil, leading to subsidence. Take care also when planting against walls that form garden boundaries—roots penetrating the earth in neighboring properties can cause problems. Never plant moisture-greedy trees, such as poplars or willows, in the ground near buildings—confine them to large containers where their growth can be kept in check.

A free-draining dry-stone wall is an ideal place to grow lewisias. Gouge out some of the soil between the stones, pack the space with potting soil, tuck the plants into it, and they will thrive.

4 *Water the soil mix thoroughly, then set the plant in the soil, firming it in gently with your fingers. A good depth of fertile, moisture-retentive soil around the roots will help the plant make strong initial growth.*

5 *Spreading rock plants, which flourish in well-drained conditions, are ideal for planting among bricks, and low-growing plants with aromatic foliage, such as thyme and chamomile, are pleasant when set where they may occasionally be stepped on by passers-by, releasing their fragrance into the air.*

Growing in containers

Growing any plant in a container is very different from growing it in the open ground and will have an effect on both the way the plant develops and the way we need to care for it. A container has a limited amount of space in which the plant's roots can develop, and it contains relatively small amounts of potting mix or soil. If the roots are restricted, this will limit the overall size of the plant; as an extreme example, the small containers and careful root-pruning used in bonsai culture are able to reduce a potentially towering forest tree to a perfect miniature replica of itself.

The small volume of soil mix in containers also reduces the amount of moisture and nutrients available to the plant, which in turn has an effect upon the plant's size and development. By watering and feeding plants in containers we can, to an extent, overcome some of these effects, but this can produce further problems; it promotes the size of the top growth of the plant while the spread of roots is still limited by the boundaries of the container. This leads to an unbalanced plant, which could be blown over easily by wind, for example, since it does not have the firm below-ground support system to balance its above-ground growth. It will also lead to problems with water supply, since the increased leaf surface is likely to lose water by evaporation more rapidly than the roots can take it up or sometimes more rapidly than the gardener can supply it.

The trick of growing plants in containers successfully is to maintain a balancing act. It is necessary to promote healthy root growth, especially of the young feeding roots, and well-shaped, balanced top growth; to supply sufficient water at all times without overwatering; to start feeding once the original supply of nutrients in the soil is beginning to run low; and to provide the right nutrients both for the plant's health and for the best display of the plant's outstanding features. Container-grown plants often need extra support because of their limited root system, and they may need pruning to keep them balanced and shapely.

Drainage

This is a priority for all containers, since water must be able to drain away freely for healthy root growth. Whenever possible, the container should have drainage holes in the base, but on their own these may not be sufficient. You can add a layer of drainage material, such as broken clay pots, coarse gravel, or stones, in the bottom of the pot. Containers on the ground will drain more freely if they are raised slightly on bricks, or decorative plastic or clay "feet" can be bought.

Some plastic tubs or wooden containers are intended for use as decorative pot covers and do not have drainage holes. But if you want to use these as plant pots, it is usually fairly simple to drill a number of holes at least ½in (1cm) across in the base.

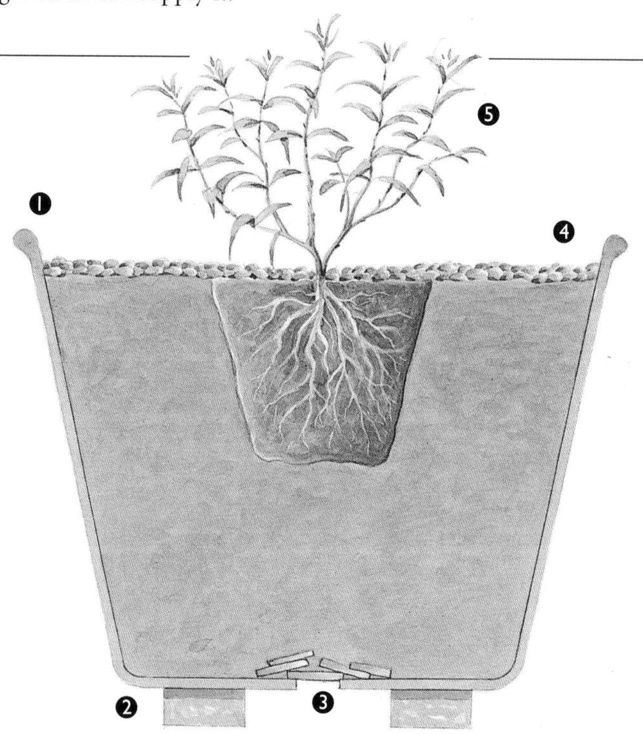

TIPS FOR CONTAINER PLANTING

1 Choose a suitable container and make sure there are sufficient drainage holes in it. It is fairly simple to drill extra holes in wood, plastic, or fiberglass.
2 Stand the container on bricks or feet to raise it off the ground so that it will drain freely and the soil mix will not become waterlogged. This also helps to prevent wooden containers from rotting.
3 Cover the drainage holes with pot shards or large pebbles so that the holes do not become blocked by the compost.
4 Fill the container to the bottom of the pot rim with damp soil mix, then press it down with your hands. Make a hole in the mix to take the plant, firm it in with your fingers, water it well, and, if desired, add a top layer of gravel.
5 Choose good-quality, sturdy plants with well-developed root systems. This is especially important if your container is to hold a single specimen plant.

A striking container is a decorative feature in itself, so keep the planting simple and let it echo the colors of the pot.

Growing in containers

An extra-deep layer of pot shards at the base of a container may help water drain more quickly, but watering must still be done carefully. A better system is to grow the plant in a smaller pot inside the container without drainage holes, setting the inner pot on the deep layer of shards. Then, if the plant is overwatered and the water level comes above the shard layer, the inner pot can be removed and allowed to drain.

Compost

Garden soil is not the best choice for containers. It is usually full of weed seeds and often disease organisms that can cause havoc among the plants. In addition, its texture and structure may be completely unsuitable for container growing. Various growing mixes are available from garden centers and plant shops; these are sterile, so they are weed, insect, and disease free, and they contain known quantities of nutrients.

The main choice is between soil-based, or loam-based potting mixes, and soilless (also called loamless or peat-based) mixes. The soil-based mixes have the appearance of garden soil. They are heavy, making them awkward to handle in the bag, and the weight of filled containers makes them difficult to move around. Some gardeners prefer these soil mixes because they behave in a similar way to garden soil; they absorb water well and contain a relatively long-lasting supply of nutrients.

Soilless mixes used to be based on peat, and although peat moss types are still available, there are now several mixes based on peat substitutes, such as coir, or coconut fiber, in order to preserve dwindling peat supplies and wildlife habitats. These are similar to peat moss in that they are lightweight, clean, and easy to handle. Soilless mixes contain relatively low levels of nutrients and hold limited supplies of water; they can be difficult to re-wet if they are allowed to dry out. Supplementary feeding must be started soon after potting, and watering must be carried out frequently.

There are also one or two special potting mixes: hanging-basket mix, for example. Some brands are soil-based, but this potting mix is often soilless, to ensure that the filled baskets are not too awkward to handle and that they will not prove too heavy for their supports. The soil mix is likely to contain a slow-release fertilizer and may also contain water-retaining granules to help avoid the common problem of drying out. Acidic soil mix is formulated without lime, so that it can be used for acid-loving plants such as heathers, pieris and rhododendrons.

Fertilizer

In order to keep producing a good display despite a limited volume of soil mix in which to grow, container plants need supplementary feeding. The full range of nutrients and fertilizers is discussed on p.137, but perhaps particularly useful for containers are slow-release fertilizers and liquid foods. There are some natural slow-release fertilizers, such as blood, fish, and bone meals, which gradually break down to make nutrients available to the plants, or there are specially formulated granules that are manufactured in such a way that particular combinations of ambient temperature and moisture levels allow the nutrients to be released slowly throughout the growing season.

Liquid foods are at the opposite end of the spectrum; they provide a quick pick-me-up for plants, since they are rapidly absorbed. They can be mixed in the watering can and applied every 10 days or so at full strength, or a diluted dose can be given with every watering.

Evergreen plants in large containers are best potted in soil-based potting mix, which is heavier, providing stability for the roots; it also holds water well and contains more nutrients.

A symmetrical grouping of identically painted pots, filled with neatly clipped boxwood, contrasts pleasingly with the otherwise informal planting in this corner of a patio garden and creates an attractive formal focal point.

Watering

Containers need regular watering during the growing season, and you should apply sufficient water each time to moisten the soil mix thoroughly, right down to the base of the pot. In many instances, watering may need to be done twice a day or more in high summer. For perennial plants, watering may still be necessary during the dormant season in order to prevent the container from drying out completely, but care must be taken not to overwet the soil, or the roots will rot. Check the state of the soil mix 2–3in (5–7.5cm) below the surface before watering in winter.

Planting containers

Several hours before planting your containers, thoroughly water the plants you intend to put in them. This will ensure that they are easy to turn out of their pots and will get them off to a good start.

Before planting, always check that there are enough reasonably large drainage holes in the container and make more or make them bigger if necessary. If the container is large, it is worth putting it in its final position before you begin—it could be too heavy to move afterwards.

If you know you are going to need to move a large container from time to time, you can buy a plant dolly with casters on which to transport it. You will probably have to put it on the dolly before planting and leave it there throughout the season, since lifting a ready-planted pot on to the dolly could be difficult.

Cover the base of the pot with pot shards and a layer of coarse gravel for drainage, then fill the container to two-thirds with your selected soil mix. If you want to use fertilizer and water-retaining granules, you can either mix them in before you begin, to ensure that they are evenly distributed, or you can add them to the soil mix in the container at this point and mix them in with your hands.

Gather the plants you intend to use and work out their locations in the container before removing them from their pots. Group them together, standing the pots on the soil surface, and check the effect from all sides, adjusting their positions as necessary. Once you have arranged them satisfactorily, knock them out of their pots and plant them with a trowel or your hands, firming them in lightly but thoroughly and adding soil mix as necessary. Begin planting from the center to avoid damage to plants already planted.

When the planting is complete, the level of the soil mix should be just below the rim of the container, to make watering easier. Water the completed pot gently and, if possible, shade it from bright sun for a day or two to give the plants a chance to get established.

This trough of alpines, in which each plant can be seen at its best, demonstrates the value of working out a plan before planting.

Growing in containers

Pots, tubs, and troughs

These are some of the most popular of all plant containers. They are very versatile, coming in a wide range of shapes and sizes and in a variety of colors and decorative finishes. They are free-standing, and smaller containers can be moved from place to place without too much difficulty. They can support many different types of plant.

The traditionally shaped plant pot is cylindrical with gently sloping sides. Its height is normally equivalent to the width across the top of the pot, tapering to about two-thirds that width at the base. There are, of course, many variations on this, including square pots and tall or wide pots. The point at which a pot becomes a tub is something of a gray area; a tub is larger than a pot, but there is no specific size at which one becomes the other. A tub is a container that is often rather more squat than a pot, with less steeply sloping sides, and probably contains something over 4 gallons of soil mix. (Plant containers are generally measured according to their volume in cubic feet or their width in inches across the widest part of the top.) A wooden half-barrel is perhaps most people's idea of a typical tub.

Decoratively shaped urns and jars such as "Ali-baba" jars also fall into the category of pots and tubs, while a trough is oblong and tends to be shallow—the typical window box shape, but used as a free-standing container on the ground.

If the window ledge is narrow, you can attach a shelf to the wall below the level of the ledge and safely stand a window box on it; since the box is lower down, the plants will block out less light.

An alpine trough is an even shallower rectangle and is broader than a window box—an old stone sink is a typical example.

Pots, tubs, and the like have usually been designed according to tradition and for convenience rather than to suit plant growth; the tapering shape of the traditional plant pot facilitates repotting and enables the empty pots to be stacked, for instance, rather than being of special value to the plant.

AN ALPINE TROUGH

1 *A wooden trough makes an attractive container, but it needs lining, otherwise the soil mix will fall between the slats. You will need a quantity of shards, broken terra-cotta flowerpots and the like, to put at the bottom to ensure drainage.*

2 *Line the trough with sphagnum moss, which is in keeping with the rustic look of the wood. Staple plastic sheeting to the top of the trough, cutting holes in it so excess water can escape, add the shards, and half-fill the trough with soil mix.*

3 *Water the pots of plants well an hour or so before planting. When you have decided on your planting plan, put your fingers around the base of each plant and carefully turn it over. Try to keep a good ball of soil around the plant roots.*

Some containers are simply designed to be decorative; tall jars, with narrow necks and bulbous middles, have a graceful and elegant appearance but are not particularly practical for growing plants, especially when it comes to repotting.

Keeping the display going

As individual plants start to die off, they can often be removed and replaced with another plant that is just coming into flower. This is made easier if the seasonal plants are kept in their individual pots, sunk into the surrounding soil mix, and disguised with a thin layer of mix over the top. Once they are ready to be replaced, the pot can simply be uncovered and lifted out, leaving a planting space for the next occupant. A little advance planning is necessary to have replacement plants in the correct size pots at the right time.

Semipermanent or permanent plants will generally need to be moved to their final-size container in stages, as they grow. A plant with a small root ball set in a large pot will not grow well—it should be moved into a container only slightly larger than the current one each time. If a plant is already in its final-size pot, it can be repotted into the same pot, but with a little fresh potting mix to give it a boost to growth.

Topdressing is a useful way to perk up large plants that cannot easily be removed from their containers. Without removing a plant from its pot, scrape away and remove as much of the potting mix from the surface as possible, then top with a layer of fresh mix, with added slow-release fertilizer granules. The techniques of repotting and topdressing are explained on pp.138–139.

Window boxes

A window box is one plant container that nearly every home can use. Different types of box are available *(see pp.84–85)*. They can be made from a variety of materials, but wood or plastic are the most common, since they are reasonably light in weight and not too difficult to attach securely to the wall or window ledge. Wooden boxes can be painted with a plant-safe wood preservative to extend their life, but it is better to choose a type that has two or three plastic inserts that will actually contain the soil mix and plants.

WINDOW BOX SAFETY It is important that a window box is fastened in place securely. You risk ruining your display and wasting your time and money if the box topples off a ground-floor window ledge; there are more serious implications with an upper-story window ledge because of the damage a falling box can do to people or property below.

There are various ways of securing a window box, depending on the style of the box itself and the surface on which it is to be fitted. If there is an outside window ledge, it is sometimes wide enough to take a window box, but it will need to be attached in position with brackets screwed to the wall for safety. Since window ledges slope downward to allow water to drain away, some wooden wedges should be inserted under the front of the box to keep it level.

4 *When all the plants have been set in place, fill up the trough with compost, water it well, and add more compost if it settles too far. A layer of coarse gravel on the top will keep the compost moist and improve the appearance of the trough.*

5 *Stand the trough in a bright, sunny spot, and within a week or two the plants will begin to flourish and grow over the edges of the trough.*

Growing in containers

Standing the box on the the window ledge is fine as long as the windows open inward or slide, but some open outward, making this position impractical. And as the plants grow, much of the view and light from the window will be obscured.

A position below the window is more suitable if there is no window ledge or only a narrow one. A casement window can still be opened outward, but this may become difficult as the plants get taller. Even if you don't usually open the window in question, you will need to do so to water and feed the plants in the window box.

Use metal brackets to support the box from below and either screw the back of the box to the wall (or, preferably, to a wooden batten fixed to the wall) or attach chains and hooks between the window box and wall to keep it in position. (See pp.16–19 for tips on securing baskets and window boxes to walls.) A permanent wrought-iron container can be attached securely to the wall, and a wooden or plastic window box placed inside it.

Bear in mind that you need to have easy access to a window box for deadheading, watering, feeding, and maintenance; don't put it in a location where it will be difficult or dangerous to reach.

PREPARING A WINDOW BOX As with other containers, plants in a window box need to be grown in quick-draining soil mix. If there is no obstruction below, holes can be drilled directly into the base of the box for drainage. If water draining from the box is likely to cause a nuisance, use a drip tray below the box that can be emptied as necessary or fill the undrilled base of the window box with drainage material and stand drilled plastic liners on this to hold the plants. Self-watering window boxes are useful; they have a reservoir for water at the base with capillary material to take the moisture up to the plants.

Window boxes should be planted in the same way as pots, tubs, and troughs.

Hanging baskets

These can be spectacular when well grown, and nearly every home can manage to find a suitable spot for a hanging basket. They can, however, be a big disappointment if they are not properly cared for.

Plenty of different types are available, but the main distinction is between wire-mesh baskets and "hanging plant-pot" types with solid sides *(see pp.84–85)*.

WIRE-MESH BASKETS The traditional basket is open plastic-coated wire mesh, hanging from three chains. This has the advantage that plants can be pushed through the wire in the sides of the basket so that the basket itself can be completely disguised with plant growth. Its disadvantages are that it is trickier to plant, needs a liner, dries out quickly, and is more difficult to water. Traditional lining for a wire basket is sphagnum moss, but this is not always easy to obtain or to

A TRADITIONAL HANGING BASKET

1 *Set the plastic-coated wire basket on top of a fairly large flower pot or bucket to keep it steady. Start to line the basket with sphagnum moss. If you prefer, you can use plastic sheeting with holes pierced in it or a fiber or plastic foam liner.*

2 *Put a plant saucer in the bottom of the basket. This will act as a water reservoir and will help to keep the soil mix moist, so the basket will not need watering as often. It will also help catch drips when it is watered.*

3 *Half-fill the basket with soil mix. Take the plants you plan to set in the sides of the basket out of their pots. Gently wash off some of the soil and push the plants, roots first, through the wire and lining; lay the roots flat on the soil mix.*

use. Various alternatives have been developed commercially, including coconut fiber, plastic foam, and recycled fabric liners. Some of these can look ugly, and it is difficult to plant the sides of the basket so as to hide them. When planting, either use special hanging basket soil mix or mix some slow-release fertilizer and water-retaining granules with soilless potting mix. This is almost essential with hanging baskets unless you are prepared to water two or three times daily at the height of the summer.

HANGING POTS These are squat pots or bowls, often with an integral clip-on saucer, hanging from three plastic or wire chains. If you want to disguise the basket you need to plant it carefully with plants that will hang over the edge, since you cannot plant through the sides of the basket. On the other hand, the solid walls prevent the compost from drying out so quickly, and the saucer provides a reservoir of water. Self-watering baskets have a deeper reservoir and may have a covering of capillary matting to wick up water into the soil. They also have a filler tube through which to fill the reservoir.

A hay rack, or manger, makes a handsome plant container, so be sure not to obscure the metalwork when filling it with plants.

PLANTING THE BASKET

Work out a rough planting plan, bearing in mind that the basket will be viewed from below as well as the sides and possibly above. Set low-growing and cascading plants towards the edge at the top of the basket, a more upright specimen in the centre, and small trailing plants, which will help to conceal the basket, around the edge or between the wires of a traditional basket. When planting the sides of a wire-mesh basket, wrap the plants' roots in a small piece of newspaper to neaten them so that they can be tucked in easily. If the basket is big enough, make two layers of trailers through the wires, and when planting the top of any basket, remember to allow for the position of the chains when it is hanging.

Water tends to run off the surface of a hanging basket, so before you add the plants at the top of a traditional basket, sink a small plant pot or piece of tube near the edge and level with the surface of the soil. By watering through this, you can be certain that the water will penetrate to the roots of the plants.

4 *Cover the roots and fill the basket with potting soil. Before planting the top of the basket, insert a small plant pot or piece of tube level with the top of the soil mix. This will make it easier to water the basket.*

5 *Plant the top of the basket, being careful not to obstruct the plant pot. Water the completed basket gently and keep it in a sheltered place for a week or two for the plants to become established. Hang it where you can enjoy it all season.*

Growing in containers

Growing bags

A growing bag is simply a plastic sack of compost, but instead of transferring the compost to a pot, the plants are set directly in the sack. When growing bags are not available, you can make your own, using a potting mix. Growing bags are widely used for raising tomatoes on patios and in greenhouses, but they are far more versatile than this.

The bags are laid flat where the plants are to be grown. Opinion is divided over whether it is advisable to cut drainage slits in the base of the bag. They were first used for commercial tomato growing when the border soil in greenhouses had become diseased, and it was important to keep the bags intact in order to isolate plant roots from the contaminated soil below. If this is not an issue, no harm is done by cutting slits in the base, especially if you are prone to overwatering containers. It is possible to conceal the bag itself by setting it in a specially designed shallow trough. Instead of the gaudily colored bags that are common, it is sometimes possible to obtain plain green ones. Trailing plants set at the edges will soon help to disguise the bag.

Tower pots

Cut planting holes in the upper surface of the bag with a sharp knife. If you intend to grow a lot of plants close together—a bedding plant display, for instance—it is easiest to cut one large rectangle from the top of the bag. Because the depth of compost a growing bag contains is shallow, it dries out quickly, so leaving as much as possible of the compost surface covered by the plastic will help to prevent this. Mix a small amount of water-retaining granules with the compost in the bag to cut down the frequency of watering.

Plastic

Plant the bag in the normal way. Tall plants that need staking can be a problem, since the depth of compost is often not sufficient to support a stake, but there are specially designed frames, which are anchored underneath the bag, and these should be put in place at an early stage. Because the bag is well-filled with compost it tends to have a rounded upper surface, which can make watering difficult since the water runs off; again, various watering devices to overcome this can be found in most garden shops. Growing bags contain similar amounts of fertilizer as general-purpose sowing and potting compost. Once the plants have become established, regular liquid feeding will help to prolong their productive period and keep them looking healthy.

Converted containers

Plants can be grown in almost anything that will hold enough compost, and inventive growers have given many different items new leases of life as plant containers. Antique cisterns, washtubs, chimney pots, stone sinks, boats, wheelbarrows—

PLANTING UP A GROWING BAG

1 *You will need a growing bag, a trough to contain it in if you intend to use one, the plants—here tomatoes, French beans, basil, and parsley—stakes to support them, and string to tie them in to the stakes.*

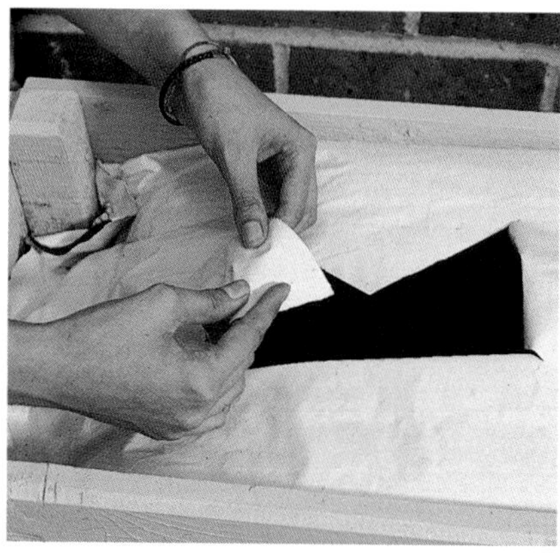

2 *Put the growing bag into the trough. If you want to grow two or three specimen plants, rather than a show of annuals, cut equally spaced crosses in the bag and tuck the flaps under to form diamond-shaped planting holes.*

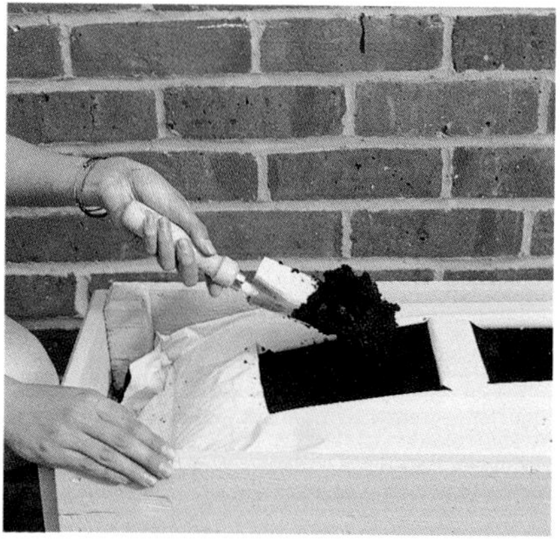

3 *Water the compost in the growing bag with a rose on the can until it is thoroughly moist but not waterlogged. With a trowel, dig out enough of the compost to make holes big enough to accommodate your plants.*

even worn-out walking boots and old car tires have been converted to horticultural use. If you want the container to last for several years, you may need to treat it in some way. Wood can be coated with boat paint on the inside to prevent it from rotting and varnished on the outside to protect it from the weather. Metal or painted surfaces may benefit from a coat of acrylic varnish to prevent flaking. Remember that many objects may be stained, scratched, or otherwise spoiled by a single season as a container, so don't use a valuable item unless you are sure it can stand up to the conditions without too much damage.

The biggest problem with many "novelty" containers is the lack of adequate drainage. Ensure that suitable drainage holes can be made and use drainage material at the base. Make sure, also, that it will hold sufficient soil mix for good growth and that you will be able to water the plants easily. The rules for cultivation are then the same as for any other container—water regularly and liquid feed as necessary throughout the growing season.

Plastic or terra-cotta "tower pots" (left) extend the growing area upward; a long, hanging plastic tube (above left) can double hanging basket space; and drainpipe pots (right) full of cascading plants will turn even that mundane object into an asset.

Miscellaneous containers

Each year new systems for growing in container are introduced. Often these promise more spectacular displays, but they may also offer easier cultivation; because container-grown plants need watering so frequently, self-watering systems are often incorporated.

Tower pots clip together to make a free-standing, vertical column in which plants can be grown to cover the pots completely. Another system uses a perforated plastic tube that is suspended to form a hanging "tower". Always follow the instructions on these kits, since the way in which they are assembled can be critical to achieving proper watering. Most have a reservoir at the base and are self-watering to an extent, but check regularly that moisture penetrates evenly all the way down the tower.

Containers that disguise unsightly items are also popular. Manhole covers are a feature of some city yards, and while they are easy enough to conceal with a planted trough, make sure it is not so heavy and awkward to move that it prevents access to the cover. Drainpipes can be graced with pots clipped to them by plastic rings, and the drains into which they flow can be fitted with a planted cover as well. These are valuable for making full use of all the available space in a small area, but you must take care to ensure that they don't interfere with the function of the object they are disguising.

4 Set the plants in the holes and push in stakes to support the tomatoes. As the plants grow, gently tie in the stems. The underplanting of herbs will quickly form bushy growth that will help to hide the plastic growing bag.

Plant supports

When plants are grown in a small space, you usually need to pay more attention to their support and training than you do in a larger garden. Supports are necessary for a several reasons. They keep plants tidy and prevent them from obstructing pathways so that they are less likely to be damaged by people pushing through or past them. Supports can also help plants grow into pleasing shapes—perhaps more attractive or practical than their natural ones.

Many plants need support to combat damage by wind and rain, which may otherwise flatten or break their branches. Flowers such as delphiniums and lupines are soon spoiled if a heavy shower beats the stems down. The tips of the flower heads continue to grow in a strongly vertical direction within hours, so even if you are able to gather up the stems and restore them to their normal position later, the flower heads will have a permanent kink in them that will ruin the display.

In exposed, windy locations, it is not just the above-ground parts of the plant that may suffer. Constant rocking of the main stem as it is blown to and fro will also cause movement of the root ball, preventing the roots from establishing themselves in the soil—a condition known as wind-rock. A stake is even more necessary where larger plants are growing in shallow soil, as is the case in containers or shallow raised beds, since their roots cannot penetrate sufficiently far to give them the anchorage they would achieve in deeper soil. While trees or shrubs in the open garden are often staked for only their first two or three years, until they become established, some plants in shallow soil are likely always to need a stake.

Plants often need to be staked in order to show off their best features, such as flowers that may otherwise be hidden behind foliage. Occasionally plants are bred that carry flowers that are too large and full for their stems to support; many varieties of double daffodil, for instance, have stems that fold under the weight of the blooms, particularly after rain. Careful staking at an early stage can prevent such problems.

Rose standards and small trees in raised beds or containers will need permanent staking. Insert the stake into the soil or compost before planting and attach the plant to the stake with a couple of small tree ties. Check the ties regularly as the plant grows to make sure that they are not too tight.

Not every plant needs support; many types have spreading growth or short or stout stems that will hold up quite well on their own. Climbers and ramblers and other plants with tall, lax growth or weak stems should nearly always be provided with some form of support, but otherwise experience will tell you which plants would do better with staking in your own particular conditions.

How to support plants

The "no-garden" often has particular problems when it comes to supporting plants. It can be difficult to find a firm base in which to secure the support because there is little or no natural soil, only a hard surface. For example, it is usually recommended that a tree stake should extend a good 20in (50cm) below the soil surface—well below the base of the root ball. In a "no-garden" situation, this is usually impossible—the base of the root ball is as low as you are likely to be able to get. Obviously this does not provide the stability that a deeper stake does.

Lightweight composts, such as those based on peat moss or peat substitutes, do not make things any easier. Because they are light and fluffy in texture, they do not hold a stake as firmly as a soil-based mix does. One way to overcome these problems of stability in a large container or raised bed is to set a cane or stake in a plastic plant pot filled with a stiff cement mix. Once this has set, the weighted stake can be buried in the container or raised bed, or even positioned behind a container, to provide a relatively stable support.

Stake set in concrete

The main rule is that the supports should be unobtrusive. Use natural-looking materials, preferably in dull green or brown shades and arrange them so that plant growth will cover them as much as possible. They may be fairly obvious initially, but once the plants they are supporting have grown they should be almost invisible. The plant's habit of growth should always appear natural, even if it isn't—few things look worse than a bunch of stems that have been gathered tightly together and firmly trussed to a single, overlarge stake. Don't be stingy with materials; three or four stakes or canes, placed among the stems of a shrub or tall perennial, give a much more natural effect than if you try to make do with one.

CREATING A SUPPORTING FRAMEWORK

1 *Spreading plants, such as* impatiens, *can be supported by inserting several small green wooden split canes into the soil at strategic positions among the stems.*

2 *Once you have made a framework of canes, tie one end of a length of green garden twine to one of them, then carefully loop the twine around the rest of the canes.*

3 *The twine will contain and support any sprawling, wayward stems, and as the plant grows and becomes more bushy, both twine and canes will disappear among the leaves and flowers.*

TYING IN PLANTS

1 *Soft-stemmed plants, such as geraniums, can be tied in to a cane. Loop green garden twine or raffia around the cane, cross the ends behind it, then bring them around the stem just above a leaf stem and knot them against the cane.*

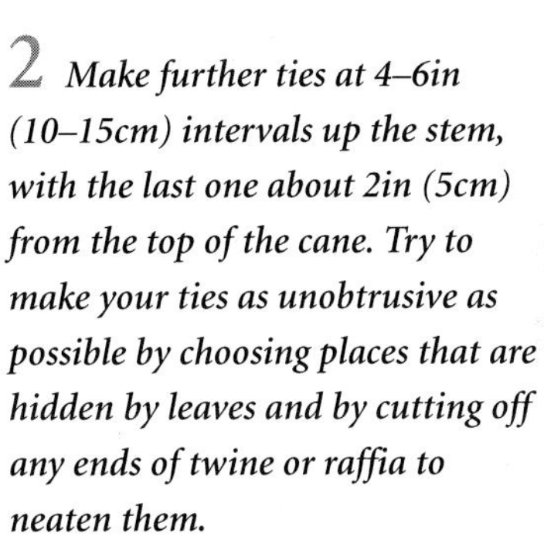

2 *Make further ties at 4–6in (10–15cm) intervals up the stem, with the last one about 2in (5cm) from the top of the cane. Try to make your ties as unobtrusive as possible by choosing places that are hidden by leaves and by cutting off any ends of twine or raffia to neaten them.*

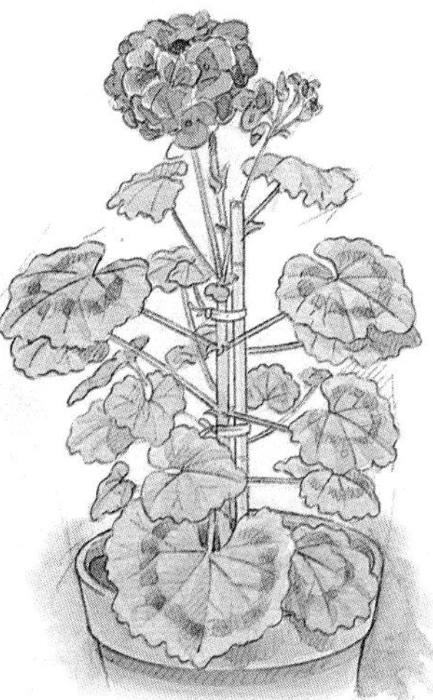

SUPPORTING PERENNIALS

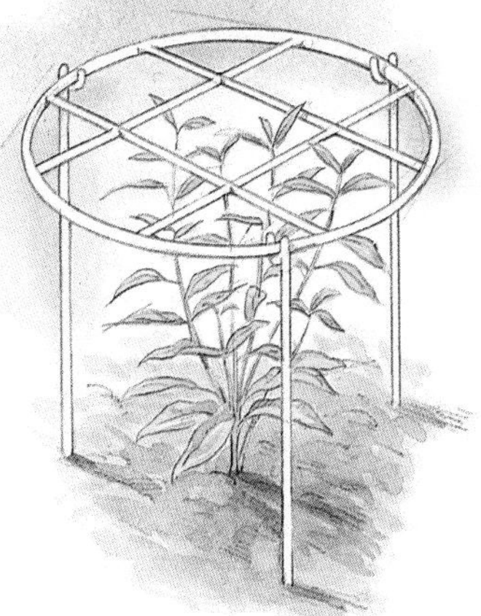

1 *Bushy herbaceous plants that tend to flop over or produce very heavy flower heads are best supported by one of several types of metal frame. The most common, the "gro-thru" type, consists of a crisscross framework supported on legs (left) or of a series of linked metal stakes that can be bent around and joined to form a support (below).*

2 *The legs of the frames must be pushed into the ground in the spring, when the plant starts growing. As the plant increases in size, the stems will grow through the framework and eventually obscure it.*

Plant supports

Always support plants from an early stage; if you leave it until they need support, it is often too late to achieve a pleasing effect. The plants should grow up into the support to give a natural outline, with branches well covered with foliage. If you try to gather in branches later on, the support may be visible due to a lack of foliage at the base or on one side.

Once you have provided a plant with its support, that is not the end of the story. Its growth needs to be tied in regularly and gently encouraged to grow in the right direction. Further supports may need to be added, or existing ones moved, as the spread of the branches increases. At all times aim for a natural-looking result.

Types of plant support

Use different methods of support according to the types of plant that are being grown and where they are growing.

In containers

CANES Bamboo canes have the advantages of being relatively cheap and having a pleasant, natural appearance. They do not last for ever, though, since they eventually split and rot where they have been below ground. Their life can, however, be extended by dipping the base (the thicker end of the cane) in a plant-safe wood preservative. Unobtrusive green plastic "canes" are also available, which do not rot. Because bamboo canes are hollow, they can form a good hiding place for plant pests, such as pill bugs and earwigs; stopping up the ends with modelling clay or putty helps to keep out undesirable creatures.

Support sweetpeas and tall runner beans on a teepee of canes, tied together at the top. Otherwise, you can buy a plastic ring with holes in it through which you pass the canes to hold them together at the top.

A single, central cane may be sufficient or, for climbers, a tepee of three or more canes evenly spaced around the edge of the pot and tied together at their tips. Sometimes a ring of canes at the edge of the pot with twine twisted around them is appropriate.

SPLIT CANES Made from wood, rather than bamboo, these are thinner and shorter than bamboo canes and are square in shape and are usually stained green. They are useful for smaller plants and can be inserted among the branches of the plant wherever they are needed.

Many serious injuries are caused by people bending down among plants and being poked in the eye by the top of a cane. Using small plastic pots, thread spools, corks or one of the proprietary cane tops available will help avoid this.

FIXING WIRE TO WALLS

1 *Plastic-covered wire stretched horizontally on a wall provides good support for climbers. Using a drill with a masonry bit, drill holes in the wall and insert eye screws—screws with a loop at one end—large enough to hold the wire slightly away from the wall surface or screw them into battens. Thread the wire through the first eye and twist the end tightly with pliers to secure it.*

2 *Screw the rest of the eye screws into position, with one every 6ft (2m) or so, spacing the horizontal wires about 18in (45cm) apart. Thread the wire through each intermediate eye screw, looping it back on itself so that it can be tensioned; when the final eye screw is reached and the wire twisted off, the tension can be adjusted by turning the eye screw itself with pliers.*

PEA STICKS OR BRUSH Perfect for annuals and perennials, pea sticks provide plenty of support while being unobtrusive. Finding suitable sticks in a city can be a problem, but occasionally they are sold at garden centers. Usually they last for only one season.

FREE-STANDING TRELLIS Usually made into a fan or other decorative shape, wooden or plastic trellis for containers has long prongs at the base that are inserted into the soil in the pot. Trellis is used for supporting climbing plants.

MESH CYLINDER Climbers such as clematis, grown in a pot, can be trained around a central cylinder made from rigid plastic mesh or chicken wire. Cut a piece of mesh to the appropriate size, roll it into a cylinder and fasten it with wire or string. Place it in the centre of an empty pot, allowing room for the plants to be set around the outside. Fill the pot with soil mix and plant it; the climbers will soon cover the cylinder and form an attractive flowering column.

In beds and in the ground

STAKES Where the depth of soil allows, a heavier wooden stake can be used to support a tree or tall shrub. Dig the planting hole, then drive the stake into position before planting; this avoids the root damage that occurs when a stake is inserted after planting. It used to be recommended that the stake should be tall enough to come just below the head of the plant. This is still the case for thin-stemmed plants, such as Rose standards, but otherwise short stakes about 24in (60cm) above ground are considered better, because they allow some movement of the trunk, which helps to strengthen and thicken it. In an exposed location, two or three short stakes can be used around the plant.

When planting a container-grown tree with a dense root ball, or if staking is necessary after planting, use an angled stake, driven in so that the tip of the stake avoids the plant roots. Cut off the top of the stake just beyond the top of the trunk once the tree has been attached to it.

Attach a tree to a stake with an adjustable tree tie, which will prevent chafing of the trunk and can be loosened as the tree grows and its girth increases.

CANES AND TWIGGY STICKS Bamboo and plastic canes can be used in open ground in the same ways as they are in containers. Pea sticks are also useful for low perennials, annuals, and bulbs in beds and borders.

COMMERCIAL SUPPORTS Various supports, such as a circle of wire mesh on legs or angled wire stakes that link to each other with hooks and eyes to form a range of shapes and sizes, can be useful for a wide variety of plants. Many save time and labor, being easier to use than traditional methods of staking, though they may not have such a natural appearance. As with all supports, for the best effect it is important to have them in place before they are needed. Some commercial products would be very expensive if used in quantities in a large garden, but are more suitable for small areas where few are needed.

On walls and fences

Self-clinging climbers, such as ivy and Virginia creeper, do not need supports in order to climb rough surfaces such as masonry walls, but you will have more control over the plants and will find it easier to train them if you do provide some form of support. Where it is necessary to maintain the surface over which you wish to grow the plants—painting a wall for instance, or treating a wooden fencing panel with preservative—you will find maintenance easier to carry out if climbing plants are grown on a trellis that can be detached from the wall. This is especially important if the wall or fence forms a boundary with an adjacent property and is the responsibility of your neighbors, since they may wish to carry out maintenance at a time of year that is not the most suitable from the point of view of the plants.

WOODEN TRELLIS This is available in a range of different shapes and styles, some of them purely functional, some more decorative. Some wooden trelliswork is very lightweight; if you need it to support heavy, vigorous plant growth, make sure you choose a sturdily constructed type. Plastic trellis is also available. Chicken wire can be used to provide a base for lightweight climbers to scramble over, but it will sag under any heavy stems.

ATTACHING A TRELLIS TO A WALL

Rather than attaching the trellis directly to the wall, screw wooden battens or spacing blocks about 3in (8cm) thick to the wall and secure the trellis to these. This will maintain a flow of air behind the plant, leading to healthier growth; it will also help to prevent self-clinging plants from attaching themselves to the wall. If you need access to the wall behind the plants, you can unscrew the trellis from the battens and lay it carefully on the ground, so make sure the sections of trellis are a suitable size to make this practical. Otherwise you can use hooks and screw eyes to attach the trellis to the battens, which will make lowering it even simpler.

Training plants

Plants are usually trained in order to make them look attractive, but various training methods can also help to display a plant's best features more prominently, to promote flowering and fruiting by restricting leafy growth, and to expose fruit or branches to maximum sunshine in order to ripen them. "Training" means making a plant grow in a way that it would not do naturally. It usually means that regular attention is required from the gardener throughout the plant's life to maintain its form.

Growing plants up the types of support just discussed is training at its simplest. Climbing plants may need to be encouraged to climb by twisting their shoots round the support, or threading them through trelliswork. Plants will usually need to be attached to the support at intervals; this can be done with plastic-covered wire ties, which are twisted into place, or soft garden twine, loosely tied. It is usually best to tie the stems just below a leaf node, and they should always be tied to the support with a figure-eight loop to prevent their being crushed. Spread the branches out equally over the supports and train shoots into place to fill in any gaps. When it is necessary to cut back plants, make the cut just above a bud that is pointing in the direction you want the new growth to take.

Training fruit trees

Vigorous plants often produce a lot of leafy growth at the expense of flowers and fruit. This can be remedied by slowing down the passage of plant foods in the stems by keeping the stems horizontal or sloping downward. Side shoots, or laterals, are trained horizontally, or they can even be trained downward; this method is used by commercial fruit growers, who attach weights to the tips of branches of apple trees to pull them down and so increase the fruit crop. Shoots off the laterals are known as sublaterals.

Fruit trees are often candidates for specific training techniques aimed at improving the crop and forming attractive plants. Many of these trees are ideal for small spaces, allowing a range of fruit to be grown where it would otherwise be impossible. They are often known as restricted forms and need dwarfing or very dwarfing rootstocks.

These restricted forms all need support. Training in the early stages can be complex, and it is best to buy trees that have been specifically produced to be grown in these forms. The initial training should then have been done for you.

TRAINED FRUIT FORMS

CORDONS

These are single-stemmed trees, usually grown at an angle of 45 degrees. Compact columnar trees, such as Minarette and Ballerina trees, are a type of vertical cordon. When planting cordons, make sure that the grafting point remains well above soil level, otherwise the grafted variety will root and overcome the effects of the dwarfing rootstock.

ESPALIERS

For an espaliered tree, suitable branches are trained horizontally to form a tree with a central stem and regular tiers of branches about 18in (45cm) apart. Fruit crops are potentially heavier than with a cordon, but the trees require considerably more space.

Grow trained trees in containers or in the open ground on wires against a wall or fence or on posts and wires.

Pruning trained trees

This is all-important for restricted forms. Most pruning is done in summer, since this slows down growth; avoid winter pruning, which tends to lead to vigorous growth the following spring.

On cordons, prune the tip of the main stem lightly in late spring once it has reached the top wire of its support. Once the shoots have reached about the thickness of a pencil, start to prune them, carrying out the whole operation over a period of several weeks in midsummer. Prune laterals, or shoots off the main stem, fairly lightly, cutting them back to the third leaf above the cluster of leaves at the base of the stem. Prune sublateral shoots (shoots arising from main-stem side shoots) more severely.

Fan-trained cherries should be pruned more lightly, with the laterals cut back to four or six leaves. Badly placed buds should be removed in early spring. Retain those that will grow on in the same plane as the wall and rub out any that point in towards the wall or straight outward.

PRUNING CORDONS

Every year, in late spring, cut off the tip of the main stem of cordons, leaving about ½in (1cm) of new wood. Tie the stem to its support.

In midsummer, when laterals (side shoots on the main stem) are about 9in (21cm) long, cut them back to the third leaf above the basal cluster. On sublaterals, cut above the first leaf beyond the basal cluster.

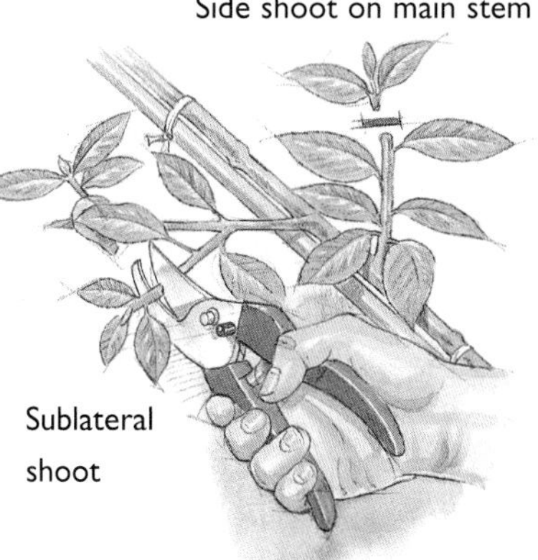

STEPOVERS

The ultimate in small trees, the stepover is an espalier with just one tier of branches. It can be grown as an edging to a bed and will bear a small crop of fruit.

FANS

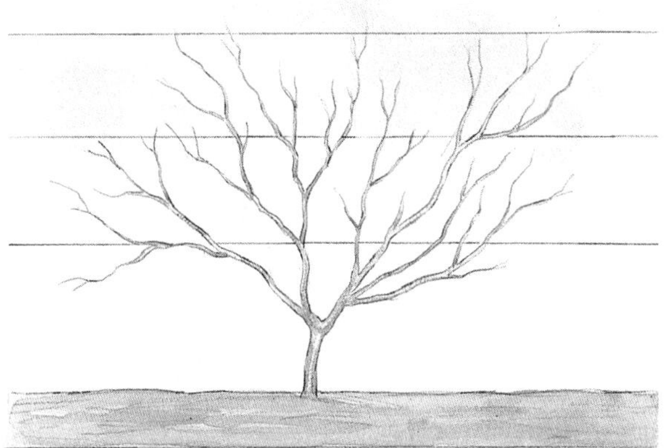

Cherry trees are perhaps the most commonly found fan-trained trees. They are usually grown against a wall or fence, with the branches spread out in a regular fan shape and the tree kept flat against the wall.

Training plants

Standards

A standard—a plant with a naked stem topped by a head—makes a good focal point in a group of plants, adding height and a touch of formality. Many foliage and flowering plants can be trained as standards; bay, fuchsia, rose, rosemary, and marguerite are popular choices. Half-standards have shorter naked stems than standards; the accepted height varies from species to species.

It requires a lot of skill to produce some standard plants. With roses, for example, one variety provides a strong-growing stem while the flowering variety, which will form the head, is budded on to the stem later, when it has reached an appropriate height. Slow-growing bay trees need several years of painstaking training before they produce a reasonably sized specimen. Usually such plants must be bought ready trained—producing them is beyond the scope of most gardeners, let alone "no-garden" gardeners.

Training a standard plant

Other plants, however, are much easier to train, and anyone with a little patience can produce a standard within a season or two, depending on the type of plant. Fuchsias make a good starting point.

Select either a young rooted cutting or a slightly older plant that has been produced specifically for training as a standard. Make sure the growing point is undamaged. Provide the plant with a cane and allow it to continue growing upward, tying it to the support regularly in order to keep the stem as straight as possible. As side shoots start to grow, pinch them back to one pair of leaves. Do not rub the shoots out completely; they help to build up the main stem. Pot the plant on in the normal way as necessary, taking extra care not to damage the growing point or stem. Continue in this manner until the stem has reached the required height. Allow the leading shoot to produce another four pairs of leaves, then pinch out the tip to stimulate the buds beneath into growth to form the head. Pinch out the tips of the shoots that develop when they have reached 6in (15cm) or so in length to encourage a bushy head to form. Thereafter, pinch out the tips of shoots to keep the head well shaped and even and rub out any shoots that develop on the main stem.

The stem lengths generally recognized for standards are 10–18in (25–45cm) for a quarter standard; 18–30in (45–75cm) for a half standard; and 30–42in (75–107cm) for a full standard.

TRAINING A FUCHSIA STANDARD

1 *Choose a strong cutting 6–9in (15–23cm) high with an intact growing tip. Pinch out any side shoots that grow in the leaf axils (where the leaves join the main stem).*

2 *Provide the plant with a cane and tie it to the cane to produce a straight stem. Continue to pinch out the side shoots as they appear, leaving one pair of leaves.*

Topiary

Small-leafed evergreens can be clipped into ornamental shapes, known as topiary. Some specimens are extremely complex, taking the form of intricately spiraled corkscrews or painstakingly produced birds and animals, but for the "no garden" situation, simpler spheres, cones, and pyramids are more suitable and effective. Topiary specimens are particularly suitable for growing in containers, but take care that the shape and style of container chosen will complement the eventual form of the plant. Good plants for clipping are yew, box-leafed honeysuckle (*Lonicera nitida*), and perhaps most popular, boxwood.

Select a strong, healthy container-grown plant with an even shape. If you have a good eye, simple shapes can be clipped freehand, but a better result is likely to be achieved by placing a wire frame—obtainable from many garden centers—over the young plant and simply clipping back shoots with hand pruners as they grow through the frame. Clip regularly during the growing season to maintain dense, bushy growth. It is also possible to "cheat" by growing vigorous, small-leafed ivies over a moss-covered wire frame, training the shoots carefully over the wires to cover it completely and tucking in or clipping back untidy growth as it forms. In this way, complex shapes can be covered in a short time to give an effect very similar to that of traditional topiary. Water the plants frequently and mist the leaves to keep the moss damp.

Corkscrew frame

Spherical frame

3 *When the fuchsia is as tall as you want it, allow it to produce three more sets of leaves, then pinch out the growing tip of the plant.*

4 *As side shoots form at the top of the stem, pinch out their growing tips. This will make them branch, and gradually a bushy head will form at the top of the stem.*

MAKING A TOPIARY CONE

1 *Littleleaf boxwood,* Buxus sempervirens, *is especially suitable for small topiary because it has small, densely packed leaves on woody stems. Choose a sturdy plant and clip it roughly into the shape with sharp hand pruners.*

2 *When the plant has grown sufficiently, either buy a wire frame or make a cutting guide from canes held in a cone shape with wire. Place the frame over the plant and cut the stems to the shape.*

3 *Once the shape is established, you will need to clip it at least twice a year to maintain it. In between, cut off new growth or pinch off the leaves with your fingers to prevent cutting marks on the leaves.*

TRAINING IVY ON A FRAME

Make a frame from a double layer of chicken wire with a layer of sphagnum moss about ¾in (2cm) thick in between. Shape the frame and put it in position, leaving room at the edge of the pot for the ivies. As they grow, train the tendrils over the frame.

Plant maintenance

One of the main objects of pruning plants is to keep their growth within bounds and to prevent them outgrowing their allotted space, and nowhere is this more necessary than where space is in short supply. But you need to prune carefully, not just cut back branches wherever they encroach.

This is not, however, the only consideration. It is important to prune plants to keep them flowering, fruiting, and looking attractive. Pruning plants correctly helps to stimulate vigorous growth, encourage more profuse flowering, improve the shape of the plant, and keep it healthy. But be wary; prune incorrectly, and it can have exactly the opposite effects to those you intend.

What is meant by "pruning"?

The term is usually associated with woody-stemmed subjects, where cutting-back has an effect on the main framework of the plant. Shrubs and climbers are the chief candidates for regular pruning, although in small spaces, some trees may require attention, too.

If a plant needs frequent, drastic pruning to keep it small enough for its space, it is probably better to replace it with a more compact, less vigorous variety. Before replacing it, however, check your pruning technique. Severe pruning in winter or early spring encourages strong, vigorous growth, so you may be making the problem worse by cutting the plant back hard. The removal of selected whole branches is often more successful than clipping back branch tips, as long as you take care not to spoil the plant's shape.

The timing and type of pruning required varies according to the particular plant, but when pruning flowering shrubs, note when the flowers are produced and on what type of wood—prune early bloomers right after the flowers fade and summer bloomers in late winter to early spring.

PRUNING RULES

1. Know why you are pruning.
2. Use well-sharpened tools to avoid damage to stems.
3. Cut out dead, damaged, and diseased branches.
4. Cut back healthy stems to a strong bud.
5. Prune at an appropriate time of year.

HARD PRUNING

Where plants are grown for characteristics other than flowers, they may need especially hard pruning. Red-twigged dogwood, Cornus stolonifera, *for example, has attractive winter stems, and eucalyptus,* Eucalyptus gunnii, *round, blue, juvenile leaves. The stems of these plants can be cut down to within a few inches of the ground in spring to promote the production of strong young shoots, rather than leaving them to form large plants. Butterfly bush,* Buddleia davidii, *also benefits from hard pruning, which improves the quality of flowers and appearance of the plant.*

DEADHEADING

The removal of faded blooms, deadheading, improves virtually all plants that do not produce attractive or useful fruits or berries. It enhances the plant's appearance, saves it from wasting energy on setting seed, and often encourages prolonged flowering periods. Pinch off dead flower heads with your finger and thumb or snip them off with a pair of hand pruners.

Follow these steps when pruning

1 Take out dead, dying, and diseased branches completely and cut right back to healthy wood. For many shrubs, this will be all that is necessary, but if the plant is too large, or fails to give a good display of flowers, colored foliage, or stems, further pruning may be needed.

2 Check when the plant flowers. Deciduous flowering shrubs fall into two main groups: those that flower in spring on last year's shoots, and those that flower in summer on the current season's growth.

Prune plants in the first group immediately after flowering, in late spring or early summer, cutting back the branches that have just flowered. This promotes the growth of strong young shoots that will overwinter and carry next season's flowers. Prune plants in the second group in late winter or early spring, as they are about to start growing.

Evergreen trees and shrubs are usually best pruned in spring or early summer.

3 On most plants, cut back branches to within a few buds of where they join the main stem, using sharp hand pruners. Cut just above a bud with a straight cut or one sloping away from the bud. Before cutting, envisage the direction in which the bud will grow away—it is usual to choose an outward facing bud so as to keep the centre of the plant open.

4 If a plant is encroaching on an open area, neighboring plant, or pathway, cut back the overhanging branches to an appropriate bud. You may need to cut back the opposite side of the plant in a similar way to retain a balanced shape. Remember to allow for regrowth when deciding how hard you need to prune.

Clipping

Some plants are grown as hedges or formal shapes, which require frequent pruning of the growing tips during the growing season. This clipping can be done with pruners, hedge shears or electric hedge trimmer, depending on the size of the plants. The constant cutting back of the tips of the branches encourages new shoots to grow, forming a dense, leafy bush.

Pinching

Many plants, particularly annual types such as marigolds, asters, snapdragons, and chrysanthemums, naturally produce a single stem with a flower on top. A more attractive and free-flowering plant will be produced if the growing point is pinched out while the plant is still young, since this stimulates buds lower down the stem to start into growth, resulting in a bushy specimen with many more flowers. This technique is also known as stopping.

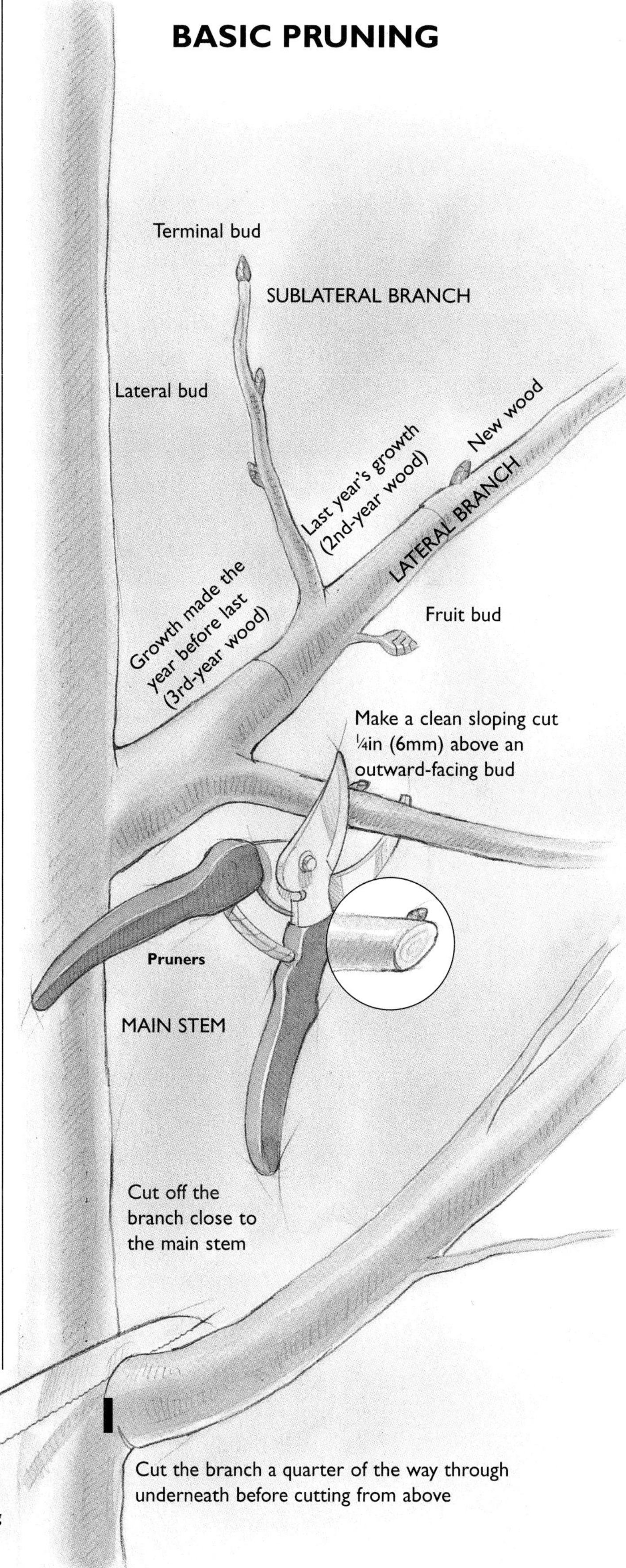

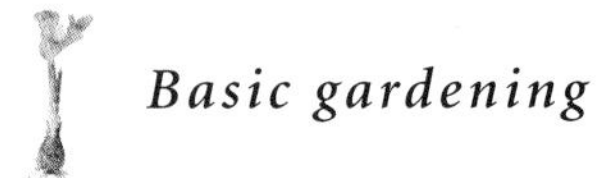

Plant maintenance

In one way or another, your plants will need care all through the year. In cold climates there may be little to do in the worst of the winter (*see pp.140–141 for details of winter care*), but the growing season, from early spring to late fall, can be as busy as you like to make it. Gardening in a small space means that jobs rarely have a chance to become tedious.

Watering

One thing almost all "no-garden" situations have in common is that there is a limited amount of soil around the plants' roots. Even when plants are not in containers, but planted out, they may be at the base of walls, in raised beds, or cracks in paving, where the soil is shallow and often of poor quality. The most important consequence of this is that water available to the plants' roots is almost certain to be in short supply, so regular watering will be an essential task.

Estimating the correct amount of water to give a plant can be difficult for inexperienced gardeners, but giving too much will eventually kill the plant just as surely as not giving enough. The aim should be to keep the growing medium moist, not wet. The spaces between the soil particles must contain air as well as water. Unimpeded drainage is necessary to let excess water run away. Containers must have sufficient drainage holes in the base and be raised off the ground if necessary. Shards, in the form of broken clay pots, or stones covering the drainage holes will enable the water to percolate through easily; similar shards and rubble should form the base of a raised bed. The soil or soil mix used for the plants must also be of the right consistency, usually containing a proportion of sand, fine gravel, or grit to ensure efficient drainage. These drainage precautions may seem ironic when the supply and conservation of water is usually a gardener's biggest worry, but they are essential for healthy growth nonetheless.

Soilless potting mixes tend to be most popular for "no-garden" situations because they are light and relatively clean to handle. They do, however, dry out more quickly than soil-based types. Once peat moss or peat substitutes are allowed to dry out completely, they are often difficult to rewet—the water simply runs off the top of the mix or drains away down the sides of the container where the dry compost has shrunk, leaving a gap. Many brands contain a wetting agent to help overcome this, but sometimes the entire container needs to be immersed in water for several hours before it will start to take up water normally again. To prevent the problem from arising, make sure the soil mix never dries out completely.

Water plants sufficiently to keep the soil or growing mix just moist; if necessary, dig a little hole so that you can check the condition of the soil a few inches below the surface.

Fertilizers are available for every type of plant. Those shown here are, clockwise from top left, potassium-rich fertilizer for tomatoes and roses; liquid concentrate for acid-loving plants; organic seaweed extract and high-potash fertilizer to promote vigorous root growth, flowering, and fruiting; sulphate of aluminum for blueing hydrangeas; chelated iron for acid-loving plants such as azaleas; general-purpose concentrated manure; and bonemeal.

The best time to water is in the evening, when the sun is off the plants, since less water is wasted through evaporation. But if plants show signs of lack of water, they should be watered immediately.

Feeding

In the same way that finding sufficient water can be a problem for plant roots in confined spaces, plant nutrients are usually in short supply, too. Plants in "no-garden" situations are usually grown at high densities, as gardeners try to cram quarts into their pint pots. This increases the competition for food and water, making the plants ever-more reliant on the grower supplementing the natural supply.

We have already noted which nutrients plants require (*see p.99*), and although good soil or growing mix contains sufficient nutrients to start the plants, after a while they will require supplementary feeding. A balanced fertilizer, with more or less equal quantities of the major nutrients, is a good basic plant food, while high-potassium foods encourage prolific flowering and fruiting and high-nitrogen foods are suitable for foliage plants to ensure healthy, lush, leafy growth.

All fertilizer packs should display the nutrients they contain as an NPK (nitrogen, phosphorus, potassium) ratio—7:7:7, for instance, indicates a balanced fertilizer, while 14:4:22 is a high-potash (potassium) food. Most fertilizers also state the types of plant and applications for which they are particularly useful, but you will find some are interchangeable if you study their NPK ratio. Rose and tomato fertilizers, for instance, are often identical, both being high-potash foods.

Pay special attention to watering and feeding plants growing between paving slabs and in other confined spaces. The soil will be sparse and probably poor, and little rain will reach the roots.

PLANTS NEED FEEDING MORE OFTEN IF THEY ARE:

- vigorous growers
- planted in soilless compost
- growing in small containers
- planted very closely
- given short-acting fertilizers

PLANTS NEED FEEDING LESS OFTEN IF THEY ARE:

- slow growing and compact
- growing in good-quality loam-based compost
- spaced well apart
- have a good depth of soil for their roots
- fed with slow-release, long-acting fertilizers

Fertilizers are formulated in a variety of ways. Powders are usually dissolved in water before application, although some can be applied dry to the soil; granules are applied to the soil surface and watered in or mixed with the soil mix when the plant is planted; sticks and tablets are pushed just below the soil surface. Liquid fertilizers are diluted with water and applied to the soil around the plants and sometimes to the foliage as well. Specially formulated foliar foods usually contain trace elements, which are taken up rapidly by the leaves. It is important to follow the directions for the application of all fertilizers carefully—they can harm the plants if wrongly applied. Powder and granule fertilizers should always be kept off leaves, since they may scorch them.

How often you need to feed plants depends on their type and the density at which they are being grown, the type and volume of compost or soil, and the brand of fertilizer.

Plant maintenance

Plants growing in containers in a small volume of soil will soon fill that soil with roots and exhaust the supplies of plant nutrients. Feeding will replace the nutrients, but in order to make healthy new root growth, fresh soil or potting mix must be supplied from time to time. This can be done by repotting the plant into a larger container, cutting the roots of the plant back, and simply replacing the soil mix or topdressing with fresh potting soil.

Potting on

A plant should always be supplied with a container in proportion to its size. Tempting though it may be to place a small plant in a large tub because that is where you want it to end up, this is not a good idea. It will be difficult to regulate the amount of moisture held by the large volume of soil mix the plant's roots do not penetrate, leading to its becoming sour and not suitable for plant growth.

Young plants should be moved progressively to slightly larger containers as they grow, enabling their roots to extend quickly into the new soil mix provided. How soon they need repotting varies according to the vigor of individual plants, but generally a good sign that it's time to move them is when roots start to emerge from the drainage holes in their current containers.

To repot, prepare the new container by placing pot shards or other drainage material in the base, then add a layer of a similar type of soil mix to the one in which the plant is already growing. You may want to change over to a mix containing a higher level of nutrients, but it is not generally a good idea to swap between between soilless and soil-based mixes when repotting.

Remove the plant from its existing pot by turning the pot upside down and striking the rim against a firm edge, or if the pot is too large for this, turn it on its side and run a large knife or thin piece of wood between the sides of the pot and the root ball and ease the plant and its root ball out carefully. (The plant will come out of its pot more easily if it has been well watered several hours in advance.)

Stand the root ball on the layer of potting mix in the new container and check that the top of the root ball is at the correct level. Fill in around the sides with fresh mix, firming it down with your fingers or a piece of wood to ensure there are no air pockets. Cover the top of the root ball with a fairly thin layer of soil mix and water the plant.

REPOTTING A PLANT

1 *To remove a plant from its pot, water it well some time beforehand. Turn it upside down, place your hand around the top of the plant to prevent its falling, and give the rim of the pot a firm tap against the edge of a table or a window ledge.*

2 *Put a layer of pot shards in the bottom of a pot one size larger than the old one and cover it with fresh potting mix. Gently tease out the roots of the plant if they are very constricted, then set the plant in the pot.*

3 *Fill the gap between the side of the pot and the plant with fresh soil mix, dribbling it in carefully by hand so as not to damage the plant. Press the mix down firmly. Then water the plant thoroughly with a sprinkler head on the can, or stand the pot in a bucket of water to soak the soil mix. Finally, drain the pot.*

Repotting and topdressing

If the plant is already in the largest practical size of pot, it can be repotted into a new container of the same size. Some plants, such as clivia, need to be slightly pot-bound in order to flower well. They, too, should be repotted into a pot of the same size, but only when roots appear on the surface of the compost.

If you cannot turn the plant out of its pot, simply top-dress it by scraping away and replacing the top layer of soil.

Staking plants

Tall or weak-stemmed plants may need staking as they grow. The earlier the supports are provided, the better the effect. It is much more difficult to achieve a natural-looking shape if stakes are put in position only when it becomes essential. Check plants frequently as they grow so that supports can be moved or ties adjusted. Never let a tie bite into the stem of a shrub or tree and tie soft stems with garden string or use a plastic-covered twist tie. Details of supports and training are given on pp.126–133.

Most weed killers can be sprayed, or watered, onto plants and paths.

Weeding and pest control

Weeds are an ever-present problem in even the tiniest pocket of soil. Besides looking untidy, they compete with your plants for nutrients, moisture, and space and should be removed, preferably while they are still in the seedling stage. In "no-garden" areas, a hoe is unlikely to be practical, and weeds should simply be pulled out by hand. This is easiest to do when the soil is moist.

Weeds with a deep taproot that cannot be pulled up easily; those such as bindweed, which are difficult to disentangle from plants without damage; and others, like creeping grasses, which are difficult to remove from the soil entirely, can be spot treated with a weed killer such as glyphosate, but care must be taken to keep the weed killer off cultivated plants. Weed killers are produced as sprays, sticks, and gels for easy use.

Regular monitoring means that any pests can be detected early, so treatment is more likely to be successful. Further details on possible pests and their control, as well as some common diseases, are given on pp.150–155.

REPOTTING INTO THE SAME SIZE POT

1 *Remove the plant from its old pot and crumble away some of the old soil from the roots and top of the root ball. Use a pointed piece of wood if necessary or cut off part of the root ball with a sharp knife to encourage the growth of strong new roots.*

2 *Put a layer of drainage material in the bottom of the pot, then a layer of soil mix, and set the plant on it so that the top of the root ball comes just below the bottom of the pot rim. Fill in around the root ball with fresh mix and press it down firmly. Add fresh mix to the top of the root ball, too, but don't bury the stem any deeper. Water thoroughly.*

TOPDRESSING

If a plant is too large and well established to turn out of its pot, you can simply top dress it. With a kitchen fork, or a small garden fork, gently scrape away the top 2–3in (5–7.5cm) of compost, being careful not to damage the roots. Fill the pot up to the old level with fresh soil mix to which slow-release fertilizer has been added, press it down, and water the plant.

Winter care

Preparations must be made for the winter season in climates where frosts and prolonged cold spells are likely. Plants vary in their degree of hardiness, or ability to cope with cold. Even those that are generally acknowledged to be fully hardy can often be killed by frost if they have not been accustomed to cold weather—plants that have been grown in a greenhouse, for example. The growth they produce is soft and sappy and much more prone to frost damage than if they had been growing in the open, where stems would have become firmer and more resilient.

Caring for plants

Having assessed your particular situation, as discussed on pp.34–43, you should have a good idea of the likelihood of damage to your plants. If you are growing annuals or bedding plants that are easy to replace, the plants can be discarded when they are past their best or as soon as frost spoils the display. Containers can then be cleaned and put away for the next summer season or, where climate permits, filled with plants for winter interest, such as winter-flowering pansies and heathers or with spring bulbs. If you are replanting for the winter, don't wait for the frost before getting rid of your summer plants; it helps to have winter-flowering plants well established before the coldest weather begins. Make sure that the new plants are fully hardened off before putting them out.

Some of the container plants you have grown may be tender but not easily replaced. Perhaps they are unusual varieties, or particularly expensive, or perennials that must be grown for several years before they assume an attractive shape, reach a reasonable size, or are able to flower or fruit.

These plants can sometimes be successfully brought into the home to overwinter; they usually require a cool, frost-free environment with plenty of light. The aim is to prevent them from being killed by frost rather than to keep them growing all year-round, and many species will not thrive in heated rooms. A frost-free greenhouse or conservatory is ideal, and you may know someone who would be willing to board out your plants until the spring. Large specimens are not easy to move and are not so adaptable to changes in conditions, so keep your most tender plants in practical-sized containers and prune them back well if necessary so that they are manageable.

Those plants that are marginally hardy are in some ways less easy to deal with. They may survive outside for several years quite well, only to be killed off by an especially sharp

Snow will do less damage to sturdy stone containers and to hardy plants such as boxwood than frost and biting winds.

WINTER PROTECTION

A large tender shrub can be protected by covering it in floating-row cover fabric and tying rope around the bush.

Place stakes in a square around a young tree, then wrap burlap or plastic sheeting around the stakes.

spell one winter, just as you have become confident of their hardiness. As an insurance policy, always take a few cuttings of treasured varieties during the summer and keep them under cover for the winter so that you have replacements if the worst happens. Give a little extra protection to borderline plants by heaping peat moss, dry leaves, or straw over dormant rootstocks or by constructing shelters around them.

Be careful about applying fertilizer. High-nitrogen fertilizers promote soft, vulnerable growth; high-potash foods help to ripen and toughen up stems for the winter. Towards the end of the summer, switch from nitrogen to potassium-based fertilizers for all the plants that you want to overwinter; withold fertilizer while plants are dormant.

Wrap vulnerable pots in bubble plastic or sacking stuffed with straw for winter protection.

Caring for containers

Plant containers can be expensive, and they all need regular maintenance and occasional cleaning. While plants are growing in them, the outside can be hosed down, scrubbed with a stiff brush, or wiped with a cloth. In winter, when they are empty, scrub the pot inside and out with a mild disinfectant solution to help prevent the recurrence of pest and disease problems. A stiff toothbrush is useful for cleaning raised decorations. Any other treatment pots may require depends on the material from which they are made.

PLASTIC Wash and scrub the pots. Discard any pots that have become brittle or cracked after exposure to sunlight.

FIBERGLASS Fiberglass can also be brittle and needs careful handling. Like plastic, it can be scrubbed and washed. On white or light-colored containers, ornate decorations often become grimy; scrubbing empty containers with a weak solution of household bleach usually solves this.

Straw packed around a tepee of canes makes good protection for borderline plants.

CLAY AND EARTHENWARE Terra-cotta, or clay, pots are fragile, so handle them carefully. They can also be prone to frost damage, and in cold areas you should buy those that are guaranteed frost-proof. Because the clay absorbs moisture, algae often grow on the outside and salts are deposited on the surface, giving a patina of age, which many people find attractive but others prefer to scrub off. There is no problem of algal growth with glazed earthenware pots; they are easy to wipe clean but, like terra-cotta, are prone to frost damage.

If you are worried about a pot's frost resistance, it will help to line the inside of the container with plastic sheeting before filling it with potting mix, but remember to cut drainage holes in the base of the plastic. A piece of plastic-coated wire encircling a pot and twisted tight before winter sets in will help to hold the pot together if it does crack.

WOOD Wooden containers will rot if they are constantly damp, so treat them with a plant-safe wood preservative and raise them off the ground so that water can drain away from the base. In winter, recoat the outside with wood preservative or paint.

METAL Treat metal containers inside and out with a suitable preservative against rust before planting. Any signs of rust that appear later can be spot-treated with an oxidizing paint.

Caring for ponds and water features

If the surface of a pond freezes over for more than a day or two in winter, you will need to melt a hole in the ice to allow oxygen in and other gases out. Don't break the ice with a heavy implement, since this causes shock waves that will harm any fish. Electrically operated pond heaters can be used to keep a small area free of ice, or you can stand a metal pan of boiling water on the surface to melt a hole.

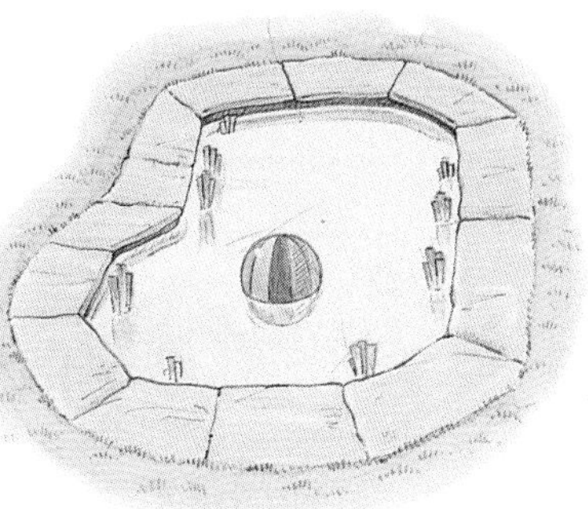

Floating a plastic ball on the surface of the water absorbs the pressure from ice and helps to prevent the sides of a concrete pond from cracking.

In cold regions, miniponds are at risk of more than just the surface of the water freezing. It is safest to transfer any fish to an indoor tank for the winter. In marginal climates, partially sinking the minipond into the ground can help to keep a sufficient depth of water free from ice.

Where there is a high risk of freezing weather, the pumps for fountains and the like should be switched off and any exposed pipes emptied so that they do not freeze and burst.

Propagation

Raising your own plants is always satisfying; it can also save money and enable you to perpetuate those that have done particularly well for you. Although propagation on a grand scale is not possible in a "no-garden" situation, some methods require a minimum of space and special equipment.

Seed

A vast number of seeds of vegetables, flowering, and foliage plants is available, many of which are very simple to raise. Annuals or plants grown as annuals are particularly popular and you can produce large numbers for a small outlay.

Seeds can be sown in ordinary pots, but seed trays are more useful. Sterile seed and cuttings soil mix, with a low level of nutrients, or a general purpose mix, is essential to prevent the seedlings from being attacked by fungal diseases. Seed kits, which contain all you need to grow the plants indoors, are often available. Trays should be watered with a can fitted with a fine rose or sprayer, or with a hand mister, to avoid disturbing the surface and dislodging the seeds. For pricking out young seedlings, a plastic dibble is handy, but a pencil will do the job just as well. For those seeds that are sown directly into the soil out-of-doors, a rake is useful to break up the soil into fine crumbs, and garden string stretched between a couple of stakes will help you to obtain straight rows in beds.

If you intend to raise a lot of plants from seed and want to try some of the more difficult species that require high temperatures to germinate, you can buy electrically heated propagators for indoor use. You will, however, need sufficient space indoors to transplant the seedlings before they are ready to be planted out, so it is probably only worth investing in a

HANDLING VERY FINE SEEDS

The best way to sow very fine seeds is to mix them with a tablespoon or two of fine builders' sand in a clean jar and spread the mixture evenly over a tray of damp compost. Then simply cover the tray with glass and newspaper.

PROPAGATING BY SOWING SEED

1 *Most seeds do not need special treatment. Simply fill a seed tray with moist seed-starting mix, level the surface, and press it lightly with the base of another seed tray to firm it. Spread the seeds thinly and evenly over the surface, either tapping them from the packet or scattering pinches of seed by hand.*

2 *Cover the seeds carefully with a layer of fine soil mix, preferably through a screen or a layer of coarse sand. This will hold them in place and keep them moist, though some seeds (very fine ones or those that need light in order to germinate) should not be covered—the seed packet will tell you if this is the case.*

3 *Water the sown tray carefully with a fine rose on the watering can or a coarse mist from a hand sprayer until the soil mix is thoroughly moist but not waterlogged.*

heated propagator if you have a conservatory or sunroom. In order to germinate, seeds require warmth and moisture. The amount of warmth varies according to the plant and its country of origin. Some seeds need a heated propagator, others the warmth of an indoor room, while yet others can be raised in trays outdoors.

The seeds of hardy annuals can be sown where they are to flower. Break down the soil until it is fine and crumbly, then make a series of shallow, parallel rows using a cane or tool handle. Sprinkle the seed evenly along the rows, rake soil over to cover, and water with a fine rose. When the flower seed germinates, the plants will be easy to distinguish from any weed seedlings because they will be growing in straight rows. As the seedlings develop, gradually thin out the rows, eventually leaving the strongest plants at the correct spacing.

Once seeds have germinated, the young plants need light, nutrients, and water, just as adult plants do, but like all babies, young plants need special care in their early stages.

WORKING WITH LARGE SEEDS

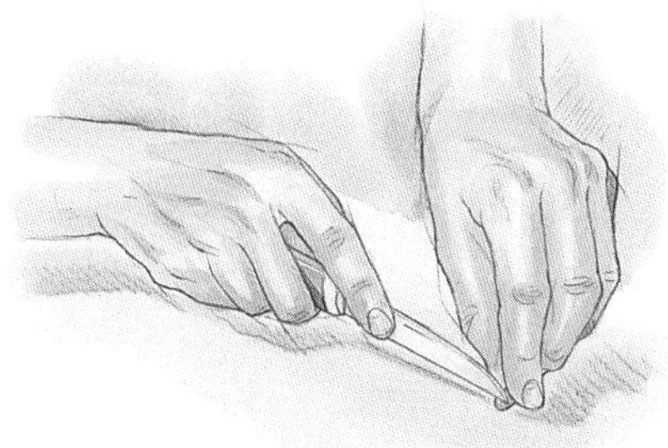

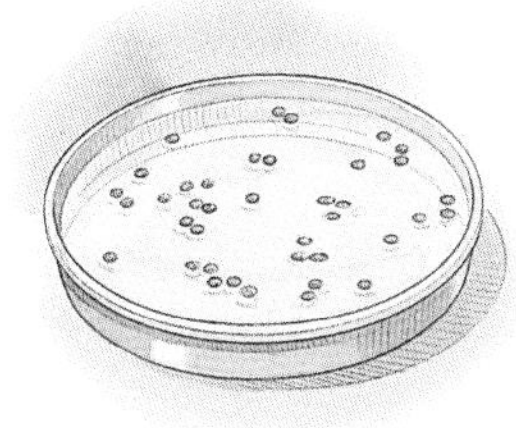

To speed the germination of hard-coated seeds, such as those of some sweet pea varieties, nick the side opposite the eye with the point of a sharp knife (left) or soak them in a bowl of water for 12 hours (right).

Sow large seeds by hand, spacing them about 1in (2.5cm) apart to avoid having to prick them out too soon. Push the seeds into the compost—the larger the seed the deeper it should be sown—then gently water the tray.

4 *Cover the seed tray to create a warm, humid atmosphere, which will induce the seeds to germinate. The traditional method is to use a sheet of glass topped with newspaper, but an upturned seed tray will also do. Best of all is a plastic propagator top with sufficient headroom for the seedlings to develop; cover it with newpaper until germination begins.*

5 *Remove the cover as soon as the first seedlings show through. Once they are up, they need bright, diffused light, but they must not be exposed to direct sun. Tissue paper taped to the window glass makes a good shade for plants on a windowsill. As the seedlings grow and become stronger, remove the shading. Give enough water to keep the soil mix just moist.*

6 *Thin out the seedlings as soon as they are large enough, handling them by their seed leaves (the first pair of leaves), never by their stems. Water the tray, then gently lever the plants up with a dibble, tease the roots free, and carefully pull the seedlings apart. Set them in fresh soil mix in another tray so that the space between them is about the same as their height.*

Propagation

Cuttings

Not all plants can be raised from seed. Some plants are sterile and do not produce seeds; others produce seed but do not breed true—plants raised from the seed they produce will not have the same characteristics as the parent. Sometimes growing plants from seed can be too slow, difficult, or laborious to be practical. In this instance, cuttings can often be used to produce plants instead. A young plant raised from a cutting is larger and more robust than a seedling and has the advantage of being genetically identical to its parent.

Many different types of cutting can be taken at various times of year, using roots and leaves as well as stems, but for the "no-garden" gardener the most useful are softwood and semiripe cuttings.

SOFTWOOD CUTTINGS These are taken mainly in spring and early summer, using vigorous young shoots. Almost any plant can be increased by this method, but perennials and bedding plants are probably the most common candidates.

First, prepare pots or trays of propagating soil mix or general purpose soil mix in the same way as for sowing seed, and sprinkle a thin layer of builders' sand on the surface. Select a strong, healthy young shoot, preferably without any flower buds, and cut or break it from the plant—cuttings of some plants, such as chrysanthemum, root better if they are snapped rather than cut. The length of the stem varies, but most softwood cuttings carry one or two pairs of fully expanded leaves when trimmed. Using a sharp knife or blade, trim the cutting just below a node (the point where the leaves join the stem) and remove the lower leaves flush with the stem.

Rooting powder or gel is optional with softwood cuttings; most root just as well without it, and some root better. If you are trying to propagate a particularly difficult species, you may want to try it. Choose a brand that contains a fungicide as well as rooting hormones, since this will help to prevent the base of the cutting from rotting. Tip out some powder into the lid of the can, dip the base of the cutting in it, then tap the stem lightly to shake off all but a fine dusting of powder.

Insert the prepared cutting into the soil mix and firm it gently but thoroughly with your fingers to ensure that the base of the cutting is in close contact with the soil mix—don't leave an air space beneath it. Once the pot or tray is filled, water well with a fine sprinkler on the can and cover it with a propagator top if you have one or a tent made from a clear plastic bag supported on split canes. Because cuttings still

SOFTWOOD CUTTINGS

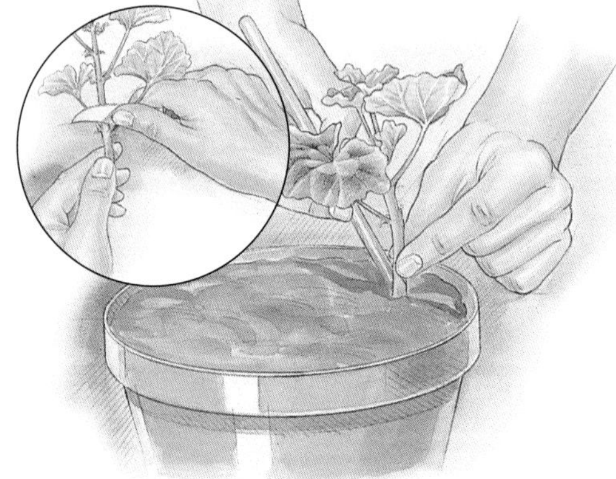

1 Soft-stemmed geraniums are excellent subjects for softwood cuttings. Cut a stem about 3in (7.5cm) long with three or four leaf nodes between the tip and the base. Remove the lower leaves with a sharp knife (inset) and trim the stem to just below a node. Fill a pot with soil mix and sprinkle a thin layer of sand on top. Make a hole with a dibble or pencil and insert the cutting, gently firming the soil around it with your fingers.

2 If you put several cuttings into the same pot, make sure that their leaves do not touch. Water the pot well. Then cover it with either a propagator top or with a clear plastic bag held away from the cuttings with canes; seal the opening with tape or a twist tie to provide the humid atmosphere the plants need to form roots. Remove the bag when the cuttings begin to show signs of growth.

SEMIRIPE CUTTINGS

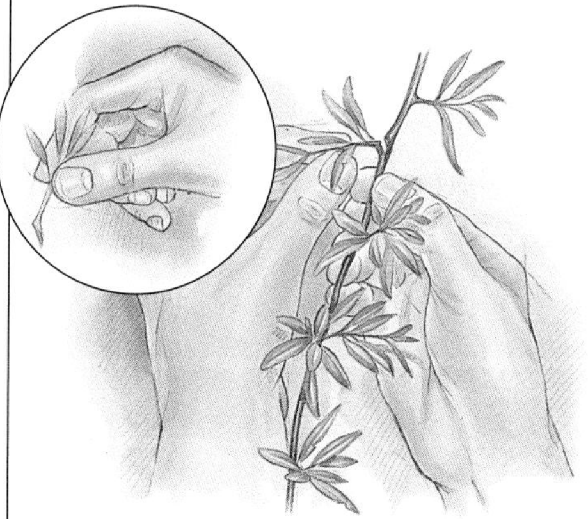

1 Shrubs are suitable plants from which to take semiripe cuttings. In summer, select a 3–6in (7.5–15cm) long side shoot of the current season's growth that is firm but still pliable, and tear it away from the main stem with a heel of the old wood.

have their leaves, they continue to lose moisture through them, so it is essential to provide a humid atmosphere. Shade the tray from direct sunlight. It is common for the leaves to droop immediately after the cuttings have been inserted, but they should pick up after a few hours.

A reasonably warm location will speed rooting, and some plants may produce new roots in only a few days. Two to three weeks is normal, but some species may be much slower. Once the cuttings have recovered from their initial shock, the ventilators on a propagator top should be opened to help avoid fungal disease; covers can often be removed altogether after a short while, as long as the soil mix is kept moist. Do not overwater—this will cause the base of the cuttings to rot.

It is usually easy to see when the cuttings have begun to root as they start to look fresh and "growy" at their tips. Be patient; never pull up a cutting to check its root development. You can check for signs of roots through the pots' drainage holes, but in general it will be obvious from the cuttings' appearance when they have rooted and need transplanting.

SEMIRIPE CUTTINGS Woody plants, such as trees and shrubs, usually produce better results from semiripe cuttings, which are taken in summer from the current season's growth, when the stems have begun to firm up and ripen.

Prepare pots or trays in advance as for softwood cuttings. Select a side shoot of the current season's growth; it should be firm at the base but still pliable. Side shoots of a suitable length can be torn away from the stem to leave a small "heel" of bark attached, otherwise they are trimmed with a sharp knife just below a node. Semiripe cuttings are generally rather larger than softwood cuttings, but again usually consist of two pairs of fully expanded leaves. If the plant has very large leaves, it is best to reduce them to a single pair to avoid excessive water loss.

Dip the base of the cutting in hormone rooting powder or gel and tap off the excess. Insert in propagating soil mix, firm in, and water as before. Cover with a propagator top at first, but this can be removed once the cuttings have recovered from the initial shock; the atmosphere does not need to be as humid as for softwood cuttings.

Semiripe cuttings do not root as quickly as softwood cuttings, but are more resilient. Keep them in a sheltered location out of direct sun for the rest of the summer, moving them to a cool spot under cover before the first frosts if necessary. Keep the soil mix just moist during the winter and remove any fallen leaves. The cuttings will not generally be rooted and ready for repotting until the following spring.

2 *Trim the base of the cutting cleanly with a sharp knife and neaten the heel if necessary. Remove the lower leaves and stalks and, if the plant has particularly large leaves, take off all but one pair and the terminal bud. Dip the base of the cutting in hormone rooting powder or gel, leaving only a fine dusting on the stem.*

3 *Insert the cutting into a prepared tray of soil mix covered with sand, using a dibble or pencil to make a hole, and firm it in with your finger. It is a good idea to take more than one cutting at a time, since they may not all root.*

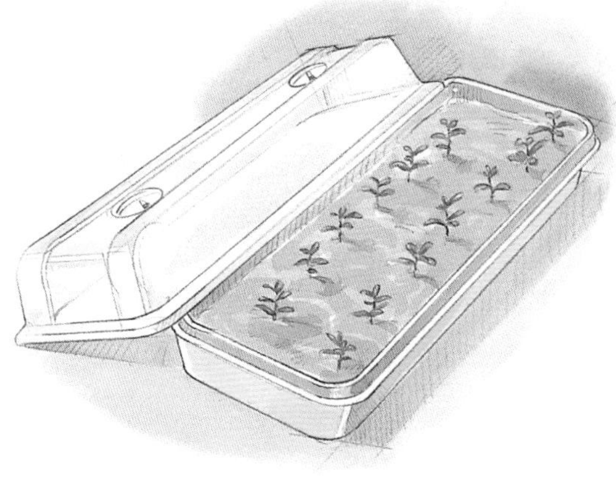

4 *Water the cuttings with a fine spray and cover the tray with a propagator top. Keep the tray in a shady spot and, after a few days, open the vents in the top. Water the cuttings as soon as the soil mix begins to dry out. Overwinter the cuttings in the tray indoors or in a cold frame and transplant them the following spring.*

Propagation

Layering

Layering is a simple way to produce new plants. It is similar to taking cuttings in that a portion of a plant is encouraged to produce its own roots, but the layer is not separated from the parent plant while rooting takes place. This means that its food and water supply are unchanged, so there is little stress on the new plant.

Plants that are generally increased by layering are those that have branches that can be bent down to soil level easily or that produce plantlets on long runners. Shrubs such as rhododendrons and dogwoods, and climbers like clematis or wisteria, are common candidates.

There are various methods of layering, according to the type of plant being increased:

SIMPLE LAYERING This is used for spreading shrubs, such as dogwoods and rhododendrons. In spring, select a healthy, vigorous branch of the previous year's growth that can easily be pulled down to ground level, allowing a portion of the stem to be buried while leaving 6in (15cm) or so of the tip above ground. If the shrub is growing in a raised bed, it can be layered into the surrounding soil; if it is in a container, you will have to bury the layer in soil mix in a pot.

Use soil-based mix, since this is less likely to dry out and will hold the layer in place more firmly. If necessary, raise the pot to a suitable level by standing it on another upturned pot or a pile of bricks. Stems layered in this manner can take up

SIMPLE LAYERING

1 In early spring, select a healthy shoot of the previous year's growth that is firm, yet still pliable. At a point about 12in (30cm) from the tip bend the stem down to the soil and mark the spot where it touches. Dig a hole about 4in (10cm) deep and 8–10in (20–25cm) long and work in some peat and coarse sand.

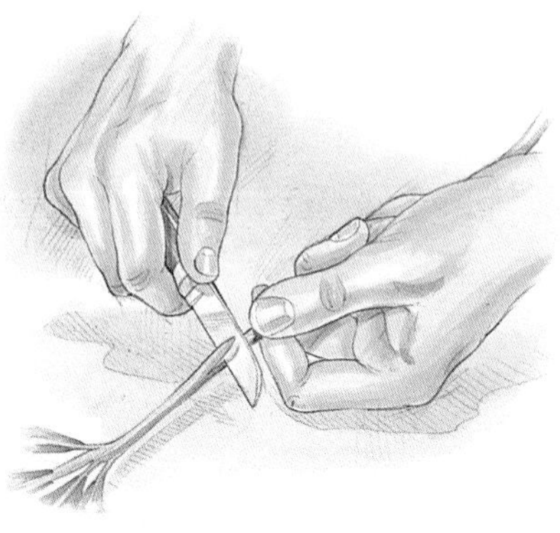

2 Starting some 6in (15cm) from the tip trim the leaves and leaf stems off the branch for about 24in (60cm). Then make an angled cut in the bare stem so that the tip can be bent at a right angle. This will encourage roots to grow from the stem just above the the cut.

3 With a bent piece of wire or forked stick, pin the stem firmly into the hole so that the tip with leaves on is above the ground. This will help to prevent the stem from springing up out of the soil.

4 Fill in the hole with soil to which you have added some peat and coarse sand. Roots will form only in the dark, so cover the stem thoroughly. Lightly firm the soil down to help hold the stem in place and water it well.

5 Insert a cane close to the tip of the layer that is showing above ground and tie the shoot to it. This will keep the layer upright so that it will form a straight-stemmed plant. Water frequently during the summer. When the layer has rooted, cut it away from the parent but do not lift it or pot it for six weeks or so.

to 18 months to root. Some may have rooted by the first fall after layering; others need to be left undisturbed until the following fall.

Whether or not layers have rooted can often be assessed by looking at the amount of growth the tip has made compared to the other, unlayered shoots on the shrub; where a branch is layered into a pot, check for root growth through the base. When a strong root system has developed, cut the stem between the layer and the parent plant with pruners; in six weeks, lift the layer carefully and pot it.

SERPENTINE LAYERING Climbers with long, sinuous stems, such as clematis, can be layered by this method, which has the advantage of producing a number of plants from one shoot. Each leaf node has the potential to form roots if buried, but two or three nodes must be left intact between buried portions; these will provide the shoots for the new plants. The completed layer, with its series of loops, looks like a snake making its way across the soil, hence the name. If you do not have a suitable patch of soil, the stem can be layered into a large pot, curling it round to take up less space.

RUNNERS Strawberries, ajuga (*Ajuga reptans*), sweet violets (*Viola odorata*), and strawberry begonia (*Saxifraga stonolifera* or *So sarmentosa)* are among the plants that produce new plantlets on stolons, or runners. If left alone, they produce a thick mat of plants, since they root readily into the soil, but by selecting the best plantlets and pinning them down into pots of soil-based mix in spring and summer, you can produce strong young plants ideal for transplanting.

SERPENTINE LAYERING

Choose a long, healthy stem of a plant such as clematis and strip off the leaves around the nodes you have selected for layering, leaving two or three nodes on the stem between each of them. With a sharp knife make a small nick in the underside of the stem to encourage rooting. Lay the stem on the soil and bury each of the prepared sections of stem, leaving the intact nodes above the ground.

LAYERING RUNNERS

1 *Disentangle the runners around the parent plant, choose those that bear strong plantlets, and cut off the other runners. Select the plantlets nearest to the parent and cut off the rest of each runner.*

2 *Sink small plant pots filled with soil-based mix into the ground around the parent plant and pin each plantlet down with a bent piece of wire. Keep the pots moist, and the new plants should be ready for lifting by fall.*

Propagation

Division

Many groups of plants can be increased by division, including those that form clumps, such as herbaceous perennials; bulbs and succulents that form offsets; and tubers and rhizomes, which can be cut into sections. It is a simple and usually very successful method of propagation.

SIMPLE DIVISION Many herbaceous plants become woody in the centre of the clump after a few years, and they can be divided as they are dying down in fall or as they are starting into growth in spring. Discard the woody centers and keep only the strong growths around the edge for replanting.

RHIZOMES Swollen underground stems of plants such as bearded irises, known as rhizomes, grow horizontally along the ground, producing leaves from their upper surface and roots from the lower. They can be cut into sections to form new plants when older parts become woody and unproductive. Lift irises once they have finished flowering. Using a sharp knife, cut 6in (15cm) sections of plump rhizome, each with a fan of leaves, and some healthy roots; discard any shrivelled, woody pieces. Then cut down the fan of leaves to about 4in (10cm) to balance the reduced stem and roots. Replant the sections, leaving the top of the rhizome just clear of the soil.

OFFSETS Many bulbs increase by forming smaller bulbs, known as offsets, around the parent. With bulbs such as narcissus, the offsets remain attached to the parent at the basal plate, the ring of tissue where the roots form. If the bulbs are not lifted, flowering is likely to deteriorate after a few years, since the offsets cause overcrowding of the clump. Offsets are also produced on short runners or around the base of the parent by several rosette-forming, succulent plants, such as hens-and-chickens. The offsets are usually left to form clumps, but one or two can be removed to provide new stock.

TUBERS Plants such as tuberous begonias and caladiums grow from disc-shaped tubers with a dished upper side where the shoots arize. When it is time to start the tuber into growth, press the lower side into a pot of moist compost. Mist the upper side with water once or twice but do not overwet it; its dished shape collects water, which can lead to rotting. When clusters of growth buds appear on the surface, lift the tuber from the soil mix and divide it into sections.

SUCKERS Several shrubs produce suckers—shoots that arise from the roots—which can be removed and grown individually to produce new plants. Plants that sucker freely include *Japanese kerria* and red-twigged dogwood.

Carefully dig away the soil to expose the root from which the sucker is growing. Ensure the sucker has plenty of fibrous root growth, then cut it off close to the parent. Dig under the sucker so it can be lifted with roots intact, cut off surplus lengths of the main root, and pot the sucker in fresh soil mix.

DIVIDING HERBACEOUS PLANTS

1 *If the plant is growing in an open bed, lift it carefully, using a fork, retaining as much soil around the roots as possible. If it is in a container, loosen the soil around the edge of the container with a stick or knife and turn the plant out.*

2 *With your hands, split the plant into several sections, each with at least one healthy shoot and some good fibrous roots. Patiently tease the sections apart without damaging them.*

3 *If the crown is too tough to tear apart with your hands, carefully split it using a pair of hand or border forks, then pull the sections apart.*

DIVIDING BULBS

Some species of lily produce bulbils, tiny black bulbs, on the stem. Remove them after the flowers have faded and plant them, well spaced, in propagating soil mix with their tips just beneath the surface. Keep them in partial shade, and they should flower in three or four years.

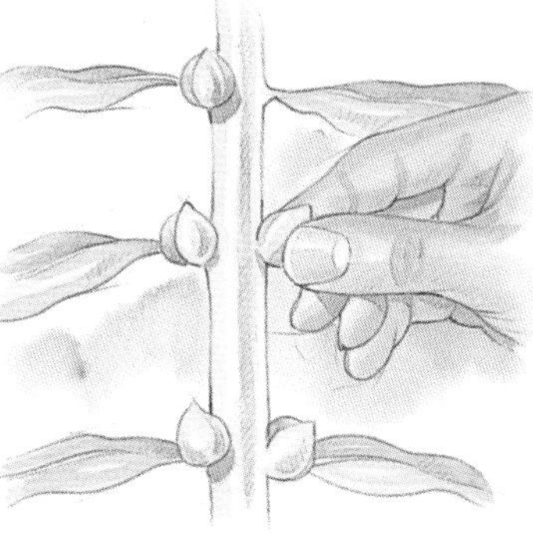

When the foliage begins to die down, lift bulbs of plants such as narcissus. Shake off loose soil to expose the offsets—there are usually two or three per bulb—and separate them from the main bulb by pushing them off gently with your thumb. Store them with the original bulbs for replanting in fall.

DIVIDING TUBERS

Divide tubers with a sharp knife. Most tubers can be cut into two or three pieces, each of which must have a group of plump buds. Dust the cut sides of the sections with fungicide powder and then replant them in individual pots of soil mix.

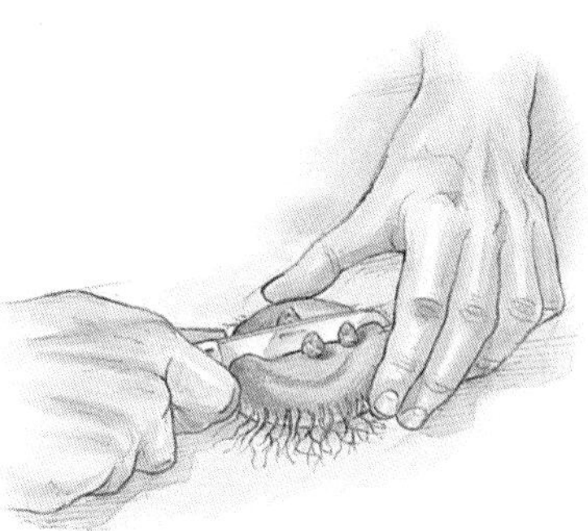

TAKING OFFSETS

Offsets are produced by some rosette-forming succulent plants, such as Echeveria *and hens-and-chickens. Plants with small plantlets directly around the base should be lifted carefully and the offsets gently teased away. The offsets should be potted in sandy soil mix.*

4 *The crowns of some plants are so tough and the roots so entangled that they must be cut into segments with a sharp knife.*

5 *Discard the old sections of the crown. At once, before the roots dry out, replant the newer sections into fresh soil mix to which slow-release fertilizer has been added. Water them in well.*

DIVIDING CHRYSANTHEMUMS

In fall, lift half-hardy florist's chrysanthemums, trim the rootstocks, or stools, then pack them in potting mix for the winter. In spring, new roots and leaves will grow on the edges of the stool; detach them and pot them to form new plants.

Keeping plants healthy

Plants seldom make it through a whole growing season without showing some disfiguring signs of infestation by disease or attack by pests. Pest and disease organisms are everywhere, in even the most sterile urban environment, just waiting for a suitable victim to arrive.

Growing plants in a "no-garden" situation has some drawbacks as far as plant health is concerned. Damage that would be insignificant in a larger area is all too obvious, and one or two unhealthy plants can ruin an entire display. The temptation to pack as many plants as possible into a limited space leads to overcrowding, which provides fungal diseases with ideal conditions in which to develop. Remedies are sometimes difficult to apply to only a few plants, and chemicals can drift on to neighboring properties.

But there are benefits to small-scale gardening, too. When you are caring for a small number of plants, it is relatively easy to spot the early signs of trouble and deal with them promptly. In a large garden, problems can go unnoticed until they are well established and far more difficult to deal with. Using sterile soil mix helps you to avoid a range of potentially harmful soil-living organisms. In addition, plants grown in containers are less likely to be attacked by some pests and diseases than those growing in the open ground. But no matter how many plants you grow, and whatever the size of your "no-garden" garden, the key to maintaining healthy plants is keen observation and prompt, appropriate action when it is needed.

Look after your plants

It is generally thought that weak, undernourished, badly grown plants are more likely to be attacked by pests and diseases than flourishing, well-cared for specimens. This is not usually the case—in fact, the opposite may well be true. However, the thriving plant is in a much better state to throw off the damaging effects of infestation than one that is already undermined by poor growing conditions, so the visible effects of the problem are usually less obvious.

Keep plants healthy by providing them, as far as possible, with ideal growing conditions. Choose subjects that are suitable for the situation in which they will have to grow—exotic plants that love high temperatures are never going to do well in a cold, exposed site, and shade-loving woodland natives will find it hard to cope with a sun-baked balcony. A relatively minor pest or disease problem could be the final straw for plants that are already struggling to survive. Keep them adequately watered at all times, apply fertilizers, and repot when necessary.

Most problems occur in the growing season, particularly spring and early summer. Pay close attention to your plants; those that are failing to make strong, healthy growth could be showing the first signs of a pest or disease attack. Favorite places for pests are the undersides of the leaves and the soft young growing tips, so check these carefully if you suspect a problem. And don't forget the roots; if a plant wilts, soil-living pests such as vine weevil and diseases like verticillium wilt could be responsible.

Control without chemicals

It is not always necessary to rely on chemical products to keep plants healthy. You cannot avoid pests and diseases entirely, but you can take simple steps to make it more difficult for them to attack your plants and to minimize the effects if they do. Taking early action helps to prevent a problem getting out of hand, and several nonchemical means of control give excellent results, particularly where a small number of plants is involved.

KEEP PLANTS TIDY Remove dying leaves and flowers, which can be a focus for fungal diseases. Leaf litter provides a perfect hiding place for slugs, snails, woodlice, and other pests, and cleaning up regularly can significantly cut down their numbers and the damage they do.

HAND-PICK PESTS If a pest is identified, hand-picking is often a surprisingly successful way to eliminate it, provided you act promptly. Leaf-eating caterpillars can be picked off individually (if you are not too squeamish), and one or two aphid-encrusted shoots can usually be cut away without spoiling the plant. Occasionally an entire plant may have to be sacrificed in order to prevent the spread of a problem. A strong jet of water from a hand sprayer can sometimes be enough to dislodge pests. For example, this is often a good way of dealing with aphids on young growing points.

"NATURAL" PESTICIDES Pests can often be controlled organically, with pesticides such as soft soap and pyrethrum.

BIOLOGICAL CONTROL The deliberate introduction of natural predators and parasites to control plant pests is most suitable for the enclosed, controlled environment of greenhouse growing. However, recognizing and encouraging common beneficial insects like ladybugs, lacewings, and praying mantis will certainly help to protect your plants against severe pest attacks.

Chemical control

There is no doubt that modern pesticides are both effective and safe—as long as they are used correctly. But garden shops carry a bewildering range of products, and it is often difficult to know where to begin when looking for the best remedy.

The first step is to identify the problem. There's no need to be too precise—it is enough to know that caterpillars are the culprits, you don't need to know the species. It is also helpful to know the plants that are affected, since not all chemicals are suitable for all groups of plants.

Having identified the problem, you can find out how to treat it. New chemicals are being developed all the time, and manufacturers' literature is often freely available in garden centers to keep you up to date. The same chemicals are available in several different combinations and formulations under a wide variety of brand names, but the active ingredients should be stated on the packaging to enable you to compare the various brands. The packaging should also tell you the range of pests or diseases the product will control.

Products are formulated in a variety of ways, some of which are much more convenient for use in small areas than others. Chemicals may have systemic or contact action. Systemic chemicals are taken up by roots and foliage and transported within the vascular system to all parts of the plant. Chemicals with contact action will affect only those pests or parts of the plant to which they are directly applied. Also, not all chemicals are legal for use in all states or provinces.

CONCENTRATES Chemicals are easier to store in concentrated form and have a longer shelf life. However, care must be taken when storing and handling the concentrate, and it must be diluted correctly before application. Check the minimum amount that can be made up; it is often not practical to prepare the small quantities needed for very small areas. Surplus solution made up from concentrates cannot be stored, and it is a problem to dispose of it safely.

Liquid concentrates are the most common; buy packages with easy-to-use measuring devices. Dry concentrates can take the form of wettable powders or granules, or effervescent tablets to make dilution particularly quick and simple. Don't be tempted to add a little extra concentrate to the solution to make it more effective—it won't, and it may damage your plants. Don't make up weaker solutions than recommended, either. They won't do the job properly and could encourage resistance to develop in pests or diseases.

READY-TO-USE CHEMICALS These are particularly useful in "no-garden" situations. Although they tend to be expensive, their convenience, and the fact that there is no waste, makes them an attractive proposition. They are often in the form of a liquid in a trigger spray or as aerosols. Insecticides applied to the soil may come as granules, and some insecticides and several fungicides are available as powders in puffer packs. Some systemic insecticides may be obtainable as tablets or cardboard stakes that are pushed into the soil to allow the active ingredients to be taken up by the plant's roots.

SAFE USE OF CHEMICALS

Garden chemicals are tested to ensure their safety, but they can still be harmful to plants, animals, and people if they are misused. Follow common-sense safety precautions.

* **Choose the right product for the job.** Spraying caterpillars with a product designed to kill aphids is a waste of time and money.
* **Mix different chemicals** only if the labels tell you it is safe to do so.
* **Choose the right pack size.** Large economy packs may seem cheaper but, remember, they have a limited shelf life.
* **Read the instructions.** Note any precautions, including recommended protective clothing, storage and how long you should keep children or pets away from treated plants.
* **When treating edible crops,** observe the stated harvest interval or witholding period between spraying and eating.
* **Don't spray plants in windy conditions.** Spray might drift on to neighboring plants or properties.
* **Store chemicals in a cool, dry place** away from children, pets, and foodstuffs, preferably in a locked cupboard.
* **Keep products in their original containers.** Never pour garden chemicals into a different container because the packaging is damaged. If the label and instructions have become unreadable, dispose of the product properly.
* **Don't store diluted concentrates.**
* **Mix only enough concentrate** to do the job—surplus solution is very difficult to dispose of. Do not pour it down drains, sinks, or toilets. If possible spray it on bare soil, gravel, or unsurfaced paths and driveways.
* **Contact your local authority** to find out how to dispose of concentrates safely if you cannot get rid of them in the ways suggested above.
* **Wear gloves and wash your hands** after you have handled chemicals.
* **Wash out any equipment you have used,** preferably under an outside faucet or using a bucket of clean water.
* **Don't mix chemicals** or rinse out equipment in the kitchen sink.
* **Dispose of sprayer rinse water** in the same way as surplus solution.

Plant pests

Aphids

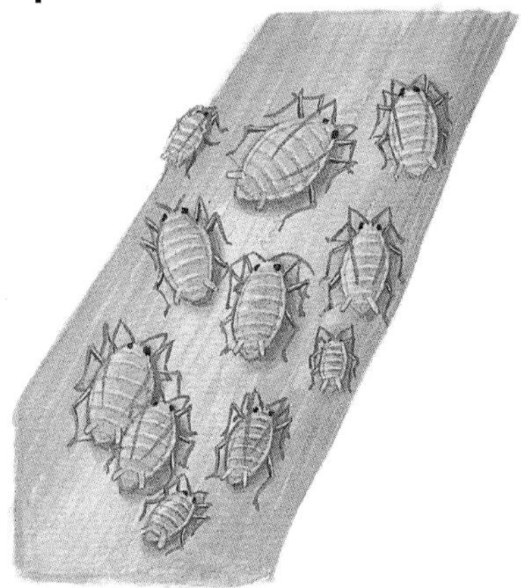

Also known as greenfly or blackfly, aphids may also be pink, yellow, brown, or white. Females can reproduce without fertilization by males, leading to rapid population increases. Aphids feed on plant sap and can usually be found clustered on growing tips or the undersides of young leaves. Plant growth may be distorted and stunted, and the sticky honeydew excreted by aphids is often colonized by sooty mold, which forms a black deposit on the foliage and stems. Aphids also help to spread viral diseases.
CONTROL In the early stages of infestation, a strong jet of water may be enough to wash away aphids. There are many over-the-counter chemical controls that are registered for this use.

Caterpillars

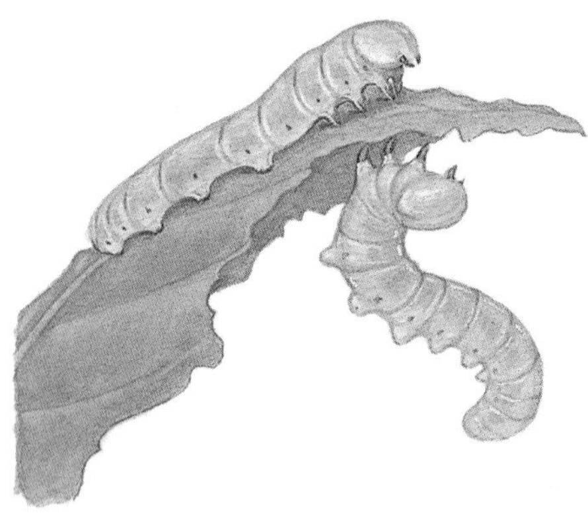

Caterpillars are often clearly visible on plants and can cause considerable damage by eating irregular holes in foliage. Some species produce grey webbing at their feeding sites, often near the shoot tips. They may be present in large numbers when clusters of eggs are laid or they may occur singly. Most caterpillars are the larvae of moths, although one species of butterfly—the cabbage white—is a serious pest of brassicas.
CONTROL Hand-picking of the caterpillars is often sufficient. Prolific infestations can be sprayed with a biological control agent, *Bacillus thuringiensis.* Chemical pesticides such as carbaryl are also very effective.

Flea beetles

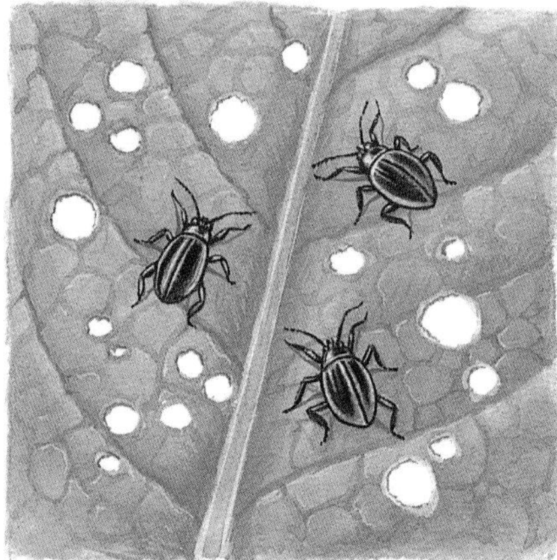

These pests may attack seedlings of the cruciferae family, as well as broccoli and cabbage; radishes, too, are often badly affected. Leaves are peppered with very small holes, and large numbers of the tiny adult beetles can often be seen leaping from the plants when the foliage is disturbed.
CONTROL Keep the growing area free from weeds and plant debris, such as dead leaves, in which the beetles can overwinter. Bad infestations can be treated with insecticides such as pyrethrins, as well as many other insecticides registered for this use.

Leaf miners

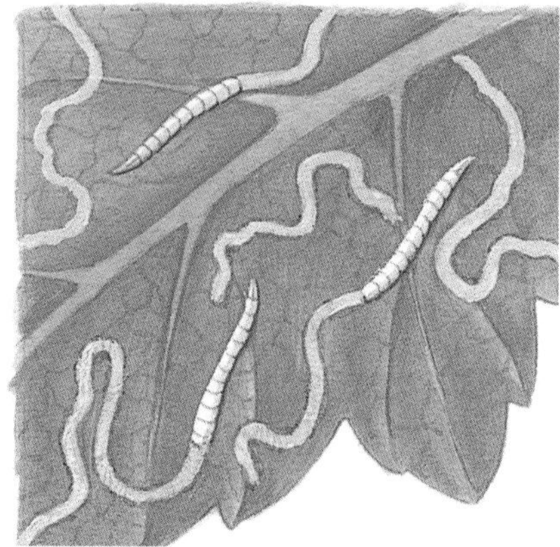

Characteristic meandering white or brown lines may appear on the foliage of a number of plants, indicating the presence of a small larva eating its way through the plant tissue between the upper and lower leaf surfaces. Chrysanthemums, columbines, and hollies are among plants affected.
CONTROL Pick off and destroy affected leaves as soon as the miners are seen.

Red spider mites

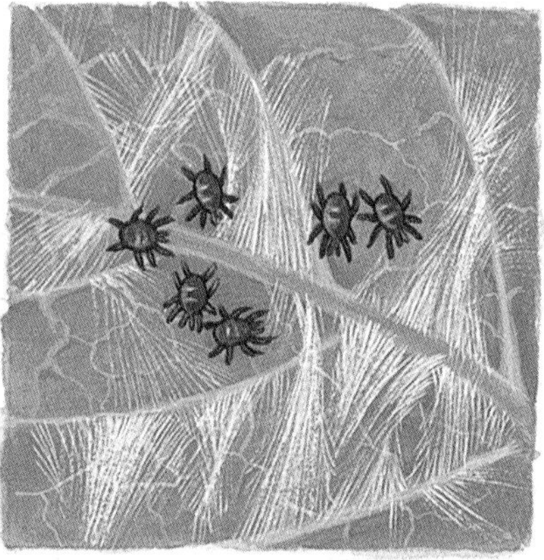

Usually a problem in greenhouses and indoors, sap-sucking red spider mites (two-spotted mites) can also be troublesome outside, particularly in hot, dry conditions. Affected foliage loses its luster and becomes dull; tiny yellow or white speckling covers the surface. Very fine webbing may be present at shoot tips or on the undersides of leaves. The tiny mites are only just visible to the naked

eye, but can sometimes be seen on the underside of the leaf or in the webbing.
CONTROL Increase the humidity by spraying plants and damping down paving with water. Registered chemicals can be used, but repeated applications are usually necessary. Insecticidal soaps are not usually very efficient.

Sawflies

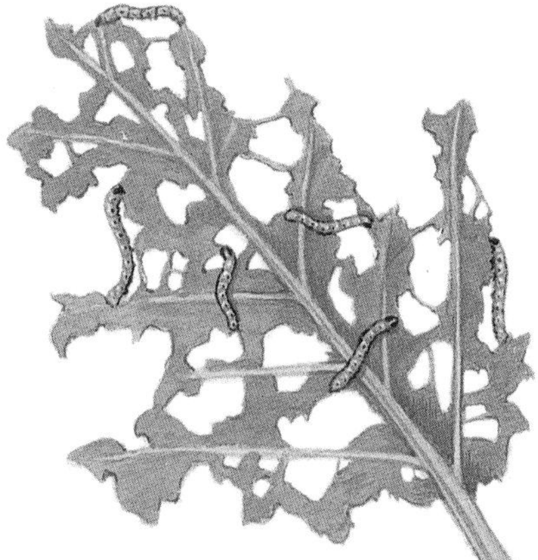

Damage is caused by the caterpillar-like larvae, which can be particularly troublesome on fruit. The foliage of gooseberries and currants is often reduced to a skeleton of veins. Other species of sawfly bore into the young fruits of apples and plums. On infested roses, the leaves become tightly rolled into narrow tubes.
CONTROL Pick off and destroy rolled rose leaves. Spray fruit at the first signs of attack with permethrin or carbaryl.

Scale insects

Limpetlike brown scales attached to stems and the undersides of leaves are the most visible stage in the life cycle of this pest. Scale insects weaken the plant through sucking sap, and the sticky honeydew they excrete attracts sooty mold fungus. Bay *(Laurus nobilis)* and succulents are very commonly attacked.
CONTROL Scrape off the scales with a fingernail. Insecticides are effective only against the mobile nymph stage, so spraying is best carried out when they are active, in late spring and early summer, using pirimiphos-methyl or malathion.

Slugs and snails

Virtually all soft-leafed plants can be attacked by these pests, often with devastating results. Seedlings may disappear entirely; older plants can have foliage reduced to tatters. They feed at night, slimy trails on and around plant remains giving away their presence the following day. They are generally less troublesome on plants growing in containers than in open ground. Young, tender plants are most at risk: lettuce and hostas are particular favorites.
CONTROL Keep the growing area free of weeds and plant debris. Use a flashlight and hand-pick the pests after dark or lure them into traps baited with beer for disposal. Several organic controls and deterrents are available, or slug pellets can be used with care (these are poisonous to pets and wildlife).

Vine weevils

The dark grey adults eat holes from the edges of leaves of a variety of plants, particularly rhododendrons, while their larvae damage roots. A collapse of the plant may be the first sign of a problem.
CONTROL Keep the area free of weeds and plant debris. Permethrin may control weevils; apply only to plants listed on the package label. Biological control exists in the form of nematodes.

Pill bugs (woodlice)

These pests may attack seedlings, but they are mainly a secondary problem, adding to the damage caused by another pest or disease. Some types of fruit, such as strawberries, can be ruined when large numbers of pill bugs begin feeding on decaying tissue.
CONTROL Keep the area free of weeds and plant debris and remove damaged foliage and fruit promptly.

Blossom end rot

This disorder affects tomatoes and sweet peppers and is the result of a shortage of calcium, generally caused by irregular watering. A brown or black, hard, shrunken patch of tissue develops at the base of the fruits, often making them inedible. Only fruits at a certain stage of development during a period of water shortage will be affected, and provided adequate water is given afterwards, subsequent fruits will not be affected.
CONTROL Never let plants dry out; those in containers are particularly at risk. Nothing can be done for fruits already affected.

Damping off

This fungus disease affects young seedlings. Damping off usually occurs where seedlings are overcrowded and causes plants to collapse at soil level.
CONTROL Sow thinly and maintain good air circulation around seedlings. Spray the seedlings with a general-purpose fungicide at the first sign of damping off.

Downy mildew

There are two types of plant mildew, downy and powdery (*see facing page*); downy mildew is the less common. It occurs on lettuce and grapevines and sometimes on a range of bedding plants. Leaves are marked with yellow or pale green patches on their upper surface, with downy gray or purplish mold on the lower surface. The disease is most damaging when plants are young.
CONTROL Pick off and destroy diseased leaves as soon as you see them; destroy badly affected plants completely. Spray with mancozeb, making sure that the undersides of the leaves are treated.

Botrytis (Gray mold)

Usually this fungus attacks dead or damaged parts of a plant first, but it soon spreads to to the rest of the plant. Affected parts become covered in gray fluffy mold. Botrytis thrives in cool, damp conditions and is a serious disease of annuals in wet seasons.
CONTROL Remove damaged plant material promptly. Avoid overcrowding and overwatering. Outbreaks on fruit and vegetables can best be treated with a fungicide, such as chlorothalonil, if labeled for use on specific plants, or one registered for ornamentals, such as carbendazim or thiophanate methyl.

Leaf spots

Leaves usually show brown or black spots or patches, with yellowing tissue between them; leaves fall early and the plant loses vigor. The best-known disease in this group is blackspot in roses, but similar fungal or bacterial leaf spots may affect a large number of plants.

Leaf spot—brownish round or oval spots—affects pansies, phlox, and polyanthus.

Leaf blotch—rings of dark spores—is common on columbine.
CONTROL Pick off and destroy diseased leaves and clean up and destroy fallen leaves in autumn. Subject plants to a program of preventive spraying with fungicides or treat plants at the first sign of attack with a baking soda solution.

Powdery mildew

This common disease affects trees, shrubs, perennials, bedding plants, fruits and vegetables. It is frequently seen on asters and myosotis, particularly in hot, dry seasons; roses and apples may also be badly affected. A white powder covers the upper surface of leaves, especially new shoots; growth is stunted and the plant's appearance is spoiled.

CONTROL Make sure plants are not overcrowded. Clean up and destroy all plant debris in fall to prevent the infection from surviving in winter. Many registered chemical fungicides can be used to treat mildew. A baking soda solution works well. Spraying with sulphur is a long-established treatment but it is not suitable for use on some plants and can be used only in temperatures below 80°F (27°C).

Rust

Rusts affect a large number of plants and are usually quite distinctive. Typically, pale yellow spots appear on the top surface of the leaf, and rings, or pustules, of orange or dark-brown powdery spores are present on the underside. The leaves fall early and the growth of the plant is weakened. Rusts are caused by a variety of fungi and can be difficult to control. Roses, chrysanthemums, and geraniums are among the plants most commonly affected.

CONTROL Ensure that plants are not overcrowded. Remove and destroy affected leaves and spray affected and nearby healthy plants with propiconazole, mancozeb, or copper compounds.

Scab

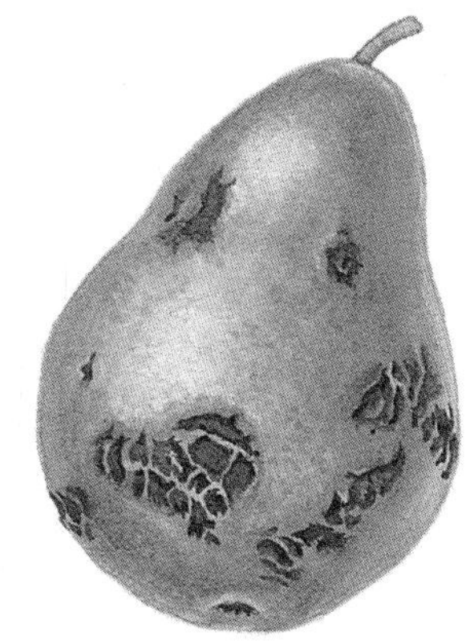

Scab is common on apples and pears. The fruit is disfigured by dark brown or black, corky scabs, and leaves develop round, brown spots and often fall early. Scab also affects potatoes and some other root vegetables; although it is not related to apple scab, the symptoms are similar, with widespread corky brown spots on the potato tubers. It is a particular problem in dry summers, especially with well-drained soils.

CONTROL For apples and pears, a program of preventive spraying with fungicides is necessary, starting when the blossoms open and continuing every two weeks until petal fall. Many fungicides are suitable, mancozeb and triforine among them. Clean up and destroy fallen leaves in autumn, since the fungus overwinters on them and will reinfect trees the following year. Spray trees with lime-sulphur in late winter.

Planting resistant varieties will reduce the incidence of potato scab. Add plenty of organic matter to light soils and water often in dry spells; potatoes grown in containers also need regular watering. Don't apply lime to the soil—this creates ideal conditions for scab to develop.

Viruses

There are many plant viruses, causing a wide range of symptoms on a large number of plants. Typical symptoms include the yellowing, mottling, and streaking of leaves, which may also be malformed, often with curled and crinkled margins. Flowers can be affected, with color-breaking causing streaks and flames, which are sometimes decorative; many bicolored tulips owe their origins to virus infection. Viruses can also affect fruits; mosaic virus is common on summer and winter squash, and can cause distorted crops.

CONTROL There is no chemical control for viral diseases, and affected plants should be destroyed. Many viruses are spread by aphids, so controlling them will help to prevent infection. Weeds may also be hosts, so keep the growing area weed-free. Wash your hands and tools after touching virus-infected plants, since the infection may be spread by handling.

Chapter Four

Plant directory

So many plants are perfect for small-space gardens that the list here can offer no more than selected suggestions, which should whet your appetite and encourage you to find out more.

In most instances, the species and cultivars particularly suitable for growing in confined spaces are mentioned, but the availability of particular cultivars will change. Don't be afraid to experiment, but remember that plants within a genus can vary in their speed of growth and ultimate size. "Dwarf", "slow-growing" and "compact" are among the plant descriptions you should look for.

Where plant size is given in the directory, it is only a very rough guide. The size of the container or available root run, the type and quality of soil, the amount and type of watering and feeding, climate and many other aspects of cultivation will also play a large part in governing a plant's ultimate size.

The cactus-flowered dahlia 'Explosion' *produces a riot of small, brilliantly colored blooms from midsummer through to fall.*

Plants for special places

Trees for containers

Most trees have a limited life in containers, but many species can make a very attractive showing for several years, adding height and an important air of maturity to the overall plant display. A reasonably large tub is required to allow the plant to assume treelike proportions.

Acer
Maple

Citrus
Citrus

Eucalyptus
Eucalyptus

Ilex
Holly

Prunus
Flowering cherry, cherry laurel

Salix
Willow

Several types of citrus tree will flourish and bear prolifically in a container, particularly Citrus sinensis, *the orange (right), and* C. limon, *the lemon.*

The rounded young leaves of Eucalyptus gunnii, *cider gum, are more attractive than the older foliage, so the tree should be cut back hard annually to prevent it from becoming too large for a "no-garden" situation.*

Conifers for containers

Choose slow-growing, well-shaped conifer species and varieties for the best results. Some dwarf forms are compact enough for very small containers, including window boxes and troughs.

Abies
Fir

Chamaecyparis
False cypress

Juniperus
Juniper

Picea
Spruce

Pinus
Pine

Taxus
Yew

Thuja
Arborvitae

Juniperus squamata *'Blue Star', with its fine blue-gray needles, is extremely slow growing and will take decades to form a dense mound some 2ft (60cm) across and 3ft (1m) high.*

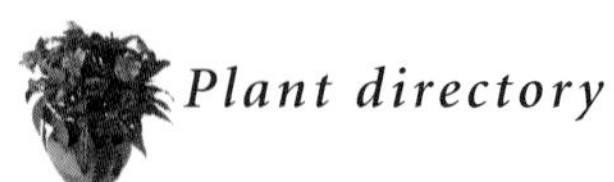

Ground cover

These plants are ideal for awkward planting locations such as sloping banks; they also reduce maintenence by suppressing weed growth. Remember that many varieties may be invasive in the wrong spot.

Ajuga
Ajuga

Aubretia
Aubretia

Bergenia
Bergenia

Campanula
Bellflower

Cornus canadensis
Bunchberry

Cotoneaster congestus
Cotoneaster

Erica
Heath

Euonymus fortunei
Wintercreeper

Geranium
Cranesbill, geranium

Hedera
Ivy

Hypericum
St-John's-wort

Lamium
Dead nettle

Thymus
Thyme

Vinca
Periwinkle

An excellent but not rampant ground cover, Hedera helix *'Buttercup' has leaves that are a bright yellow-green when it is grown in the sun and pale green in a shady site.*

In late winter, the large yellow-green, cup-shaped flowers of Helleborus lividus *appear in clusters above pale green leaves that are tinged with purple on the underside.*

Early-flowering plants

After a dull, cold winter, the sight of some of the earliest flowering plants coming into bud is always a delight. Several of the following species bring the promise of spring to even the chilliest winter weather.

Anemone
Windflower

Camellia
Camellia

Chionodoxa
Glory-of-the-snow

Crocus
Crocus

Eranthis
Winter aconite

Erica
Heath

Erythronium
Dog's-tooth violet

Galanthus
Snowdrop

Helleborus
Hellebore

Leucojum
Snowflake

Narcissus
Daffodil, narcissus

Primula
Primrose

Prunus
Almond, cherry, plum

Tulipa
Tulip

Viola
Violet, pansy

Scented plants

Plants with fragrant flowers are especially suitable for seating areas near the house, where their perfume can be fully appreciated. Many are most strongly scented in the evening.

Brugmansia
Datura, angel's trumpet

Buddleia
Butterfly bush

Choisya
Mexican orange blossom

Cytisus
Broom

Daphne
Daphne

Dianthus
Pink, carnation

Hamamelis
Witch hazel

Hyacinthus
Hyacinth

Jasminum
Jasmine

Lavandula
Lavender

Lilium
Lily

Lonicera
Honeysuckle

Mahonia
Oregon grape

Nicotiana
Flowering tobacco

Philadelphus
Mock orange

Rosa
Rose

Viburnum
Viburnum

The short, magenta-colored blooms of Buddleia davidii *'Dartmoor', full of nectar, scent the air and act as a magnet for butterflies.*

Dianthus *'Emile Pare' is a relatively modern pink, which resembles the old-fashioned pinks in its tendency to sprawl and in its fully double flowers with a sweetly spicy perfume.*

Choisya *'Aztec Pearl' has almond-scented white flowers, which are pink in bud, and darker, more finely divided leaves than those of* C. ternata, *whose flowers are pure white and citrus-scented.*

Plants tolerant of air pollution

Air quality in crowded and industrial areas is often poor, leading to difficult growing conditions. The following plants have been found to grow well in polluted areas.

In spring, the arching, spiny stems of Berberis x stenophylla *'Corallina Compacta' are covered with strongly fragrant, bright yellow flowers. It is a useful plant that rarely grows taller than 12in (30cm).*

Acer
Maple

Berberis
Barberry

Buddleia
Butterfly bush

Buxus
Boxwood

Camellia
Camellia

Chaenomeles
Flowering quince

Cornus
Dogwood

Cotoneaster
Cotoneaster

Cytisus
Broom

Elaeagnus
Elaeagnus

Escallonia
Escallonia

Eucalyptus
Eucalytus

Fatsia japonica
Japanese aralia,
Japanese fatsia

Euonymus
Wintercreeper

Hibiscus
Hibiscus

Hypericum
St-John's-wort

Ilex
Holly

Laburnum
Golden chain

Lonicera
Honeysuckle

Magnolia
Magnolia

Malus
Crab apple

Philadelphus
Mock orange

Prunus
Prunus

Pyracantha
Firethorn

Pyrus
Ornamental pear

Robinia
False acacia

Salix
Willow

Viburnum
Viburnum

Shade-tolerant plants

Hardy, herbaceous Lamium *'Beacon Silver' is a low-growing plant with silvery leaves, ideal for planting at the front of a shady bed. Here it is teamed with purple-pink asters.*

Few plants thrive in permanent, dense shade, but those that grow naturally in woodland conditions are well adapted to low light levels and will do especially well in dappled shade.

Adiantum
Maidenhair fern

Ajuga
Ajuga

Alchemilla mollis
Lady's mantle

Aucuba japonica
Japanese laurel,
Japanese acuba

Bergenia
Bergenia

Camellia
Camellia

Dryopteris
Wood fern

Elaeagnus
Elaeagnus

Euonymus
Euonymus

Fatsia japonica
Japanese aralia,
Japanese fatsia

Fritillaria
Fritillary

Hedera
Ivy

Hosta
Hosta

Lamium
Dead nettle

Vinca
Periwinkle

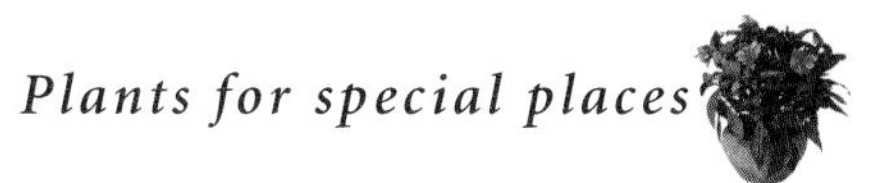

Sun-loving plants

The following plants will thrive in bright light and direct sun; full sunlight is often necessary to ensure that the flower buds open.

Anemone coronaria
Poppy anemone

Cistus
Rock rose

Cytisus
Broom

Dimorphotheca
African daisy, Star-of-the-Veldt

Dorotheanthus
Mesembryanthemum, ice plant, Livingstone daisy

Eschscholtzia
California poppy

Genista
Broom

Hakonechloa
Hakonechloa

Helichrysum
Everlasting, strawflower

Ipomoea
Morning glory

Kniphofia
Red hot poker, torch lily

Lavandula
Lavender

Rosmarinus
Rosemary

Salvia
Salvia, sage

Yucca
Yucca

Shrubby Salvia officinalis 'Purpurascens' *is the purple-leafed culinary sage. It is also reputed to have medicinal value, and an infusion of two sage leaves in a cup of boiling water will act as an aid to digestion either before or after a heavy meal.*

Plants for dry places

Plants that are naturally adapted to dry growing conditions usually have silver-grey, succulent, or waxy foliage to help them cope with water shortages.

Achillea
Yarrow

Agave
Agave

Aloe
Aloe

Armeria
Thrift

Buddleia
Butterfly bush

Buxus
Box

Cistus
Rock rose

Lavandula
Lavender

Sedum
Stonecrop, ice plant

Sempervivum
Houseleek

Senecio
Senecio

Yucca
Yucca

Waxy-leafed aloes are excellent for growing in dry conditions, but they should be planted in pots and brought indoors where winters are cold and frosty.

Plants for fall color

Just before many deciduous plants lose their leaves for winter, the foliage may turn remarkable shades of red, yellow, orange, and gold, making a short-lived but spectacular display. Fall is also the time when some of the most showy flowering plants are at their best, and many plants are full of fruits or berries or, in the case of some roses, brilliantly colored hips.

Acer
Maple

Berberis
Barberry

Cercidiphyllum
Katsura tree

Cotinus coggygria
Smokebush

Cotoneaster
Cotoneaster

Dahlia
Dahlia

Dendranthema
Chrysanthemum

Hamamelis
Witch hazel

Malus
Crab apple

Parrotia
Parrotia

Parthenocissus
Virginia creeper
Boston ivy

Prunus
Flowering cherry, cherry laurel

Pyracantha
Firethorn

Rosa rugosa
Japanese rose

Sorbus
Mountain ash

Vitis
Grape

In midsummer, Cotinus coggyria *'Flame' produces clouds of pinkish flowers, which turn gray later in the season, hence its common name of smokebush. In fall the dark green, rounded leaves change to many shades of orange and red.*

Cotoneaster horizontalis, *or rockspray cotoneaster, has bright green leaves, which turn red in fall, when a mass of red berries also appears.*

Plants for winter interest

It is not only evergreens that maintain interest in the garden during the winter; berries, flowers, stems, and bark also play their part, coming into their own in the dormant season.

Viburnum tinus *'Gwenllian' is a bushy evergreen shrub with shiny leaves. The buds appear from midfall and the pinkish flowers, which open from midwinter onwards, are followed by blue-black berries.*

Acer griseum (bark)
Paperbark maple

Calluna (foliage)
Heather

Chimonanthus praecox (flowers)
Wintersweet

Cornus stolonifera (stems)
Red-twigged dogwood

Corylus avellana 'Contorta' (stems)
Harry Lauder's walking stick

Erica (flowers)
Heath

Eucalyptus (bark)
Eucalyptus

Hamamelis (flowers)
Witch hazel

Iris unguicularis (flowers)
Winter iris

Lonicera × *purpusii*, *L. standishii*, *L. fragrantissima* (flowers)
Shrubby honeysuckles

Mahonia (flowers)
Oregon grape

Prunus serrula (bark)
Prunus

Salix alba 'Britzensis'; *S. matsudana* 'Tortuosa' (stems)
Willow, dragon's claw

Viburnum (flowers)
Viburnum

Euphorbia characias *is evergreen and hardy in Zone 7 and warmer (Zone 8 Can). It forms a large shrubby plant with yellow-green flower heads up to 8in (20cm) long in mid to late spring.*

Plants for year-round interest

Some plants maintain their good looks throughout the year, even in the dormant season. A selection of the following will help give continuity of interest from month to month.

Arundinaria (foliage)
Bamboo

Berberis (evergreen varieties—foliage, flowers, berries)
Barberry

Calluna (foliage, flowers)
Heather

Choisya (foliage, flowers)
Mexican orange blossom

Cordyline (foliage)
Dracena

Erica (foliage, flowers)
Heath

Euphorbia (evergreen varieties—foliage, flower heads, architectural shape)
Euphorbia

Festuca glauca (foliage, flower heads)
Blue fescue

Hedera (foliage)
Ivy

Ilex (foliage, berries)
Holly

Mahonia (foliage, flowers, architectural shape)
Oregon grape

Pyracantha (foliage, flowers, berries)
Firethorn

Climbers and wall plants

Climbing plants are an ideal way to maximize growing space in small areas, and many other plants will also benefit from the protection offered by a sunny wall. There are some plants that will thrive when planted in deep shade, although most prefer at least a little sunshine. You need to choose the plant to suit the exposure. In the Northern Hemisphere, north- and east-facing walls are generally cool and shady, while south- and west-facing walls are suitable for plants that love warmth and sun; in the Southern Hemisphere south- and east-facing walls are cool, while north- and west-facing walls are warm.

Climbers and plants for warm, sunny walls

Grown in a warm, protected location, such as that offered by a warm sunny wall, the edible fig, Ficus carica, *will produce a rewarding crop.*

Rosa *'Mme Grégoire de Stachelin' is a vigorous climber, which produces quantities of strongly scented double flowers. It is a particularly useful rose, since it will also do well on a cool, shady wall.*

Actinidia kolomikta
Kolomikta vine

Bougainvillea
Bougainvillea

Campsis
Trumpet vine

Ceanothus
Californian lilac

Chaenomeles
Flowering quince

Eccremocarpus scaber
Chilean glory flower

Fatsia
Japanese aralia, Japanese fatsia

Ficus carica
Fig

Hebe
Hebe

Hibiscus
Hibiscus

Humulus lupulus 'Aureus'
Golden hops

Ipomoea
Morning glory

Jasminum officinale
Common jasmine

Lathyrus
Sweet pea

Magnolia liliiflora
Lily magnolia

Passiflora caerulea
Passionflower

Rosa
Rose

Climbers and wall plants for cold walls with little sun

Garrya elliptica *produces festoons of silky, silver-gray catkins from midwinter to early spring. Those on male plants are more showy, but after flowering the branches of female plants are hung with long tassels of purple-brown fruits.*

Aucuba japonica
Japanese laurel, Japanese acuba

Bergenia
Bergenia

Cotoneaster horizontalis
Rockspray, cotoneaster

Euonymus fortunei
Wintercreeper

Garrya elliptica
Silk tassel bush

Hedera
Ivy

Hydrangea petiolaris
Climbing hydrangea

Jasminum nudiflorum
Winter jasmine

Mahonia
Oregon grape

Parthenocissus quinquefolia
Virginia creeper

About the plants

Lack of space means that this list of plants suitable for "no-garden" gardens contains no more than suggestions to whet your appetite and encourage you to find out more.

The plants are listed alphabetically by botanical name; the family name and the most frequently used common names are also given. In most instances, the species and cultivars that are particularly suitable for growing in confined spaces are discussed. Don't be afraid to experiment but remember that plants within a genus can vary greatly in their speed of growth and ultimate size. Dwarf, miniature, slow-growing, and compact are among the catalog descriptions to watch for. Sizes are usually those likely to be attained by established plants growing in open ground; plants growing in containers or confined spaces will generally be much smaller.

Brief notes about the type of soil, location, and general care the plants require, with details of how they may be propagated, are given under the heading "Cultivation." If plants are liable to suffer from any particular pest or disease this is also mentioned (*see also pp.150–155*).

A plant's suitability for the "no-garden" situations identified in this book is indicated alongside the common name. Where a genus is noted as suitable for situation 1, this usually means that only selected species will be appropriate.

① No ground space (window boxes, hanging baskets, wall pots)
② Small amount of ground space (standing room for a small tub, planting space for climbers)
③ Slightly larger ground space (roof garden, patio)

Abies Pinaceae

Fir ③

- *Evergreen conifer*
- *Various dwarf and slow-growing forms*
- *Hardy*

Abies generally makes a large forest tree, but several dwarf types are suitable for growing in small spaces. Dense, needlelike foliage is often silvery; the tree outline is rounded or flattened according to variety.

Abies balsamea nana makes a rounded shrub growing slowly to around 2–3ft (60–90cm). Zone 3 US; 2 Can.

The low-growing ***A. cephalonica* 'Meyer's Dwarf'** reaches some 2ft (60cm) high and in time will spread to 5ft (1.5m). Zone 5 US, 6 Can.

***A. lasiocarpa arizonica* 'Glauca Compacta'** has a more conical outline; it eventually reaches some 12ft (4m) but is very slow growing. **'Argentea Compacta'**, another conical variety, grows to only 30in (75cm) and has silver-blue needle. Zone 5 US, 6 Can.

Cultivation

Quick draining but moisture-retentive soil is required; strongly alkaline soils are not suitable. Give young plants shelter from cold winds until they become established.

Prune lightly, if necessary, to keep a compact shape in early to midspring. New plants can be raised from seed sown outdoors or in a cold frame in spring.

Firs may be attacked by adelgids, sap-sucking pests that leave waxy white tufts on the branches. A systemic insecticide may be necessary to control severe infestations.

Acanthus Acanthaceae

Bear's breeches 

- *Herbaceous perennial*
- *Bold, striking foliage and imposing spikes of summer flowers*
- *Hardy* *Zone 5 US, 6 Can*

Bear's breeches, with a mound of large, deeply cut, dark green leaves tipped with spines, makes a good specimen plant for a border or large container. The hooded, funnel-shaped flowers are purple and white and are carried in tall, stately spires. ***Acanthus spinosus*** grows 3–4ft (1–1.2m) tall and has a spread of around 2ft (60cm).

Cultivation

Grow in a sunny or lightly shaded location in fertile but well-drained soil. In cold areas, protect the roots with a mulch of organic matter or chipped bark over winter, particularly until young plants get established. Plants in containers need moderate watering in summer.

Clear away top growth and cut the stems back to within a few inches of ground level in fall. Plants can be increased by division in the dormant season.

Acer palmatum dissectum

Acer Aceraceae

Maple ②③

- *Deciduous tree*
- *Ornamental foliage, often with brilliant fall leaf color*
- *Attractive bark*
- *Hardy* *Zone 5 US, 6 Can*

There are hundreds of species and varieties of maple, many of which are excellent compact specimens that grow as medium to large shrubs. Commonly grown types are deciduous, with palmate leaves that are usually colorful in fall.

The Japanese maple, ***Acer palmatum***, has given rise to many cultivars. **'Osakaszuki'**, known for its fine fall color, is one of the most popular. **'Atropurpureum'** has purple-red leaves, which turn bright scarlet red in autumn, while **'Dissectum Atropurpureum'** has finely divided, lacy leaves and eventually forms a mound up to 4ft (1.2m) high and the same across. **'Butterfly'** is variegated with creamy white, and spreading **'Garnet'** has finely cut red foliage. All can be kept to under 6ft (2m). **'Sango-Kaku'** is valuable for its pinkish red winter stems and pink-tinged spring foliage.

Cultivation

Maples are best in full sun but will grow in light shade. Shelter from strong wind will extend their fall display. They need fertile, well-drained acidic soil. Plants in containers need regular watering.

Any pruning should be done in early spring; strong growths can be pinched back in summer as necessary. Propagation is not practical for small-scale gardeners.

Achillea Compositae

Yarrow ③

* *Herbaceous perennial*
* *Flat heads of long-lasting, colorful flowers*
* *Deeply cut, ferny, aromatic foliage*
* *Hardy* *All Zones 4 US, 5 Can*

The tall border plant *Achillea filipendulina*, with wide flat heads of many tiny yellow flowers, is perhaps the best-known yarrow, but many new and more compact varieties have been bred in recent years, extending the color range and suitability of these plants for small spaces. Some plants are semievergreen, and their feathery foliage can be attractive through mild winters.

A. **'Moonshine'**, growing to about 24in (60cm), has silver foliage and heads of light yellow flowers in summer; **'The Beacon'**, growing to a similar size, has crimson blooms. For smaller spaces, *A.* × *lewisii* **'King Edward'** forms a rounded, spreading plant only 4in (10cm) high, with tightly packed heads of light yellow flowers from early summer.

A. ptarmica **'The Pearl'** has abundant round white pompons of blooms in large sprays; it grows to 30in (75cm) and can be invasive.

Cultivation

Yarrows are generally best in borders and raised beds rather than containers, although the compact **'King Edward'** can be grown in pots as well as in walls and rock gardens. Full sun and well-drained soil are required. Cut back the flower stems in fall and tidy up the foliage as necessary. Plants can be divided in spring.

Achillea filipendulina **'Gold Plate'**

Actinidia kolomikta

Actinidia Actinidiaceae

Actinidia, Chinese gooseberry, kiwi, kolomikta vine ② ③

* *Climbing plant*
* *Bold or colorful foliage*
* *Edible fruits sometimes produced*
* *Hardy*

Actinidia are vigorous twining plants with bold, heart-shaped leaves. They grow well on walls or over pergolas.

In suitable conditions, Actinidia deliciosa (A. chinensis), the Chinese gooseberry or kiwi fruit, produces edible, egg-shaped fruits that are densely covered in brown hairs. A male and female plant must be grown close together if fruits are required; in cool temperate areas fruiting is unreliable in the open, but these plants do well in sheltered, enclosed garden spaces. The coarse, strong stems and midgreen foliage are covered in bristly hairs. Zone 7 US, 9 Can

More decorative is the less vigorous *A. kolomikta*, with heart-shaped leaves that are pink at the tips, merging to creamy white, then green. Zone 4 US, 5 Can.

Cultivation

Actinidia will grow well in sun or light shade, but *A. kolomikta* needs full sun for the best leaf coloration. Moderately fertile, well-drained soil is required.

Train the young shoots on wires or trelliswork on walls. If pruning is necessary, thin out the branches in early spring and tip back the leading shoots.

Adiantum Adiantaceae

Maidenhair fern ① ② ③

* *Deciduous or evergreen fern*
* *Delicate, attractive foliage*
* *Shade loving*
* *Hardy or tender*

The maidenhair fern is well known as a houseplant in cool temperate regions, but there are also fully hardy members of the family. They are good for damp, shady spots, and in sheltered locations even the more tender species may survive outside.

Adiantum capillus-veneris, or common maidenhair fern, is tender but can be grown outdoors in warm areas. The individual leaves, which are triangular and pale green, are carried in dainty fronds on very slender black stems. It reaches a height of about 12in (30cm). Zone 8 US, 9 Can.

A. pedatum is taller, at up to 18 in (45cm), with pale green, arching fronds. It is hardy, but dies down after the first frosts. Zone 3 US, 3 Can. The broadly triangular, delicate fronds of *A. venustum* turn rusty brown after frost and persist until the new foliage emerges in spring. The plant grows to around 9in (23cm), with a greater spread. Zone 5 US, 6 Can.

Cultivation

These ferns grow well in containers. Plant in light shade in moisture-retentive, fertile, preferably acidic soil, containing plenty of well-rotted organic matter. Keep the soil moist but not waterlogged.

Remove dead leaves unless they are kept for winter interest. In cold areas, move container-grown tender varieties indoors in the winter. Plants can be divided in spring.

Agapanthus Liliaceae

Lily-of-the-Nile, African lily ② ③

* *Herbaceous perennial*
* *Striking summer flowers*
* *Good specimen plant*
* *Hardy* *Zone 6 US, 7 Can*

This is an eye-catching plant, with rounded heads of blue, funnel-shaped flowers carried on tall, stout stems above long, strap-shaped, glossy leaves. It can be grown as a specimen plant in a container.

'Headbourne Hybrids', with variable blue flowers, is among the hardier strains, with plants reaching some 36in (90cm). Particularly suitable for small spaces is **'Lilliput'**, which grows to around 12in (30cm) and has deep blue flowers. There are also white-flowered varieties, including **'Bressingham White'**.

Cultivation

It needs a fairly sheltered location in full sun in a mild region to thrive outdoors. Use well-drained but moisture-retentive, fertile soil; feed and water plants regularly in the growing season. Cut down faded flower stems.

Protect the crowns with a mulch in winter in all but very mild areas or overwinter indoors. Divide every few years.

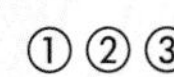

Agave Agavaceae

Agave ③

- ***Succulent, rosette-forming plant***
- ***Specimen plant with exotic appearance***
- ***Sword-shaped, spine-tipped leaves***
- ***Tender*** ***Zone 10 US***

These bold, succulent plants lend an exotic touch to a warm, sheltered spot. All are rosette-forming perennials with spiny leaves; take care if planting them where there are children or a lot of foot traffic. Agaves will not stand frost and need winter protection in cold areas.

Agave americana, the century plant, is one of the most popular species, growing to some 3–5ft (1–1.5m). Its narrow leaves are armed at the tips with tough, needlelike spines. *A. americana* **'Striata'** (often sold as **'Marginata'** or **'Variegata'**) has broad creamy bands along the leaf edges. In warm, frost-free zones only it may flower in summer, producing creamy yellow, bell-shaped flowers on towering 15ft (5m) stems; but as a container plant it will remain reasonably compact for some years.

The smaller *Agave filifera* has midgreen leaves edged with white, which peels away to hang in attractive fibrous threads.

Cultivation
Agaves require very well-drained soil; container-grown plants need regular watering in summer, but take care not to overwater or the roots will rot. A sheltered location in full sun is essential.

Mulch around the base of the plant with chipped bark or similar material in fall and protect the roots from excess rain during the winter. Where temperatures drop to freezing and below, overwinter the plants in a frost-free place. The plants can be propagated by offsets in spring.

Ajuga Labiatae

Ajuga, bugleweed ①②③

- ***Herbaceous perennial***
- ***Spreading ground cover***
- ***Semievergreen with colorful foliage***
- ***Hardy*** ***Zone 3 US, 3 Can***

This mat-forming, groundcover has rounded, toothed leaves and short spikes of purple-blue, hooded flowers in late spring. *Ajuga pyramidalis* grows to about 6in (15cm) high, with deep green leaves, but more popular are *A. reptans* and its many cultivars. **'Atropurpurea'** has bronzy purple, metallic foliage; **'Burgundy Glow'** has leaves marked and splashed with cream, pink, and purple. **'Catlin's Giant'** has particularly large, lush, shiny bronze leaves.

Ajuga reptans 'Multicolor'

Cultivation
Ajuga prefers light shade and a fertile, moisture-retentive soil but will grow adequately in most conditions.

The spikes of flowers can be picked off as soon as they appear if a low carpet is required, otherwise they can be removed when the flowers have faded. Tidy up the foliage in late fall; in all except very cold areas, the foliage persists throughout the winter. Plants are easily propagated by division of the roots in spring.

Alchemilla Rosaceae

Lady's mantle ②③

- ***Herbaceous perennial***
- ***Attractive, scalloped leaves and summer flowers***
- ***Hardy*** ***Zone 4 US, 4 Can***

The light green, palmate, lobed leaves of alchemilla have a furry texture and scalloped edges; they are particularly attractive after light rain or heavy dew, when glistening drops of water are held by the hairs around the edges and on the surface of the leaf. In summer, loose sprays of tiny, lime-green flowers (bracts) are carried in frothy profusion.

Alchemilla mollis, growing in loose, rounded clumps to around 12in (30cm) high, is the most popular species. Smaller and more dainty is *A. alpina,* reaching some 6in (15cm) high. The leaves are finely pleated as they open and more densely covered with silky, silvery hairs. The flowers are similar to those of *A. mollis,* though on a smaller scale.

Cultivation
Plant lady's mantle in well-drained soil, in full sun or partial shade. It grows well in containers.

Cut down the faded flowers and foliage in late fall to tidy the plant for winter.

Divide plants in spring or fall to increase your stock.

Allium Liliaceae

Ornamental onion 

- ***Perennial bulb***
- ***Spring and summer flowers in a wide range of forms and colors***
- ***Foliage smells of onion when crushed***
- ***Hardy***

There are many species of allium, providing a wide range of attractive plants. Flowers are generally carried on tall stems and may be in tightly rounded umbels or loose sprays. Colors range from purple and blue through pink and rose to white and yellow. Dried umbels of taller species are good for flower arrangements.

Among the many species appropriate for small spaces are ***Allium oreophilum*** (***A. ostrowskianum***), Zone 4 US, 5 Can, with rounded, loose umbels of rosy red flowers in late spring and summer, and ***A. moly,*** Zone 3 US, 4 Can, with sprays of bright yellow, star-shaped flowers in early summer. Both are suitable for containers, raised beds and rock gardens, growing to no more than 10in (25cm) high.

Slightly larger is ***A. narcissiflorum,*** with nodding, bell-shaped, pink flowers, Zone 4 US; 5 Can. ***A. cristophii*** (***A. albopilosum***) reaches some 18in (45cm) and has rounded heads of narrow-petaled, star-shaped purple-pink blooms. Among the most dramatic specimens is ***A. schubertii,*** growing to around 24in (60cm). The large umbels carry dozens of purple-pink, starry flowers on slender stems of varying lengths, which create the impression of exploding fireworks. Both Zone 4 US, 5 Can.

Cultivation
Allium like an open position in full sun, in quick-draining soil. Plant the bulbs to a depth of three times their size; keep the soil moist but do not overwater. Remove faded flower stems; some make good dried flowers. Divide crowded clumps in fall.

Aloe Liliaceae
Aloe ①②③

* *Succulent, rosette-forming perennial*
* *Exotic summer bedding plant for warm areas*
* *Tender* *Zone 10 US*

Aloes have succulent, sword-shaped leaves and bear some resemblance to agaves. Like agaves, they are useful to give an exotic appearance to warm, sheltered garden areas. They will not stand frost and in cool areas need to be overwintered under cover.

Aloe variegata is one of the hardiest species and will survive to a minimum of 45°F (7°C). It is suitable for a summer trough and grows 9in (23cm) high. Known as the partridge-breasted aloe, it has dark green leaves banded with pale green to white stripes and salmon flowers.

A. arborescens has long, bluish leaves with spiny margins; there is also a variegated form with creamy striped leaves.

Cultivation
Plant aloes in full sun in a sheltered location in well-drained soil. Water regularly during the summer but make sure that the soil is never waterlogged. Overwinter at a minimum temperature of 40°F (5°C) and water very sparingly during the winter.

Plants can be propagated during the summer from the freely produced offsets.

Mealy bugs may attack aloes, forming white tufts like cotton on the leaves. It is usually necessary to treat severe infestations with a systemic insecticide.

Anemone Ranunculaceae
Anemone, windflower ①②③

* *Herbaceous perennials with tuberous or rhizomatous roots*
* *Cup-shaped or daisy-like spring and summer flowers*
* *Some species good for shaded areas*
* *Hardy*

Many different species of anemone exist, nearly all are easy to grow and trouble free.

Anemone blanda produces bright, daisylike flowers from late winter through midspring in shades of blue, white, mauve, and pink. Growing to around 6in (15cm), with gray-green, attractively lobed leaves, it makes good ground cover under deciduous trees or shrubs and is also an excellent container plant. Zone 3 US, 4 Can.

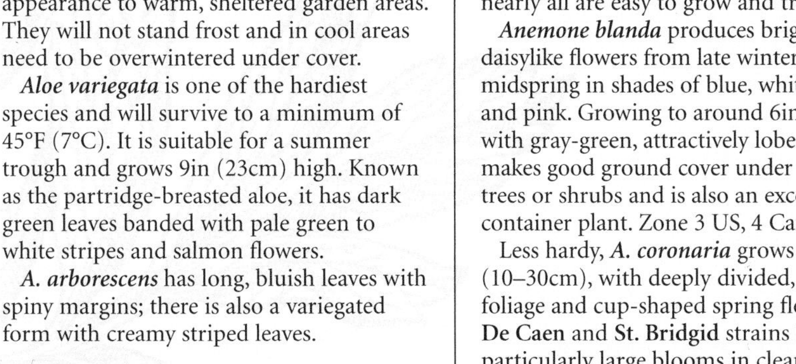

Less hardy, *A. coronaria* grows to 4–12in (10–30cm), with deeply divided, ferny foliage and cup-shaped spring flowers. The **De Caen** and **St. Bridgid** strains have particularly large blooms in clear shades of red, white, and blue. Zone 8 US, 9 Can.

For summer and early fall flowers, *A.* × *hybrida* (*A. japonica*) is a border plant up to 5ft (1.5m) tall, with cup-shaped single or double blooms in white or pink on delicate, branching stems. Zone 4 US, 5 Can.

A woodland plant, *A. nemorosa* produces a mass of delicate, white, starry flowers above deeply cut foliage, to form a 6in (15cm) high carpet in early spring. Zone 4 US, 4 Can.

Cultivation
A. coronaria does best in full sun, but most other varieties prefer light shade. Plant in well-drained, humus-rich soil that should be kept moist during the growing season. Leave *A.* × *hybrida* undisturbed as far as possible, but *A. coronaria* is best discarded and replaced after two or three years.

Viral diseases can cause mottling of the foliage and stunting and distortion of plants. Destroy affected specimens and control aphids, which spread the diseases.

Aquilegia Ranunculaceae
Columbine ③

* *Herbaceous perennial*
* *Delicate, nodding, spurred flowers*
* *Suitable for rock gardens, raised beds and borders*
* *Hardy* *Zone 3 US, 3 Can*

These old-fashioned, cottage-garden favorites have been much improved by selective plant breeding. The lobed, gray-green, ferny foliage forms a soft mound, topped with graceful, pendent, usually long-spurred flowers.

There are several alpine species especially suitable for small spaces, including the dainty ***Aquilegia flabellata*** **'Alba'** (**'Nana Alba'**), with white-spurred spring flowers, which is about 6in (15cm) tall. The early summer-flowering border varieties grow to around 3ft (1m) and are usually represented by hybrids such as **'Mrs. Scott Elliott'** and **'McKana Hybrids'**, which have more upward-facing flowers in a good range of colors and bicolors.

Cultivation
Alpine species like partial shade and moisture-retentive, humus-rich soil; border varieties prefer open, sunny locations and well-drained soil. Plants cross-pollinate and self-seed freely and can become a nuisance.

Plants are easy to raise from seed, or clumps can be divided in fall or spring.

Leaf miners are often a problem, leaving white tracks on the leaves. Control by picking off and destroying affected leaves.

Anemone blanda

Aquilegia **'McKana Hybrids'**

Argyranthemum Compositae

Marguerite daisy ② ③

- *Evergreen perennial*
- *Daisylike summer flowers and ferny foliage*
- *Excellent for training as a standard*
- *Tender* *Zone 10 US*

Also know as chrysanthemum, *Argyranthemum frutescens* is a tender evergreen with aromatic, ferny, deep green foliage and large, daisylike flowers. It produces a woody stem and, supported by a stake, can be trained as a standard, which makes an imposing container specimen.

The species has white flowers, but named varieties with colored flowers are available, including the pale yellow **'Jamaica Primrose'** and pink **'Mary Wootton'**.

Cultivation

Plant in spring in a fertile, well-drained soil; in cool regions, keep plants under protection until warm weather arrives, then set out in a sunny, sheltered location. Water freely in summer.

Pinch leading shoots regularly to form a rounded bush or train one shoot upward for a standard. Move plants back under cover before the first frosts and take stem cuttings in spring to provide the following season's plants.

Aphids may attack the young growth and can be controlled with a nonpersistent contact insecticide.

Armeria maritima

Armeria Plumbaginaceae

Thrift, sea pink ① ② ③

- *Evergreen perennial*
- *Cushionlike mounds of foliage and summer flowers*
- *Hardy*

A native of coastal areas, thrift is an easily grown, undemanding plant that has a long flowering season. *Armeria maritima* forms a neat, compact (6–9in/15–23cm) hummock of thin, midgreen leaves. From this arise many stiff stems topped with round heads of papery pink flowers during the early summer. Named varieties include **'Bloodstone'**, **'Vindictive'**, and the white-flowered **'Snowball'**. Zone 3 US, 3 Can.

A. caespitosa (***A. juniperifolia***) grows to only 2–3in (5–8cm), with grayish leaves and an abundance of round pink flower heads in early summer. Varieties include the deep pink **'Bevan's Variety'** and white **'Alba'**. Zone 5 US, 6 Can.

Cultivation

Well-drained soil and full sun suit these plants. Water container-grown specimens fairly sparingly during the growing season.

Remove faded flower heads in late fall to enjoy the neat mounds of evergreen foliage throughout the winter. Increase by taking semiripe cuttings in late summer.

Artemisia ludoviciana

Artemisia Compositae

Wormwood, southernwood ② ③

- *Shrubby perennials*
- *Finely cut, aromatic, silver foliage*
- *Hardy*

There are several species of artemisia, mostly grown for their attractively ferny, silver foliage. They withstand drought well and most are reasonably hardy. Plants often become leggy and ungainly after a few years and many are best replaced by new cuttings annually.

Artemisia ludoviciana, which grows to 3ft (1m) or more, usually has entire, lance-shaped leaves covered in woolly white hairs, which give it a striking silver-white appearance. The top growth dies down in winter. Zone 7 US, 8 Can.

A. schmidtiana **'Nana'**, known as silver mound, is a low-growing, semievergreen perennial, with very finely cut, threadlike silver foliage that forms a spreading, 3in (8cm) high dome. It is suitable for a rock garden or the top of a wall, as well as for containers. Zone 4 US, 5 Can.

The well-known **'Powis Castle'** is a vigorous, woody, evergreen shrub with deeply cut, aromatic, silver leaves. It reaches about 3ft (1m) and becomes leggy after a year or two. Zone 4 US, 5 Can.

Cultivation

Full sun, light, quick-draining soil and a sheltered location are required for the smaller species. Take care not to overwater container-grown plants.

Prune evergreen species back hard in early spring to promote neat growth. In summer, take semiripe cuttings and overwinter them in a frost-free place to guard against winter losses, which can occur in severe weather.

Arundinaria Poaceae

Bamboo ③

- *Evergreen*
- *Good container plants for an exotic look*
- *Can be invasive*
- *Hardy* *Zone 7 US, 8 Can*

The bamboos have undergone a variety of confusing name changes, and some species of *Arundinaria* are also known as *Pleioblastus*. Many species of bamboo are very invasive and unsuitable for small areas, but dwarf species can make excellent container plants.

Pleioblastus variegatus (*Arundinaria fortunei, A. variegata*) is a slow-spreading, tufted variety growing to around 4ft (1.2m). The narrow, midgreen leaves are striped white along their length. Although this species is not as invasive as some, it should nevertheless be confined to a container in small gardens.

Cultivation
Fertile, moisture-retentive soil is necessary for bamboos; keep the soil moist at all times. Plants can be grown in full sun or light shade but need protection from winds, which can discolor the foliage.

Divide crowded plants in spring to keep growth healthy and vigorous.

Pleioblastus auricoma (Arundinaria viridistriata)

Aster × frikartii

Aster Compositae

Michaelmas daisy, aster ③

- *Herbaceous perennial*
- *Late season, daisylike flowers*
- *Good for cutting*
- *Hardy* *Zone 4 US, 5 Can*

Michaelmas daisies can grow up to 6ft (2m), but there are also some excellent dwarf alpine species. Asters are valuable for their colorful flowers, which are produced well into the fall; the cultivars of *Aster × frikartii* are particularly free flowering.

A. alpinus is a spreading rock plant growing to 6in (15cm). It has dark green foliage and in midsummer bears purple flowers with yellow centers; there are also lilac-pink and white varieties.

A. amellus reaches about 18in (45cm) and is usually represented by lavender-blue **'Rudolph Goethe'**, although there are several other purple and pink varieties.

Native Michaelmas daisies include *A. novae-angliae* and *A. novi-belgii*. There are many varieties: the red **'Jenny'**, **'Little Pink Beauty'**, and **'Royal Ruby'**; white **'Kristina'** and **'Lady in Blue'** are good dwarf varieties.

A. thomsonii **'Nana'** reaches about 16in (40cm) and has pale lilac flowers.

Cultivation
Grow asters in an open, sunny location in rich, free-draining but moisture-retentive soil and support the stems with pea sticks where necessary. In containers, they need frequent watering while flowering. Cut down and remove the top growth in fall and divide plants after two or three years to maintain vigor.

Asters are very prone to powdery mildew, and preventive spraying with a suitable fungicide is often necessary.

Aubrieta Cruciferae

Aubrieta ②③

- *Evergreen perennial*
- *Trailing stems with colorful spring flowers*
- *Useful for the tops of walls and banks*
- *Hardy* *Zone 4 US, 5 Can*

This popular rock plant makes a carpet of color in spring and early summer and is trouble-free to grow. The gray-green leaves are elongated; the small, four-petaled flowers, in shades of red and purple, are carried in great profusion and last well.

There are several varieties in different shades, including **'Dr. Mules'**, **'Gurgedyke'**, and **'Purple Gem'**, all forming spreading mats under 4in (10cm) high. Even more compact is *Aubretia deltoidea* 'Variegata', which has leaves edged with creamy white and pale purple flowers.

Cultivation
Grow aubrieta in full sun in well-drained soil. Water sparingly if required.

Keep plants neat by cutting them back hard once the flowers have faded.

Soft tip cuttings can be taken in early summer, or plants can divided in fall.

Aucuba Cornaceae
Aucuba ②③

* *Evergreen shrub*
* *Shade tolerant*
* *Female plants produce colorful berries*
* *Some varieties have colored leaves*
* *Hardy* *Zone 6 US, 7 Can*

Although *Aucuba japonica* will form a shrub up to 10ft (3m) high when allowed to, it makes an excellent container plant, and with regular pruning will remain small and compact for many years. The leathery, glossy green foliage is tolerant of dense shade but will also cope with full sun. You need both male and female varieties for berries to form on the female plants.

'Nana Rozannie' is a very compact, small-leaved female variety. It usually berries well and is unusual in that it is self-pollinating, although berrying is usually better with a male plant for pollination.

There are several varieties with colored leaves, of which the male **'Crotonifolia'**, with large, gold-spotted foliage, is one of the most reliable. **'Gold Dust'**, with oval leaves speckled with gold, is a berry-bearing female.

Cultivation
Moist, but not waterlogged, fertile soil is required. Variegated types are best in full sun, but aucubas grow well in shade and are useful for planting in gloomy areas.

Prune the branches back hard in early spring to maintain a neat, compact shape.

Increase your stock by taking semiripe cuttings in summer.

Begonia Begoniaceae
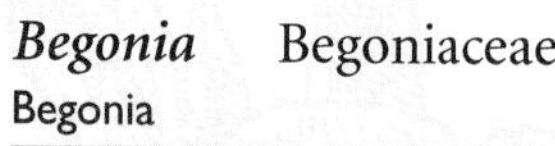
Begonia ①②③

* *Perennial, sometimes tuberous*
* *Summer flowers in a wide color range*
* *Tender* *Zone 9 US*

There are many species and varieties of begonia, but the two groups most suitable for growing outside are ***Begonia* × *tuberhybrida*** and ***B. semperflorens***. Stems are soft and succulent, and the colorful flowers may be single or double.

B. semperflorens is a low, bushy, branching plant with rounded, often bronze-red foliage. Small, simple flowers are carried in loose panicles in shades of red, pink, and white.

The flowers of ***B.* × *tuberhybrida*** are much larger; the central, male flower in each group of blooms is the most showy, and the females each side are often pinched off. Many named varieties exist.

Cultivation
Plant tubers dished-side up, with the top above soil level; water sparingly until growth starts, then more frequently. Start the tubers into growth under cover in early spring. Plant out ***B. semperflorens*** after all risk of frost has passed. Both types like fertile, well-drained soil and are excellent for containers.

Lift ***B.* × *tuberhybrida*** before the first frosts; let the leaves die down and store the tubers in dry peat for replanting the following spring.

Begonias are often affected by powdery mildew, which can be treated with fungicide.

***Begonia* × *tuberhybrida* cv.**

***Bellis perennis* Pomponette Hybrids**

Bellis Compositae
English daisy ①②③

* *Perennial, usually grown as a biennial*
* *Very double, daisy flowers in spring*
* *Hardy* *Zone 4 US, 6 Can*

English daisies, ***Bellis perennis***, are grown for their cheerful, buttonlike flowers carried on short stems in spring and summer. The leaves are midgreen, oval, with toothed edges; flower stems, about 8in (20cm) high, carry fully double blooms in shades of red, pink, and white, with a yellow eye. These little plants are good for bedding out, for containers, and as edging plants.

Strains include **Goliath Hybrids**, with extra-large flowers, and the compact, miniature-flowered **Pomponette Hybrids**.

Cultivation
English daisies grow best in the sun but will tolerate light shade. They prefer fertile, well-drained soil. Deadhead the plants to keep them neat and encourage flowering. Divide established clumps in spring.

Berberis Berberidaceae
Barberry ③

* *Evergreen, semievergreen, or deciduous shrub*
* *Prickly foliage, spring or summer flowers*
* *Fall color (deciduous types)*
* *Hardy*

This versatile group of plants may be grown for a variety of purposes. They make good hedges, their spines deterring

intruders, and many varieties have a spectacular flowering season, with bright yellow or orange flowers carried in great abundance and followed by blue-black or red berries.

Among the varieties particularly suitable for small spaces are ***Berberis* × *stenophylla*** **'Corallina Compacta'**, a dwarf evergreen growing only to some 10in (25cm), with plenty of orange-yellow flowers in spring, Zone 5 US, 6 Can; ***B. thunbergii*** **'Atropurpurea Nana'**, a purple-foliaged, deciduous plant up to 24in (60cm) tall; and the similar but smaller 12in (30cm) high **'Bagatelle'**. Zone 4 US, 4 Can.

Cultivation
Barberries will grow in most soils, even poor soil, but cannot stand waterlogging. Plant in sun or light shade; deciduous varieties give better fall color in full sun.

To maintain a neat shape, prune plants in early spring or after flowering (depending on type). Propagate from semiripe cuttings in late summer.

Bergenia Saxifragaceae
Bergenia ③

- *Evergreen perennials*
- *Large, leathery leaves*
- *Good ground cover*
- *Shade tolerant*
- *Hardy* *Zone 3 US, 4 Can*

The rounded or heart-shaped, leathery leaves of bergenia form a mound up to 24in (60cm) high; in some varieties they turn red or russet in fall and winter.

Panicles of deep pink drooping bell flowers are carried in late spring. Most popular cultivars are hybrids and include **'Abendglut'**, with luminous rosy flowers and deep crimson foliage, and **'Silberlicht'**, with midgreen leaves and white flowers. **'Baby Doll'** is a particularly compact variety, with low-growing foliage and clusters of pale pink flowers.

Cultivation
Bergenia is not fussy about soil or location and will tolerate sun or shade. Foliage colors are most pronounced in full sun and in well-drained, not-too-rich soils. Plants in containers need regular watering during the growing season.

Remove any damaged or yellowed leaves in fall and winter and cut down faded flower stems. Crowded clumps can be divided in spring or fall, but plants should otherwise be left undisturbed if possible.

Bougainvillea Nyctaginaceae
Bougainvillea ②③

- *Evergreen or semievergreen climber*
- *Colorful flowerlike bracts in summer*
- *Tender* *Zone 9 US*

This climber has woody, scrambling stems, which are sometimes thorny, and oval, midgreen leaves. Plants bear showy clusters of bracts in several shades; purple is the most common, but many named cultivars have been bred with bracts of crimson, scarlet, salmon-orange, cream, and white. In some varieties the bracts are bicolored, and some have double bracts.

Bougainvilleas are frost tender, but can be grown outdoors in a warm, sunny, sheltered location in the summer; move them under cover before fall in colder areas.

There are many hybrid bougainvilleas in a range of colors. **'Barbara Karst'** has red bracts from summer to fall. **'Raspberry Ice'** (also called **'Tropical Rainbow'**) has variegated leaves and cerise bracts.

B. glabra has rosy-purple bracts with a conspicuous, long-tubed, cream flower in the centre; ***B. g.*** **'Harrissii'** (**'Variegata'**) has a narrow cream margin to the leaves.

Cultivation
Bougainvilleas need well-drained soil and a bright, sunny location. Train the stems up a trellis or similar support or around a hoop.

Keep the plants well watered during the active growing season, but water sparingly when dormant. In cold areas, move bougainvilleas to a heated sunroom well before the first frost is likely.

Prune back the previous year's lateral shoots to within 1in (2.5cm) of the main stem in spring.

Plants can be propagated by semiripe cuttings in summer.

Whitefly can be a problem; spray with a suitable insecticide as soon as they appear. Several applications will be necessary.

Brassica Cruciferae
Ornamental kale, flowering kale ①②③

- *Biennial grown as an annual*
- *Attractive, colorful foliage throughout the winter*
- *Hardy* *Zone 8 US, 9 Can*

Ornamental forms of ***Brassica oleracea*** (cabbage or kale) make neat, compact plants for winter containers and bedding. Plants form curly-leafed rosettes, with pink or green central leaves, which become green toward the edge, or have deeply cut, feathery foliage in shades of rose, pink, and white. They are easy to raise from seed but are usually bought as potted plants in late summer or spring.

Strains include **Tokyo Hybrids** and the **Peacock Hybrids**. Particularly suitable for containers are **Kamome Hybrids**, a dwarf type with tightly packed, frilly foliage in red or white.

Cultivation
Plant in full sun in a fertile, moisture-retentive soil. Cold conditions (nights below 40°F/5°C) produce the most intense coloration of the foliage.

Discard plants when they are past their best or begin to show signs of blooming. Plants can be raised from seed sown outdoors in spring.

Ornamental kale is not usually troubled by insect pests, except the caterpillars of cabbage white butterflies, but like all brassicas it is subject to clubroot disease.

Brassica oleracea

Briza maxima

Briza Gramineae

Quaking grass ②③

- *Annual or perennial grass*
- *Delicate, pendent panicles of spikelets*
- *Good for cutting and for drying*
- *Hardy* *Zone 4 US, 5 Can*

These tuft-forming grasses grow up to 24in (60cm) tall and have very slender stems carrying gracefully drooping heads that give a delicate, shimmering effect when planted in a mass.

Briza maxima is an annual species with a dozen or so purplish green heads to each stem, while *B. media* is a hardy perennial, bearing more numerous but smaller purple-brown spikelets. Both plants flower in summer.

Cultivation

Grow *Briza* in well-drained soil and in a sunny location. *B. maxima* can be raised from seed sown directly in spring; *B. media* can be increased by division in midspring. Once established, it will often seed itself.

Brugmansia Solonaceae

Angel's trumpet, datura ②③

- *Semievergreen shrub*
- *Fragrant flowers in midsummer*
- *Good for containers*
- *All parts poisonous*
- *Tender* *Zone 9 US*

Often still known by its old name of *Datura*, *Brugmansia* produces large, trumpet-shaped, exotic flowers with a heady scent. The midgreen, oval leavs are rather coarse in appearance; the plant makes a rounded or conical shrub up to 8ft (2.5m) tall. The white, cream, orange, yellow, or peach pendulous flowers, often with attractively waved rims, may be up to 10in (25cm) long.

Among the most popular species are *Brugmansia arborea*, with white flowers, and *B.* × *candida* **'Grand Marnier'**, with orange-red blooms.

Cultivation

Angel's trumpet needs a warm, well-lit spot and frost-free conditions. Light, well-drained but fertile soil is required. Water plants moderately while in growth, sparingly at other times; in cold areas, grow plants in containers that can be taken under cover to protect them in winter.

Prune stems back hard in early spring. Propagation is possible from semiripe cuttings in summer.

Red spider mites and whiteflies often attack the plants: spray with plain water to increase humidity and use a suitable pesticide when necessary.

Buddleia Loganiaceae

Butterfly bush ③

- *Deciduous or semievergreen shrub*
- *Strongly scented summer flowers*
- *Attractive to butterflies*
- *Hardy*

These spreading, easily grown shrubs produce panicles of small, strongly fragrant flowers in white, purple, lilac, purple-red, or orange. Buddleias are also valuable because they attract large numbers of butterflies, which feed on their nectar.

The most popular species is *Buddleia davidii*, a vigorous, arching shrub with long panicles of flowers. Many cultivars have been raised, including the deep purple **'Black Knight'** and compact **'Border Beauty'**. **'Harlequin'**, with variegated leaves, is also reasonably low growing, Zone 5 US, 6 Can. *B. globosa*, the orange ball tree, grows to 10ft (3m) and has attractive, spherical heads of fragrant orange flowers in early summer, Zone 7 US, 8 Can.

Cultivation

Grow in full sun in a moderately fertile, well-drained soil in a reasonably protected location.

Prune *B. davidii* hard each spring, cutting all the branches back to within a few inches of the older wood; this keeps plants compact and improves flowering. *B. globosa* should be pruned after flowering, by cutting back flowered branches by about one-third. Semiripe cuttings can be taken in summer.

Buxus Buxaceae

Boxwood ②③

- *Evergreen shrub*
- *Good for hedging and topiary*
- *Hardy*

Boxwood has small, neat, deep green leaves and forms a compact bush that responds well to clipping. It is widely used for dwarf hedges and edging borders; container-grown specimens can be clipped to ornamental shapes.

Buxus microphylla is littleleaf boxwood, which forms a dense shrub about 3ft (1m) high. **'Compacta'** is a tiny, rounded, dwarf form suitable for rock gardens and containers; **'Green Pillow'** is slightly larger but still forms a low, dense mound of bright green foliage. Zone 6 US, 7 Can.

B. sempervirens, common box, has given rise to many named varieties, of which **'Suffruticosa'** is widely used as an edging plant or low hedge. It will grow to just under 3ft (1m) tall but is generally clipped to keep it lower. Zone 5 US, 6 Can.

Cultivation

Boxwood grows well in most soils, except very heavy ones, in sun or light shade.

Prune to shape in late spring and clip hedges and trained forms throughout the summer. Take semiripe cuttings in summer.

Buxus sempervirens

Calluna vulgaris 'Golden Feather'

Calluna Ericaceae

Heather ①②③

- *Evergreen subshrub*
- *Valuable for both foliage and flowers*
- *Good winter color*
- *Requires acidic conditions*
- *Hardy* *Zone 3 US, 3 Can*

This versatile plant forms a bushy, low evergreen shrub up to about 24in (60cm) tall, but there are many lower-growing cultivars. Slender branches are densely packed with needlelike leaves in red, orange, and yellow, as well as green and gray-green; some varieties have foliage that changes color during the year. Spikes of small, bell-shaped flowers are carried at the tips of the branches from late summer into fall. The dead flower spikes may persist and remain attractive through the winter.

There are hundreds of cultivars of *Calluna vulgaris,* varying in their size and habit, as well as in their leaf color and flower form and color. Reliable varieties include **'Anthony Davis'** (gray leaves, white flowers); **'Beoley Gold'** (golden leaves, white flowers); **'Blazeaway'** (gold leaves turning red in winter, purple flowers); **'County Wicklow'** (compact, double, pale pink flowers); **'Darkness'** (compact, purple-pink flowers); **'Elsie Purnell'** (gray-green leaves, double, silvery pink flowers); **Foxii Nana'** (compact, midgreen leaves, sparse pink flowers); **'Golden Feather'** (gold to orange foliage, purple flowers); **'Gold Haze'** (bright gold leaves, white flowers); **'H. E. Beale'** (midgreen leaves, double, rose pink flowers in long spikes); **'Spring Cream'** (bright green leaves tipped cream in spring, white flowers); and **'Wickwar Flame'** (yellow and orange leaves intensifying in color in winter, mauve flowers).

Cultivation

Heather requires very well-drained, acidic soil. Add a little coarse sand to heavier soils to improve them. Grow the plants in full sun. Regular clipping keeps plants compact. This is usually done in spring, but trim varieties grown for colorful spring foliage in early fall to give a good flush of new growth for spring.

Camellia Theaceae

Camellia ②③

- *Evergreen shrub*
- *Very early spring flowers*
- *Hardy* *Zone 7 US, 8 Can*

The large, showy flowers of camellias are well known, but because they are carried so early in the season plants often need a protected location to prevent the blooms from being damaged. The foliage is leathery, dark green, and oval or lance-shaped; flowers are cup-shaped and may be double, semidouble or single in shades of pink, red, and white. Plants grown in the open ground may reach 30ft (9m), but they grow well in large pots or tubs where they can usually be kept below 6ft (2m).

There are many cultivars of *Camellia japonica,* including the old favorite **'Adolphe Audusson'** with semidouble, deep red flowers; **'Donckelaeri'**, slow-growing with red, semidouble flowers marbled white; and **'Mary Charlotte'**, with pale pink, anemone-type flowers.

Camellia japonica 'Akashigata'

The hybrid *C.* × ***williamsii*** has produced a large number of very successful varieties such as **'Brigadoon'**, with rosy-pink, semidouble flowers; **'Donation'** with large, semidouble pink flowers; and **'J.C. Williams'**, a pure pink single variety.

Cultivation

Grow in fertile, acidic soil with some added organic matter. In cool areas, plant in a sheltered location where the flowers will not receive early morning sun, which will damage them in frosty weather, or where there is heavy dew. Most camellias grow well in semishade. They make successful container plants.

Remove dead flower heads and prune back long shoots in midspring after flowering if necessary to maintain the shape. Propagation by semiripe cuttings is often tricky, but plants can also be layered.

Campanula Campanulaceae

Bellflower ①②③

- *Annuals, biennials, and herbaceous perennials*
- *Bell-like flowers in spring and summer*
- *Hardy* *Zone 4 US, 5 Can*

There are many different types of campanula, from prostrate or trailing alpine varieties to tall, stately border plants. They mainly have lance-shaped, midgreen leaves, and blue or white, bell-like flowers.

Among species suitable for rock gardens, troughs, and baskets are ***Campanula isophylla,*** which is tender but invaluable, and ***C. portenschlagiana,*** which forms mats of midgreen, heart-shaped leaves and violet-blue, open bell-shaped flowers; it can be invasive. The low-growing ***C. cochleariifolia*** has small, round leaves and dainty bells on slender stems.

The Canterbury bell, ***C. medium,*** is a biennial border plant growing to 3ft (1m) or more. The perennial ***C. glomerata,*** with violet or purple flowers, is another good border plant.

Cultivation

Campanulas prefer quick-draining, fairly fertile soil and full sun. Remove the flower spikes of tall varieties once the flowers have faded. Divide plants in fall or spring or take basal cuttings in spring.

Border varieties are often attacked by froghoppers (spittlebug), but this rarely causes damage and can be washed off with water. Slugs and snails may damage young growth and can be controlled with slug bait or an organic alternative.

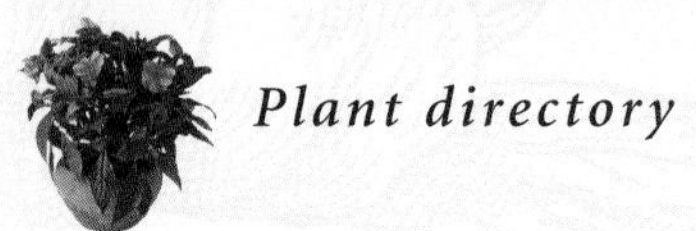

Campsis radicans

Campsis Bignoniaceae

Trumpet vine ② ③

* *Deciduous climber*
* *Showy, trumpet-shaped flowers*
* *Hardy* *Zone 5 US, 6 Can*

An attractive climbing plant with light green, pinnate, toothed leaves that clings by aerial roots. In summer, large, red, yellow or orange flowers are produced. ***Campsis radicans*** is the most popular species; ***C. grandiflora*** is less hardy and flowers well only in warm locations. The hybrid ***C. × tagliabuana*** **'Mme. Galen'** has attractive salmon pink blooms but can be invasive.

Cultivation

Grow in fertile, moisture-retentive but well-drained soil in a sunny, sheltered location; against a warm wall is ideal. Water generously in dry spells during the growing season.

Prune back shoots to within a few inches of older growth in late winter. New plants can be raised from semiripe cuttings, by layering or from seed.

Canna Cannaceae

Canna 

* *Herbaceous perennial*
* *Showy foliage and flowers*
* *Striking specimen plants*
* *Tender* *Zone 9 US*

Its exotic appearance makes Canna a good plant to grow as a specimen in a container. The roots are rhizomatous, sending up a strong stem clasped by broad leaves that may be midgreen or purplish brown. Tall flower spikes, up to 4ft (1.2m), carry large, orchidlike flowers in shades of red, orange, and yellow.

Hybrids are most commonly available under the name *Canna hybrida,* or more recently *C. × generalis.* **'Black Knight' has dark red flowers and bronze foliage;** the red flowers of bronze-leafed **'Lucifer'** are edged with yellow, while **'Orange Beauty'** has orange flowers and midgreen leaves.

Cultivation

A moisture-retentive soil with added organic matter suits these plants best. Plants in containers need regular watering during the growing season. Start the rhizomes growing in pots under cover in early spring, setting them out in a sheltered, warm location once all risk of frost has passed.

Lift the plants before the first frost, remove the top growth, and store the rhizomes in just-moist peat in a frost-free place over winter.

Plants can be increased by dividing the rhizomes in spring, as soon as they have started growing.

Slugs and snails find the succulent leaves attractive; to deal with these pests, use slug bait or an organic alternative.

Ceanothus Rhamnaceae

Californian lilac 

* *Evergreen or deciduous shrub*
* *Dense heads of blue flowers in summer*
* *Hardy*

Californian lilac is grown for its clouds of tiny, powder-blue flowers, which appear in early summer. In cool areas, the plant appreciates the protection offered by a sheltered wall.

Some cultivars, such as **'Trewithen Blue'**, tend to make large, spreading bushes, but there are reasonably compact varieties. **'Blue Mound'** is evergreen, making a dense, bushy mound up to 5ft (1.5m) high, which is covered in deep blue flowers in early summer. **'Burkwoodii'**, with deep blue flowers in midsummer and fall, is hardier than some. Both Zone 9 US. **'Gloire de Versailles'** is deciduous, with powder-blue flowers throughout summer and fall. Zone 7 US, 8 Can. All grow up to a height of 5ft (1.5m).

C. thyrsiflorus var. *repens* is a dense, spreading evergreen less than 3ft (1m) high,

Ceanothus arborus 'Trewithen Blue'

with abundant light blue flowers in spring and early summer. Zone 8 US, 9 Can.

Cultivation
Light, well-drained soil, preferably acidic, is required. In cool areas, plant evergreen varieties in the shelter of a wall.

Prune deciduous varieties back almost to the old wood in spring; prune evergreens lightly to keep them within bounds at this time. Increase plants from semiripe cuttings taken in summer.

Cercidiphyllum Cercidiphyllaceae
Katsura tree ③

* *Deciduous tree*
* *Spectacular fall color*
* *Hardy* *Zone 4 US, 5 Can*

Only one species of this small to medium-sized tree is grown—***Cercidiphyllum japonicum***. The leaves are deep green in summer, turning to attractive yellow, purple, and pink shades in fall, when they give off a strong and distinctive smell of burnt sugar. Suitable for growing in slightly larger garden spaces.

Cultivation
Plant in moisture-retentive, fertile soil, preferably acidic. Katsura will grow in sun or light shade.

Propagation is by seed sown in fall, but it takes several years to produce a good-sized plant. If necessary, prune the tree lightly in early spring to keep its shape.

Chaenomeles Rosaceae
Flowering quince ③

* *Deciduous shrub*
* *Early spring flowers*
* *Hardy* *Zone 4 US, 5 Can*

These spiny, spreading shrubs grow particularly well against walls or fences. Long before the rounded, toothed, glossy green leaves appear, cup-shaped, bright red or orange-red flowers can be seen in clusters on the bare stems. They are often followed by small, aromatic, quincelike fruits.

Chaenomeles japonica grows to about 3ft (1m), with a spread of twice that. Orange-red flowers appear in early spring. Free-flowering ***C. × superba*** is of similar size: **'Crimson and Gold'**, **'Knap Hill Scarlet'**, and **'Texas Scarlet'** are popular varieties.

The taller ***C. speciosa*** flowers earlier, in late winter, with slightly larger, deep red flowers; **'Geisha Girl'** and **'Moerloosei'** are popular cultivars.

Chaenomeles japonica

Cultivation
Well-drained, moderately fertile soil and an open, sunny location, preferably against a wall or fence, suits flowering quince.

Keep plants tidy by cutting back the previous season's branches to two or three buds in late spring after flowering. Take semiripe cuttings in summer.

Fireblight disease, which causes branches to look as though they have been scorched, is common on flowering quince. Cut out affected branches as soon as they are seen.

Chamaecyparis Cupressaceae
False cypress ② ③

* *Evergreen conifer*
* *Exhibits a range of different shapes, foliage colors, and textures*
* *Hardy*

False cypress can grow to 50ft (15m) or more, but there are many excellent dwarf and slow-growing forms. The aromatic leaves, whose color varies widely, are carried in flattened sprays.

Chamaecyparis lawsoniana **'Ellwoodii'**, with gray-green foliage, is slow growing; it eventually makes a 10ft (3m) column, but can be grown successfully in a container or rock garden for many years. **'Gnome'**is a true dwarf, making a blue-green sphere some 20in (50cm) tall. **'Minima'**, to 3ft (1m) tall, is another rounded variety, with fresh green foliage. Zone 5 US, 6 Can.

C. obtusa provides several good dwarf varieties. **'Kosteri'** is a spreading bush growing very slowly to some 4ft (1.2m).

Chamaecyparis lawsoniana 'Gnome'

'Nana' forms a small, flat-topped, rounded bush growing slowly to 3ft (1m); **'Nana Aurea'** has golden foliage. Zone 4 US, 5 Can. ***C. pisifera*** is probably most commonly represented by **'Boulevard'**, a medium-sized bush with soft, silver-blue foliage. Zone 4 US, 4 Can.

Cultivation
This conifer is happy in most soils as long as they are not waterlogged. An open, sunny location is preferred, although light shade can be tolerated.

Plants may need occasional pruning in late spring to keep them in shape. Conical varieties sometimes produce forked leaders, which should be reduced to the strongest to give the best effect.

Take semiripe cuttings with a heel of older wood in summer.

Chimonanthus Calycanthaceae
Wintersweet ③

* *Deciduous shrub*
* *Sweet-scented winter flowers*
* *Hardy* *Zone 6 US, 7 Can*

Chimonanthus praecox, which grows up to 8ft (2.5m) tall and forms a rounded, bushy shape, is grown primarily for its winter flowers, carried on bare stems. They are cup shaped, yellow with a central purple blotch, and strongly fragrant. The leaves that follow are oval and dark green.

Cultivation
Plant in fairly fertile, well-drained soil in full sun. Although the plants are hardy, a sheltered location against a warm wall will protect the flowers in cold regions.

Shoots that have carried flowers can be cut back hard once the flowers have faded to keep plants neat.

Low-growing shoots can be layered to provide new plants.

Chionodoxa forbesii

Chionodoxa Liliaceae

Glory-of-the-snow ① ② ③

- *Bulb, producing early spring flowers*
- *Suitable for rock gardens, containers, and raised beds*
- *Hardy* *Zone 3 US, 3 Can*

These bulbs generally produce two long, narrow, erect leaves and clusters of open-faced blue or pink flowers with a central cluster of stamens. ***Chionodoxa luciliae*** (*C. gigantea*) has relatively large, blue flowers with white eyes and is less than 4in (10cm) tall. ***C. forbesii*** (***C siehei***) formerly known as *C. luciliae*, is slightly taller, with pale blue flowers, but the most popular form is the large-flowered **'Pink Giant'**. ***C. sardensis*** has pendent, rich blue flowers with no contrasting eyes. All flower in late winter or early spring.

Cultivation
Well-drained soil with added organic matter is preferred. Chionodoxa thrives in full sun. Seed germinates freely in fall, or plants can be divided in late summer.

Choisya Rutaceae

Mexican orange blossom ② ③

- *Evergreen shrub*
- *Fragrant flowers in spring*
- *Aromatic foliage*
- *Hardy* *Zone 7 US, 8 Can*

This plant makes a rounded shrub some 6ft (2m) high, with glossy, fresh green leaves, consisting of three leaflets. They have a pleasant aroma when crushed. Small, starry, very fragrant white flowers are carried in spring and early summer, often with a further flush in fall that sometimes persists throughout a mild winter.

Choisya ternata **'Sundance'** has shiny, bright yellow leaves.

Cultivation
Grow in well-drained soil in a sunny but sheltered location, especially in colder areas, where it will benefit from the protection of a wall, since it is prone to frost damage.

Prune straggly shoots where necessary in late spring, removing frost-damaged shoots.

Propagate by taking semiripe cuttings in summer.

Cistus Cistaceae

Rock rose ② ③

- *Evergreen shrubs*
- *Excellent for seaside areas*
- *Summer flowers*
- *Hardy* *Zone 6 US, 7 Can*

These plants can form a spreading, lax shrub up to 6ft (2m) high where conditions suit them, but most remain smaller than this. The long, crinkled, gray-green leaves of rock rose are sometimes sticky to the touch. In summer, open, cup-shaped flowers, with delicate, paper-thin petals, cover the branches. Flowers may be white or pink, often with contrasting blotches at the base of the petals, and with a showy golden boss of stamens. Each flower lasts only a day, but further buds open in quick succession to give a long season of interest.

Cistus × corbariensis grows to about 3ft (1m) but spreads more widely; it carries white flowers with a central yellow blotch. Slightly taller is ***C. ladanifer***, with slightly tacky leaves and white flowers with maroon blotches at the base of each petal.

C. × purpureus has rose-pink flowers with deeper red markings at the center.

The popular hybrid **'Silver Pink'** has gray-green foliage and large, clear pink flowers with golden stamens, which are produced in abundance in early summer.

Cultivation
Provide rock roses with light, very well-drained soil, and a location in full sun. Some shelter is necessary in colder areas, and plants should be protected from prolonged frosts.

Prune back dead wood in spring. Plants can be increased by softwood cuttings taken in summer.

Citrus Rutaceae

Citrus ② ③

- *Evergreen shrubs*
- *Fragrant spring flowers and colorful fruit*
- *Excellent in containers*
- *Tender* *Zone 10 US*

Members of the citrus family have deep green, glossy, ovate leaves, which are aromatic when crushed, and starry, fragrant white flowers in spring. These are usually followed by attractive, sometimes edible fruits. Plants are not frost hardy and should be overwintered under cover in cold areas.

The calomondin, × ***Citrofortunella microcarpa*** (***Citrus mitis***), is one of the most successful plants, with small, orange-yellow fruits freely carried. It grows to around 2ft (60cm) in a container.

C. limon (lemon) and ***C. sinensis*** (orange) can also be grown; they reach 4ft (1.2m) in suitable conditions.

Cultivation
Citrus plants need a minimum temperature of 40°F (5°C) to do well, although established plants will sometimes withstand short periods of lower temperatures. In cold regions, they are best grown in a sun room, greenhouse, or a well-lit location indoors during the winter; place them in a sunny, sheltered spot outdoors when all risk of frost has passed.

Use well-drained, soil-based growing mix and water plants freely during the growing season, sparingly in cooler weather.

Cut back or cut out straggly shoots in spring.

Plants can be increased from semiripe cuttings in summer, but a heated propagator is generally needed to produce good results.

Citrus sinensis

Clematis 'Bill Mackenzie'

Clematis Ranunculaceae

Clematis ②③

* *Evergreen or deciduous climber*
* *Showy flowers from early spring to fall, depending on species*
* *Hardy*

There are three main groups of clematis: early-flowering species, which are largely evergreen and have small, nodding flowers in early spring; early-flowering hybrids, with larger, flat-faced flowers with colorful sepals in early to midsummer; and hybrids and species that bloom in late summer or early fall.

Early-flowering species such as ***Clematis alpina*** (Zone 4 US, 4 Can) with pendent, purple-blue flowers, and ***C. armandii*** (Zone 5 US, 6 Can) with small, white, strongly scented blooms, are particularly suitable for containers and small gardens.

C. montana is a vigorous scrambler with an abundance of small to medium, white spring flowers; **'Tetrarose'** is a less rampant form, with deep pink blooms and reddish-tinged leaves, Zone 5 US, 6 Can.

C. florida **'Sieboldii'**, with ivory-white sepals and purple stamens, needs a warm sheltered position, Zone 5 US, 6 Can.

The large-flowered cultivar **'H. F. Young'** is compact and has pale violet-blue blooms in midsummer. Yellow **'Bill Mackenzie'** blooms from midsummer to early fall and often bears flowers and seedheads together. Both Zone 3 US, 4 Can.

Cultivation

Clematis like their heads in the sun and their feet in the shade, to give them a cool, moist root run. Keep containers moist at all times; never let the compost dry out. Give high-potash liquid feedings regularly.

When necessary to keep them within bounds, spring-flowering species can be pruned after flowering by removing all the flowered wood.

Early-flowering hybrids should have young shoots shortened by up to one-third in spring; and the previous season's shoots on late-flowering hybrids should be pruned back to a pair of healthy buds near the base in spring.

Plants can be increased by semiripe cuttings in summer or by layering low-growing shoots in spring.

Clematis wilt causes the sudden, dramatic wilting of the top growth; affected plants should be mulched. Heaping the mulch around the base of the plant encourages adventitious roots from the base of the stem and new shoots are often produced. Do not plant replacement clematis in affected soil or potting mix.

Colchicum Liliaceae

Autumn crocus ②③

* *Corm*
* *Crocuslike fall flowers, appearing before the leaves*
* *Hardy* *Zone 4 US, 5 Can*

Although similar in appearance, colchicum and crocus are not related. Colchicum produces relatively large, goblet-shaped flowers in early autumn. The flowers rise on slender, fragile-looking stems directly from the ground; the untidy mounds of broad leaves are produced in spring. There is one spring-flowering species, but it is not widely grown.

Colchicum agrippinum grows to some 4in (10cm) tall and has deep, rosy-pink flowers with pointed petals. The 6in (15cm) high ***C. autumnale*** has pink, white, or purple flowers on delicate stems.

Free-flowering ***C. byzantinum*** has funnel-shaped, pale lilac flowers and grows to some 6–8in (15–20cm).

C. speciosum, at about the same height, is a vigorous grower with purple-pink flowers; **'Album'** is a pure white form.

The hybrid **'Waterlily'** produces fully double flowers that are often too heavy for their slender stems, while **'The Giant'** has large, mauve-pink flowers, fading to white at the base.

Cultivation

Plant the corms 4in (10cm) deep in groups in late summer. Colchicums like an open, sunny location and may be grown in well-drained soil in borders, containers, and raised beds or naturalized in grass. Remember, however, that the spring foliage may look untidy and can smother grass.

Lift the corms in early summer and break away the offsets to increase your stock before replanting.

Colchicum speciosum 'Atrorubens'

Cordyline australis 'Albertii'

Cordyline Agavaceae

Dracena ②③

- *Evergreen shrub*
- *Foliage plant with a tropical appearance*
- *Excellent for containers*
- *Tender*

The long, strap-shaped leaves of cordyline are carried in rosettes at the ends of the stem, giving the plant a palmlike appearance. The most commonly grown species is *Cordyline australis,* which can grow slowly to become a branching tree more than 25ft (8m) tall but usually remains restricted to below 6ft (2m) in a container. Many forms with colored and variegated leaves are available, including **'Atropurpurea'** with bronzy green leaves, and the purple-leaved **'Purpureus'**. Zone 10 US.

C. indivisa produces a single stem up to 10ft (3m) high, with long, grayish green leaves in loose rosettes. Zone 9 US.

Cultivation

Fertile, well-drained soil and a warm location are necessary; in cold regions protect young plants during the winter.

Cordylines prefer full sun but will tolerate light shade. Water moderately in the growing season but sparingly otherwise. Prune only to remove frost-damaged growth. Plants can be propagated by potting up suckers in spring.

Red spider mites may attack plants in summer although they are more common on specimens grown as houseplants. Spraying the foliage with plain water helps avoid infestation.

Cornus Cornaceae

Dogwood ②③

- *Deciduous shrub*
- *Colorful winter stems*
- *Hardy* *Zone 2 US, 1 Can*

There are several useful members of the dogwood family, but perhaps the most popular is *Cornus alba,* grown for its bright red winter stems. Plants reach about 6ft (2m), forming a cup-shaped bush. **'Sibirica'** (also known as **'Westonbirt'**) has shining red bark, while **'Kesselringii'** has deep red bark and colorful fall foliage. **'Elegantissima'** has white-variegated foliage and **'Spaethii'** golden-variegated leaves, giving these two cultivars summer interest in addition to their red winter stems.

Cornus alba 'Spaethii'

Cultivation

Dogwoods like fertile, moisture-retentive soil in sun or light shade. Plants grown for their winter stems should be pruned back hard in spring, cutting them to within a few inches of the ground; this ensures the formation of vigorous young shoots, which have the best color.

Propagate plants by semiripe cuttings in summer or by layering low-growing branches in fall.

Corylus Corylaceae

Hazel ③

- *Deciduous shrub*
- *Attractive catkins in late winter and spring*
- *Bears edible nuts*
- *Hardy* *Zone 4 US, 5 Can*

Corylus avellana is a vigorous plant, forming a large bush that bears hazelnuts in fall. The most attractive form for gardens is **'Contorta'**, known as Harry Lauder's walking stick, which forms a bushy shrub 6ft (2m) or more in height. Its shoots are curiously twisted and corkscrewed, making it very attractive in winter, particularly when it is hung with catkins. Oval, toothed leaves cover the branches in summer.

Cultivation

Plant in well-drained soil in a sunny or lightly shaded spot. Position the plant against a suitable winter background that will display the stems well.

Cut out at the base any straight shoots and suckers that develop.

Plants can be increased by layering low-growing branches.

Cotinus Anacardiaceae

Smokebush ③

- *Deciduous shrub*
- *Attractive foliage and flowers*
- *Good fall color*
- *Hardy* *Zone 4 US, 4 Can*

Smokebush makes a bushy shrub, eventually growing to about 10ft (3m), with soft, oval, midgreen leaves which often color well in fall.

Cotinus coggygria bears fluffy, feathery plumes of flower heads in midsummer, which persist until fall and give the plant its common name of smokebush. The variety **'Royal Purple'** has deep purple foliage, which turns light red in fall, and clusters of pink flowers.

Cultivation
Light shade is tolerated, but purple-leafed forms have better color in sun. Grow in quick-draining, light soil; over-rich soil leads to disappointing fall color.

Prune lightly to shape, if required, in early spring. Plants can be increased by semiripe cuttings or layering in early fall.

Cotoneaster Rosaceae
Cotoneaster ②③

- *Evergreen or deciduous shrub*
- *Attractive foliage, flowers, and fruits*
- *Hardy*

This is a large and varied family, containing many valuable plants. Cotoneasters can be grown as ground cover, specimen shrubs, hedges, or wall plants, depending on variety. On deciduous species, the round, deep green leaves generally turn bright red in fall and the small, pink-tinged white flowers are followed by little, round, red fruits.

Among ground cover types are *Cotoneaster congestus* (Zone 5 US, 6 Can), a dense-growing, spreading evergreen forming low 8in (10cm) hummocks with sparse red berries. *C. salicifolius* has more pointed, glossy green leaves, and **'Autumn Fire'** (Zone 5 US, 6 Can) is a slightly taller, evergreen or semievergreen, spreading plant with arching stems and freely borne bright red berries.

C. **'Coral Beauty'** is a compact, arching, evergreen shrub up to 3ft (1m), with orange-red berries in fall, which can be grown as a specimen shrub or as ground cover. Zone 4 US, 4 Can.

C. horizontalis, or rockspray cotoneaster (Zone 4 US, 5 Can), is a wall plant that produces flattened branches in a herringbone arrangement. The deciduous, dark green leaves turn flame-red in fall. A profusion of pale pink flowers is carried in early summer, and these are followed by bright red berries, clustered tightly on the stems.

Creeping cotoneaster, *C. adpressus,* (Zone 3 US, 4 Can) grows close to the ground and bears white-tipped pink flowers and large dark red fruit. The most commonly grown cultivar is **'Little Gem'**.

Cultivation
A sunny location and light, well-drained soil will give good results. Evergreen species are tolerant of light shade. Prune back overlong shoots in early spring. Propagate plants by semiripe cuttings in summer.

Fireblight disease may attack cotoneasters, causing leaves, flowers, and berries to shrivel and blacken suddenly, with a scorched appearance. Cut out and destroy affected branches immediately.

Crocus Iridaceae
Crocus ①②③

- *Corm*
- *Spring or fall flowers*
- *Ideal for containers*
- *Hardy* — *Zone 3 US, 4 Can except as noted*

Crocus is one of the best-known flowering corms, with low-growing, goblet-shaped flowers in a wide range of colors in early spring. However, one or two species do flower in fall. The leaves are narrow, stiff, deep green and pointed, and usually accompany the flowers.

There are dozens of species and hundreds of varieties. Among the early spring-flowering species are *Crocus ancyrensis* (golden bunch crocus) with deep yellow flowers; *C. angustifolius* (cloth-of-gold crocus), with yellow flowers that are marked bronzy brown on the outside; and *C. tommasinianus,* with flowers in a range of purple-blue shades.

C. vernus has a large number of popular spring-flowering cultivars, among which are the reliable **'Enchantress'**, light purple inside, glossed with silver outside; **'Flower Record'**, strong purple, paler inside with a white throat; **'Golden Yellow'**, good fragrance; **'Jeanne d'Arc'**, large, white flowers; and **'Pickwick'**, striped purple and white.

Fall-flowering types (Zone 4 US, 5 Can) include *C. kotschyanus,* with purple-pink, yellow-centered flowers; *C. laevigatus,* which has pale lilac flowers with gold and white centers; and *C. speciosus,* with purple flowers and a prominent orange stigma.

Cultivation
Plant corms in fall, in well-drained soil in full sun or light shade, about 3in (8cm) deep. They can be grown in beds or containers or naturalized in grass.

Once the foliage has died down, the corms can be lifted, cleaned, and dried for storage before replanting, or they can be left in place. Increase plants by dividing clumps of corms when the leaves begin to turn brown after flowering. Birds may damage the flowers by shredding the petals; use bird scarers if they are a problem.

Cyclamen Primulaceae
Cyclamen ①②③

- *Tuberous perennial*
- *Fall, winter, and spring interest from flowers or foliage*
- *Hardy*

The dainty flowers of cyclamen have a very distinctive form, having strongly reflexing, swept-back petals and nodding heads. Besides their attractive flowers, many species have strongly marked, decorative foliage, with heart-shaped, marbled leaves. Plants grow from tubers, which can become very large; some species self-seed freely. Height is around 4–6in (10–15cm).

There are many valuable hardy species, but the best known is *Cyclamen hederifolium* (*C. neapolitanum*). Zone 8 US, 9 Can. Pale to deep pink flowers are produced in fall, usually before the slightly pointed, silver-marbled leaves appear. **'Album'** is a white cultivar. The foliage remains attractive until early summer.

C. coum (Zone 4 US, 5 Can) has more rounded, sometimes marbled foliage; the winter flowers are a stronger, deeper pink shade and not quite so dainty as those of *C. hederifolium.*

C. repandum, with purple-pink or white flowers and heart-shaped, silvery leaves, flowers in spring. Zone 7 US, 8 Can.

Cultivation
Plant the tubers shallowly in early fall. Cyclamen like light shade and a well-drained but fertile, humus-rich soil. Allow the tubers to dry off in summer. For best results, do not disturb the tubers.

Propagate by seed collected in summer.

Crocus vernus

Cytisus Leguminosae
Broom ③

* *Deciduous, evergreen, or semievergreen shrub*
* *Pealike flowers carried in profusion*
* *Hardy*

For the most part, cytisus are spreading shrubs with wiry, green, arching branches and three-lobed or linear leaves. The flowers, typical of the pea family, appear in large numbers in spring or summer, in shades of cream, yellow, or red.

Cytisus battandieri, Moroccan broom, will grow into a small tree up to some 12ft (4m) high. The three-lobed leaves are covered in silvery hairs, and racemes of golden yellow flowers are carried in early summer. The blooms have a strong, rich pineapple scent. Zone 6 US, 7 Can.

C. × ***kewensis***, with pale yellow flowers in late spring, is smaller, growing to 24in (60cm) high and spreading to 4ft (1.2m). Zone 6 US, 7 Can.

The Warminster broom, *C.* × ***praecox***, forms a mound of slender, arching branches eventually reaching some 4ft (1.2m); in spring the branches are densely packed with pale, creamy, scented flowers. The variety **'Allgold'** has deeper yellow flowers. Zone 5 US, 6 Can

C. ***scoparius*** is the common, or Scotch, broom, of vigorous, upright habit. Several named cultivars exist, with flowers in varying shades of yellow, cream, red, and brown. Most readily available are **'Burkwoodii'**, with carmine red and brownish flowers, and **'Moonlight'**, with creamy white flowers. Zone 6 US, 7 Can.

Cultivation
Grow in full sun in very well-drained, light soil; broom tolerates lime. Try to leave plants undisturbed; some species tend to be short lived.

If necessary, thin out the branches after flowering to shape plants. Propagate by semiripe cuttings taken in summer.

Dahlia Compositae
Dahlia ②③

* *Tuberous-rooted, herbaceous perennial*
* *Colorful late-summer and fall flowers*
* *Good for cutting*
* *Tender* *Zone 8 US*

Toward the end of summer, dahlias produce long-lasting, colorful flowers that continue until the first frosts. There are many different forms of border dahlia, classified according to the type of flower: pompom, collerette, anemone-centered, cactus, and so on. Colors include red, orange, yellow, pink, white, and purple. More compact types suitable for small spaces, which usually grow to less than 3ft (1m), include: **'Bishop of Llandaff'**, single, deep red flowers and bronzy foliage; **'David Howard'**, deep orange flowers and dark foliage; **'Fascination'**, with pale violet-pink flowers; and **'Giraffe'**, with strikingly marked, orange-yellow flowers.

Bedding dahlias are raised from seed and are usually treated as annuals. They are more compact and shorter growing than border varieties; the flowers may be single, double, or semidouble, and colors are usually mixed. The **Redskin Hybrids**, growing to 12in (30cm), have bronze-tinted foliage and double flowers in many colors; **Coltness Hybrids** have single flowers and reach 18in (45cm).

'Explosion' is a small cactus-flowered type *(see illustration on pp.156–157)*.

Cultivation
Dahlias like a rich, moisture-retentive soil and full sun. Border dahlias are planted out as dormant tubers in midspring or as young plants or rooted cuttings in late spring, after the risk of frosts has passed. Bedding dahlias are planted out after the frosts. Keep the plants well watered during dry spells and feed with a high-potash fertilizer every 14 days.

Stake the flowering stems of taller varieties. When flowering is over and frosts have blackened the top growth, lift the tubers and store them in dry peat or similar material in a cool but frost-free place over winter, ready for planting out the following spring. Bedding dahlias also form tubers that can be stored, but the plants are often discarded and replaced with fresh stock.

Aphids can be a problem on young growth and flower buds; wash them away with water or spray with a non-persistent contact insecticide. Earwigs may eat holes in petals and cause malformed flowers. They feed at night and hide among the plants during the day. Trap the earwigs with straw-lined flowerpots, then shake out and destroy them.

Daphne Thymelaeaceae
Daphne ②③

* *Deciduous or evergreen shrubs*
* *Very sweet-scented winter or early summer flowers*
* *Poisonous*
* *Hardy*

Daphnes range from small, creeping alpines to medium-sized shrubs, all with tubular, pink or white, fragrant flowers. ***Daphne alpina***, a small, upright, deciduous plant, with slightly furry, grayish green leaves and white flowers in late spring, grows to 18in (45cm). Variegated *D.* × ***burkwoodii*** **'Carol Mackie'** grows to 5ft (1.5m); it is semi-evergreen, with clusters of pink flowers in early summer. (Both Zone 4 US, 5 Can).

Evergreen *D.* ***cneorum*** is usually represented by **'Eximia'**; the small, deep green leaves and deep pink and white spring flowers are carried on a plant some 6in (15cm) high, spreading to 2ft (60cm). Zone 3 US, 2 Can.

D. mezereum makes a rounded bush about 4ft (1.2m) tall; in winter and spring its bare stems bear thick clusters of deep pink flowers. The purple-pink flowers of evergreen *D.* ***odora*** (Zone 3 US, 3 Can), appearing from midwinter to early spring, are among the most fragrant of all. This species can be rather tender and needs a protected location; the variety **'Aureomarginata'**, with a fine gold rim to the leaves, is hardier. Zone 7 US, 8 Can.

Cultivation
Plant in full sun in fertile, well-drained but moisture-retentive soil containing plenty of organic matter. The smaller species are very suitable for rock gardens and containers. Prune plants lightly to shape, if required, in early spring.

Propagate by semiripe cuttings in summer; they are not, however, very easy to root.

Dendranthema Compositae
Chrysanthemum ②③

* *Herbaceous perennial*
* *Colorful late summer and fall flowers*
* *Hardy* *Zone 5 US, 6 Can*

These plants are more familiarly known as garden chrysanthemums and along with dahlias provide a bright show of color in late summer and fall. There are many different flower forms and hundreds of

Daphne odora

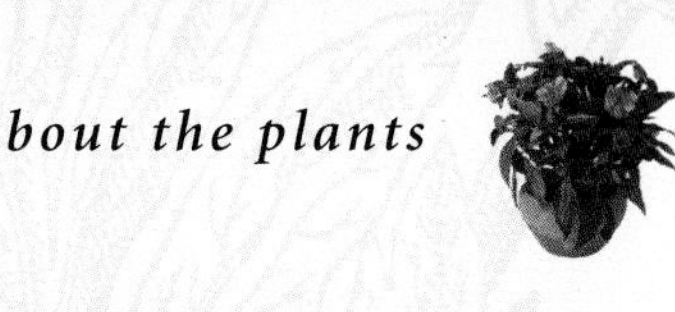

***Dendranthema* 'Cherry Emily'**

cultivars. Midgreen foliage is lobed and aromatic; the stems can be tough and woody.

Suitable for smaller spaces are the pompom types, which grow to 12–18in (30–45cm). They include varieties such as **'Legend'**, which is gold and spreading; and the bright purple **'Barbara'**, a compact, strong grower, and its coral and bronze sports. **'Goldmine'** is golden yellow and long lasting; **'Shelley'** is a red and yellow bicolor; **'Raquel'** is single, lilac; and **'Starlet'** single, bronze, with spoon-shaped petals.

Cultivation

Grow in well-drained but moisture-retentive, fertile soil, in full sun. Water plants regularly and feed with a high potash fertilizer every 14 days.

In late fall, when flowering is over, cut down the stems and lift the roots to store in dry peat or similar material over winter. Plant out again in spring or start the roots into growth under cover and take cuttings of the young shoots that arise.

In cool, damp weather, botrytis can be a problem on incurving varieties, causing the petals to rot. Shelter blooms from excessive rain to try to prevent it.

Dianthus Caryophyllaceae

Pink, carnation ① ② ③

* *Evergreen perennials*
* *Scented, summer flowers*
* *Hardy*

Mainly cushion-forming plants, with narrow, blue-gray leaves, dianthus have flat-faced or double, often sweetly scented flowers in red, white, or pink shades. Tallest members of the group are the carnations, including border and perpetual-flowering carnations. These grow up to 3ft (1m) high, with semidouble or double flowers, some of which require greenhouse cultivation.

Suitable for smaller spaces outdoors are varieties such as **'Bookham Fancy'**, which is yellow and red; **'Golden Sun'**, yellow; and **'Merlin Clove'**, white and red. Zone 6 US, 7 Can.

Pinks provide a large number of plants suitable for small gardens and containers. The alpine pink, ***Dianthus alpinus,*** forms a compact bun of rosy pink flowers in summer; the deep green, narrow leaves make an attractive evergreen mat. The maiden pink, ***D. deltoides,*** has 6in (15cm) high summer flowers over tufts of evergreen foliage; **'Flashing Light'** is a brilliant cerise shade. Both Zone 3 US, 3 Can.

Old-fashioned pinks form spreading mats of gray foliage and produce huge numbers of flowers in summer; they are often heavily laced or have fringed petals, and all are strongly fragrant. **'Dad's Favorite'** is white with purple-brown lacing; **'Mrs. Sinkins'** is a double white with fringed petals; and **'Sops-in-Wine'** has single, purple flowers with white markings. Zone 4 US, 5 Can.

Modern pinks have been bred to combine the best attributes of old-fashioned pinks with robust growth and repeat flowering. Good examples are **'Doris'**, pale pink semidouble, marked with deeper pink; **'Helen'**, small carnation-like flowers in salmon; and **'Aqua'**, with double, pure white flowers. Zone 5 US 6 Can.

Cultivation

Pinks and border carnations like light, well-drained soil, preferably containing some lime. An open, sunny location is necessary.

Cut down dead flower stems to encourage repeat flowering. Propagate plants by "pipings"—soft-stem cuttings—in summer.

Dicentra Papaveraceae

Bleeding heart ③

* *Herbaceous perennial*
* *Attractive foliage and early summer flowers*
* *Hardy* *Zone 4 US, 5 Can*

Bleeding hearts are among the earliest border plants to push up their shoots in spring. The leaves are fresh green and attractively fernlike; the flowers are heart shaped in shades of pink and white.

The best-known species is ***Dicentra spectablis,*** which has arching flower stems some 2ft (60cm) or more tall, bearing racemes of dainty rose pink and white flowers in spring and early summer. By midsummer the top growth has usually died away completely. **'Alba'** has creamy white flowers. ***D. eximia*** is a more compact plant, up to 18in (45cm), with finely divided grayish green foliage and narrow pink flowers all summer; ***D. formosa,*** about the same height, has bright green ferny leaves and deep pink blooms in early summer.

Dicentra spectabilis

The several hybrid varieties include **'Adrian Bloom'**, with compact mounds of foliage and sprays of rose pink and crimson blooms; **'Bacchanal'**, with relatively short-stemmed flowers of deep crimson; and **'Luxuriant'**, with cherry red flowers above blue-green foliage.

Cultivation

Bleeding hearts thrive in well-drained soil containing plenty of organic matter, in sun or light shade. Early spring foliage can be damaged by late frosts, so choose a reasonably sheltered location.

Divide plants in the dormant season, but otherwise avoid disturbing the roots.

Dimorphotheca Compositae

African daisy, Cape marigold
Star-of-the-Veldt ① ② ③

* *Annual*
* *Daisylike summer flowers*
* *Tender* *Zone 9 US*

Many of the plants previously known as dimorphotheca have now been reclassified as osteospermum. ***Dimorphotheca pluvialis*** (***D. annua***) is a bushy annual up to 12in (30cm), with deep green, downy leaves. The daisylike flowers have white petals with purple undersides and purple-brown centers. ***D. sinuata*** (***D. aurantiaca***), Star-of-the-Veldt, has similar daisy flowers in a range of orange and red shades.

Cultivation

African daisies thrive in poor, dry soils; they must have quick-draining conditions and full sun, since the flowers will not open in shade. They grow best in a warm, sheltered spot.

Deadhead the plants to extend the flowering season. Raise new plants from seed sown in spring. Plants may rot in cool, wet weather, particularly in heavier soils.

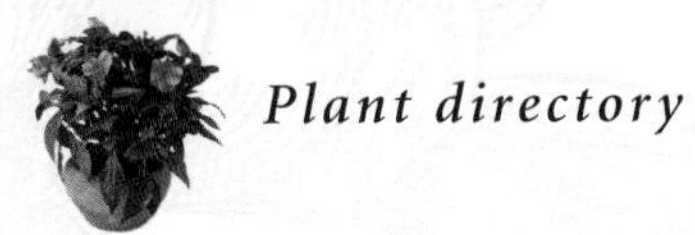

Dorotheanthus Aizoaceae

Mesembryanthemum, ice plant, Livingstone daisy ① ② ③

- *Annual*
- *Succulent plant suitable for very dry conditions*
- *Brightly colored summer flowers in profusion*
- *Tender* *Zone 11 US*

Dorotheanthus bellidiformis is probably still better known under its previous name of ***Mesembryanthemum criniflorum.*** It is a 15cm (6in) high spreading plant, with fleshy, succulent leaves. These have a crystalline appearance, which gives the plant its common name of ice plant. Many-petaled, daisylike flowers in white, red, yellow, and pink shades, often with centers of a contrasting color, are carried throughout the summer.

Dorotheanthus are usually available in mixed colors, including strains such as **Magic Carpet Hybrids** and **Splendid Hybrids.**

Cultivation

These plants must have very well-drained soil and full sun; they are excellent subjects for poor, light soils. The flowers will not open in dull weather or in shade.

Deadheading the plants will prolong the flowering season. Raise from seed sown in midspring.

Over-moist soil conditions will lead to rapid rotting of the roots and collapse of the plants. Slugs and snails are serious pests, and plants should always be protected with slug bait or an organic alternative.

Dorotheanthus bellidiformis

Dryopteris Aspidiaceae

Wood fern ② ③

- *Deciduous or semievergreen perennial fern*
- *Frondlike, divided foliage*
- *Hardy*

These generally easy-to-grow ferns have midgreen, pinnate, arching fronds arising from a woolly brown crown. In a sheltered location the foliage may last well into the winter. ***Dryopteris filix-mas,*** the male fern, grows to around 3ft (1m); there are several cultivars, including **'Crispa Cristata',** with frilled leaf margins. Zone 4 US, 5 Can.

D. erythrosora, the Japanese shield fern, with coppery-red young foliage, is a little more tender. Zone 6 US, 7 Can.

Cultivation

Dryopteris like shade or semishade and rich, moist soil. Keep plants well watered (but not waterlogged) in dry spells. Dead foliage is attractive and also a useful protection for the crowns of ***D. erythrosora*** in winter. Divide plants in midspring.

Eccremocarpus Bignoniaceae

Chilean glory flower ② ③

- *Evergreen perennial climber*
- *Showy, tubular flowers*
- *Tender* *Zone 10 US*

The only species commonly grown is ***Eccremocarpus scaber.*** Although this is a perennial in warm areas, in colder zones it is grown as an annual. The dark green leaves are bipinnate, with tendrils twining at the tips that coil around any convenient support to enable the plant to scramble upward. It is a fast grower, soon covering a pergola or growing over a wall or fence. In summer, and into early fall, clusters of scarlet, orange, or yellow tubular flowers are freely produced. Selected color forms can sometimes be obtained, including ***E. s. aureus, E. s. carmineus,*** and ***E. s. roseus.***

Cultivation

Plant against a suitable support in a sunny, sheltered, warm location in well-drained soil. Trellis or netting should be provided. Water plants regularly in dry conditions.

Deadhead the plant to encourage prolonged flowering. Plants will be killed by frost and are usually raised new from seed each year.

Elaeagnus Elaeagnaceae

Elaeagnus ② ③

- *Deciduous or evergreen shrub*
- *Attractive foliage*
- *Insignificant but strongly scented flowers*
- *Good for coastal or exposed areas*
- *Hardy* *Zone 6 US, 7 Can*

These tough, medium-sized shrubs are often grown for their sometimes attractively variegated leaves. They are not fussy about soil, and several species are useful for shady spots or exposed positions.

Eleagnus × ebbingei is a hybrid with leathery, evergreen, grayish leaves; the cultivar **'Gilt Edge'** has golden margins to the foliage. It is more compact than the species, growing to about 10ft (3m). Scented white flowers are carried in fall.

E. pungens is slightly more vigorous in growth. The tough, evergreen leaves are glossy above, with gray, scaly undersides; those of **'Maculata'** have a broad, golden center. White, bell-shaped, fragrant flowers appear in fall.

Cultivation

Well-draind, light soil and a sunny location are preferred, although elaeagnus will grow well in light shade. Variegated cultivars need bright light to maintain their colored foliage.

Shrubs can be shaped if necessary and overlong shoots reduced by pruning in mid-spring. Variegated cultivars may produce all-green shoots, which should be cut out at the base as soon as they are noticed.

Plants can be increased by semiripe cuttings in summer.

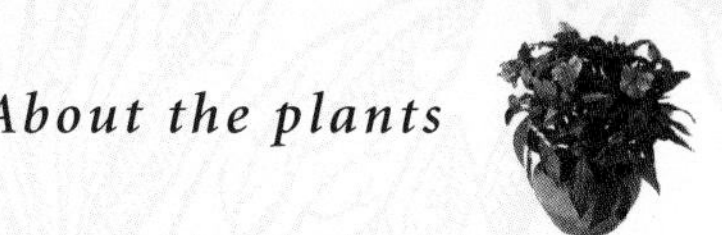

Eranthis Ranunculaceae

Winter aconite ①②③

* *Tuberous perennial*
* *Winter or early spring flowers*
* *Hardy* *Zone 4 US, 5 Can*

The bright golden, buttercup-like flowers of winter aconite have glossy, lacquered petals, backed by bracts which form an attractive green ruff. The blooms appear in late winter or very early spring, growing to some 4in (10cm) high, and the plant becomes dormant in summer. ***Eranthis hyemalis*** is the true winter aconite.

Cultivation

The oddly shaped tuberous roots should be planted in fall in moisture-retentive soil containing plenty of organic matter, preferably in partial shade. Keep them well watered during dry spells in spring.

Plants can be increased by lifting and dividing clumps in the green (after flowering, but while the plants are still in leaf), when they are easier to establish than dormant tubers.

Erica Ericaceae

Heath ①②③

* *Evergreen subshrub*
* *Winter or summer flowers and attractive foliage*
* *Good ground cover*
* *Prefers acidic soil*
* *Hardy*

These are some of the most useful plants for year-round color in small-space gardens. Some cultivars flower in summer, others during the winter months; some are grown mainly for their attractive foliage.

Probably the most popular species is the winter-flowering ***Erica carnea***, which contains dozens of different cultivars. Plants can reach 12in (30cm) but are usually about half that height. The foliage consists of whorls of tiny, deep green needles; flowers are bell shaped in shades of white, red, and pink. Unlike most heaths, this species will tolerate some lime in the soil.

Among the many excellent cultivars are **'Ann Sparkes'**, purple flowers and bronze-gold foliage; **'Foxhollow'**, yellow foliage with orange-red winter tints and pale pink flowers; and **'Myretoun Ruby'**, with deep purple-red flowers and deep green foliage. The long stems of vigorous **'Springwood White'** are packed with white, brown-tipped flowers; **'Springwood Pink'** is similar, but with pink flowers; and **'Vivellii'** has bronze-red winter foliage and deep purple flowers. Zone 4 US, 4 Can.

E. ciliaris, the fringed heath, which flowers from midsummer through fall, carries its rounded, bell-shaped flowers at the tips of the branches. **'David McClintock'** has white flowers with pink tips and gray foliage. Zone 5 US, 6 Can.

The Scotch heath, ***E. cinerea***, blooms from midsummer to midfall. **'Atrorubens'** has long stems of ruby red flowers; **'Pink Ice'** is a low grower with pale pink flowers; and **'Golden Drop'** has gold foliage that turns shades of orange and red in winter. Zone 5 US, 6 Can.

Bushy, winter-flowering ***E. × darleyensis*** grows up to 18in (45cm) or so; the tips of the young shoots are often creamy white or pink in late spring. Like ***E. carnea***, this hybrid tolerates lime. **'Arthur Johnson'** has rosy pink flowers and creamy pink spring foliage; the long-lasting flowers of **'Darley Dale'** are clear pale pink; and **'Ghost Hills'** has pink flowers and cream-tipped spring foliage. The long-lasting, fragrant flowers of **'Silberschmelze'** (Molten Silver) are white, and it has creamy spring foliage. Zone 4 US, 5 Can.

E. tetralix (cross-leaf heath) grows to 12in (30 cm) and produces dense heads of usually deep pink flowers from summer to midfall. **'George Frazer'** has pale pink flowers over olive green foliage; **'Pink Star'** has lilac-pink flowers, held upright, and spreading gray foliage. Zone 4 US, 5 Can.

Cultivation

Heaths grow best in a sunny location in well-drained but moisture-retentive, acid soil containing plenty of organic matter.

Varieties of ***E. carnea*** and ***E. × darleyensis*** will tolerate lime, but they usually perform better in acid soil. Water the plants regularly in dry spells.

Prune lightly after flowering or in early spring to keep the plants compact. Heaths can be propagated by semiripe cuttings in summer or by layering.

Erica carnea 'Foxhollow'

Erysimum 'Bowles Mauve'

Erysimum Cruciferae

Wallflower ①②③

* *Annuals, biennials, and evergreen perennials*
* *Spring flowers*
* *Hardy* *Zone 5 US, 6 Can*

These plants are related to, and sometimes listed as, cheiranthus. Best known are varieties of ***Erysimum cheiri*** (***Cheiranthus cheiri***); many selections are available, including the dwarf **'Tom Thumb Mixed'**, orange-scarlet **'Fire King'**, yellow **'Golden Monarch'**, and the compact, dwarf **Prince Series**. ***E. × allionii*** is the slightly taller Siberian wallflower, of which **'Orange Bedder'** and **'Golden Bedder'** are popular varieties. These wallflowers are sometimes grown as biennials for spring bedding in mild climates.

There are several attractive perennial varieties of erysimum, including **'Bowles Mauve'**, with dark green leaves and mauve flowers, growing to some 2ft (60cm) tall; **'Harpur Crewe'**, with scented, double, yellow flowers, to 12in (30cm); **'Moonlight'**, a low-growing, spreading plant some 4in (10cm) high with pale yellow flowers; and **'Jacob's Jacket'**, with flowers that change to pale pink, yellow, red, and bronze tones. All tend to be short lived.

Cultivation

Grow in full sun in light, well-drained neutral to lightly alkaline soils. Varieties grown as perennials need a sheltered location. Deadhead after flowering.

Sow seed of varieties grown as biennials in early summer; increase perennial types by softwood cuttings taken in early or midsummer. Take cuttings each year as a precaution against unexpected losses.

Erythronium 'Pagoda'

Erythronium Liliaceae

Dog's-tooth violet ①②③

* *Tuberous perennial*
* *Spring flowers and attractive foliage*
* *Hardy* *Zone 3 US, 4 Can, except as noted*

Dog's-tooth violets have attractive, nodding, spring flowers in shades of white, pink or yellow. The leaves of some species are attractively mottled and marbled.

Erythronium dens-canis (dog's-tooth violet) grows to 6in (15cm) and has lilac or purple-pink, pendent flowers with lightly reflexed petals. The leaves are often mottled grey and deep purple.

'White Beauty' has spikes of several slightly pendent flowers that are white and marked with reddish brown in the center, and leaves that are lightly mottled.

E. revolutum can reach 12in (30cm) tall, with brown and green mottled leaves and spikes of pink flowers. Zone 5 US, 6 Can.

'Pagoda' is an attractive hybrid with unmottled leaves and a flower stem up to 18in (45cm) tall, bearing 8–10 pendent, yellow flowers with reflexed petals and prominent stamens.

E. tuolumnense has plain green, shiny leaves and bright yellow flowers in clusters of half a dozen or more.

Cultivation

Dog's-tooth violets prefer cool, moist soil containing plenty of organic matter, and a location in light shade.

Do not let the tubers dry out during the growing season.

Plants can sometimes be increased by offsets in late summer; replant the offsets immediately.

Escallonia Escalloniaceae

Escallonia ③

* *Evergreen or deciduous shrub*
* *Early summer flowers and glossy foliage*
* *Good for mild coastal regions*
* *Hardy* *Zone 7 US, 8 Can*

This medium-sized shrub usually requires a sheltered spot in a mild climate; in cooler areas it can be grown against a wall. Leaves are oval, glossy, and mid- to deep green; white or pink flowers are carried from early to midsummer.

Most of the commonly grown types are evergreen hybrids. Good choices include **'Apple Blossom'**, a bushy shrub up to 6ft (2m), with pink and white flowers; **'Langleyensis'** with arching branches to 6ft (2m), loaded with deep pink flowers in early summer; and **'Donard Gem'**, a compact grower with large, pink, scented flowers.

Cultivation

Well-drained soil is required, as is an open, sunny position, or the shelter of a wall in exposed areas. Plants can be clipped lightly after flowering to keep them shapely.

Increase escallonia by taking semiripe cuttings in summer.

Eschscholzia Papaveraceae

California poppy ③

* *Annual*
* *Brightly colored, poppylike flowers*
* *Tolerates poor soils*
* *Hardy* *Zone 8 US, 9 Can*

California poppy, ***Eschscholzia californica***, has finely cut, fernlike, blue-green leaves and open, cup-shaped flowers in summer. The poppylike flowers have silky petals and are carried on slender 8–12in (20–30cm) stems; they may be white, cream, yellow, red, or orange. Mixed shades are common—**Monarch Hybrids** is a popular strain—but single color selections are also available, including **'Aurantiaca'**, **'Carmine King'**, **'Golden West'**, **'Milky White'**, **'Purple Gleam'**, **'Orange King'**, and the scarlet and gold, semidouble **'Dali'**.

E. caespitosa has smaller, rather less showy yellow flowers in late summer and grows to some 6in (15cm).

Cultivation

Well-drained soil is essential, as they thrive in poor, thin, sandy soils. The plants need a location in full sun. Deadheading will ensure a long-lasting display of flowers.

Grow from seed sown in early to mid-spring; earlier-flowering plants can be obtained from a fall sowing in all but very cold, exposed areas.

Eucalyptus Myrtaceae

Eucalyptus ②③

* *Evergreen tree*
* *Attractive foliage and bark*
* *Hardy* *Zone 7 US, 8 Can*

Fast-growing, vigorous trees from Australia, eucalyptus can top 100ft (30m) in their natural habitat. However, if they are cut back hard annually, they make attractive shrubs suitable for smaller spaces. The gray-green leaves have a characteristic aroma when crushed.

The most popular species of eucalyptus is probably the cider gum, ***Eucalyptus gunnii.***

Eschscholzia californica

It is one of the hardiest of the eucalyptus, and grows rapidly to make a large tree. The juvenile foliage is round and a bright silver-blue; adult foliage is sickle shaped and blue-green. The plant can be cut back to within a few inches of the base each year to maintain the juvenile foliage and keep it a manageable size. The bark is attractively patched cream and tan on larger plants.

E. pauciflora niphophila, the snow gum, grows relatively slowly. The bark is a striking silver-white on young plants; on older trees it peels to form green, gray, and cream patches. Young shoots are bright red.

Cultivation

Eucalyptus likes well-drained, reasonably fertile soil and a sunny, sheltered location, especially when young; the vigorous growth is prone to wind damage. Make sure the soil does not dry out during the summer.

In small spaces, plants will need frequent pruning. Cut them back to the base in early spring and pinch out the strongest-growing branches regularly to form a rounded shrub. Plants may need cutting back twice a year if they start to outgrow their space.

Plants can also be grown as small trees by allowing them to reach just over the required height before removing the growing tip. Rub out most of the new shoots that appear on the stem as soon as they develop, leaving those at the top of the stem to form a head. These shoots can then be cut back close to the main stem every spring, to form a "pollarded" tree.

Severe frosts or cold winds will damage or kill plants, so give winter protection if necessary until they become established.

Plants can be raised from seed sown in spring.

Euonymus Celastraceae

Euonymus, burning bush, wintercreeper ①②③

- *Deciduous or evergreen trees and shrubs*
- *Attractive foliage*
- *Suitable for ground cover*
- *Hardy*

These are versatile plants with a wide range of uses. ***Euonymus alatus***, burning bush, is a slow-growing, deciduous shrub; it has unusual branches with attractive corky wings. The leaves color well in fall. Inconspicuous white flowers are followed by showy, fleshy, purplish red fruits with exposed, bright orange seeds. The form **'Compactus'** is particularly suitable for small spaces, growing to about 3ft (1m) tall, although it will spread to two or three times that. Zone 3 US, 3 Can.

E. fortunei, wintercreeper, is a popular

***Euonymus fortunei* 'Emerald 'n' Gold'**

evergreen, with prostrate, creeping stems that will climb if they are provided with a suitable support. Leaves are oval, glossy, and dark green. When the stems reach the top of their climb, a different, adult form of growth develops, with larger foliage and green-white flowers followed by pink and orange fruits.

'Emerald 'n' Gold' forms a dense, bushy shrub to 2ft (60cm) or so tall, with bright, gold-margined leaves. **'Minimus'** is a dainty miniature form with slender stems and very small leaves; it is ideal for a rock garden, raised bed or container. Zone 4 US, 3 Can.

Cultivation

Moisture-retentive, reasonably fertile soil and sun or light shade are required. Variegated types need sun to maintain good leaf color. Cut plain green shoots to their base as soon as they are seen.

Plants can be propagated from semiripe cuttings in summer.

Scale insects are a serious problem.

Euphorbia Euphorbiaceae

Euphorbia ②③

- *Evergreen, semievergreen or deciduous perennials and shrubs*
- *Striking flower heads and foliage*
- *Good for cutting for flower arrangements*
- *Hardy*

The large family of spurges contains many different types of plant, including succulents and popular houseplants, but they excel as striking border perennials. ***Euphorbia amygdaloides* 'Purpurea'** (**'Rubra'**) is semi-evergreen, with stems up to 12in (30cm) long clothed with narrow, oblong, deep reddish purple leaves. The color is most pronounced in spring. Zone 6 US, 7 Can.

The stems of *E. characias wulfenii* are upright or rather lax, growing up to 5ft (1.5m), with evergreen, blue-gray foliage. In spring, it bears large, elongated heads of long-lasting lime-green flowers with brown centers in spring. The plant is a good architectural subject. Zone 7 US, 8 Can.

E. griffithii has midgreen leaves, and in late spring and early summer, the small flowers are surrounded by showy, orange-red bracts. **'Fireglow'**, reaching about 3ft (1m), is a particularly good form. Zone 4 US, 5 Can.

Cultivation

Plants need well-drained soil but should not be allowed to dry out, particularly in spring and early summer. Full sun or light shade are suitable. Cut down the flower stems once the flowers have faded to maintain a compact, bushy shape.

Propagate plants from seed or by softwood cuttings of basal shoots in late spring.

Fatsia Araliaceae

Japanese aralia, Japanese fatsia ②③

- *Evergreen shrub*
- *Bold, palmate leaves and late-summer flowers*
- *Architectural value*
- *Hardy* *Zone 7 US, 8 Can*

Fatsia japonica makes a rounded shrub up to 10ft (3m) tall. It is valuable for its large, glossy, dark green, deeply lobed leaves. In late summer it bears distinctive round umbels of tiny white flowers, followed by blue-black fruits. **'Variegata'** has narrow, creamy white margins to the leaves.

Cultivation

A sheltered location is required for this plant, with protection from cold winds. Any reasonably fertile soil is suitable, and plants grow well in shade or full sun.

Propagate by semiripe cuttings in summer. Severe frosts will damage plants, killing shoot tips and causing distorted growth. Prune back damaged branches.

***Fatsia japonica* in flower**

Festuca Gramineae

Blue fescue ①②③

* *Evergreen perennial grass*
* *Colorful foliage gives year-round interest*
* *Hardy* *Zone 4 US, 5 Can*

This grass makes neat tufts of narrow, steely blue foliage around 6in (15cm) high. By far the most popular species grown is ***Festuca glauca***, with fine, silver-blue foliage and dainty panicles of pale fawn spikelets in summer. **'Elijah's Blue'** has an especially intense silvery blue color. ***F. amethystina*** grows to 12in (30cm) high, with spreading tufts of blue-green leaves.

Cultivation

Light, well-drained soil and an open, sunny location are preferred.

Flower spikelets are sometimes thought to detract from the foliage and they can be cut off if they are not required.

Plants should be divided and replanted in fall or spring every few years, to keep growth neat and vigorous.

Ficus Moraceae

Fig ②③

* *Deciduous shrub or small tree*
* *Attractive, bold foliage*
* *Edible fruits in favorable conditions*
* *Hardy* *Zone 5 US, 6 Can*

The common edible fig, ***Ficus carica***, has large, lobed leaves on spreading branches. Fruits are regularly produced in warm climates, but in cool temperate zones fruiting is not reliable.

The fruits are carried toward the ends of the branches; in cold areas only, small, undeveloped fruits should be allowed to remain on the bush over winter to ripen the following summer. Large, unripe fruits still on the tree in late fall should be removed, since they will not mature.

'Brown Turkey' is the most popular fruiting variety; **'White Adriatic'** is good for warmer areas.

Cultivation

Grow figs in the shelter of a warm, sunny wall or a similar location. Restricting the roots ensures better fruiting, so these plants are ideal for container culture. Use moisture-retentive, fertile soil and water regularly during the growing season, giving liquid fertilizer every 14–21 days.

Remove frost-damaged branches in early spring.

Plants can best be propagated by layering the lower branches.

Fritillaria imperialis 'Rubra Maxima'

Fritillaria Liliaceae

Fritillary ①②③

* *Perennial bulbs*
* *Showy spring flowers*
* *Hardy*

The showiest of the fritillarias is the crown imperial, ***Fritillaria imperialis***. The large, lilylike bulb, with overlapping scales, has a hollow center; both the bulb and the shoots it sends up have a distinctive skunky smell. The tall 3ft (1m) high stems, with linear, midgreen leaves, bear clusters of large, pendent, bell-shaped flowers in late spring; these are topped with a leafy cluster. The flowers may be orange, yellow, or orange-red; **'Lutea'** has yellow flowers, while **'Rubra Maxima'** is deep orange-red. Zone 4 US, 5 Can.

The snake's head fritillary, ***F. meleagris***, is quite different. Growing to some 12in (30cm), it has linear leaves, with dainty, pendent flowers on slender stalks; the petals may be white, purple, or pink, and usually show an attractive white speckled pattern. Zone 3 US, 3 Can.

F. persica **'Adiyaman'** grows to around 3ft (1m) or more and has gray-green leaves and a dozen or more deep plum-purple, bell-shaped flowers at the top of the stems. Zone 4 US, 5 Can.

Cultivation

Fritillaries like well-drained but moisture-retentive soil, in sun or light shade. ***F. meleagris*** grows well naturalized in grass, in rockeries, or in the front of a border; ***F. imperialis*** and ***F. persica*** are good border plants or accent plants. All these plants are suitable for containers.

Plant the large bulbs on their sides to avoid water collecting in the hollow centers, which can lead to rotting. Do not disturb the bulbs unless essential. Plants can be raised from seed or from offsets, which take several years to reach flowering size.

Slugs and snails can damage both the bulbs and the young shoots as they emerge; use slug bait or an organic alternative.

Fuchsia Onagraceae

Fuchsia ①②③

* *Deciduous shrub*
* *Summer flowers*
* *Hardy* *Zone 8 US, 9 Can except as noted*

There are hundreds of different varieties of fuchsia, some tender, some hardy in warm temperate regions. Flowers, which are carried throughout the summer, are usually pendulous and tubular, with overlapping petals and colorful sepals forming a bell shape. Petals may be single or double, waved and ruffled; the sepals are often of a contrasting shade. Leaves are oval and mid- to dark green, sometimes tinged red. Plants usually grow to around 2–3ft (60–90cm), but hardy cultivars often exceed that in mild, sheltered locations.

Some types are bushy and upright, others trailing; they are excellent in containers and can be trained as standards. The choice is vast and increasing. Good forms include **'Dark Eyes'**; trailing, deep red sepals, and double, violet blue petals; **'Autumnale'**; upright, single violet blue petals and red sepals, and variegated leaves; **'Lena'**; trailing, single, very pale pink sepals, magenta petals; **'Marinka'**; trailing, single, bright red sepals, darker red petals; and **'Swingtime'**; upright, double red sepals, white petals.

Fuchsia magellanica **'Tricolor'** has cream, green, and pink variegated foliage and small flowers with red sepals and purple petals. Zone 6 US, 7 Can.

Among good cultivars for use in containers and as summer bedding are **'Marinka'**, trailing, red sepals and petals; **'Swingtime'**, lax, semitrailing, full double flowers with white petals and red sepals; and **'Thalia'**, very long tubes with small orange-red sepals and petals.

Cultivation

Plant hardy varieties in a fairly sheltered location in sun or light shade, in well-drained but fertile soil. Tender varieties should not be planted out until all risk of frost is past. Keep plants well watered during the flowering season and feed every 14 days with a high-potash liquid fertilizer.

Move tender varieties under cover before the first frosts; softwood cuttings can be taken from new growth in spring. Leave the old stems on hardy plants over winter for protection, cutting them down to near the base in early spring. Buds may grow from the old stems or spring directly from the

roots. In colder areas, extra protection can be given by mulching the root area with peat, chipped bark or straw.

Take softwood cuttings in early summer.

If aphids infest young shoots, spray with a non-persistent contact insecticide.

Galanthus Amaryllidaceae

Snowdrop ①②③

* *Bulb*
* *Very early, pendulous flowers*
* *Hardy Zone 3 US, 4 Can*

For many people, snowdrops are the first sign of approaching spring. The bulbs send up pairs of spear-shaped, mid-green leaves and pendent white flowers on slender stems. The flowers have three large, all-white outer petals and three short inner ones that are white tipped with green. They grow to about 4–6in (10–15cm).

The common snowdrop is ***Galanthus nivalis***, and there are many cultivars, including **'Viridi-apice'**, with pronounced green markings on the outer as well as the inner petals.

G. elwesii, with broader, strap-shaped leaves and larger, more rounded flowers, can reach 10in (25cm).

Cultivation

Plant the bulbs in late summer in moisture-retentive soil in light shade; they can be difficult to establish if they have dried out. The most reliable time to plant snowdrops is "in the green," just after flowering, but they are not available at that time in the trade. Established clumps of bulbs are best divided at this time.

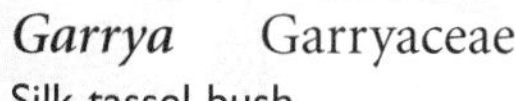

Garrya Garryaceae

Silk tassel bush ②③

* *Evergreen shrub*
* *Long, showy catkins in winter and spring*
* *Grows best against a wall*
* *Hardy Zone 7 US, 8 Can*

Garrya elliptica forms a bushy shrub up to 10ft (3m) or so if given the shelter of a wall. The deep green, leathery leaves are oval, with waved edges; in winter and spring the branches are profusely draped with long, pale green catkins.

Male and female are on separate plants ; the males produce longer, more handsome gray-green catkins, although the females' short, silver-gray catkins are followed by long, knobby clusters of purple-black berries, which can be an attractive feature. The sexes must be grown in close proximity for the berries to be produced.

'James Roof' is a vigorous male variety with particularly long, striking catkins with yellow anthers.

Cultivation

Plant in spring in well-drained soil in a sheltered location, preferably protected by a wall. Plants will grow in sun or shade but they will flower better in sun.

Garrya do not like being transplanted, and container-grown plants will establish more quickly.

Cut back overlong or damaged shoots once the catkins have shrivelled.

Propagate by taking semiripe cuttings in late summer.

***Galanthus nivalis* 'Flore Pleno'**

Genista pilosa

Genista Leguminosae

Broom ②③

* *Deciduous shrub*
* *Profusion of flowers, often fragrant, in early summer*
* *Grows well in poor soils*
* *Hardy*

Brooms generally make spreading shrubs with slender green branches; the leaves are thin and linear, and the stems often appear leafless. In late spring and early summer, typical pea-shaped, usually yellow flowers are carried in great numbers.

Some species of broom make small trees, but there are several low-growing, compact forms particularly suitable for small spaces. The Spanish gorse, ***G. hispanica,*** must be sited carefully, since it is extremely spiny. It grows some 2ft (60cm) high and forms a mound of dense clusters of golden flowers in early summer. Zone 7 US, 8 Can.

Genista lydia is a dwarf shrub less than 3ft (1m) high; its pendulous shoots are covered with yellow flowers in late spring and early summer. Zone 3 US, 5 Can.

G. pilosa makes a neat hummock about 12in (30cm) high and the same across, with yellow flowers in early to midsummer. It is particularly good on dry banks or in rock gardens. Zone 4 US, 5 Can.

Cultivation

Plant in full sun in well-drained, light soil. Brooms resent being transplanted and fairly small, container-grown plants will establish most quickly. Plants do not normally require watering or feeding, but watering will be necessary if they are in containers.

Trim with hand pruners after flowering to keep the bushes in shape.

Softwood or semiripe cuttings can be taken in summer, but they may be difficult to root.

Gentiana Gentianaceae

Gentian ①②③

- ✻ *Semievergreen or evergreen perennial*
- ✻ *Intensely blue flowers in early summer or fall*
- ✻ *Excellent for rock gardens*
- ✻ *Hardy* *Zone 4 US, 5 Can*

Well known for their brilliant blue flowers, gentians also have a reputation for being difficult to grow. They are fussy about soil and position and are sometimes reluctant to bloom. Among the easiest and most reliable is ***Gentiana acaulis***, which produces dense mats of slender or oval leaves; the flowers are relatively large, trumpet shaped, and often of a deep, intense blue.

The most commonly grown species are the evergreen ***G. septemfida*** and ***G. sino-ornata***, which flower in late summer or fall. ***G. septemfida*** has oval leaves and grows to about 12in (30cm); the midblue flowers have white centers. ***G. sino-ornata*** has narrow leaves and deeper blue flowers with less conspicuous white throats than those of ***G. septemfida***, but the outsides of the trumpets are strongly marked with black and white stripes.

Cultivation

Plant gentians in acidic, moist, humus-rich soil in full sun or semishade. Water as needed to keep the soil moist but not waterlogged during the growing season.

Divide the clumps of plants every few years in spring.

Gentiana acaulis

Geranium **'Johnson's Blue'**

Geranium Geraniaceae

Cranesbill, geranium ①②③

- ✻ *Herbaceous perennial*
- ✻ *Flowers carried freely in summer*
- ✻ *Hardy* *Zone 4 US, 5 Can and possibly hardier*

The cranesbills are colorful, easy-to-grow plants, ideal for rock gardens and paved areas, as well as containers. They form low mounds 6–24in (15–60cm) high, with downy, deeply cut or lobed leaves. In summer, they carry open, cup-shaped flowers, often with prominent stamens, in shades of pink, purple, white, and blue.

Among the best known are ***Geranium cinereum*** **'Ballerina'**, with pink, strongly veined petals; ***G. clarkei*** **'Kashmir Purple'** and **'Kashmir White'**, with finely cut foliage and nodding flowers. ***G. × oxonianum*** **'Wargrave Pink'** is often evergreen, with a long season of bright pink flowers. **'Ann Folkard'** has golden yellow foliage and deep magenta, black-eyed and veined flowers. **'Johnson's Blue'** has attractively divided foliage and lavender-blue flowers. The scented foliage of ***G. maccrorrhizum*** makes it ideal for small gardens. ***G. himalayense*** **'Plenum'** and ***G. pratense*** **'Plenum Violaceum'** are good double varieties.

Cultivation

Grow in sun or light shade in well-drained soil. In early summer, after the first flush of flowers, clip untidy plants back hard to encourage fresh, compact growth.

Gypsophila Caryophyllaceae

Baby's breath ③

- ✻ *Annual or perennial*
- ✻ *Tiny flowers in summer; good for cutting*
- ✻ *Thrives in alkaline soil*
- ✻ *Hardy* *Zone 3 US, 3 Can*

Gypsophila bears clouds of tiny, delicate white or pink flowers in panicles, making it a valuable texture plant and a fine addition to vases of cut flowers. The border perennial ***Gypsophila paniculata***, with narrow leaves and heads of white flowers, grows to 3ft (1m); **'Bristol Fairy'** is a double form; and **'Flamingo'** has double, pale pink flowers. The annual ***G. elegans*** has larger flowers; **'Covent Garden White'** reaches a height of about 18in (45cm).

G. repens is a semievergreen, trailing perennial, ideal for a rock garden or bank. Its white or pink flowers on wiry stems spring from spreading mats of grey-green leaves. **'Dorothy Teacher'** is a reliable form.

Cultivation

These plants like well-drained soil and an open, sunny location. They prefer alkaline soils, and plants in acid soils will benefit from the addition of a little lime. Although perennials may cope well with poor, light soils, they tend to be short-lived in these conditions.

Stake flowers with stakes or pea sticks where necessary and cut down flowering stems as they fade.

Sow seed of annual species in early spring. Divide ***G. repens*** in spring; named cultivars of ***G. paniculata*** cannot be propagated successfully by small-scale gardeners.

Hakonechloa Graminaea

Hakonechloa ②③

- ✻ *Perennial grass*
- ✻ *Attractive foliage and architectural form*
- ✻ *Hardy* *Zone 4 US, 5 Can*

This slow-growing grass produces a fountain of attractive foliage throughout summer and into fall and winter, making it a good specimen plant for a container. The usual form is ***Hakonechloa macra*** **'Aureola'**, with boldly striped green and yellow leaves that become tinged with red as they age. They are accompanied in fall by panicles of long-lasting red flower spikes. The plant grows to around 2ft (60cm). **'Alboaurea-variegata'** is slightly more compact and has more golden foliage.

Cultivation

Fertile, moisture-retentive soil is required; keep the roots moist at all times throughout the growing season.

A position in full sun is preferred and will ensure the best-colored foliage. Divide plants in spring.

Hamamelis Hamamelidaceae

Witch hazel ②③

- *Deciduous shrub*
- *Fragrant winter flowers*
- *Colorful fall foliage*
- *Hardy* *Zone 5 US, 6 Can*

The witch hazels make spreading shrubs or small trees, with oval leaves that generally turn rich shades of yellow and red in fall. The flowers have strap-shaped petals, which gives them a spider-like appearance. They are carried on the bare branches in winter and early spring and often have an intensely sweet scent.

Hamamelis* × *intermedia is a hybrid between *H. mollis* and *H. japonica*; the flowers, carried throughout the winter, have crinkled petals and are delicately scented. Many cultivars are available, including **'Jelena'** (**'Copper Beauty'**), with large, rich orange-yellow flowers, and a rather vigorous, spreading habit; and **'Diane'**, with striking red-orange flowers and particularly good fall color.

H. japonica, Japanese witch hazel, makes a large shrub about 10ft (3m) in height. The yellow petals are sometimes red-tinged, and the foliage is a glossy midgreen, turning yellow in fall. In early spring, **'Arborea'** has masses of yellow flowers; it also has good yellow fall colours.

H. mollis grows to 6ft (2m) or more; the scented, golden yellow, flat-petaled flowers are carried in late winter. **'Pallida'** has large, paler yellow flowers.

Cultivation

Witch hazels prefer acid soil, which should be moisture retentive, with well-rotted organic matter added before planting. Full sun or semishade are suitable, in a location sheltered from cold winds.

Straggly shoots can be cut back after flowering.

Propagation is not practical for the small-space gardener.

Hamamelis mollis

***Hebe* 'Midsummer Beauty'**

Hebe Scrophulariaceae

Hebe ②③

- *Evergreen shrub*
- *Spikes of summer flowers and attractive foliage*
- *Hardy*

Hebes are particularly suitable for mild coastal areas, since they stand up well to salty winds. There are many species and cultivars, varying from prostrate rock plants to medium-sized shrubs. Dense spikes of bottlebrush-type flowers are carried in summer, often in shades of purple but also in white, pink and red.

'Autumn Glory' grows to some 2ft (60cm); it forms a rounded bush, with dark green leaves and violet-blue flowers from late summer well into fall. Zone 9 US. **'Cranleigh Gem'** is a compact, round shrub around 2ft (60cm) tall, with densely packed spikes of white flowers from early summer. Zone 9 US.

'Youngii' (**'Carl Teschner'**) is more or less prostrate, making a low, spreading shrub with small, dark green leaves on dark stems and short spikes of purple flowers in summer. It is a good plant to grow in rock gardens or around the edges of a bed. Zone 6 US, 7 Can.

The flower spikes of **'Great Ornby'** are deep pink, becoming pale pink from the base as the flowers age. The dark stems are clothed with glossy, midgreen foliage; the bush grows to around 3ft (1m). Zone 9 US. The evergreen **'Midsummer Beauty'** is a little taller, with glossy, green leaves tinted red on their undersides. It bears long spikes of pale lilac flowers from midsummer to fall. Zone 8 US, 9 Can.

As valuable for its foliage as for its flowers is ***H. pinguifolia* 'Pagei'**, a dwarf shrub growing to 9in (23cm) with dense, blue-gray leaves and short spikes of white flowers in spring and early summer. This variety is an excellent plant for rock gardens and can be grown as ground cover, as well as in containers. Zone 6 US, 7 Can.

Cultivation

Well-drained soil is essential; hebes tolerate alkaline soils. Grow in full sun and in a warm, sheltered location.

Trim plants back hard in spring to keep growth neat and compact. Take semiripe cuttings in summer and overwinter them in a frost-free place.

Hedera Araliaceae

Ivy ①②③

- *Evergreen self-clinging climber*
- *Attractive foliage*
- *Shade tolerant*
- *Hardy*

Ivies are very adaptable and easy-to-grow plants, good for difficult places such as cold, shady walls. Once established, they grow quickly, their woody stems clinging to any rough surface with little rootlets.

Leaves are generally lobed or triangular, variable in shape and size, and those of many cultivars are attractively variegated. Once ivy has reached the top of its support, it produces short, stiff branches bearing round heads of tiny yellow-green flowers in fall, which are followed by black berries.

Hedera canariensis is a rather tender species but thrives in sheltered sheltered spots. **'Gloire de Marengo'** has large, dark green unlobed leaves variegated with silver and white at the margins. Zone 7 US, 8 Can.

Somewhat similar but hardier is the rapid climber ***H. colchica* 'Dentata Variegata'**, whose large, unlobed leaves have a creamy variegation. Zone 6 US, 7 Can.

There are dozens of cultivars of the common English ivy, ***H. helix***. Leaves are generally small and deeply lobed; growth is vigorous and can be invasive. Reasonably restrained varieties include **'Buttercup'**, which needs full sun to develop its yellow foliage; **'Ivalace'**, with glossy, deep green, wavy leaves; and **'Little Diamond'**, dwarf and bushy, with green and cream, diamond-shaped leaves. Zone 4 US, 5 Can.

Cultivation

Ivies thrive in most soils and situations, although variegated varieties need full sun.

Plants can be pruned in spring to keep them within bounds; if required, they can be cut back hard to produce fresh young growth. Soft tip cuttings can be taken in early summer. If cuttings are taken of the flowering shoots, they will produce non-climbing, rounded shrubs.

Red spider mite may attack plants in dry conditions. Increase the humidity around plants by spraying them regularly with plain water, especially under the leaves.

Helichrysum bracteatum nanum

Helichrysum Compositae

Everlasting, strawflower ① ② ③

* *Annuals, perennials and evergreen shrubs*
* *Colorful, papery summer flowers or attractive foliage*
* *Hardy or tender*

Helichrysum are well known for their brightly colored flowers, which can easily be dried to give everlasting flowers for arrangements, but there are also valuable foliage types.

The annual *Helichrysum bracteatum* bears papery textured, daisy flowers in a wide range of red, pink, yellow, orange, and white shades. Plants can be rather straggly, growing to some 3ft (1m), but dwarf strains such as **Bright Bikini Hybrids** are suitable for smaller spaces. Zone 10 US.

H. italicum (*H. angustifolium*) is a low-growing evergreen shrub some 2ft (60cm) or more high, with long, silver leaves. The leaves have a strong, spicy aroma, which is released when they are touched, even just by sunlight. It is known as the curry plant, and its aroma is not universally popular. Zone 8 US, 9 Can.

H. petiolare, with its trailing, downy, silver-leaved shoots, is particularly valuable for hanging baskets. **'Variegatum'** has creamy variegated leaves, and those of **'Limelight'** are pale yellow. Although this species is moderately hardy, it is usually grown as a bedding plant, since it quickly becomes leggy and untidy. Zone 9 US.

Cultivation

Everlastings like a sunny, open location in well-drained soil. The evergreen species need shelter from excessive rain in winter. Sow *H. bracteatum* directly where desired, or sow in pots indoors and plant out after any likelihood of frost has passed.

Propagate *H. petiolare* and *H. italicum* from softwood cuttings in summer, keeping the young plants under cover during the following winter. Prune *H. italicum* fairly hard in spring to prevent the plants from becoming straggly.

Everlastings can be attacked by downy mildew, which causes moldy white patches on the leaves. If the attack is bad, spray with a suitable fungicide or discard the plant.

Helleborus Ranunculaceae

Hellebore ② ③

* *Herbaceous or evergreen perennials*
* *Showy flowers in winter and early spring*
* *Hardy*

The lobed leaves of hellebores are often as attractive a feature as their flowers, and in reasonably mild areas the foliage is retained throughout the winter. The plants form hummocks 12–24in (30–60cm) high. The green, white, pink, or purple flowers are cup-shaped, often nodding, with prominent golden stamens.

Helleborus argutifolius (*H. corsicus*) has deeply divided, spiny-edged, deep green leaves forming a spreading clump. The green, nodding flowers are carried in clusters in late winter.

H. foetidus has divided leaves, and elegant panicles of pale green flowers with red margins are produced in early spring. The best variety is **'Wester Flisk'**, with striking red stems, which tolerates the dry soil under trees. Both Zone 6 US, 7 Can.

The Christmas rose, *H. niger,* has relatively broad, divided, deep green leaves and pure white flowers with golden stamens, carried in late winter. **Millet Hybrids 'Medallion'** has particularly large, showy flowers. *H. orientalis,* the Lenten rose, flowers slightly later. Flowers may be cream, pink, or purple, often with darker freckling inside the cup. Both Zone 4 US, 5 Can.

Cultivation

Light or moderate shade and well-drained but moisture-retentive, humus-rich soil is ideal for hellebores. Once established, they resent disturbance.

Do not let the soil dry out in spring and early summer. Mulch around *H. niger* with straw or chipped bark as the buds develop to prevent the blooms from being splashed with soil.

Faded flowers can be removed, but plants seed themselves freely if allowed. Species and varieties crossbreed readily, giving rise to interesting new hybrids.

Slugs and snails can damage plants in early spring and should be controlled with slug bait or an organic alternative. Black spots on the leaves are caused by fungal leaf spots. Remove and destroy affected leaves and spray plants with a suitable fungicide.

Hemerocallis Liliaceae

Daylily ② ③

* *Perennial*
* *Short-lived but plentiful lilylike flowers*
* *Hardy* *Zone 3 US, 3 Can*

The colorful, lilylike blooms of daylilies are carried on tall stems above clumps of arching, grassy foliage. Although each flower lasts only a day, the succession of blooms persists for several weeks throughout the summer.

Many garden hybrids have been bred, some up to 3ft (1m) or more, but others are compact and suitable for small spaces. **'Corky'** has small, pale yellow trumpets on dark stems to 2ft (60cm); **'Cream Drop'**, has creamy yellow flowers 18in (45cm) tall; and **'Children's Festival'**, with ruffled petals in pale peach, grows to 2ft (60cm). **'Little Wine Cup'** has dainty, deep red and gold blooms on compact 18–20in (45–50cm) plants.

Cultivation

Grow in sun or light shade and rich, moisture-retentive soil. Don't let the soil dry out in the growing season. Once the plants are established, don't disturb them.

Cut down the flower stems when the flowers have faded. Slugs and snails can be very damaging to the young shoots in early spring; control with slug bait or an organic alternative. Deer are a serious problem.

Heuchera × brizoides

Heuchera Saxifragaceae

Coral bells ②③

* *Evergreen perennial*
* *Attractive foliage and summer flowers*
* *Good ground cover*
* *Hardy* *Zone 4 US, 4 Can*

The round, lobed leaves of coral bells, in green, bronze, purple, or silver, form a large, rounded clump. Dainty stems of small, bell-shaped flowers are carried well above the foliage in summer; the flowers may be rich red, pink, or white.

Good garden hybrids include **'Firefly'**, with scarlet flowers; **'Red Spangles'**, bright crimson; and **'White Cloud'**, white. **Bressingham Hybrids** include a range of mixed colors.

For foliage effect, **'Palace Purple'** has deep purple-red leaves against which the small white flowers are an effective contrast; **'Snow Storm'** has mottled cream and green leaves; and **'Pewter Moon'** has silver, veined leaves with red backs and pale pink flowers on a compact plant.

Cultivation

Coral bells like well-drained but moisture-retentive soil, preferably containing plenty of well-rotted organic matter, and a location in semishade.

If the plants are required for foliage effect alone, flower stems can be removed as they form; cut flowers last well in water.

Plants should be divided every 3–4 years in fall.

Hibiscus Malvaceae

Hibiscus, rose-of-Sharon ②③

* *Evergreen or deciduous shrub*
* *Large trumpet-shaped flowers in summer*
* *Hardy or tender*

This plant makes a rounded shrub up to some 5ft (1.5m) tall. ***Hibiscus rosa-sinensis*** is a tender species with oval, midgreen leaves with toothed margins and funnel-shaped flowers with prominent anthers. Flowers may be red, pink, white, or yellow. Zone 10 US.

More popular for growing outside is the hardy rose-of-Sharon, ***H. syriacus***, with deep green, lobed leaves and large flowers from late summer into the fall. **'Blue Bird'** has violet-blue flowers with a deeper colored center; **'Red Heart'** is white with a deep red eye; and **'Woodbridge'** is rosy pink with a carmine center. **'Diana'** has large pure white flowers, and **'Hamabo'** is pale pink with a crimson center. **'Ardens'** has pale, reddish purple flowers on a compact plant. Zone 5 US, 6 Can.

Cultivation

Grow *H. syriacus* cultivars in fertile, humus-rich, well-drained soil and a sunny, sheltered spot. In colder gardens they will benefit from the protection of a wall.

H. rosa-sinensis makes a good patio plant for the summer, but must be moved under cover before the first frost or treated as an annual and replaced.

Water plants in containers regularly; buds and flowers will fall if the roots dry out. Cut plants back hard in spring. Take softwood cuttings in early summer or semiripe cuttings later in the season.

Hibiscus attracts aphids and whitefly, which should be treated with a suitable insecticide. Several applications will be needed to control whitefly.

Hosta Hostaceae

Hosta, plantain lily ②③

* *Herbaceous perennial*
* *Bold, attractive foliage*
* *Shade tolerant*
* *Hardy* *Zone 3 US, 3 Can*

Hostas form large clumps of striking leaves, which vary widely in form and size and are often attractively textured or variegated. Stems of pale, delicate, trumpet- shaped flowers in summer can be a bonus.

Many varieties are vigorous, large-leafed, spreading plants, so take care when selecting them for small spaces and containers. **'Ginko Craig'** has deep green leaves with narrow white margins and grows to 12in (30cm); **'Ground Master'** is a little larger, with a much broader white edge to the leaves. **'Golden Prayers'** has textured, yellow-green leaves, and **'Golden Tiara'** has heart-shaped, deep green leaves edged with lime green. Both reach about 6in (15cm) high. **'Shade Fanfare'**, growing to 18–24in (45–60cm), is a reliable variety with pale green, cream-edged, heart-shaped leaves and pale lavender flowers in summer.

Cultivation

Hostas thrive in shade and fertile, moisture-retentive soil, which must not be allowed to dry out. Add well-rotted organic matter to the soil before planting. Remove faded flowers and dead foliage at the end of the season. Divide plants in spring.

Slugs and snails, which destroy the foliage, are a major problem, but container-grown plants are less likely to be damaged. Deer are a serious problem.

Humulus Cannabidaceae

Hops ②③

* *Perennial herbaceous climber*
* *Attractive lobed leaves*
* *Hardy* *Zone 3 US, 4 Can.*

Humulus lupulus is the common hop, whose papery fruit clusters are used to flavor and preserve some types of beer. The plant produces vigorous twining, scrambling stems and has deeply lobed, toothed leaves. The golden-leafed **'Aureus'** is most commonly grown in gardens.

Cultivation

Plant hops in sun or light shade where it can scramble up a support such as a pergola. Well-drained soil is preferred. Propagate plants from softwood cuttings in spring.

Aphids may attack young shoots; control them with a non-persistent insecticide or use beneficial insect predators.

Humulus lupulus 'Aureus'

Hyacinthus Liliaceae

Hyacinth ①②③

* *Bulb*
* *Fragrant flower spikes in spring*
* *Hardy* *Zone 4 US, 5 Can*

The densely packed flower spikes of hyacinths are one of the familiar sights of spring. The rounded bulbs produce glossy, midgreen, strap-shaped leaves and, usually, a single, fleshy flower spike packed with many fragrant, open, bell-shaped flowers in a wide range of colors. Hyacinths are ideal for containers, indoor forcing, or spring bedding.

The dozens of cultivars in existence arise from ***Hyacinthus orientalis.*** Reliable garden cultivars include **'Amsterdam'**, rosy red; **'Anna Marie'**, pale pink; **'City of Haarlem'**, light yellow; **'Delft Blue'**, violet-blue; **'Jan Bos'**, red, **'L'Innocence'**, white; and **'Ostara'**, deep blue.

Multiflora hyacinths have less formal, looser spikes of flowers and produce several spikes to each bulb; they are available in blue, white, and pink.

Cultivation

Plant in fall in well-drained soil and in an open, sunny or lightly shaded location. Best results are obtained by lifting the bulbs as soon as the foliage has died down, drying them off, storing them over the summer, and replanting them the following fall.

Overwet soil conditions will cause the bulbs to rot.

Hyacinthus 'Ostara'

Hydrangea Hydrangeaceae

Hydrangea ②③

* *Deciduous shrubs and climbers*
* *Showy, rounded flowerheads in summer*
* *Hardy*

Most familiar is the bigleaf hydrangea, ***Hydrangea macrophylla,*** a bushy shrub growing to some 4ft (1.2m), with light green, oval, toothed leaves and rounded heads of colorful flowers from mid- to late summer. Florets may be sterile or fertile, the sterile ones being largest and most colorful.

Mophead (hortensia) hydrangeas consist mainly of sterile florets; lacecaps have sterile florets around the outside of the flower head and smaller fertile florets in the middle, giving a lacy effect. Flower color is affected by soil acidity: acid soils give blue flowers and alkaline soils give pink or red; white varieties are unchanged by the type of soil. Zone 5 US, 6 Can.

Mophead varieties that have good, clear colors in suitable soils include **'Générale Vicomtesse de Vibraye'**, rosy pink or light blue; **'Hamburg'**, deep pink or deep blue; **'Nikko Blue'**, rich blue. **'Ami Pasquier'** is a dwarf variety usually better in alkaline soil, where it has deep crimson flowers. **'Madame Emile Mouillère'** has white flowers, becoming tinged pink as they age.

Good lacecaps include **'Blue Wave'**, lilac pink or blue; **'Lanarth White'**, with white sterile florets and pink or blue fertile florets; and **'Mariesii'**, rosy pink or rich blue.

The hybrid *H.* **'Preziosa'** is similar in habit to a mophead, with round heads of deep rosy red flowers and neat foliage tinged with bronze-purple.

H. paniculata grows up to 10ft (3m) tall and has arching shoots with dense, terminal panicles of white flowers. Those of **'Grandiflora'** are particularly large and turn pink as the flowers age. Zone 3 US, 4 Can.

The climbing hydrangea, ***H. anomala petiolaris,*** with toothed, pointed leaves and flat, lacy heads of cream flowers in early summer, is a vigorous grower that will quickly cover a shady wall. Zone 4 US, 5 Can.

Cultivation

Hydrangeas like moisture-retentive soil containing plenty of organic matter, and a sheltered location in sun or light shade. They make excellent container plants, and they should be watered freely during the growing season. For blue flowers, use acid soil mix and apply aluminium sulphate.

Prune ***H. macrophylla*** back to a strong pair of buds near the base of the shoots in early spring. ***H. paniculata*** should be cut back to within 2in (5cm) or so of the previous year's growth at the same time.

Plants may be propagated from softwood cuttings in early summer.

Hypericum Clusiaceae

St-John's-wort ③

* *Perennials and deciduous or evergreen subshrubs and shrubs*
* *Colorful summer flowers*
* *Some varieties suitable for groundcover*
* *Hardy*

The bright golden, cup-shaped flowers of St-John's-wort, with their prominent stamens, are attractive in summer. Leaves are oval, mid- to deep green. Plants vary from prostrate creepers to upright shrubs, suitable for rock gardens, borders, or banks.

The evergreen or semievergreen ***Hypericum calycinum*** makes a spreading shrub some 12in (30cm) tall, which is spangled with large, golden flowers during summer and well into fall. It is excellent for poor, dry soils and makes a good ground cover, but it can be invasive, so take care to plant it where it can be contained. Zone 4 US, 5 Can.

H. **'Hidcote'** flowers profusely from midsummer to fall and forms a compact, semievergreen shrub about 4ft (1.2m) tall. The saucer-shaped flowers are larger than those of most hypericums. Zone 6 US, 6 Can. *H.* **'Elstead'**, with deep green leaves and little starry yellow flowers with long stamens, is slightly smaller. The flowers are followed by attractive salmon pink berries. Zone 6 US, 7 Can.

Cultivation

Any reasonably fertile, well-drained soil is suitable, preferably in an open, sunny spot.

Cut upright shrubs back by about one-third in spring. ***H. calycinum*** usually

benefits from harder pruning and should be cut to within a few inches of the base. Plants can be propagated from softwood cuttings in summer.

Many of these plants, particularly ***H.* 'Elstead'**, are prone to rust disease; use fungicide sprays as a preventive.

Ilex Aquifoliaceae

Holly ②③

- *Evergreen or deciduous shrub or tree*
- *Attractive berries in fall and winter*
- *Hardy* *Zone 7 US, 8 Can*

Hollies are generally grown for their colorful red (occasionally yellow) fruits, but many cultivars are worth growing for their attractive foliage alone. Male and female are on separate plants, so if berries are required a female plant must be obtained and a male plant grown nearby to pollinate it. Do not be misled by the variety names: King or Queen in the name does not necessarily indicate the expected sex.

Ilex* × *altaclarensis is a vigorous hybrid, growing to more than 6m (20ft) where space allows; the dark green, glossy leaves are often almost spineless. **'Camelliifolia'** is upright, with purple-black stems, deep green, glossy, virtually spineless leaves, with plenty of large red berries.

I. aquifolium, English holly, has deep, green, wavy-edged leaves armed with sharp spines. **'Ferox'**, the hedgehog holly, has prickles over the whole leaf surface as well as at the margins; **'Ferox Argentea'** has silver-edged leaves. Both plants are male and relatively slow growing.

'J. C. van Tol' or **'Pyramidalis'** are the cultivars to grow if you have room for only one plant; they are self-pollinating and produce reliable crops of bright red berries when grown alone. **'Winter Queen'** (a male) is a dense, fairly compact shrub with cream-edged leaves; young leaves are pink.

The native winterberry, ***I. verticillata***, 10ft (3m) tall, is deciduous and is grown for its brilliant red-orange berries. **'Afterglow'** is a compact form with orange-red-fruits; **'Red Sprite'** (**'Nana'**, **'Compacta'**) grows 3–5ft (1–1.5m) tall and bears large, bright red berries on rounded shrubs.

Cultivation

Hollies will grow in almost any soil but prefer one that is well drained. Grow variegated types in sun for the best leaf color; green varieties will do well in shade.

Holly makes a good specimen plant in a tub and can be clipped to shape in summer. Cut out plain green shoots on variegated types as soon as they are seen. Propagate plants from semiripe cuttings in summer.

***Impatiens*, New Guinea hybrid**

Impatiens Balsaminaceae

Impatiens, busy Lizzie ①②③

- *Annual or perennial grown as annual*
- *Profuse summer flowers in a wide colour range*
- *Tender* *Zone 10 US*

These plants, growing to 6–18in (15–45cm), are popular for summer bedding and are excellent in containers. They have succulent stems and soft, pointed leaves which may be colored. The flowers are spurred, with open, flat faces in white, red, pink, lilac, and salmon shades; the petals may be marked with white to give a star effect.

Most bedding impatiens are hybrids. Popular strains are the **Accent Hybrids**, in mixed or single colors, including stars; the **Deco Hybrids**, with bronzy leaves; the **Super Elfin Hybrids**, compact plants in a good color range; and the **Spectra Hybrids**, a New Guinea impatiens with extra-large flowers and bronze or variegated foliage. **'Double Rosette Mixed'** has double or semidouble flowers like tiny rosebuds.

Cultivation

Busy Lizzies grow well in light shade and in moist, fertile but well-drained soil. Plant them out after the risk of frost has passed and keep them well watered during summer but never allow them to become waterlogged. Feed with a liquid high-potash fertilizer every 14–21 days.

Particularly good plants may be potted up and overwintered under cover. Cut them back hard in early spring to promote new growth for use as softwood cuttings. Plants may also be raised from seed.

Control aphids with a non-persistent contact insecticide. Slugs and snails can also be a problem when young plants are set out. Use slug bait or an organic alternative.

Ipomoea Convolvulaceae

Morning glory ①②③

- *Perennial climber usually grown as an annual*
- *Showy, funnel-shaped summer flowers*
- *Tender* *Zone 10 US*

The twining stems of morning glory will quickly trail from a hanging basket or cover a pillar. Most of these plants are short-lived perennials that are most satisfactory when grown as annuals. The leaves are heart shaped, and from midsummer to early fall a succession of funnel-shaped flowers unfurls. These open in the morning and close in the afternoon.

Most popular is ***Ipomoea tricolor* 'Heavenly Blue'**, with abundant, sky-blue, white-throated flowers for a long season. It rapidly reaches 10ft (3m) or so. ***I. nil* 'Early Call Mixed'** has heart-shaped or lobed leaves and funnel-shaped flowers in scarlet, deep red, salmon, pink, and white and flowers earlier than ***I. tricolor***.

Cultivation

Well-drained, fertile soil containing plenty of well-rotted organic matter is required. Grow in a sheltered position in full sun. Provide a support for the stems to twine around or let them trail from a basket or container. Do not let the soil dry out.

Raise plants from seed sown in spring.

Control aphids with a contact, non-persistent insecticide where necessary.

***Ipmoea tricolor* 'Heavenly Blue'**

Iris danfordiae

Iris Iridaceae

Iris ①②③

* *Rhizomes or bulbs*
* *Distinctive, colorful flowers in spring and summer*
* *Hardy*

Irises can be divided into the rhizomatous, or German, types, which flower mainly in early summer, and early-blooming bulbous varieties, which include the Reticulata group of dwarf irises.

Rhizomatous irises have stiff, sword-shaped leaves and tall stems of flowers with three large, downward-curving petals; known as falls, and three smaller, upright ones, known as standards. Some have bristly beards of colored hairs in the center of the falls.

Among rhizomatous irises growing to 12–18in (30–45cm) are **'Banbury Ruffles'**, deep blue with ruffled petals; **'Eyebright'**, yellow flowers with purple-brown markings; and **'Curtsy'**, which is white with lavender falls. Zone 3 US, 4 Can.

Bulbous irises include the Dutch, Spanish, and English irises, which grow to about 3ft (1m) and flower in succession from early to late summer in a wide range of colors.

Particularly suitable for small spaces are Reticulata irises (Zone 4 US, 5 Can), no more than 8in (20cm) tall. ***Iris danfordiae*** produces lightly fragrant, bright yellow flowers in late winter or early spring, when the narrow leaves are only just appearing. ***I. histrioides***, with blue flowers marked with darker blue, white, and yellow on the falls, flowers even earlier. **'Major'** is a deep blue.

The flowers of ***I. reticulata*** bloom a little later; they are fragrant and deep purple, with yellow markings on the falls. **'Cantab'** has light blue flowers, **'J.S. Dijt'** is purple-red.

Other Reticulata hybrids include **'Joyce'**, blue with white and yellow markings; **'Harmony'**, pale blue with white and yellow markings; and **'Katharine Hodgkin'**, with flowers delicately marked with yellow, pale blue feathering, and deeper violet-blue spots and streaks on the falls.

Cultivation

German irises like well-drained but moisture-retentive, fertile soil and an open, sunny location. Plant with the tops of the rhizomes just showing. Increase plants by dividing the rhizomes after flowering.

Bulbous and dwarf irises are ideal for shallow pans and containers or the rock garden. They like light, well-drained soil. Plant the bulbs in fall; they can be lifted and divided after the foliage has died down.

Slugs and snails may attack the young foliage; use slug bait or an organic alternative if necessary.

Jasminum Oleaceae

Jasmine ②③

* *Deciduous or semievergreen shrubs and climbers*
* *Starry flowers at various seasons, often scented*
* *Hardy or tender*

Jasmines are scrambling twiners or wall-shrubs with delicate, trumpet-shaped flowers; many species are tender and are grown as houseplants. Of the hardiest species, two are particularly popular.

Jasminum nudiflorum (winter jasmine) is a lax, arching, deciduous shrub best grown against a wall; it needs to be tied to a support to keep it neat. The bright green, leafless stems carry starry yellow, unscented flowers throughout winter and early spring. Zone 6 US, 7 Can.

The common jasmine, ***J. officinale***, is a summer-flowering climber. The leaves are midgreen, divided into leaflets, and are semievergreen in mild locations. White, very sweetly scented flowers are carried in clusters throughout the summer. Zone 7 US, 8 Can.

Jasminum nudiflorum

Cultivation

Grow jasmine in well-drained soil in a sunny location. ***J. officinale*** needs a sheltered spot, but ***J. nudiflorum*** is hardier.

After flowering has finished, cut back the flowered shoots of ***J. nudiflorum*** almost to the base and trim back outward-facing shoots. Thin out ***J. officinale*** after flowering as required.

Propagate by semiripe cuttings in summer.

Juniperus Cupressaceae

Juniper ①②③

* *Evergreen conifer*
* *Handsome foliage and architectural shapes*
* *Hardy*

Junipers are versatile plants suitable for a wide range of different locations. Although they can make tall, forest trees, there are many dwarf and slow-growing forms suitable for small spaces. Some species are narrow and columnar, others wide-spreading and prostrate; foliage may be green, blue, silver, or gold. Instead of cones, they carry round berries with a distinctive aroma, which are used for flavoring gin.

One of the most popular of all dwarf conifers, ***Juniperus communis* 'Compressa'**, forms a neat column about 30in (75cm) tall. It is widely used in rock gardens and as a companion for heathers. Zone 2 US, 3 Can.

On a larger scale, ***J. scopulorum* 'Skyrocket'** is exceptionally narrow and upright, with bluish foliage. Although it can eventually reach 20ft (6m), it is very slow growing and will remain suitable for a small space for many years. Zone 3 US, 3 Can.

J. virginiana is another slow-growing species, more or less conical in shape; **'Grey Owl'** has silver-gray foliage and forms a spreading, low-growing specimen up to 10ft (3m) tall. Zone 2 US, 2 Can.

Among prostrate and spreading forms, ***J. squamata* 'Blue Carpet'** makes a low, silver-blue mat about 12in (30cm) high. ***J. s.* 'Blue Star'**, which forms a low, rounded bush to 20in (50cm), has attractive, steely blue leaves, and ***J. s.* 'Holger'** is a low shrub to 3ft (1m), with silvery foliage that has creamy yellow tips when young. Zone 3 US, 4 Can.

Cultivation

Most well-drained soils are suitable. A location in full sun is preferred, particularly for the forms with colored leaves, but junipers tolerate shade well.

Prune out damaged branches in late spring.

Plants may be increased from semiripe heel cuttings in late summer.

Kniphofia 'Little Elf'

Kniphofia Liliaceae

Red hot poker, torch lily, poker plant ③

* *Herbaceous or evergreen perennial*
* *Bright, pokerlike flowers in summer*
* *Hardy* *Zone 5 US, 6 Can*

Red hot pokers make a mound of grassy foliage from which arise tall flowering stems bearing dense spikes of overlapping, tubular flowers. Orange-red is the usual color, but there are also yellow and cream varieties.

Most garden plants are hybrids growing to about 3ft (1m). **'Alcazar'** produces bright orange spikes in early summer; **'Royal Standard'** has rich yellow flowers opening from scarlet buds; **'Little Maid'**, with creamy yellow flowers, grows to 2ft (60cm); and **'Wayside Flame'** (**'Pfitzer'**) has tall, glowing scarlet flower spikes in mid- to late summer.

Cultivation

Light, well-drained soil is essential; grow red hot pokers in full sun. Do not let the soil dry out during the growing season.

Cut down faded flower stems and tidy the leaves in late fall. Do not remove all the dead leaves, since they help to protect the crowns against excessive winter weather.

Laburnum Leguminosae

Golden chain, laburnum ③

* *Deciduous tree*
* *Abundant flowers in spring and early summer*
* *All parts poisonous, especially the seeds*
* *Hardy* *Zone 5 US, 6 Can*

The pendent racemes of golden, pealike flowers make golden chain a beautiful specimen in late spring and early summer. It forms a spreading tree up to 6m (20ft) tall but is usually about half that height in gardens. Leaves consist of three light green leaflets with silky hairs on the undersides.

Most common is ***Laburnum anagyroides,*** which carries dense flower clusters in late spring. **'Erect'** has more upright branches, making it a good choice for small spaces. A weeping variety, **'Pendulum'**, is often grafted on to a stock to make a small, graceful tree.

The Scotch laburnum, ***L. alpinum,*** has slightly larger leaves and longer racemes of flowers than ***L. anagyroides*** and blooms a few weeks later.

L. × ***watereri*** is a hybrid between ***L. anagyroides*** and ***L. alpinum;*** **'Vossii'** is the most popular variety, with very long racemes of flowers, freely carried.

Cultivation

Golden chains grow well in any soil except heavy, poorly drained types. The trees prefer full sun but will tolerate light shade.

Pruning is not normally required, but where children may have access to the tree, the seed pods should be removed and destroyed safely as soon as they form; fallen pods should also be removed.

The species can be raised from seed sown in fall; propagation of named varieties is not practical for small-space gardeners.

Lamium Labiatae

Dead nettle ②③

* *Herbaceous or semievergreen perennial*
* *Attractive foliage*
* *Useful ground cover*
* *Hardy* *Zone 4 US, 5 Can*

Dead nettles are easily grown plants that tolerate poor soils and growing conditions. While they provide excellent ground cover, they can also become troublesome weeds if care is not taken to curb their spread.

The midgreen leaves are oval, with toothed edges, but most cultivars have colored or variegated foliage. Flowers are hooded and carried in whorls on the square stems in early summer. They may be purple-pink, white, or yellow but are usually of secondary interest to the foliage.

Lamium galeobdolon **'Florentinum'** grows 9in (22cm) tall; the leaves are attractively silvered, with green veins, and yellow, rather straggly flowers appear in summer. This is an invasive plant that is suitable only for containers in small gardens.

L. maculatum can also be invasive. Its leaves have a broad central stripe or splash of silver, and the flowers are deep purplish pink. **'Beacon Silver'** has silver, heavily veined foliage with green margins and mauve-pink flowers; **'Pink Pewter'** and **'White Nancy'** have similar foliage and soft pink and white flowers respectively.

Cultivation

Dead nettles will grow in any well-drained soil and are good for poor, dry, sandy sites. They tolerate shade well.

When the plants are being grown for their foliage effect, the flowers can be cut off as they form. Divide plants in fall or spring or increase them by softwood cuttings in early summer.

Lathyrus Leguminosae

Sweet pea 

* *Annual or perennial climbers or bedding plants*
* *Usually fragrant, colorful summer flowers*
* *Hardy or tender* *Zone 4 US, 5 Can*

The annual climbing sweet pea, ***Lathyrus odoratus,*** with its tendril-tipped leaflets, is well loved for its large pea-type flowers in a wide range of colors and fancy forms. Many varieties have a strong, sweet scent, but some modern varieties, grown specifically for flower size, form, and color, have lost their fragrance.

A number of low-growing, bushy, non-climbing varieties have been bred and are particularly suitable for confined spaces and containers. They include strains such as the **Knee Hi, Bijou, Snoopea**, and **Patio Mixed Hybrids**. There are hundreds of climbing cultivars in red, pink, salmon, cream, white, lilac, purple, and bicolors.

Perennial species include ***L. grandiflorus,*** climbing to around 5ft (1.5m), with pink and purple-red flowers, and ***L. latifolius,*** a vigorous climber, which reaches 6ft (2m) or more, with deep rosy pink flowers .

Cultivation

Sweet peas need well-drained but moisture-retentive soil with plenty of well-rotted organic matter. Give plenty of water while the buds are forming and a high-potash liquid fertilizer every 10 days from the time flowering starts. Provide supports in the form of netting or stake tripods to which plants can cling.

Remove faded flowers regularly for a long flowering season. Cut down perennials almost to soil level in fall.

Sow seed in early spring; soaking the seed overnight or nicking the seed coat carefully with a sharp knife will speed germination, which can otherwise be slow.

Mildew and botrytis can be a problem; use a fungicide where necessary.

Laurus Lauraceae
Bay laurel, sweet bay ②③

* *Evergreen tree*
* *Aromatic deep green foliage*
* *Suitable for growing as a standard*
* *Hardy* *Zone 8 US, 9 Can*

The bay tree, ***Laurus nobilis,*** has a long history of cultivation. The strongly aromatic leaves are lanceolate and glossy deep green; the tree grows to some 10m (30ft) or more where space allows but can be kept neat and compact by pruning. It is popular as a clipped specimen in tubs.

In spring, clusters of fluffy, greenish yellow flowers wreathe the branches; they are most conspicuous on clipped plants in containers. The leaves can be used in cooking and form part of a classic *bouquet garni.* Tear the edges of the fresh leaf to bring out the flavor.

Cultivation
Well-drained, reasonably fertile soil is required. Even where plants are hardy, the foliage can be damaged by cold winds and prolonged frosts, so a sheltered spot is necessary; overwinter indoors in colder zones. Keep the soil moist but never waterlogged during the growing season.

Clip plants to shape in summer and propagate by semiripe cuttings. Rub out any shoots growing from the stems of standards as soon as they are noticed.

Brown leaves with curled edges may be caused by cold winds or hard frosts; trim off affected shoots and move plants to a more protected location.

Scale insects are a common problem; inspect the reverse of the foliage frequently and scrape off any scales that are found there. Bad infestations usually need treating with a systemic insecticide; don't use the leaves of treated plants in cooking.

Black, sooty deposits on the foliage are caused by sooty mold, which forms on the secretions of scale insects; the mold can usually be wiped off, but you must deal with the scale insects to prevent a recurrence of the problem.

Lavandula Labiatae
Lavender ②③

* *Evergreen shrub*
* *Fragrant summer flowers*
* *Aromatic gray foliage*
* *Hardy* *Zone 5 US, 6 Can except as noted*

Lavender is well known for its strongly scented, tubular flowers, which are carried in dense spikes on stiff stems. It is a valuable decorative shrub, with silver-gray foliage, sometimes divided, which is also aromatic when lightly crushed. Flowers dry well, retaining their strong scent. For best results, pick them just before they open.

English lavender is ***Lavandula angustifolia,*** but hybrids are most frequently available. **'Hidcote'** is a reliable, compact cultivar with gray-green leaves and dense spikes of purple-blue flowers; it grows to 30in (75cm) and flowers in midsummer. Another compact grower is **'Munstead'** (Zone 4 US, 5 Can), with narrow leaves and intense blue flowers from mid- to late summer. **'Twickel Purple'** has broader leaves and long flower spikes. For a change of color, there are **'Loddon Pink'**, with early, pale pink flowers, and the white-flowered, dwarf **'Nana Alba'**, which is 1ft (30cm).

Less hardy French lavender, ***L. stoechas,*** is a small, early flowering, dense shrub with purple flowers, each spike being topped by a tuft of long-lasting, rosy purple bracts. (Zone 8 US, 9 Can.) These are particularly prominent on Spanish lavender, ***L. stoechas pedunculata.***

Cultivation
These Mediterranean natives like fertile, well-drained soil and a warm, open, sunny location.

Deadhead plants after flowering and trim them lightly to maintain a neat appearance. In spring, carry out further trimming to encourage bushy growth; plants often look bedraggled after a cold winter and will benefit from being cut back quite hard.

Propagate by semiripe cuttings in summer.

Lavandula angustifolia 'Hidcote'

Leucojum Amaryllidaceae
Snowflake ①②③

* *Bulb*
* *Pendent white flowers in spring or fall*
* *Hardy* *Zone 4 US, 5 Can*

The flowers of snowflake bear a slight resemblance to those of snowdrops: they are pendent, bell shaped, and white with green markings on the petals. The spring snowflake, ***Leucojum vernum,*** grows to 6–8in (15–20cm) and flowers in late winter and early spring. The summer snowflake (***L. aestivum***) is confusingly named, since it flowers in mid- to late spring. The nodding heads of white and green blooms are carried on stems up to 3ft (1m) tall, amid clumps of spear-shaped, dark green foliage.

Much less common is the fall snowflake, ***L. autumnale.*** Growing to around 6in (15cm), it has very fine, grassy leaves and slender, wiry stems bearing a dozen or more delicate, bell-shaped, white-flushed-pink flowers in early fall.

Cultivation
Plant the bulbs in fall. The spring and summer snowflakes both thrive in moisture-retentive soil in dappled shade; fall snowflake prefers well-drained soil and full sun. Keep spring and summer snowflakes moist throughout the growing season. Divide the clumps after flowering.

Lewisia Portulacaceae
Lewisia ①②③

* *Herbaceous or evergreen perennial*
* *Showy flowers in late spring and early summer*
* *Ideal for rock gardens and walls*
* *Hardy* *Zone 4 US, 5 Can*

Lewisia form rosettes of fleshy, midgreen, oblong leaves and produce a profusion of flowering stems up to 12in (30cm) long, bearing open-faced flowers. Colors range from pink, rose, and salmon to yellow, orange, red, purple, and white. Some species are rather difficult and need specialized conditions in an alpine house, but many of the hybrid strains are easy to grow in a rock garden or in containers.

The evergreen **Cotyledon Hybrids** are the most popular lewisia, but there are various reliable selections, including **Alba** and **Sunset Strain.**

Cultivation
Lewisia need moisture-retentive but well-drained, acidic soil and sun or semishade. Mulch around the neck of the plants with chippings or small gravel to ensure good

drainage around the crowns. They are often best planted on a slope or sideways in a rock crevice to ensure that water drains away from the center of the rosettes. Excess moisture, especially in winter, causes the crowns to rot. Shallow pans, or stone or clay troughs, make suitable containers; lewisias do not usually do well in plastic pots.

The plants produce offsets that can be detached in summer and rooted in sandy soil mix. They can also be raised from seed sown in spring.

Slugs and snails may damage the foliage.

Lilium Liliaceae

Lily 

- *Bulb*
- *Fragrant summer flowers*
- *Hardy*

Many species and cultivars of the stately lily are grown. The unusual bulbs consist of overlapping, fleshy scales with no tunic (papery covering) and are prone to damage and drying out before planting. Each bulb produces a single stem with lanceolate leaves, often in whorls, along almost its entire length. The flowers are carried in groups at the top of the stem and are generally large and trumpet shaped, with six petals and prominent stamens. They may be white, pink, orange, or yellow, sometimes striped or freckled, and are usually fragrant. In some species, the tips of the petals curl back to form a Turk's-cap shape.

Almost all lilies make excellent container plants. ***Lilium auratum,*** the golden-rayed lily of Japan (Zone 5 US, 5 Can), grows to 5ft (1.5m) and has wide, open flowers up to 10in (25cm) across. They are white, with a central golden band on each petal and a heavy sprinkling of purple-brown spots. This lily requires acidic soil and is often short-lived. The Madonna lily, ***L. candidum,*** (Zone 6 US, 7 Can) has pure white, funnel-shaped, strongly fragrant flowers on 4ft (1.2m) stems. It is good for containers but likes a little lime added to the soil.

L. regale (Zone 4 US, 5 Can) is easier to grow; the trumpet-shaped flowers are white, flushed gold in the throat, and the petals have purple backs. Another popular white lily is ***L. longiflorum,*** the Easter lily (Zone 7 US, 8 Can). It grows up to 3ft (1m), with strongly fragrant blooms.

Flowers of the tiger lily, ***L. lancifolium*** (***L. tigrinum***), have strongly recurving petals giving a Turk's-cap effect. They are a glowing orange, freckled with purple spots.

There are many hybrid varieties. Well-established, reliable cultivars include: **'Enchantment'**, orange, funnel-shaped flowers with black speckled throats;

Lilium auratum

'Mrs. R.O. Backhouse', lightly reflexing petals, rich yellow with purple freckles; **'Stargazer'**, rosy red with narrow white margins and darker spots in the throat; and the pure white **'Casa Blanca'**, with large, very fragrant blooms. All Zone 3 US, 4 Can.

Cultivation

Plant lilies in fall in well-drained, fertile soil. Most like an open, sunny location but with cool, moist roots. In containers, water sparingly until growth appears, then water more freely to keep the soil moist but never waterlogged. Feed with a high-potash liquid fertilizer every 10 days in the growing season.

Bulbs can be propagated from bulb scales or, in some species, from bulbils, which appear in the leaf axils.

Aphids and the larvae of the European (red) lily beetle may attack the plants. Slugs and snails may also cause damage, and deer are a serious problem. Wet soil conditions can lead to rotting of the bulbs.

Lithodora Boraginaceae

Lithodora ①②③

- *Evergreen subshrub*
- *Prostrate or trailing*
- *Showy, early summer flowers*
- *Hardy* *Zone 5 US, 6 Can*

The most popular species is ***Lithodora diffusa,*** often known as ***Lithospermum diffusum.*** It forms a low mat of narrow, evergreen leaves; the stems trail over rocks and walls and in early summer bear clusters of intense blue, funnel-shaped flowers, which often cause the plant to be mistaken for a gentian. **'Heavenly Blue'** is the most common cultivar; **'Grace Ward'** has slightly larger flowers.

Cultivation

L. diffusa requires acid soil, which must be moisture retentive but well drained. Grow in full sun. Lithodora is excellent for rock gardens and does well in containers and at the edge of raised beds. Trim the plants after flowering and take semiripe cuttings in summer.

Lobelia Campanulaceae

Lobelia ①②③

- *Annual or herbaceous perennial*
- *Freely produced flowers in summer*
- *Trailing varieties ideal for hanging baskets*
- *Tender except* **Lobelia cardinalis**

Trailing lobelia is an indispensible basket and container plant, flowering continually through the summer. The plants grown are usually hybrids of ***Lobelia erinus,*** a tender perennial grown as an annual. Leaves are small, oval or lanceolate, and midgreen or bronze; flowers are small, lipped, and, typically, blue. Plants grow to around 6in (15cm) high; some have a trailing habit and others are more upright and bushy.

Among trailing types are **'Sapphire'**, deep blue with a white eye; **Cascade Series** in red, blue, and white; and **'Regatta Blue Splash'**, white with light blue markings. Bedding lobelias include **'Cambridge Blue'**, pale blue flowers; **'Crystal Palace'**, deep blue flowers and bronzy foliage; and **'Rosamund'**, rosy red with a white eye.

Less well known is the perennial border lobelia, ***L. cardinalis.*** It reaches 30in (75cm), with midgreen or deep bronze-red, lanceolate leaves and brilliant scarlet, lobed flowers in midsummer. Zone 3 US, 4 Can.

Cultivation

Moisture-retentive soil and a sheltered location in sun or semishade suit bedding lobelias best, but some species are shade tolerant. Water regularly and feed with high-potash liquid fertilizer every 7–10 days. Grow bedding lobelias from seed sown in spring. Flowering may cease in high temperatures

L. cardinalis likes fertile, damp soil. It will also grow in shallow water at the edge of a pond. In cold areas, protect the roots with a mulch of chipped bark or straw. It can be raised from seed or divided in spring.

Lobelia 'Rosamund'

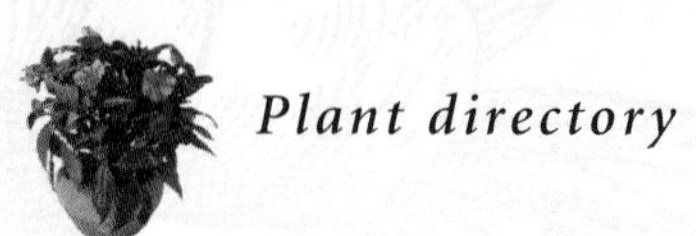

Lonicera Caprifoliaceae

Honeysuckle ②③

* *Deciduous or evergreen climbers and shrubs*
* *Sweet-scented, tubular flowers at various seasons*
* *Hardy*

The climbing species are the best known honeysuckles, but there are also several attractive shrubby ones. The long, tubular flowers, with prominent stamens, are mainly yellow or cream, often flushed with red or purple. Most are strongly fragrant.

Climbing plants produce strong, twining, woody stems. The Woodbine honeysuckle, ***Lonicera periclymenum*** (Zone 4 US, 5 Can), is a vigorous scrambler, with creamy yellow, red-flushed flowers in summer. It has given rise to two popular deciduous varieties: **'Belgica'** (early Dutch honeysuckle), which has yellow and red flowers in early summer, and **'Serotina'** (late Dutch honeysuckle), which flowers from late summer into fall with deep red and white blooms.

Invasive ***L. japonica*** (Zone 5 US, 6 Can) is evergreen or semievergreen, with oval, light green leaves and small, creamy white, fragrant flowers in summer and early fall. **'Aureoreticulata'** has leaves marked with an attractive network of gold, but it is less likely to keep its leaves during cold winters.

Of the nonclimbing species, the winter-flowering honeysuckles are, perhaps, the most valuable. ***L. fragrantissima*** and ***L. standishii*** are similar. Both grow to around 6ft (2m), but ***L. standishii*** tends to be narrower; it is also more likely to be evergreen. Both bear creamy white, fragrant flowers from midwinter to early spring. (Both Zone 5 US, 6 Can)

Cultivation

Grow honeysuckles in ordinary, well-drained soil that has had some well-rotted organic matter added. The climbers like a cool, moist root run and will grow well in sun or semishade. Provide some support for young stems; they will soon twine over posts, pergolas, sheds, and arches.

When climbers have finished flowering, prune out some or all flowering stems. Prune scrubby species to shape in midspring. Propagate plants by semiripe cuttings in summer.

Lysimachia Primulaceae

Loosestrife, creeping Jenny, moneywort ①②③

* *Herbaceous or evergreen perennial*
* *Attractive foliage and flowers*
* *Hardy* *Zone 4 US, 5 Can*

Lysimachia nummularia 'Aurea'

The most useful loosestrife for small garden spaces and containers is the prostrate, spreading ***Lysimachia nummularia***, creeping Jenny. The small, round, fresh green leaves are carried in pairs on long, trailing stems, and cheerful, bright yellow buttercup-type flowers appear in summer. The plant is easy to grow in most locations, and can be invasive. Golden-leafed **'Aurea'** is slightly more restrained than the species and is more commonly grown.

Cultivation

This plant prefers, cool, moist, fertile soil, but adapts well to dry conditions. It can be grown in sun or shade and will thrive on a bank or tumbling over the top of a wall, but take care to plant it only where its spread can be restricted. It makes an excellent hanging basket plant, and should be watered freely when grown in containers.

Plants are easily propagated by softwood cuttings in late spring and summer.

Magnolia Magnoliaceae

Magnolia ②③

* *Deciduous or evergreen trees or shrubs*
* *Showy flowers, usually in spring*
* *Hardy*

Magnolias make stately, noble plants, often with spectacular, large, waxy blooms. Some species are fussy about soil and location, and may take many years to flower; several make large trees that demand a large space.

But two in particular are good for small areas. ***Magnolia liliiflora*** makes a rounded bush up to 10ft (3m) high, with broad, oval, glossy green, deciduous leaves. From mid- to late spring into summer, it carries large, erect, chalice-shaped flowers, which are rosy purple on the outside, creamy white inside, and have a delicate perfume. **'Nigra'**, with deep wine-red flowers, is popular. Zone 5 US, 6 Can.

M. stellata, the star magnolia, is a wide, spreading shrub some 6ft (2m) high. In

Magnolia stellata

midspring it bears a profusion of starry, fragrant flowers with narrow white petals, which appear before the midgreen, lanceolate leaves. **'Waterlily'** has larger flowers with more petals; **'Dawn'**, **'Rosea'**, and **'Rubra'** have flowers tinged with varying degrees of pink. Zone 4 US, 5 Can.

Hybrids between ***M. liliiflora*** and ***M. stellata*** have been produced; they have a long flowering season and produce abundant, narrow-petalled flowers with strong, purple-pink coloring. **'Susan'** is the most commonly available.Zone 5 US, 6 Can.

Cultivation

Magnolias require acid, fertile, well-drained but moisture-retentive soil, which should be enriched with plenty of well-rotted organic matter before planting. They will not grow well in light, dry soils. Keep the roots moist throughout the growing season and mulch in fall.

Plants can be propagated by semiripe cuttings in summer or by layering.

Flowers will be damaged by frost, which causes the petals to turn brown.

Mahonia Berberidaceae

Mahonia, Oregon grape ③

* *Evergreen shrub*
* *Handsome foliage and architectural form*
* *Scented early spring flowers followed by blue berries*
* *Hardy*

The leathery, glossy, dark green leaves of mahonia are composed of a number of leaflets with spiny tips, shaped rather like holly leaves. Small, bell-shaped, yellow flowers are borne in early spring in dense clusters, or in drooping or upright racemes; they have a strong, sweet scent.

The Oregon grape, ***Mahonia aquifolium***, grows to 3–6ft (1–2m) tall and blooms in early spring, producing large numbers of conical flower clusters. These are followed by blue-black berries in grapelike clusters. **'Apollo'** is a vigorous, dense-growing form, and **'Atropurpurea'** has foliage that is burnished purple-red in winter. Zone 4 US, 5 Can.

M. japonica carries its flowers in long, slightly drooping racemes in late winter. Its growth is stiffly upright to about 6ft (2m). Plants of the Bealei Group (sometimes listed as ***M. bealei***) have shorter, more upright racemes of flowers. Zone 9 US.

The vigorous hybrid *M.* × ***media*** grows to about 4ft (1.2m), with leaves in tiers, which gives it a strong, architectural shape. **'Charity'** has shuttlecocks of flowers in long, spreading racemes at the tips of the stems in early winter; these are fragrant but less strongly scented than in some other species. Zone 9 US.

Cultivation

Grow mahonias in a lightly shaded spot in fertile, moisture-retentive soil. Protect from windburn in winter. Prune to shape in midspring; *M. aquifolium* responds well to being cut back hard every few years. Propagate by semiripe cuttings in summer.

Powdery mildew can sometimes cause white, powdery patches on the foliage.

Malus Rosaceae

Crab apple 

* *Deciduous tree*
* *Spring blossom and fall fruits*
* *Hardiness varies*

Crab apples are good-value trees for small gardens; they provide interest in spring, when the cup-shaped, apple blossom flowers appear, and again in fall and into the winter, with their small, colorful fruits. The fruits are edible and can be used for making crab-apple jelly; if they are left on the tree they often attract birds. Many crab apple cultivars have the added bonus of attractive fall foliage.

Of the species commonly grown, ***Malus floribunda*** makes a spreading tree up to 15ft (4.5m) high. In late spring, it bears a profusion of blossom. The flowers are deep pink in bud, opening to pinkish white, and are followed by berrylike yellow fruits. ***M. sargentii*** is a small, shrubby, spreading tree, up to about 10ft (3m) tall. In mid-spring the branches are covered with white flowers, which are followed by long-lasting, bright red fruits. Both Zone 4 US, 5 Can.

M. tschonoskii has a narrowly conical habit; although it may ultimately reach more than 30ft (10m), it remains suitable for a small space for several years. The flowers are white, tinged with pink, and are sometimes followed by small green and red fruits; in fall, the leaves take on shades of yellow, red, orange, and purple. Zone 5 US, 6 Can.

Easy to find, disease-resistant cultivars include **'Donald Wyman'**, with white spring blossoms and small red fruit that birds enjoy; and **'Madonna'**, which grows to about 20ft (6m) with double white flowers and cherry-sized yellow fruit that can be used for making jelly. Another good variety is the smaller **'Sugar Tyme'** with white blooms and dark red fruit that last well. All Zone 4 US, 4 Can.

Cultivation

Crab apples thrive in nearly all soils except badly drained clays. Don't let the roots dry out while trees are flowering. Prune trees to shape when they are dormant, cutting out weak, damaged, or crossing branches.

Crab apples are prone to the same diseases that affect ordinary apples, including scab and fireblight. Scab can be controlled by a preventive fungicide spraying program; fireblight is difficult to control, but affected branches should be cut out well beyond the damaged area and burned if possible.

If aphids and caterpillars infest the tree, they can be dealt with by spraying with a nonpersistent pesticide.

Monarda Labiatae

Bee balm, bergamot ②③

* *Herbaceous perennial*
* *Aromatic foliage and summer flowers*
* *Hardy* *Zone 4 US, 5 Can*

The oval, light green, hairy leaves of bee balm, with their strong citrus scent, are valuable in perfumery and for potpourri; an infusion of the leaves is known as Oswego tea.

The plant forms a rounded mound up to 3ft (1m) high and bears tiers of shaggy-headed flowers in pink, red, or mauve in summer. The blooms are attractive to bees.

Monarda **'Croftway Pink'** has soft pink flowers; those of **'Cambridge Scarlet'** are an intense, brilliant red.

Cultivation

Bee balm likes a fertile, moisture-retentive soil and an open, sunny location, although it will tolerate light shade. Plants can be invasive, so choose their site carefully.

Cut down stems in fall and mulch the roots with well-rotted compost or other organic matter. Powdery mildew may become a serious problem.

Myosotis Boraginaceae

Forget-me-not ①②③

* *Annuals and short-lived perennials, usually grown as biennials*
* *Small, usually blue flowers in spring*
* *Hardy* *Zone 4 US, 4 Can.*

The small, bright blue, white-eyed flowers of forget-me-nots are carried in loose sprays. They are often used as underplanting for tulips. Plants have pale green, lance-shaped leaves and branch freely.

Myosotis alpestris, the alpine forget-me-not, growing to 6in (15cm) high or less, is a short-lived perennial very much at home in a rock garden. The clusters of bright blue flowers with yellow eyes are borne just above the mound of hairy leaves in late spring and early summer.

This species is thought to be a parent of many of the hybrid varieties grown from seed as spring bedding and treated as biennials. **'Blue Ball'** is compact and bushy, reaching about 8in (20cm), with deep blue flowers; **'Rosea'** is a pale lilac-pink and forms a neat mound about 6in (15cm) high; **'Royal Blue'** is early, free flowering, and taller, at about 12in (30cm).

M. sylvatica reaches about the same height and makes vigorous, branching growth. The deep blue flowers are larger than those in other species.

Cultivation

Forget-me-nots are usually easy to grow and they are not fussy about soil or location. They do best in well-drained but moisture-retentive soil in sun or semishade. Sow seeds directly in summer and overwinter plants in their desired locations, or buy young plants for bedding in spring. Discard the plants as soon as the flowers are past to avoid excessive self-seeding. If powdery mildew is a problem, use a fungicide.

Monarda didyma

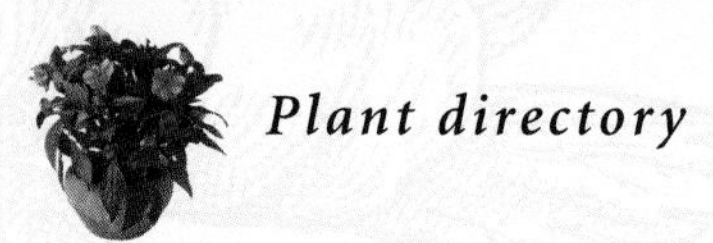

Narcissus Amaryllidaceae

Daffodil, narcissus ①②③

* *Bulb*
* *Spring flowers in a range of forms*
* *Hardy* *Zone 3 US, 4 Can*

Narcissus is probably the most popular of all spring bulbs, and hundreds of cultivars exist. These cover an enormous variety of sizes and flower forms in a color range of white, cream, yellow, pink, and orange.

The most familiar flower form is the trumpet daffodil, with six pointed, flat petals and a central trumpet at least as long as the petals. Among the rest of the 12 official divisions of the genus are large- and small-cupped varieties, which have a short central cup instead of a trumpet; double and semidouble varieties; and split-cupped types, which often have flat, orchidlike blooms.

There are also several divisions of dwarf narcissus, which are particularly attractive for small gardens and containers, where they can be appreciated at close quarters. ***Narcissus bulbocodium,*** the petticoat daffodil, grows to around 6in (15cm), with narrow, rushlike leaves. The 1in (2.5cm) long flower cup is cone shaped, with prominent curving stamens; the slender petals behind it are insignificant. Colors range from pale lemon to deep yellow.

The flowers appear in late winter and early spring, as do those of ***N. cyclamineus.*** This species has golden-yellow flowers with large trumpets around 2in (5cm) long and petals swept sharply back like those of a cylamen flower.

N. triandrus (angel's tears), with nodding, cream flowers that have cupped centers and reflexing petals, is very dainty; it grows to around 6in (15cm).

Among the named cultivars, **'February Gold'** (all yellow); **'February Silver'** (yellow trumpet and white petals); **'Tête-à-Tête'** (yellow with deeper trumpet, several flowers per stem); and **'Dove Wings'** (cream petals and pale yellow cups), all growing to about 12in (30cm) high, have a typical trumpet daffodil shape in miniature. **'Hawera'** is a ***triandrus*** type with pale yellow, nodding flowers, while **'Minnow'** (8in/20cm) has clusters of four rounded flowers per stem, with cream petals and a yellow cup.

'Pipit', a jonquil with several flowers on a stem, usually reaches 4–6in (10–15cm) and has small-cupped flowers, whose pale yellow cups and petal centers turn white as they age. The 6in (15cm) **'Rip van Winkle'** is entirely different, with starlike, shaggy double flowerheads of lemon yellow.

Cultivation

Virtually all divisions and sizes of narcissus make excellent container plants or can be grown in beds or naturalized in turf. Small varieties are excellent for rock gardens. They like fertile, well-drained, moisture-retentive soil and a spot in sun or partial shade.

Plant the bulbs in fall; in borders they may be left in place to flower for several years or they may be lifted annually and replanted. Plant to twice the depth of the bulb. Water container-grown plants regularly and feed all bulbs with a high-potash fertilizer once or twice after flowering and before the leaves die down.

Cut down faded flowers before they set seed. If possible, allow the foliage to die down naturally, until the leaves yellow, or about six weeks from the time the flowers begin to fade, in order to build up the bulbs for flowering the following year.

Increase plants by bulb offsets.

Narcissus fly larvae destroy the bulbs below ground; draw soil up around the necks of the growing bulbs in early summer to help prevent the fly from laying its eggs. Failure to flower may be caused by overcrowding and poor soil fertility, bulbs planted too shallowly, or leaves being prematurely removed the preceding year.

Narcissus 'Tête-à-Tête'

Nicotiana Solanaceae

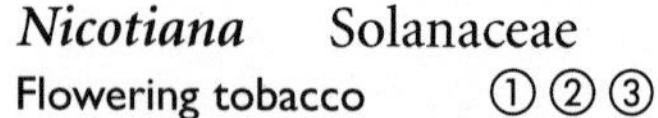

Flowering tobacco ①②③

* *Annuals or perennials usually grown as annuals*
* *Scented summer flowers*
* *Tender* *Zone 9 US*

Set flowering tobacco where the sweet fragrance can be appreciated in the evening, when it is most intense. Plants may be tall and stately, with white, trumpet-shaped flowers, or short and compact with flowers in a wide color range. Most are scented, but some of the more compact and colorful bedding varieties have lost much of their fragrance. Some species have flowers that open only in the evening, but modern hybrids have been bred to produce flowers that remain open all day long.

Among popular types are the **Domino Hybrids,** growing to around 12in (30cm) high, which are available in red, green, pink, salmon, purple, and white, with some bicolors; and the **Nicki Hybrids,** growing to 16in (40cm) with flowers in a similar color range. **Sensation Hybrids** are taller, at up to 3ft (1m). Particularly suitable for containers are the compact **Starship Hybrids** in burgundy, lime-green, pink, red, and white.

Cultivation

Full sun and reasonably fertile, well-drained soil are required. Deadhead plants to encourage a long flowering season. Raise plants from seed sown in spring.

Aphids can be a nuisance, particularly on young plants; spray with a nonpersistent insecticide where necessary.

Oenothera Onagraceae

Evening primrose, sundrops ②③

* *Annuals, biennials and perennials*
* *Summer flowers*
* *Hardy* *Zone 4 US, 5 Can except as noted*

The open, funnel-shaped, yellow, pink or white flowers of evening primrose are short-lived, but they are produced in profusion for a long period. They tend to open only in the late afternoon and evening. Leaves are mid-green and lance shaped. Oil from the seeds is used in pharmaceuticals.

Oenothera fruticosa glauca (***O. tetragona***) **'Fireworks'** forms a spreading clump some 16in (40cm) tall. Spikes of lightly fragrant, cup-shaped, glossy yellow flowers are carried from midsummer; buds and stems are tinged red.

O. macrocarpa (***O. missouriensis***) has goblet-shaped, lemon-yellow flowers, sometimes marked with red on the outside of the petals. The buds open in the evening, but the flowers last for several days; the seed pods are also decorative. Stems are lax and sprawling, and plants usually reach only 4in (10cm) tall. ***O. speciosa*** has white flowers which turn pink as they age; **'Pink Petticoats'** is pale pink with white and gold centers. The flowers are strongly scented, especially in the evening. The plant reaches 18in (45cm) and makes good ground cover, but it can be invasive. All three species are perennial. Zone 5 US, 6 Can.

Cultivation
Oenotheras demand light, well-drained soil and full sun. Do not let the roots dry out once the buds have started to form. Cut the stems down to soil level in fall.

Although perennial, the plants are often short-lived. Take softwood cuttings in early summer to guard against losses, divide plants in fall, or sow seed in spring.

Ophiopogon Liliaceae

Lilyturf, mondo grass ② ③

- *Evergreen perennial*
- *Showy foliage*
- *Hardy* *Zone 6 US, 7 Can*

Lilyturf is a grasslike plant with long, narrow, arching leaves. The white lilyturf is ***Ophiopogon jaburan;*** the variety **'Vittatus'** (also known as **'Variegatus'**) has green and white striped leaves but is rather tender. Small, round, white flowers are carried in short spikes. More popular is ***O. planiscapus*** **'Nigrescens'**, with deep purple, almost black foliage in arching clumps. Lilac and white flowers are followed by purple-black fruits. This plant makes a particularly effective contrast with gold- or silver-leafed plants.

Cultivation
Grow lilyturf in sun or light shade, in fertile, well-drained soil with plenty of organic matter. Choose a sheltered position; ***O. j.*** **'Vittatus'** particularly may be killed by cold winters, so move it under cover or mulch it for winter protection. Propagate plants by division in spring.

Osteospermum Asteraceae

Osteospermum ① ② ③

- *Evergreen perennial*
- *Showy, daisylike flowers in summer*
- *Tender* *Zone 10 US*

Osteospermum is related to and sometimes confused with *Dimorphotheca.* The plants grow to 12–24in (30–60cm) high, have

Osteospermum 'Whirligig'

lance-shaped, gray-green leaves and bear daisylike flowers in profusion in summer.

Many named plants have been raised. **'Buttermilk'** has creamy yellow flowers with purple-brown eyes; **'Cannington Roy'** has pink flowers on prostrate stems. **'Whirligig'** has petals that are crimped in the center and open out to a spoon shape at the tips; the flowers are white, tinged blue, with blue centers, and have a dazzling effect. **'Pink Whirls'** has lilac, spoon-shaped petals. **'Silver Sparkler'** has white and blue flowers and cream-variegated foliage.

O. jucundum (***Dimorphotheca barbersae***), with rosy pink flowers in summer, some of which have deeper colored eyes, forms neat clumps up to 12in (30cm) high.

Cultivation
Osteospermums require a mild climate and a sheltered, sunny location. Soil must be well drained; very fertile soils will promote leaf production at the expense of flowers.

Propagate plants by softwood cuttings in early summer, using nonflowering shoots.

Paeonia Paeoniaceae

Peony ③

- *Herbaceous perennial or deciduous shrub*
- *Large, fragrant early summer flowers*
- *Handsome foliage*
- *Hardy* *Zone 3 US, 3 Can except as noted*

Peonies produce some of the finest, most striking flowers of early summer. The blooms may be single, semi- or fully double. The Japanese type have the center of the flower filled with fluffy, stamenlike petaloids. Herbaceous varieties are most popular; their burgundy-red shoots are among the earliest border plants to put in an appearance in spring. Most cultivars grow to about 3ft (1m) and are derived from ***Paeonia lactiflora.***

The fully double, strongly scented **'Duchesse de Nemours'** is one of the oldest named varieties but still one of the best whites. **'Festiva Maxima'**, an heirloom cultivar 3ft (1m) tall, also remains among the best. Its fragrant, double white flowers are flecked with red and bloom early. The reliable **'Sarah Bernhardt'** has large, globe-shaped, double flowers of a clear silvery pink. **'Kelway's Glorious'** has huge, mounded, double white flowers, sometimes tinted pink or red, with a strong perfume. **'Bowl of Beauty'** is a favorite anemone-flowered type, with rich pink petals and creamy white petaloids.

Tree peonies are deciduous shrubs and include ***P. delavayi***, an upright plant to 6ft (2m), with deeply divided, rich green leaves and red, semidouble flowers with gold stamens, and varieties of ***P. suffruticosa.*** These usually grow to around 4ft (1.2m) and carry cup-shaped, single or semi-double flowers in late spring and early summer. They have a silky texture and are strongly fragrant. Zone 4 or 5 US, 5 or 6 Can.

Many Japanese and Chinese cultivars are listed, with suitably romantic names. **'Kao'** (king of flowers) has large, semidouble, crimson flowers with gold stamens; **'Gessekae'** (kingdom of the moon) has huge, white flowers with crimped petals; and **'Hana-kisoi'** (floral rivalry), cherry pink flowers and a strong scent. Chinese varieties include **'Da jen fen'** (gold dusted pink) and **'Fen dan bai'** (white phoenix).

'Souvenir de Maxime Cornu' is a large shrub, notable for its unusually colored, peachy yellow, fully double flowers, each ruffled petal margined with red.

Cultivation
Herbaceous peonies like fertile, well-drained but moisture-retentive soil, in sun or very light shade. Shade them from early morning sun, which may damage the flowers after a cold night. Because they start growing so early, a sheltered location helps to protect the new shoots. Tree peonies are more difficult to grow and need more protection.

Plant the top of herbaceous peony crowns no more than 2in (5cm) below the soil surface; plants will fail to flower if set too deeply. Do not disturb peonies once planted; they usually take a season or two to flower but when established are not demanding. Deadhead plants and cut down the foliage of herbaceous types in fall.

Paeonia suffruticosa

Parrotia persica

Parrotia Hamamelidaceae

Parrotia, iron tree, Persian ironwood ③

* *Deciduous tree*
* *Good fall colour*
* *Hardy* *Zone 5 US, 6 Can*

There is only one species of iron tree grown, *Parrotia persica.* While this can reach 25ft (8m) tall, in gardens it generally forms a spreading shrub or small tree. It has attractive flaking, gray bark, but it is for its brilliant red and gold fall leaves that it is chiefly grown.

Cultivation

Unlike most other members of the Hamamelidaceae family, iron tree tolerates alkaline soils well. It requires a fertile, well-drained but moisture-retentive soil and a location in full sun. Take softwood cuttings in summer.

Parthenocissus Vitacaeae

Virginia creeper, Boston ivy ②③

* *Deciduous climber*
* *Spectacular fall color*
* *Hardy*

A strong-growing, self-clinging climber, Virginia creeper attaches itself to its support with sticky-tipped tendrils. Some species are rampant growers that need to be checked.

The true Virginia creeper is *Parthenocissus quinquefolia.* The leaves consist of five (sometimes three) oval leaflets with toothed margins; midgreen in summer, they turn spectacular shades of red and orange in autumn. (Zone 3 US, 3 Can.)

The plant sometimes confused with Virginia creeper is *P. tricuspidata* (Boston ivy). This usually has entire, three-lobed leaves, although they may be divided into leaflets on young plants. It, too, has excellent fall color; the foliage of **'Veitchii'** becomes a deep purple. Zone 4 US, 5 Can.

One of the best-value species for smaller areas is *P. henryana,* or silver vein creeper. It is a vigorous grower, but not as rampant as other species. The three- or five-lobed leaves, are dark purplish green with silver veins, making them attractive in spring and summer, and when they turn red in fall. Zone 7 US, 8 Can.

Cultivation

Virginia creeper grows well against walls and fences or up trees, pillars, and pergolas in shade or semishade. Well-drained soil is required. *P. henryana* needs a sheltered location, but the attractive variegation tends to disappear in a sunny site. Provide support for young shoots until the plants get established and start to cling on their own. Prune plants in summer to keep their growth under control.

Parthenocissus can be propagated by softwood cuttings in early summer.

Passiflora Passifloraceae

Passionflower ②③

* *Evergreen or semievergreen climber*
* *Spectacular summer flowers*
* *Tender* *Zone 8 US, 9 Can except as noted*

Most of the passionflower family are tender climbers that need warm, frost-free conditions, although one species, *Passiflora caerulea,* (Zone 6 US, 7 Can) is unreliably hardy. It has mid- to dark green, lobed leaves on scrambling woody stems, which climb by means of tendrils. In summer, large, complex flowers appear, with white, petal-like sepals and a corona of slender filaments banded deep purple, white, and blue. The stamens and stigmas are prominent.

The plant derives its common name from the flowers, which some interpret as a symbol of Christ's Passion: the sepals represent the 10 apostles (minus Peter and Judas); the five anthers, the five wounds; the stigmas, the nails; and the corona, the crown of thorns. The leaves represent the hands of the persecutors, and the tendrils, the whips and scourges.

Passiflora caerulea

In warm, sunny conditions, egg-shaped yellow fruits follow the flowers; they are attractive but of no value for eating. The variety **'Constance Elliott'** has large, pure white flowers.

Cultivation

Plant passionflowers in well-drained but fertile and moisture-retentive soil and provide a trellis or similar support for the tendrils to twine around. Water regularly in spring and summer. In cold areas, provide winter protection for young plants; once established, *P. caerulea* is reasonably frost tolerant to Zone 6 US, 7 Can.

Prune out frost-damaged growth in spring. Thin out and tip back branches to keep plants tidy.

Propagate by means of semiripe cuttings in summer or from seed in spring.

Pelargonium Geraniaceae

Geranium ①②③

* *Evergreen perennial, often grown as an annual*
* *Colorful summer flowers*
* *Aromatic foliage*
* *Tender* *Zone 10 US*

Geraniums are among the most popular summer bedding plants, ideal for growing in containers. There are hundreds of cultivars, split into several groups: regals, or Martha Washington types, with oval, toothed, rough-textured leaves and relatively large, more or less trumpet-shaped flowers; zonals, the bedding geraniums, with leaves marked by a distinct dark band and uneven, five-petaled flowers; ivy-leaf, with flowers like those of zonals

***Pelargonium* 'Ringo Scarlet'**

but rather succulent leaves and trailing stems; and scented-leaf, with notably aromatic foliage in a diverse range of forms and colors.

Regal and scented-leaf geraniums are popular as houseplants and in summer gardens; zonals and ivy-leaf geraniums are often used for summer bedding and for containers.

Zonals generally grow to around 12–24in (30–60cm), though they can become taller; miniature varieties are under 12in (30cm). Flowers are carried in rounded heads on tall stems; they may be single, semidouble, or double, in many shades of white, red, pink, salmon, orange, and purple. Some varieties have flowers that fall readily (shatter) when the stems are knocked.

Reliable varieties include **'Apple Blossom Rosebud'**, with tightly packed, double, pink and white flowers; and **'Irene'**, deep crimson-pink, semi-double flowers. Plants that can be raised from seed include the **Elite Hybrids** and **Multibloom Hybrids**.

Ivy-leaf cultivars have less spectacular heads of flowers but are excellent trailing plants for baskets and containers. They are derived from ***Pelargonium peltatum***. **'Rouletta'** has semidouble, striking red and white flowers; **'L'Élégante'** has pale lilac flowers and midgreen foliage with creamy white margins that turn pink in cool conditions. The **Summer Showers Series** is one of the few ivy-leaf types that can be raised from seed.

Cultivation

Easy to grow in a wide range of conditions, but well-drained soil and an open, sunny location are preferred. Keep the plants moist at all times once the buds start to form but do not overwater. Feed every two weeks with a high-potash liquid fertilizer.

Deadhead regularly to ensure a succession of blooms. At the end of the season, plants may be discarded or overwintered in pots under cover. Cut them back hard in early spring and take cuttings from the new growths that arise. Sow seed of suitable varieties under cover in early spring.

Rust can be a troublesome fungus disease; pick off and burn affected leaves and spray plants with a suitable fungicide.

Penstemon Scrophulariaceae

Penstemon ②③

* *Semievergreen perennial*
* *Long season of summer flowers*
* *Slightly tender to hardy* *Zone 7 US, 8 Can*

The elegant spikes of penstemon flowers resemble those of foxgloves. The blooms are trumpet shaped, in shades of pink, red, purple, and white, sometimes with throats of a contrasting color; they are borne from midsummer to fall. Leaves are lanceolate, mid- to light green, and the plants are evergreen in suitable conditions. They usually grow to some 2ft (60cm) tall.

Many named varieties exist. **'Andenken an Friedrich Hahn'**, commonly known as **'Garnet'**, has wine-red flowers. **'Apple Blossom'** is very pale pink, with a deeper pink margin to the petals; **'Firebird'** has deep red flowers; and the similar **'Ruby'** has less intensely red flowers. **'Sour Grapes'** has flowers of a deep wine-purple.

Cultivation

A sunny location in moisture-retentive but well-drained soil suits penstemons. In cold areas, mulch the crowns in winter; plants tend to be short lived.

Cut down faded flower stems. Take softwood cuttings from nonflowering shoots in summer.

Petunia 'Pampas Blue'

Petunia Solanaceae

Petunia ①②③

* *Perennial grown as an annual*
* *Fragrant, showy summer flowers*
* *Half-hardy* *Zone 7 US, 8 Can*

Petunias have large, funnel-shaped flowers, usually strongly honey scented, which are carried on bushy or trailing plants all through the summer. They are excellent plants for containers, including hanging baskets. Leaves are oval, mid-green, and slightly sticky to the touch; stems are lax, growing 6–12in (15–30cm) tall. The flowers may be double or single, in shades of blue, pink, red, lavender, purple, yellow, and white, including bicolors. Star types have a bold white stripe down the center of each petal.

The large flowers of **Grandiflora** petunias are prone to weather damage; **Multifloras** have smaller but more weather-resistant blooms. Of the many varieties available, good grandiflora selections include the **Express Series**, including **'Express Star'**; the **Fluffy Ruffles Hybrids**, with huge ruffled flowers; and the **Daddy Series**, with heavily veined single flowers. **'Prism Sunshine'** is a nonfading yellow, with deep yellow centers and creamy yellow margins.

Multiflora types include the **Total Madness** and **Primetime Series**, and the relatively new milliflora **Fantasy Series**, which produces compact, free-flowering plants with small, neat flowers in a wide range of colors.

Cultivation

Petunias are best grown in reasonably sheltered, sunny locations where the flowers will not be damaged by wind. They prefer well-drained soil. Water regularly and liquid feed with a high-potash liquid fertilizer every 10–14 days. Deadhead plants frequently to prolong the flowering season.

Sow seed indoors in early spring or buy young bedding plants.

Petunias can be affected by various viral diseases, for which there is no cure; these are spread by aphids, so control aphid infestations promptly, using a non-persistent insecticide where necessary.

Philadelphus 'Belle Etoile'

Philadelphus Hydrangeaceae

Mock orange ③

* *Deciduous shrub*
* *Fragrant summer flowers*
* *Hardy* *Zone 3 US, 3 Can*

An easy-to-please plant, mock orange makes an arching shrub up to some 6ft (2m) tall. The leaves are ovate, fresh green and deeply veined and the white, usually four-petaled flowers have a central boss of golden stamens and are strongly scented. They are carried in early summer.

Philadelphus coronarius is a dense shrub with creamy white flowers. Smaller hybrids include **'Belle Etoile'**, with creamy white flowers stained red at the petal base; **'Buckley's Quill'**, a Canadian introduction which has double blooms with strap-like petals; and **'Galahad'**, single petals but very fragrant. The vigorous, prolific-flowering *P* × **virginalis** has semidouble or fully double blooms.

Cultivation
Mock orange like well-drained soil and full sun or partial shade.

Prune out some of the older branches to the base after flowering, retaining strong new shoots, which will start flowering the following year.

Increase plants by softwood cuttings in early summer or semiripe cuttings later in the season.

Aphids often infest the young shoots in spring; use a nonpersistent contact insecticide to control them.

Phormium Agavaceae

New Zealand flax ③

* *Evergreen perennial*
* *Striking, sword-shaped leaves*
* *Slightly tender* *Zone 9 US*

Phormiums are good "architectural" plants, with their bold clumps of sharply pointed, strap-shaped leaves. They are reasonably hardy but may be killed by prolonged cold spells. Their tall panicles of summer flowers are of secondary interest to the leaves.

The two species grown are *Phormium cookianum* and *P. tenax*; there are also several hybrids between these two species. *P. cookianum* is a smaller, more compact plant, growing to around 4ft (1.2m) with a spread of 1ft (30cm). *P. c.* **'Tricolor'** has midgreen leaves edged with cream and red.

P. tenax reaches 6–10ft (2–3m) and has stiff, leathery foliage, broader than that of *P. cookianum. P. t.* **'Purpureum'** has bronzy purple leaves. **'Bronze Baby'** is a dwarf hybrid with bronze foliage at the tips, while the leaves of **'Variegatum'** have a creamy-yellow margin.

There are several variegated **'Maori'** varieties, including **'Maori Sunrise'** which has pink leaves edged with bronze.**'Yellow Wave'** has slightly drooping leaves striped with green and yellow. **'Sundowner'** has upright bronzy-green leaves edged with cream to pink. Spikes of yellow flowers appear in summer.

Cultivation
Plant New Zealand flax in fertile, moisture-retentive but well-drained soil in a sunny, sheltered location. A covering of straw or some similar material will protect the crowns in winter in areas where they are marginally hardy.

Plants can be divided in spring.

Phyllitis Aspleniaceae

Hart's-tongue fern ②③

* *Evergreen or semievergreen fern*
* *Bright green fronds*
* *Grows well on alkaline soils*
* *Hardy* *Zone 4 US, 5 Can*

The hart's-tongue fern is *Phyllitis scolopendrium* (also known as *Asplenium scolopendrium*). The shiny, bright green fronds are entire and strap shaped, with undulating margins; the plant grows to about 40cm (16in). There are several types with more strongly waved, crisped, or frilled leaf margins, usually listed as **Crispum**, **Cristatum**, **Marginatum** and **Undulatum Groups**.

Cultivation
This fern grows well in a moisture-retentive alkaline soil that contains plenty of humus; compost can be added to light soils. Grow in a shady spot and keep the plants well watered through the growing season. Remove faded foliage regularly. Established plants can be divided in spring.

Picea Pinaceae

Spruce ②③

* *Evergreen conifer*
* *Attractive foliage and tree shapes*
* *Hardy* *Zone 2 US, 3 Can*

While many species of spruce make large trees, there are also several excellent dwarf and slow-growing cultivars, ranging from compact little buns to medium-sized shrubs. The branches are carried in whorls, with slender, needlelike leaves and pendulous cones.

Picea abies, the Norway spruce, has given rise to several good dwarf cultivars. **'Little Gem'**, which grows to about 18in (45cm) after many years, makes a small, dense, flat-topped globe suitable for a rock garden. **'Ohlendorffii'** is rounded when young, extending slightly to become more conical as it grows. Eventually it may reach about 5ft (1.5m). The spreading **'Pumila'** has branches in distinct layers, making a flat-topped bush no more than 2ft (60cm) tall but up to twice that in width.

P. glauca makes a neat, conical conifer with blue-green leaves; one of the most popular varieties is *P. g.* **'Conica'**, a dense, cone-shaped tree with small, soft needles of bright green. After many years' growth it may reach as tall as 6ft (2m). The variety **'Alberta Blue'** has silver-blue foliage, which is most intensely colored in late spring and early summer.

Cultivation
Spruces like moist, fertile, preferably acid soil; they do not thrive in strongly alkaline soils. Grow them in sun or partial shade in a sheltered location.

Picea glauca 'Conica'

Young shoots may be damaged by frost; prune out the dead portions, retaining the plant's shape as far as possible, and provide protection or move the plant to a more sheltered position.

In hot, dry conditions, red spider mite can be troublesome. Spray plants regularly with plain water to increase humidity and use a suitable miticide when necessary.

Pieris Ericaceae

Pieris, lily-of-the-valley bush ②③

- *Evergreen shrub*
- *Colorful young foliage and late spring flowers*
- *Hardy or slightly tender* *Zone 5 US, 6 Can*

Like most of the Ericaceae, pieris requires acid soil; in limestone areas, it can be grown successfully in a tub filled with acid soil mix. The plants are very striking, making more or less rounded, compact shrubs with lanceolate or oblong leaves that are often brightly colored when they are young. Panicles of waxy, white, bell-shaped flowers may be produced in profusion in late spring and early summer.

Pieris **'Bert Chandler'** has leaves which develop from bright salmon pink through cream and white to dark green as the season progresses; the best colors are produced on plants in an open, sunny location. This variety is grown solely for its foliage, as flowers are rarely produced. It is a compact plant, growing to about 5ft (1.5m).

The popular *P. floribunda* **'Mountain Fire'** is larger, reaching 10ft (3m) or more, which makes it less suitable for small spaces. The foliage colors are similar to those of **'Bert Chandler'**, but **'Mountain Fire'** does have the advantage of bearing large, spreading sprays of flowers.

P. formosa has also produced some good garden cultivars, but again most of these are tall and vigorous.

Varieties of *P. japonica* are a better bet; these make dense, rounded, medium-sized shrubs with young leaves of a coppery shade that turn glossy green. **'Coleman'** has flowers that are red in bud, opening pale pink; **'Debutante'** is a low-growing, compact form with white flowers in upright panicles; **'Grayswood'** has spreading, drooping panicles of numerous small, white flowers on a small, compact shrub.

'Little Heath' is a dwarf variety with small, glossy leaves variegated silver and flushed pink when young; **'Little Heath Green'** is similar, but without the variegation.

Cultivation

Give pieris the same treatment as rhododendrons. They like rich, acid, moisture-retentive soil, preferably with added peat, and a sheltered location in light shade. Do not allow the roots to dry out during the summer.

Deadhead the plants when the flowers fade and prune back frost-damaged young shoots in early spring. Take semiripe cuttings in summer.

Pinus Pinaceae

Pine ②③

- *Evergreen conifer*
- *Attractive foliage and tree forms*
- *Hardy* *Zone 2 US, 2 Can*

The pines range from dwarf, rock garden forms to tall trees, and often make attractive weatherbeaten shapes. The needlelike leaves are carried in bundles of two, three, or five.

Pinus mugo, the mountain pine, has given rise to several dwarf varieties: **'Gnom'** grows slowly to 6ft (2m), forming a dense, deep green globe; **'Mops'** is a similar shape but not so tall, at around 3ft (1m); **'Compacta'** that forms a very dense globe to 4ft (1.2m) tall; **'Alan'** is dense-growing to 1ft (30cm) high, with short, rich green needles; and **'Valley Cushion'**, with very short needles, has a low spreading habit, reaching only 10–12in (25–30cm) high.

There are also some good dwarf forms of the Scots pine, *P. sylvestris*. **'Beuvronensis'** forms a domed shrub up to 3ft (1m); **'Watereri'** is larger, growing slowly to 6ft (2m) or more, although it remains small and compact for several years.

Cultivation

Pines generally grow well in light, rather poor soils. Acid soil is preferred, but some species tolerate alkaline. Choose an open, sunny location.

Propagation is not practical for the small-space gardener.

Pinus mugo **'Mops'**

Potentilla fruticosa **'Elizabeth'**

Potentilla Rosaceae

Cinquefoil, potentilla ②③

- *Herbaceous perennial or deciduous shrub*
- *Summer flowers in a range of colors*
- *Hardy* *Zone 2 US, 2 Can*

Potentillas have foliage and flowers rather similar to those of strawberry plants. The palmate leaves are covered with silvery hairs, and the flowers are open and cup shaped, with conspicuous stamens.

The herbaceous perennial types grown in gardens are usually hybrids derived mainly from *Potentilla atrosanguinea*. **'Gibson's Scarlet'** has bright red flowers; **'Gloire de Nancy'** has large, semidouble, orange-red flowers; and **'William Rollison'**, semidouble, orange flowers with yellow centers. They all grow to 12–18in (30–45cm) high and flower from early or midsummer onwards.

Shrubby potentillas have deeply cut leaves and grow to around 4ft (1.2m), depending on the cultivar. Most are varieties of *P. fruticosa*, which has bright yellow flowers like buttercups, but new varieties have flowers in a much wider range of colors, including red, pink, orange, and white; however, these shades tend to fade in hot sunlight.

'Goldstar' has large, yellow flowers; **'Princess'** has pale pink flowers that fade to white in hot, dry weather. The flowers of **'Red Robin'** are an intense, deep red, and **'Snowbird'** has semidouble white blooms.

Cultivation

Potentillas need light, well-drained soil and an open, sunny location or partial shade.

The branches of shrubby species can be pruned back by one-third in spring to keep them compact.

Perennials can be divided in spring or fall, and shrubs can be increased from softwood cuttings in early summer.

Primula Primulaceae

Primrose, primula ①②③

* *Herbaceous perennial*
* *Showy flowers in spring and summer*
* *Hardy* *Zone 4 US, 5 Can*

The *Primula* family is wide and diverse, with plants suitable for many locations. Most are easy to grow and are suitable for containers, rock gardens, raised beds, and borders. Some like the damp soil beside water features.

Primula auricula has rosettes of pale gray-green leaves that are often covered with a white meal (known as farina). The flat-faced, often strikingly colored flowers are carried in umbels on 9in (23cm) stems in spring; they have a sweet, honey scent. Some of the most spectacular are the so-called show auriculas, with flowers that have a brilliant white center and petals of various colors with green, white, or gray edges. These are good for containers and are mostly grown indoors, where the flowers can be admired at close quarters. Other auriculas are less fussy and grow well in rock gardens or containers in the open.

The drumstick primrose, ***P. denticulata***, has globular heads of flowers on 12in (30cm) stems, in shades of rose, pink, lilac, and mauve. ***P. pulverulenta***, known as the candelabra primula because of the way its whorls of flowers are carried in tiers on the stems, grows to 2ft (60cm) and has flowers in shades of pink, red, or orange-red. ***P. japonica*** also bears tiers of flowers in pinks, cerise, and crimson. The flowers of ***P. vialii***, carried in erect spikes, open from the bottom of the spike and are pale lilac, while the buds are red.

Among the most familiar primulas is the English primrose, ***P. vulgaris***, whose short-stalked, pale yellow flowers, nestling in their rosettes of crinkled leaves, are one of the first signs of spring. The cowslip, ***P. veris***, has taller, 8in (20cm), stems topped with clusters of tubular, yellow, fragrant flowers. Crossbreeding between these two species has given rise to the polyanthus primroses, with large, primrose-type flowers carried in clusters on stout stems. There are many named selections of seed-raised polyanthus available, also primrose varieties with large, colorful flowers similar to polyanthus but carried singly on the stems; both types are valuable for bedding and for containers. Flowers are available in red, yellow, white, purple, orange, and pink, usually with a pronounced yellow eye.

Among good hybrid primula strains are the **Pacific Giant Hybrids** in assorted colors and **Wanda Hybrids** with early flowers in mixed colors, with a small, or no, eye.

Cultivation

Primulas like fertile, moisture-retentive soil and an open, sunny, or lightly shaded location. Plants can be divided after flowering or raised from seed.

Aphids may be troublesome and should be treated with a nonpersistent insecticide where necessary. Plants are subject to various viral diseases that cause stunting and distortion of growth; there is no treatment, and affected plants must be destroyed. Controlling aphids will help to prevent the spread of viruses.

Prunus Rosaceae

Flowering cherry, cherry laurel ③

* *Deciduous or evergreen shrub or tree*
* *Spring blossom or handsome foliage*
* *Hardy* *Zone 6 US, 7 Can except as noted*

The *Prunus* family is large and includes plums, peaches, almonds, apricots, and laurel, as well as cherry—but it is perhaps the flowering cherry that is most widely grown and admired. The size of the plants varies from medium shrubs to large trees; the foliage of deciduous types is generally lanceolate and light green, sometimes coloring attractively in fall.

Among the flowering cherries are **'Amanogawa'**, a narrow, columnar tree with bronzy leaves and soft pink flowers, growing up to 22ft (7m); and **'Hally Jolivette'**, with double, blush-white flowers, that blooms very young and grows to 15ft (4.5m). **'Shôgetsu'**, with arching branches densely covered in spring with semidouble pale pink flowers, also reaches 15ft (4.5m).

'Spire' (***P. × hillieri*** **'Spire'**), a narrow, vase-shaped tree, grows to 26ft (8m), with pale pink flowers and attractive fall color; and ***P. subhirtella*** **'Autumnalis'**, a winter-flowering cherry, with semidouble, pale pink flowers sporadically throughout the winter months, reaches 22ft (7m) or so.

The evergreen ***P. laurocerasus*** (cherry laurel) is a bushy shrub to 15ft (4.5m); it has glossy, oblong leaves and long racemes of small white flowers followed by cherry-like fruits ripening to black. **'Otto Luyken'** is a low-growing, compact form to around 3ft (1m) high, but spreading more widely; it has upright spikes of flowers in spring. Zone 7 US, 7 Can.

P. lusitanica (Portugal laurel) is similar to ***P. laurocerasus*** but it is hardier and easier to grow in poor soils.

Cultivation

These plants prefer an open, sunny location in well-drained, reasonably fertile soil; ***P. laurocerasus*** and ***P. lusitanica*** are both shade tolerant.

Evergreens can be pruned hard in spring to keep them compact and shapely. Flowering cherries do not normally require any pruning. Evergreens can be increased by semiripe cuttings in summer; flowering cherries are usually grafted, and it is not practical for the small-scale gardener to try to propagate them.

Caterpillars and aphids can be a problem on young growth and should be treated with a suitable insecticide. Flowering cherries are sometimes attacked by the bacterial disease fireblight; affected branches should be cut out and destroyed.

Pyracantha Rosaceae

Firethorn ③

* *Evergreen shrub*
* *Summer flowers and fall and winter berries*
* *Hardy* *Zone 5 US, 6 Can*

Firethorns are among the most valued garden shrubs, having such a long and varied season of interest. In early summer, small, creamy white flowers with prominent stamens are clustered thickly on the spiny branches among fresh green, oblong leaves. These are followed by long-lasting clusters of red, orange, or yellow berries.

Firethorn can be grown as a free-standing shrub, when it may reach 10ft (3m) or so, although its prickly growth is generally too vigorous for small spaces. It is easier to keep under control when trained as a wall shrub, and this is the way it is most often grown.

Pyracantha **'Mohave'**

Pyracantha angustifolia has narrow, oblong leaves, which are dark green above and felted gray beneath; the berries are bright orange-yellow and last well into the winter. **'Apache'**, semievergreen, with a compact habit, grows to about 5ft (1.5m) and produces brigt red fruit about ⅓in (9mm) across.

The berries of **'Navajo'** are later than some others to ripen; they are carried in dense clusters, are slightly flattened, and turn from orange to deep orange-red.

'Rutgers' is a hardier shrub with a spreading habit; it reaches 3ft (1m) tall and 9ft (2.7m) across. It has abundant orange-red fruits.

Cultivation

Firethorn will grow in most reasonably fertile, well-drained soils, in sun or partial shade. Keep the soil moist at flowering time to encourage the berries to set.

Provide a trellis or similar support for wall shrubs and train in young shoots as they grow.

Prune back wall-trained shrubs after flowering, cutting outward-growing shoots right back to the main stem; free-standing plants can also be clipped at this time.

The plants can be propagated from semiripe cuttings in summer.

Firethorns are prone to several diseases, including fireblight and scab. Scab attacks in wet summers and can be treated with a suitable fungicide; fireblight cannot be chemically controlled and affected branches must be pruned out and destroyed.

Some varieties, such as **'Lalandei'**, are particularly susceptible to disease; more modern varieties are claimed to be disease resistant, but opinion is often divided as to how resistant they really are.

Pyrus Rosaceae

Ornamental pear ③

- *Deciduous tree*
- *Attractive foliage and tree shape*
- *Hardy Zone 4 US, 5 Can*

The most widely grown ornamental pear is ***Pyrus calleryana***, which is often grown as a street tree; it reaches a height of 30ft (9m), so it is mostly too large for small-space gardening. It forms a broadly conical shape and has small white flowers in mid- to late spring. Leaves may turn red in fall. **'White House'** makes a slender column.

Especially ornamental is ***Pyrus salicifolia***, the willow-leafed pear, with silver, lance-shaped leaves and creamy white flowers in spring. The graceful weeping variety **'Pendula'** grows to about 6m (20ft), but is suitable for small spaces for many years.

Cultivation

Pears do best in well-drained, fertile soil, in sun or light shade. Prune to shape in fall. Propagation is not practical for small-space gardeners.

Ornamental pears, like edible pears, may be affected by scab and fireblight.

Rhododendron Ericaceae

Azalea, rhododendron ②③

- *Evergreen or deciduous shrub*
- *Colorful spring and early summer flowers*
- *Needs acid soil*
- *Hardy*

The *Rhododendron* genus is vast, containing hundreds of species, to which can be added many more hundreds of varieties and cultivars, all of whose hardiness differs. Check with your local nursery so that you plant only those suitable for your area.

Some rhododendrons make towering shrubs with huge leaves, while others are dwarf, alpine plants. In between, there is a good range of small to medium-sized shrubs suitable for containers and small growing areas.

Rhododendrons have funnel-shaped flowers in a wide range of colors, including white, cream, pink, violet, lilac, salmon, yellow, orange, and red. The flowers often have prominent stamens and may be sweetly scented. The leaves are usually dark green, lance shaped, sometimes leathery, and frequently hairy.

There are many hybrids ideal for small-space growing, among them **'Blue Diamond'**, lavender-blue, funnel-shaped flowers, slow growing to 3ft (1m); **'Curlew'**, open, pale yellow flowers, proportionately large, on a dwarf bush 1ft (30cm) high; **'Elizabeth Lockhart'**, deep rosy red, bell-shaped flowers and bronze leaves, 2ft (60cm); and **'Ptarmigan'**, pure white, funnel-shaped flowers on a spreading 1ft (30cm) shrub. All these are evergreen.

Rhododendron yakushimanum has given rise to a large number of varieties known as **Yakushimanum Hybrids**; all are compact shrubs with usually bell-shaped flowers in a wide color range. Zone 5 US, 6 Can.

Azaleas are often regarded as a different group. They are small shrubs with proportionately smaller leaves and flowers and may be deciduous or evergreen. They tend to be very free flowering and are most suitable for containers and small spaces.

Deciduous azaleas growing to 5ft (1.5m) or under include **'Homebush'**, semidouble, rosy purple shaded pink; **'Narcissiflora'**, pale yellow, semidouble, scented flowers; and **'Strawberry Ice'**, pale pink with deeper pink petal tips and yellow throats; and the **Northern Lights** series from Minnesota. Many deciduous azaleas also have good fall foliage color.

Among the evergreen azaleas are the beautiful, compact, small-flowered **Kurume** azaleas from Japan, such as **'Azuma-kagami'**, deep pink hose-in-hose flowers, 4ft (1.2m); **'Hershey's Red'**, plentiful bright red flowers 4ft (1.2m); **'Hinode-giri'**, bright crimson, 5ft (1.5m); **'Hino-crimson'**, deep red, and **'Surprise'**, pale orange-red, both 5ft (1.5m). Several other types are also suitable.

Cultivation

Rhododendrons need acid soil, that is moisture retentive but well-drained, and rich in organic matter. They grow well in light shade in a sheltered location, where they will not be exposed to cold, drying winds.

Dryness at the roots will cause flower buds to fall, so keep the soil just moist, and feed container-grown plants regularly, preferably with fertilizers specifically for acid-loving plants. Deadhead after flowering. Cut back straggly plants in spring.

Plants can be increased by layering or cuttings, but they are not easy to propagate.

Mottled yellow foliage is often caused by nutrient deficiency, which may be due to lime in the soil; feed affected plants with chelated iron.

Rhodendron **'Blue Diamond'**

Robinia Leguminosae

False acacia ③

* *Deciduous tree or shrub*
* *Attractive foliage and flowers*
* *Hardy*

False acacias have attractive, pinnate leaves composed of pairs of light to dark green leaflets, usually on spiny stems. Racemes of pealike flowers are carried in early summer.

The rose acacia, ***Robinia hispida***, produces brittle, bristly, suckering stems, which can be trained successfully against a wall, and will grow to 6ft (2m) or more. The pinnate leaves are midgreen, and racemes of rosy pink flowers are carried in late spring. Zone 4 US, 5 Can.

The most commonly planted form is ***Robinia pseudoacacia* 'Frisia'**, with its golden yellow foliage, which gradually turns more green during summer. Flowers are creamy white and fragrant. This variety makes a graceful tree, which can be grown successfully as a shrub if it is cut back hard (stooled) annually. A less common variety is **'Pyramidalis'** (**'Fastigiata'**), a narrow, columnar tree with spineless branches. Zone 3 US, 4 Can.

Also useful for small spaces is ***R.* × *slavinii* 'Hillieri'**, which makes a small, round-headed tree with attractive ferny foliage and lilac-pink flowers. Zone 4 US, 5 Can.

Cultivation

False acacia require a light, well-drained soil and are particularly suitable for dry areas. They prefer a sunny, reasonably sheltered location.

To grow ***R. pseudoacacia*** as a shrub, cut the branches back almost to the base in spring. Tie in the shoots of wall-trained shrubs to their supports in the growing season. Separate any suckers from parent plants during the dormant season and replant them.

Rosa Rosaceae

Rose ①②③

* *Deciduous shrub or climber*
* *Colorful, often fragrant summer flowers*
* *Hardy*

Among the most popular garden plants, roses have been cultivated for many hundreds of years. They are divided into a number of main groups.

Old roses (Old-fashioned roses) include groups such as Alba, Bourbon, China, Damask, Gallica, and Moss roses. They tend to have large, double blooms with a strong fragrance. Most flower only once in a season. They usually make fairly large, open shrubs.

Modern roses include modern shrubs, Large-flowered bush (Hybrid Tea), Cluster-flowered bush (Floribunda), ground cover, climbing, and rambling roses. Most have been bred to give a long season of bloom.

Species roses often have simple, single flowers and include wild species and natural and cultivated species hybrids.

Old roses have been enjoying a revival in popularity for some years, but most are not really suitable for small spaces. Their growth tends to be lax and spreading, and their brief flowering season does not give good value. But ***Rosa gallica* 'Versicolor'** (Rosa Mundi) is a neat-growing shrub to around 4ft (1.2m) and has striking crimson and white striped flowers; it is known to have been cultivated for at least 400 years. Zone 3 US, 4 Can.

Some old roses, such as China, Bourbon and Hybrid Perpetuals do have the ability to repeat flower. **'Irène Watts'** has peach-pink flowers on neat 2ft (60cm) bushes; **'Comte de Chambord'** has rich pink, full, quartered flowers and grows to 4ft (1.2m); **'Reine des Violettes'** is an almost thornless 4ft (1.2m) plant, with flat, full-petaled flowers in purple, red, and lilac. All Zone 5 US, 6 Can.

Modern shrub roses, including English, or David Austin, roses, are often more suitable for small areas. Some of them combine the best attributes of old roses with more compact growth, disease resistance and repeat flowering. These include **'Mary Rose'**, with rose-pink, loose-petaled flowers, 4ft (1.2m); **'Cottage Rose'**, cupped blooms in deep pink, 3ft (1m); **'The Countryman'**, clear pink, rosette-shaped blooms, 3ft (1m); and **'Fair Bianca'**, pure white, 3ft (1m). Zone 4 US, 5 Can.

Patio and **Miniature roses** are perhaps the most suitable for small-space growing. Patio (dwarf cluster-flowered) roses grow to 18–24in (45–60cm), while miniatures are below 15in (37cm). Both are ideal for containers. Patio rose varieties include **'Anna Ford'**, orange-red; **'Corn Silk'**, yellow; **'Cider Cup'**, deep apricot; **'June Laver'**, deep gold; and **'Hot Tamale'**, orange tinted with gold. Among the miniatures, ideal for window boxes, are **'Jennifer'**, shell-pink; **'Snow Bride'**, ivory white; **'Julie Ann'**, orange-red; and **'Yellow Doll'**, soft yellow. All Zone 4 US, 5 Can.

***Rosa gallica* 'Versicolor'**

Climbers and **Ramblers** are perfect for growing up walls and pillars and over pergolas and arches. Among those making reasonably restrained growth are **'Breath of Life'**, apricot pink; **'Golden Showers'**, freely produced, semidouble, creamy yellow flowers; **'New Dawn'**, silver-pink, fragrant flowers; and **'Zéphirine Drouhin'**, carmine-pink, freely produced, fragrant flowers on almost thornless stems. Hardiness varies.

Cultivation

Roses like a sunny location in fertile, well-drained but moisture-retentive soil. Water the plants well during dry spells and feed with a rose fertilizer.

Prune in spring, just as the buds are starting into growth. Remove all dead or dying stems. Then prune modern bush roses back by two-thirds, or slightly more, of the previous year's growth, cutting to an outward-facing bud. Prune old roses, climbers, and ramblers more lightly.

Old roses can be grown from semiripe and hardwood cuttings, but modern roses are budded on to rootstocks, and plants from cuttings tend to be less robust.

Pests and diseases that attack roses include black spot, rust, mildew, aphids, and caterpillars. Use combined insecticides and fungicides where necessary; otherwise use fungicides as a preventive spray and nonpersistent, contact insecticides only where pest damage is apparent.

Rosmarinus Labiatae

Rosemary ②③

* *Evergreen shrub*
* *Aromatic foliage and summer flowers*
* *Culinary herb*
* *Hardy* *Zone 6 US, 7 Can*

One of the most useful and attractive herbs, rosemary is just as valuable as a decorative plant as it is for the kitchen. The slender, needlelike leaves are dark green on the upper side and silver beneath and give off a strong scent when bruised. Pale to mid-blue, hooded flowers appear towards the tips of the branches in summer.

Rosmarinus officinalis (common rosemary) is a dense, bushy shrub to about 5ft (1.5m); **'Miss Jessopp's Upright'** has a more erect habit and forms a good hedge. **'Prostratus'** makes dense mats of foliage

Rosmarinus officinalis

sprinkled with blue summer flowers and needs a warm, sunny location; it is a good plant for a rock garden or the top of a stone wall in a sheltered garden. **'Severn Sea'** is a dwarf variety, with arching branches up to about 3ft (1m), and has intense blue flowers.

Cultivation
Rosemary is marginally hardy, but does best in a reasonably sheltered, sunny location; it is not suitable for very cold, exposed gardens. Well-drained, light soil is necessary; in containers, use fertile potting mix with a little sharp sand. Water when conditions are very dry but make sure the soil is never waterlogged.

Prune back hard in spring when plants become straggly and ungainly. Propagate from semiripe cuttings in summer.

Salix Salicaceae

Willow ③

* *Deciduous tree*
* *Attractive foliage and tree shape*
* *Hardy* *Zone 4 US, 5 Can except as noted*

Willows are plants to be wary of in small spaces; many species are fast-growing, large trees that quickly become an embarrassment. They are thirsty plants that take large quantities of water from the soil and can cause problems with drainage and the subsidence of buildings on certain soils. Fortunately there are several types that do not pose a problem for small-space gardens.

Leaves are usually lance shaped and silvery gray, or oval and deep green. Male and female plants are separate; the males generally bear more striking catkins (pussy willow) in late winter and early spring.

Salix alba is a large, fast-growing, spreading tree unsuitable for all but the largest gardens, but ***S. a. vitellina*** and ***S. a.* 'Britzensis'** (**'Chermesina'**) are different. When cut back hard (stooled), you can enjoy their shining, colored winter stems—bright red for **'Britzensis'** and orange yellow for ***S. a. vitellina***.

For a miniature weeping willow, plant ***S. caprea* 'Pendula Weeping Sally'**, a small tree growing to some 6ft (2m), with drooping branches bearing attractive catkins in late winter.

***S. matsudana* 'Tortuosa'** is a curiosity, with its twisted, spiraling branches making a good winter feature, although for small spaces ***Corylus avellana* 'Contorta'** (Harry Lauder's walking stick) gives much the same effect and is easier to keep under control and within bounds.

Cultivation
Willows like moisture-retentive soil and location in full sun. Plants grown for their colored winter stems should be cut back hard to within about 2in (5cm) of the base in early spring every other year, or remove a third of the older stems annually.

Propagate by semiripe cuttings in summer or hardwood cuttings in winter; most are easy to root.

Anthracnose can be a serious disease; it causes reddish spotting, early fall of leaves, and die-back of shoot tips. Regular fungicide sprays from early spring to summer may help to prevent it.

Salvia Labiatae

Sage, salvia ①②③

* *Annuals, perennials, and semievergreen or evergreen shrubs*
* *Attractive flowers; often aromatic foliage*
* *Culinary herb*
* *Hardy or tender* *Zone 8 US, 9 Can except as noted*

Salvias have the square stems and hooded flowers that are typical of Labiatae, but they are otherwise very varied and versatile plants. They may be grown for their flowers, colorful bracts, or ornamental or fragrant foliage.

Salvia farinacea is a perennial usually grown as an annual. It has lance-shaped leaves and 18in (45cm) erect spikes of summer flowers. **'Victoria'** is an intense violet-blue shade, with dark purple stems.

S. viridis (***S. horminum***), clary, is an annual up to 18in (45cm). The leaves are oval, and veined blue, white, or pink bracts toward the top of the stems make a colorful show in summer and are good for cutting.

There are several attractive, tender perennial salvias that deserve a sheltered spot. They include ***S. patens***, with whorls of deep or pale blue hooded flowers, and ***S. microphylla*** (***S. grahamii***) with bright crimson flowers.

S. splendens, a perennial treated as annual, is a well-known bedding plant, with neat mounds of oval, toothed leaves. It produces large spikes of hooded, usually scarlet, flowers, around 12in (30cm) tall, all through the summer. **'Blaze of Fire'** is a popular red variety; salmon, purple, white, and lavender flowers are also available in mixtures such as **Phoenix Hybrids** or as separate colors in the **Sizzler Series**.

Culinary sage (***S. officinalis***), with its strongly aromatic, oval, wrinkled, and slightly furry leaves, is a useful plant for a herb garden, but there are several ornamental varieties, too. **'Purpurescens'** has purple young foliage that turns purple-green as it matures; the irregularly margined leaves of **'Icterina'** are midgreen and splashed with pale green and yellow. Zone 5 US, 6 Can.

Cultivation
Sage likes a sunny location in moderately fertile, well-drained soil. Plant out tender types after all risk of frost is past. Tender perennials need a sheltered location or winter protection.

Take cuttings and overwinter them under cover to guard against winter losses.

Plants can be raised from seed sown in spring or from softwood cuttings in early summer. Perennials can be divided in fall or spring.

***Salvia farinacea* 'Victoria'**

Sambucus Caprifoliaceae
Elder ②③

* *Deciduous shrubs or trees*
* *Decorative foliage, flowers and fruits*
* *Hardy* *Zone 3 US, 3 Can*

Sambucus canadensis (American elder) grows to around 12ft (4m) and has slightly domed heads of creamy flowers. ***S. c.*** **'Aurea'** has golden foliage and red berries.

The flattened heads of white flowers carried by the European elder (***Sambucus nigra***) in early summer have a refreshing, sweet scent; both they and the round black berries that follow can be used to make jelly and wine. Leaves are composed of five to seven leaflets and may be attractively colored. There is also a golden-leaved form of this elder, ***S. nigra*** **'Aurea'**, which is more vigorous and can reach 15ft (5m), although it is usually smaller. ***S. n.*** **'Guincho Purple'** has purplish green to purple-black leaves and pink flowers opening to white.

The red-berried elder, ***S. racemosa***, grows to 10ft (3m). ***S. r.*** **'Plumosa Aurea'** has yellow leaflets with finely cut and serrated margins. The ferny, finely divided leaves of ***S. r.*** **'Tenuifolia'** give it a strong similarity to a cut-leafed Japanese maple. ***S. nigra laciniata*** also has finely divided foliage.

Cultivation
Elders are easy to grow, preferring an open location in moisture-retentive, fertile soil but tolerating poor soils well.

Plants can be cut back hard each winter if they are being grown for their decorative foliage; this encourages the formation of strong young shoots. If flowers and fruits are required, cut young shoots back by half in winter and remove older branches entirely. Propagate plants by softwood cuttings in summer or hardwood cuttings in winter.

Aphids often attack the tips of the shoots; where necessary, spray with a non-persistent contact insecticide. Do not use insecticide when the flowers are open.

Saxifraga Saxifragaceae
Saxifrage ①②③

* *Evergreen perennial*
* *Attractive leaves and spring flowers*
* *Alpine and rock garden plants*
* *Hardy* *Zone 5 US, 6 Can*

This extensive genus of low-growing plants includes many suitable subjects for small spaces and containers. Plants are very varied, although they usually have attractive silvery rosetted or mossy foliage and open, five-petaled flowers in white or pink.

Saxifraga longifolia 'Tumbling Waters'

Saxifraga cochlearis has rosettes of oblong, silver leaves with white encrustations on the leaf margins. Loose sprays of white, yellow-centered blooms on dainty, dark stems 8in (20cm) high are produced in early summer. ***S.*** **'Elizabethae'** is sometimes listed as **'Carmen'**; it forms a cushion only 1in (2.5cm) high, with rosettes of spiny leaves. In spring the foliage is almost hidden by pale primrose, saucer-shaped flowers. The foliage mats of ***S.*** × ***irvingii*** **'Jenkinsiae'** are a little larger and silvery green; this plant carries soft lilac-pink flowers in spring.

S. longifolia **'Tumbling Waters'** is among the showiest saxifrages when flowering. The white-encrusted foliage forms gray rosettes, from which arise long, arching panicles densely packed with small white flowers—very effective cascading over rocks or walls. The rosette dies after flowering but is replaced by offsets.

Cultivation
Hardiness can vary greatly. Generally the mossy-foliaged saxifrages like moisture-retentive but well-drained soil and a partially shaded location; the silver-rosetted types like full sun and can withstand dryer conditions. Those with encrusted leaves like some lime in the soil. All saxifrages are good for planting in rock gardens and troughs.

Mulch the necks of the plants with stone chips to facilitate water run-off.

Plants can be divided after flowering. If the small rosettes do not yet possess their own roots, insert them in pots of sandy soil mix, which should be kept only just moist until roots have formed.

Scaevola Goodeniaceae
Scaevola, fan flower ①②③

* *Perennial grown as an annual*
* *Fan-shaped summer flowers*
* *Trailer*
* *Tender* *Zone 10 US*

This plant has become increasingly popular as a trailer for the edges of containers and for hanging baskets. The lopsided and fan-shaped flowers, carried in profusion on lax stems, are usually purple-blue. Most plants available are varieties of ***Scaevola aemula***; **'Blue Fan'** and **'Blue Wonder'** are the ones usually offered. **'Saphira'** is a fairly new, very floriferous, compact variety in deep purple-blue; **'White Charm'** has yellow-eyed white flowers.

Cultivation
Plant in moisture-retentive but well-drained soil. Once flowering starts, feed every 10–14 days with a high-potash liquid fertilizer. Softwood cuttings can be taken in early summer.

Scilla Hyacinthaceae

Squill ①②③

* *Bulb*
* *Early spring flowers*
* *Hardy* *Zone 3 US, 4 Can*

These generally dwarf bulbs are easy to grow in containers, beds, and rock gardens. They have glossy, strap-shaped leaves and nodding, or starry, usually blue flowers.

Scilla bifolia produces one pair of leaves per bulb, which appear before the flowers in early spring. The 6in (15cm) flower spike carries a dozen or more light blue, pink, or white flowers. A more intense, rich blue are the flowers of *S. siberica* **'Spring Beauty'**, the Siberian squill. These nodding, bell-shaped flowers are carried in groups of two to four on 6in (15cm) stems; several flower stems may be produced per bulb. The wide, strap-shaped leaves are glossy green and are produced before the flowers.

Cultivation

Plant the bulbs to twice their depth in well-drained but moisture-retentive soil in fall. They will grow in full sun or partial shade.

Offsets are sometimes produced and can be lifted and separated from the parent bulbs as the foliage dies down.

Sedum Crassulaceae

Stonecrop, sedum ①②③

* *Evergreen or semievergreen perennial*
* *Attractive foliage and flowers*
* *Hardy* *Zone 4 US, 4 Can except as noted*

Stonecrops are succulent plants, well adapted to dry conditions. Some species can be grown on walls or in rock gardens, others as border plants; all those described will do well in containers.

Sedum acre (wallpepper) is a spreading, mat-forming plant that grows well on bare rocks and walls. The fleshy leaves are tiny, and the shoots are densely covered in brilliant yellow flowers in summer. The variety **'Aureum'** has yellow foliage. Plants spread widely but are easily restrained.

S. spathulifolium **'Cape Blanco'** has clustered rosettes of thick, fleshy, blue-gray leaves tinged with red. They form a spreading mat and in early summer bear heads of small yellow flowers on short stems. Zone 5 US, 6 Can.

A larger plant for borders, or as a specimen in a container, is ***S. spectabile***. This grows to about 18in (45cm) and has broad, gray-green, fleshy leaves and lax, succulent stems. Wide, flat flower heads of small, starry flowers with prominent stamens appear in mid- to late summer and persist into the fall; they are rosy pink and very attractive to butterflies.

***Sedum spathulifolium* 'Cape Blanco'**

Cultivation

Well-drained soil and full sun suit most stonecrops. Cut back the spread of mat-forming varieties as necessary.

Plants are easily propagated by division or softwood cuttings in summer. Plants that have been overwatered, or are growing in poorly drained soil, may rot at the base.

Sempervivum Crassulaceae

Houseleek, hen-and-chickens ①②③

* *Evergreen perennial*
* *Attractive rosettes of leaves; starry flowers*
* *Hardy* *Zone 3 US, 4 Can*

Sempervivum belongs to the same family as *Sedum* and, like those plants, have fleshy, succulent leaves, sometimes tipped with red, which form tight rosettes. They are suitable for rock gardens, walls, and troughs.

Sempervivum arachnoideum, the cobweb houseleek, forms crowded clusters of red-tipped, fleshy leaves covered in fine white webbing, which makes them look as though spiders have been busy among its leaf tips. In summer, rose pink flowers are carried in clusters on 6in (15cm) stems.

S. tectorum, the common hen-and-chickens, has similar rosettes without the webbing; the leaves are touched with purple or deep red. Deep red flowers appear in summer on 12in (30cm) stems.

S. **'Commander Hay'** has large, dull red rosettes with green tips.

Cultivation

Plant houseleeks in full sun and very well-drained soil; they need little aftercare.

They are easy to propagate by offsets; break off a rosette and replant it at once if it already has roots or pot it in gritty soil if roots have not yet formed.

Senecio greyi

Senecio Compositae

Senecio ①②③

* *Annuals, herbaceous perennials, and evergreen shrubs*
* *Attractive foliage and summer flowers*
* *Hardy* *Zone 8 US, 9 Can*

Senecios have the familiar daisy flowers of the *Compositae* family, but they tend to be grown more for their silver foliage.

Senecio cineraria (***S. maritima***), dusty miller, is an evergreen shrub nearly always treated as an annual. It has deeply lobed leaves covered in dense, fine hairs that give them a bright silver color; they make a mound about 12in (30cm) tall. The most popular variety is **'Silver Dust'**, with very finely cut, lacy, silver-white foliage; **'Diamond'** has silver-green leaves that are not so finely divided.

S. greyi (***Brachyglottis greyi***) is an evergreen shrub growing to around 3ft (1m). The oval leaves are felted and silver when young, becoming mid- to dark green as they age. Loose clusters of bright yellow flowers are carried from early summer.

Cultivation

Like all gray-leafed plants, senecios can cope well with dry soil and like full sun. *S. greyi* prefers a sheltered location and grows well in coastal areas.

S. cineraria can be raised from seed, and the young plants set out after the risk of frost has passed. Any flowers that are produced are generally removed, since they detract from the foliage.

S. greyi can be increased by taking semiripe cuttings in summer. Remove flowers when they fade and cut back straggly shoots in fall.

Sorbus Rosaceae

Mountain ash ③

* *Deciduous tree*
* *Attractive foliage, flowers and berries*
* *Hardy* *Zone 3 US, 3 Can except as noted*

The European mountain ash, ***Sorbus aucuparia***, is an elegant, medium-sized tree with ferny, pinnate leaves. Heads of small white flowers in spring are followed by bunches of red berries. **'Fastigiata'**, with dark green leaves and brilliant red fruits, is slow growing and columnar, reaching about 15ft (4.5m) after several years.

S. commixta is noted for its fall foliage color: the remarkable purple-red leaves remain on the tree until late in the season. Zone 5 US, 6 Can.

Less commonly seen is the dwarf shrub ***S. reducta***, which has upright stems around 18in (45cm) tall, with pinnate leaves that turn bronzy red in fall. The small, round berries are rosy pink or pinkish white. This shrub usually produces many suckers, but nonsuckering selections are sometimes available. Zone 4 US, 4 Can.

The Swedish whitebeam ***S. intermedia***, has leaves that are green above and silvery below making it attractive as the leaves move in a breeze. It is fairly resistant to fireblight.

Cultivation

Well-drained, reasonably fertile soils are suitable, preferably acid, since many sorbus are not long-lived in alkaline soils. Most mountain ash are grown as specimen trees, but ***S. reducta*** can be grown in a rock garden or as a border plant.

Plants can be propagated by softwood cuttings in summer.

Mountain ash may be attacked by fireblight, which causes flowers and foliage to wither, turn brown, and hang on the tree with a scorched appearance; prune out and destroy affected branches immediately.

Taxus Taxaceae

Yew ②③

* *Evergreen conifer*
* *Attractive foliage and tree shapes*
* *Poisonous*
* *Hardy*

Although the dark green, needlelike leaves of yew make it a useful foil for brighter-leafed plants, among the many varieties of English yew (***Taxus baccata***, Zone 5 US, 6 Can) are several with golden foliage.

Yew trees are tough and hardy and will put up with poor growing conditions; they

Taxus baccata 'Standishii'

are notoriously slow growing but can survive to a great age. They are amenable to hard pruning, and very useful for topiary.

Male and female forms exist; the females bear fleshy, red, berrylike arils. The flesh of the aril is harmless, but the single seed it encloses, and all other parts of the tree, are extremely poisonous.

T. b. **'Fastigiata'** is a popular upright, columnar yew, growing very slowly to about 30ft (9m). The semiprostrate **'Repandens'** grows to some 2ft (60cm), and is good for ground cover, while **'Standishii'**, with rusty gold foliage, has a compact, columnar shape very suitable for containers.

Hardier ***T. cuspidata***, Japanese yew, is not as large as *T. b.*'Fastigiata'. Slow-growing **'Nana'** has a spreading shape. Zone 4 US, 4 Can.

T. × media has olive green needles; **'Brownii'** grows to 9ft (2.7m) and has a rounded habit; **'Taunton'**, with a spreading habit, tolerates summer heat and resists winter burn. Zone 4 US, 5 Can.

Cultivation

Yews will grow in virtually any soil except a heavy, waterlogged one. They will grow in sun or shade.

Pruning can be carried out to shape the plants at any time of year. Cuttings with a heel can be taken in fall.

Deer are a serious problem.

Thymus Labiatae

Thyme ①②③

* *Evergreen shrub or perennial*
* *Aromatic foliage and summer flowers*
* *Culinary herb*
* *Hardy* *Zone 4 US, 4 Can*

The small, oval or lanceolate leaves of thyme have a warm, sweet fragrance and are widely used in cooking, but the plants are of great decorative as well as culinary value. They are low-growing, creeping or upright plants, with clusters of lipped, pink or white summer flowers that are very attractive to bees.

Garden thyme, ***Thymus vulgaris***, has narrow, dark green leaves and grows to about 8in (20cm). Upright heads of mauve flowers are carried in summer. *T. v.* **'Silver Posie'** is a compact, silver-margined variety. ***T. × citriodorus***, with its sharp citrus scent, is lemon thyme; the golden-foliaged **'Aureus'** forms a spreading shrub up to 10in (25cm) tall with pale lilac flowers. The dense mats of ***T. pseudolanuginosus*** have hairy stems and furry gray-green leaves; ***T. herba-barona*** has deep green leaves that smell of caraway.

T. serpyllum, wild thyme, makes spreading mats of tough stems with tiny green leaves. **'Annie Hall'** has pale pink flowers while those of **'Coccineus'** are rich crimson.

Cultivation

Thymes may be planted in containers, rock gardens, raised beds, and borders; they need well-drained soil and full sun. They will also grow well when planted in cracks in paving, releasing their full aroma when lightly trodden on.

Cut off the faded flowers with pruners and trim straggly plants in fall. Take heel cuttings in late summer.

Thymus serpyllum 'Coccineus' *(left) and* ***Thymus*** 'Winter Beauty'

Trachycarpus Arecaceae

Fan palm, windmill palm ②③

* *Evergreen palm*
* *Attractive foliage and architectural shape*
* *Hardy* *Zone 7 US, 8 Can*

A slow-growing palm that gives an exotic appearance to a garden, *Trachycarpus fortunei* is comparatively hardy but needs shelter from cold winds. Provide winter protection for young plants in cool areas.

The leaves are pleated like a fan and may be up to 1m (3ft) wide. They are carried on long, toothed stalks arising from a stout, hairy trunk. In early summer, panicles of small, cream flowers may appear.

Cultivation
Grow in moderately fertile, well-drained soil in full sun in a sheltered location. Remove dead leaves when necessary.

Propagation is not practical for small-space gardeners.

Tulipa Liliaceae

Tulip ①②③

* *Spring-flowering bulb*
* *Colorful flowers; some types have attractive foliage*
* *Hardy* *Zone 4 US, 4 Can*

Along with daffodils, tulips are perhaps the best known spring bulbs, valued for their typically goblet-shaped flowers carried on long stems. There are many different types of tulip, flowering from early spring to early summer, and ranging in height from 4in (10cm) or less to more than 3ft (1m). The flowers may be open and flat, cup-shaped, double, frilled, or waisted, in a range of colors including bicolors and feathered or streaked varieties. Botanically, they are split into 15 divisions, each division containing a large number of cultivars.

Among the most useful for containers and small spaces are the shorter-growing types such as **Kaufmanniana, Fosteriana** and **Greigii** hybrids. **Kaufmannianas** flower from early spring, with blooms that are generally bicolored and open out flat in full sun. The foliage is usually attractively mottled with purple-brown streaks. Varieties include **'Ancilla'**, pink outside, white inside with a red and gold throat; and **'Heart's Delight'**, deep pink outside, pale pink inside, with a red and yellow throat.

Fosterianas have large, single flowers from early to midspring and include **'Juan'**, bright orange-red, waisted flowers with a yellow-splashed base; and **'Madame Lefeber'**, brilliant red.

The foliage of all **Greigii** hybrids is striped

***Tulipa* 'Estelle Rijnveld'**

and variegated with reddish brown, and the leaf margins are usually undulating. **'Red Riding Hood'** has particularly attractive foliage and bright red flowers with a black base to the petals; **'Toronto'** produces up to three flowers on a stem, with rosy red, pointed petals.

Among the species tulips, one of the most rewarding is ***Tulipa tarda***, which produces four or five flowers on short stems in early spring; they have pointed petals, which are white with a large, central gold blotch.

Cultivation
Plant tulips in late fall in well-drained soil in a sunny location. When the leaves have died down, the bulbs may be lifted and stored in a cool, dry place until it is time to replant them; in light, well-drained soils they may be left in the ground. Young bulbs can be separated from the parent and replanted at lifting time.

Remove dead blooms during the flowering season.

Aphids sometimes attack the young shoots and can be controlled with a non-persistent insecticide where necessary. Slugs may also cause damage; use slug bait or an organic alternative. Tulips are a prime deer food.

Viburnum Caprifoliaceae

Viburnum ③

* *Deciduous and evergreen shrubs*
* *Attractive foliage and flowers; sometimes fruits*
* *Hardiness varies*

The viburnum genus is wide and diverse, but contains some excellent early-flowering shrubs. Among the best known is ***Viburnum* × *bodnantense* 'Dawn'**, an upright, deciduous shrub to 8ft (2.4m), with clusters of very fragrant, pink flowers, deep pink in bud, carried on the bare stems during mild spells throughout the late fall and winter. Zone 6 US, 7 Can.

V. carlesii, (Zone 4 US, 5 Can.) and ***V.* × *juddii*** (Zone 4 US, 5 Can.) are also early blooming, with flattened clusters of very fragrant, very pale pink or white tubular flowers on rounded deciduous shrubs, which grow up to 5–8ft (1.5–2.4m) tall and wide. They lack the brilliant fall color or fruits of some viburnums.

One of the showiest for fruiting is the tea viburnum, ***V. setigerum***. Slow-growing to 8ft (2.4m) or so, its flat clusters of white flowers in late spring give way to brilliant red or orange egg-shaped berries that hang in groups in fall. (Zone 5 US, 6 Can.)

The American cranberry viburnum, ***V. trilobum***, is very cold-hardy and grows to 10ft (3m) tall. Its white flowers, in handsome clusters some 4in (10cm) across in early summer, are followed by red berries, which are attractive to birds; it also has good fall foliage color. Zone 2 US, 2 Can.

Cultivation
Viburnums prefer fertile, moisture-retentive soil, although many will cope well with dry soils. A location in sun is best, but light shade is tolerated.

After flowering, prune out some older shoots from deciduous species to keep the plants compact; when necessary, evergreens may be thinned out in early summer.

Propagate viburnums by taking cuttings in summer—semiripe cuttings for evergreen species and softwood cuttings for deciduous species. Seed can be sown in fall.

Aphids may infest young leaves.

Viburnum bodnantense

Vinca Apocynaceae

Periwinkle, vinca ① ② ③

* *Evergreen shrub*
* *Trailing or prostrate habit*
* *Summer flowers*
* *Hardy*

The glossy, dark green leaves of periwinkle make an excellent ground cover, with starry, bright blue flowers peeping out from the mat of foliage from late spring through to fall. Like most effective ground cover plants, it can be invasive and must be located with care.

Vinca major (greater periwinkle) is a vigorous plant growing to 18in (45cm) tall, with large blue flowers throughout the summer; it is strong-growing and invasive. **'Variegata'** has leaves edged with creamy white; the leaves of **'Elegantissima'** have a central golden splash. Zone 6 US, 7 Can.

Less rampant is the lesser periwinkle, *V. minor*. Its appearance is similar to that of *V. major*, but it is smaller in all its parts, growing to only about 6in (15cm) high but still spreading widely. **'Alba'** and **'Gertrude Jekyll'** have white flowers; **'Argenteo-variegata'** has creamy-white variegated leaves. The azure blue flowers of **'La Grave'** are particularly large; those of **'Flore Pleno'** are double. Zone 3 US, 3 Can.

Cultivation

Vincas can be grown in most well-drained soils in sun or shade, but flower better in sun. They are good plants for containers, where their spread can be controlled.

The spreading stems root at the nodes as they go, and plants are easily propagated by division or by pegging sections of the stems into moist soil.

Vinca major

***Viola* 'Ardross Gem'**

Viola Violaceae

Violet, pansy ① ② ③

* ***Annuals and perennials, deciduous or semievergreen***
* ***Summer or winter flowers***
* ***Hardy*** *Zone 4 US, 5 Can*

Violets have oval or heart-shaped leaves and usually distinctively flat-faced, five-petaled flowers. They are suitable for growing in a large number of situations, including containers, rock gardens, beds, and borders.

Viola odorata, the sweet violet, flowers in spring, producing small, sweetly fragrant flowers amid mounds of heart-shaped, light green leaves 4in (10cm) high. The plants spread by means of runners and form dense clumps. Flowers are violet-blue, pink, or white; named varieties include **'Princesse de Galles'**, deep blue; **'Marie-Louise'**, double mauve; and **'Coeur d'Alsace'**, which is pink.

Pansies (*V.* × ***wittrockiana***) are perennials usually grown as annuals. They have oval leaves and relatively large, flat-faced flowers in a wide range of colors and bicolors; they may flower in late winter, spring or summer. **Majestic Giants Hybrids** are summer flowering, with large blooms in many colors. **Universal Hybrids**, with blotched or plain flowers in orange, red, pink, violet, blue, white, and yellow is one of the best winter-flowering strains.

Cultivation

These plants can be grown in sun or light shade in any fertile, reasonably moisture-retentive soil. Deadheading plants will give a longer succession of bloom.

Perennials may be propagated by division, those grown as annuals by seed.

Violets are subject to viral diseases, which cause deformed, stunted growth, sometimes with mottled foliage. Destroy badly affected plants and control aphids to help curb the spread of viruses.

Violets are often attacked by red spider mite; infestations show as dry, flecked foliage and failure of the plants to thrive. Infestations usually occur in dry, hot conditions; spray the plants with water to increase humidity and move them into a shady location.

Vitis Vitaceae

Vine ③

* ***Deciduous climber***
* ***Attractive foliage and fruits; fall color***
* ***Hardy*** *Zone 5 US, 6 Can*

These climbers have lobed or heart-shaped leaves and can be grown up walls or over pergolas; they climb by means of tendrils. The grape vine, ***Vitis vinifera***, is widely cultivated around the world for its fruits, both for eating and for wine making. There are also several decorative varieties.

V. ***coignetiae***, the crimson glory vine, has large, slightly hairy, heart-shaped leaves, which turn an attractive rich crimson in fall; it is a vigorous grower which will quickly cover a large wall. *V.* ***thunbergii*** has young foliage that is rusty-brown on the underside. Divided into three lobes, the leaves look like those of the Amur maple and in fall they turn a carmine red. The fruit are purple-red in small clusters.

There are many varieties of *V. vinifera* that will produce edible fruits in a warm, sheltered location; two grown for their foliage are **'Incana'**, with leaves thickly covered in a white meal, and **'Purpurea'**, with deep red or purple leaves and insignificant fruits.

Cultivation

Plant in moisture-retentive but well-drained, fertile soil in an open, sunny, warm, and sheltered location. Provide support for the shoots to twine around.

Prune by shortening young shoots and thinning out older branches in early fall.

Propagate by hardwood cuttings taken during the dormant season or by semiripe cuttings in summer.

Aphids may be a problem on young shoots and can be treated with a non-persistent insecticide. If mildew occurs, use a suitable fungicide.

Weigela Caprifoliaceae

Weigela ③

* *Deciduous shrub*
* *Early summer flowers*
* *Hardy* *Zone 4 US, 5 Can*

Weigela forms a medium-sized, rounded bush with trumpet-shaped flowers in early summer. These are sometimes followed by another flush of bloom later in the season. The midgreen, oval leaves are deeply veined.

Weigela florida is the most popular species grown; it has slightly arching branches up to 6ft (2m) and pink flowers in late spring. *W. f.* **'Variegata'** is slower growing and reaches some 4ft (1.2m). Its leaves have a broad, creamy white margin, and the flowers are pale pink. *W. f.* **'Foliis Purpureis'** is even more compact, and its deep purple-green foliage contrasts well with the flowers, which are deep pink on the outside, offset by the pale pink within.

There are many hybrid varieties of weigela, among them **'Minuet'**, a dwarf shrub growing to 2ft (60cm) with bright pink flowers and purple-tinged foliage, and **'Rumba'**, which is twice as tall, and has red flowers with a yellow throat.

Cultivation

Grow in well-drained, moderately fertile soil, preferably in sun, although weigelas will tolerate partial shade.

Prune out a proportion of the older branches each year after flowering, cutting them back to the ground; this encourages the formation of strong, new shoots that will flower in their second year.

Varieties grown for their foliage can be pruned back hard in early spring but they will then not bear flowers.

Propagate by semiripe cuttings in summer.

Yucca Agavaceae

Adam's needle, Spanish dagger, yucca ②③

* *Evergreen shrub*
* *Bold foliage and architectural shapes*
* *Hardy*

Exotic-looking yuccas have rosettes of narrow, sword-shaped foliage, which is often sharply spiny. Tall stems of showy, bell-shaped, creamy flowers are carried on established plants in summer.

Yucca filamentosa (Adam's needle), with stemless rosettes of stiff, blue-green leaves margined with fibrous threads, grows to 3–6ft (1–2m). Creamy white, bell-shaped flowers are carried on tall stems in summer when the plants are a few years old. **'Bright Edge'** has leaves with a fine yellow margin. (Zone 3 US, 4 Can.) *Y. flaccida* is a smaller plant with narrow, deep green leaves that tend to bend down at the tips; creamy white flowers on 3ft (1m) tall stems appear from mid- to late summer. **'Golden Sword'** has leaves with a central yellow stripe. Zone 3 US, 4 Can.

Y. gloriosa, known as Spanish dagger, has a short, stout stem and forms a small tree about 6ft (2m) tall. On top of the stem is a tuft of stiff, spiky, blue-green leaves. Panicles of flowers appear from midsummer through early fall; they are creamy white, sometimes tinged red on the outside. Zone 6 US, 7 Can.

Y. recurvifolia also has a short stem that, unlike that of *Y. gloriosa*, tends to branch; the leaves are blue-green and curve backwards. The white, late-summer flowers are produced only after several years. Zone 6 US, 7 Can.

Cultivation

Yuccas like well-drained soil and full sun; plant them in a location sheltered from wind. They grow very well in containers. Some species, particularly *Y. gloriosa*, need to be sited carefully in small spaces because of the dangerously sharp, spiky foliage. Take care that the plants are not overwatered in the dormant season or the roots will rot. Remove the flowering stems once the flowers have faded.

Plants can be increased by the suckers that form naturally; remove them from the parent plant in spring.

Large, gray, brown-edged spots on the leaves are caused by leaf spot fungus. Remove any badly damaged leaves and spray the plants with a suitable fungicide.

Yucca gloriosa

Zantedeschia Araceae

Calla lily ②③

* *Deciduous or evergreen, tuberous-rooted perennial*
* *Bold foliage and showy summer flower spathes*
* *Hardy or tender* *Zone 8 US, 9 Can except as noted*

The exotic flowers of the calla lily are formed from a club-shaped spadix (flower spike) surrounded by a large spathe (bract), which may be white, green, pink, or yellow. Plants are mostly tender, and even the hardy varieties prefer a sheltered location and a warm climate.

Zantedeschia aethiopica has glossy, deep green, arrow-shaped leaves with distinct veins. The plant forms a mound up to 3ft (1m) high, and in early to midsummer produces long stems topped by a large, showy, funnel-shaped white spathe surrounding a fleshy yellow spadix. **'Crowborough'** is one of the hardier forms; **'Green Goddess'** is also relatively hardy and has a green spathe with a white throat.

The golden calla, *Z. elliottiana*, grows to about 2ft (60cm). The heart-shaped leaves are marked with white spots and streaks; the spathe is a rich golden yellow.

The pink calla, *Z. rehmannii*, reaches about 18in (45cm); it has plain green leaves and a narrow, funnel-shaped, pale pink to deep maroon spathe. Both these species are tender. Zone 10 US.

Cultivation

Plant calla lilies in fertile, moisture-retentive soil in a warm, protected location in sun or partial shade. Water plants regularly during the growing season to keep the soil moist at all times. *Z. aethiopica* can be grown as a marginal plant in a water garden, with the roots covered by 6in (15cm) of water.

Gradually dry off container-grown plants after flowering and overwinter the tender species under cover at a minimum of 45°F (7°C). If *Z. aethiopica* is overwintered outside in cool areas, mulch the planting area with straw or similar material.

Plants can be increased by offsets in the dormant season.

Round, dark gray blotches caused by a fungal leaf spot disease may form on leaves, spathes, and leaf stalks, sometimes resulting in leaves falling. Destroy the affected foliage and spray the plants with a suitable fungicide.

Index

Page numbers in *italic* refer to captions to pictures or to text in boxes.

Acknowledgements

Picture credits

t = top; **b** = bottom; **l** = left; **c** = center; **r** = right

2 Clive Nichols, **5t** Steven Wooster/The Garden Picture Library, **5b** Photos Horticultural, **6t** Friedrich Strauss/The Garden Picture Library, **6b** Elizabeth Whiting & Associates, **6-7t** Garden Matters, **6-7b** Harry Smith Collection; **8t** Jerry Harpur, **8b** Elizabeth Whiting & Associates; **10** Lynne Brotchie/The Garden Picture Library, **10-11** Friedrich Strauss/The Garden Picture Library; **12l** Niall McDiarmid/Robert Harding Syndication, **12r** Clive Nichols/ Designer: Jill Billington; **13** Amateur Gardening/Your Garden; **14** Elizabeth Whiting & Associates; **15** Ron Sutherland/The Garden Picture Library; **16** John Glover/The Garden Picture Library; **17** Lynne Brotchie/The Garden Picture Library; **18t & c** Chas Wilder, **18b** Amateur Gardening/Your Garden; **19l** Chas Wilder, **19r** Garden Matters; **20** Garden Matters; **21** Steven Wooster/The Garden Picture Library; **22** Garden Matters; **23** Jerry Harpur; **24t** Linda Burgess/The Garden Picture Library, **24b** Chas Wilder; **25** Ron Sutherland/The Garden Picture Library; **26t** Elizabeth Whiting & Associates, **26b** Clive Nichols/Designer: Victor Shanley; **27** Clive Nichols/Designer: Randle Siddeley; **28t** John Glover/The Garden Picture Library, **28b** Elizabeth Whiting & Associates; **29t** Ron Sutherland/The Garden Picture Library, **29b** Garden Matters; **30-31** Elizabeth Whiting & Associates; **32** Spike Powell; **33** Elizabeth Whiting & Associates; **34l** Andrew Sydenham, **34r** Peter McHoy; **35t** Elizabeth Whiting & Associates, **35b** Harry Smith Collection; **36-37** Elizabeth Whiting & Associates; **38t** Photos Horticultural, **38b** Elizabeth Whiting & Associates, **38-39** Elizabeth Whiting & Associates, **39** Andrew Lawson; **40** Chas Wilder; **41** Amateur Gardening/Your Garden; **42t** Simon Butcher/Houses & Interiors, **42b** Clive Nichols; **43** Jerry Harpur; **44** Amateur Gardening/Your Garden; **45** Help the Aged/Designer: Andrea Parsons; **46t** Amateur Gardening/Your Garden, **46b** Chas Wilder; **47t** Tim Shepherd/Oxford Scientific Films, **47b** Harry Smith Collection; **48** Chas Wilder, **48-49** Garden Matters; **50** Elizabeth Whiting & Associates; **51t** Jerry Harpur, **51b** Clive Nichols/Designer: Louise Hampden; **52tl** Clive Nichols/Designer: Sue Guerney, **52tr** Andrew Lawson, courtesy: Mirabel Oster, **52b & 53** Harry Smith Collection; **54** Chas Wilder; **55** Harry Smith Collection; **56** Clive Nichols/Mrs Dymock; **57t** Clive Nichols, **57b** Jane Legate/The Garden Picture Library; **58** Chas Wilder, **58-59** Chas Wilder, **59** Garden Matters; **60** Andrew Lawson; **61** Steven Wooster/The Garden Picture Library; **62-65** Elizabeth Whiting & Associates; **66** Photos Horticultural; **67 & 68t** Harry Smith Collection, **68b & 69** Chas Wilder; **70** Zooid Pictures/Garden Matters; **71** Clive Nichols/Designer: Mrs Preston; **72** Amateur Gardening/Your Garden; **73** Chas Wilder, **73tr** Clive Nichols; **74** Chas Wilder; **75tl** Harry Smith Collection, **75tr & b** Chas Wilder; **76l** Ken Muir, **76r & 77** Chas Wilder; **78** Amateur Gardening/Your Garden, **78-79** Elizabeth Whiting & Associates; **80** Chas Wilder; **81t** Clive Nichols/Home Farm Trust-Chelsea 94, **81b-85** Chas Wilder; **86l** Clive Nichols/Designer: C. Cordy, **86r** Andrew Lawson, **86-87** Andrew Lawson, **87** Harry Smith Collection; **94** Chas Wilder; **94-95** Elizabeth Whiting & Associates; **96** Chas Wilder; **99** Charles Krebs/Tony Stone Images; **100tl & tr** Chas Wilder; **100bl** Garden Matters, **100br** Harry Smith Collection; **101t** Peter McHoy, **101c** Chas Wilder, **101bl & cb** Garden Matters, **101br** Chas Matters, **101br** Chas Wilder; **102tl** Garden Matters, **102bl & r** A-Z Botanical Collection; **103** A-Z Botanical Collection; **104t** Harry Smith Collection, **104b** Garden Matters; **105tl** Harry Smith Collection; **105tr** Peter McHoy, **105bl** A-Z Botanical Collection, **105br** Martin P. Land/Garden Matters; **106-108t** Chas Wilder, **108b** Photos Horticultural; **110-114** Chas Wilder; **115t** Harry Smith Collection, **115b** Chas Wilder; **117** Clive Nichols/Daniel Pearson, Chelsea 93; **118** Clive Nichols/Designer: Claus Scheinert; **119t** Clive Nichols/Designer: Anthony Noel, **119b** Clive Nichols/Designer: Anne Dexter; **120-122** Chas Wilder; **123t** Elizabeth Whiting & Associates, **123b** Chas Wilder; **124-139** Chas Wilder; **140** Clive Nichols/Designer: Anthony Noel; **156** Chas Wilder, **156-157** Harry Smith Collection; **158l** A-Z Botanical Collection, **158r** Harry Smith Collection; **159** Bjorn Svensson/A-Z Botanical Collection; **160l** Bjorn Svensson/A-Z Botanical Collection, **160r** Harry Smith Collection; **161t & bl** Garden Matters; **161br-163l** Harry Smith Collection; **163r** Garden Matters; **164** Garden Matters; **165t** Harry Smith Collection; **165b** Geoff Kidd/A-Z Botanical Collection; **166l** David Henderson/A-Z Botanical Collection, **166r & 167** Harry Smith Collection; **168** Geoff Kidd/A-Z Botanical Collection; **169t** Harry Smith Collection, **169** Sandra Ireland/Houses & Interiors; **170 & 171l** Harry Smith Collection, **171r** A-Z Botanical Collection; **172t** Harry Smith Collection, **172b** Steffie Shields/Garden Matters; **173t** Geoff Kidd/A-Z Botanical Collection, **173b** Geoff Kidd/A-Z Botanical Collection; **174** Garden Matters; **174-175** Garden Matters, **175** Chas Wilder; **176** Harry Smith Collection; **177t** Garden Matters, **177b** Harry Smith Collection; **178l** Geoff Kidd/A-Z Botanical Collection, **178r** Garden Matters; **179l** Harry Smith Collection, **179r** Terence Exley/A-Z Botanical Collection; **180t** Steffie Shields/Garden Matters, **180b** Bjorn Svensson/A-Z Botanical Collection; **181-182** Harry Smith Collection; **183** A-Z Botanical Collection; **184** Harry Smith Collection; **185l** Garden Matters, **185r** M.P. Land/A-Z Botanical Collection; **186** Jeremy Hoare/Garden Matters; **187l** Terence Exley/A-Z Botanical Collection, **187r** Sheila Orme/A-Z Botanical Collection; **188** Harry Smith Collection; **189l** Garden Matters, **189r** Harry Smith Collection; **190** Harry Smith Collection; **191l** Sheila Orme/A-Z Botanical Collection, **191r** Garden Matters; **192-193** Harry Smith Collection; **194** A-Z Botanical Collection; **195** Garden Matters; **196** Harry Smith Collection; **197t** Garden Matters, **197b** A-Z Botanical Collection; **198** Harry Smith Collection; **199** Garden Matters; **200** Geoff Kidd/A-Z Botanical Collection; **201l** Harry Smith Collection; **201r** J. Brunsden Rapkins/A-Z Botanical Collection; **202l** Geoff Kidd/A-Z Botanical Collection, **202r & 203** Garden Matters; **204** Harry Smith Collection; **205l** Harry Smith Collection, **205r** A-Z Botanical Collection; **206t** Garden Matters, **206bl** Harry Smith Collection, **206br** Garden Matters; **207** Harry Smith Collection; **208l** Michael R. Chandler/A-Z Botanical Collection, **208r** Harry Smith Collection; **209l** Adrian Thomas/A-Z Botanical Collection, **209r** Harry Smith Collection; **210** Geoff Kidd/A-Z Botanical Collection; **211** Martin P. Land/Garden Matters; **212** Steffie Shields/Garden Matters; **213l** Geoff Kidd/A-Z Botanical Collection, **213r** Anthony Cooper/A-Z Botanical Collection; **214-218l** Harry Smith Collection, **218r** Garden Matters; **219** David Henderson/A-Z Botanical Collection

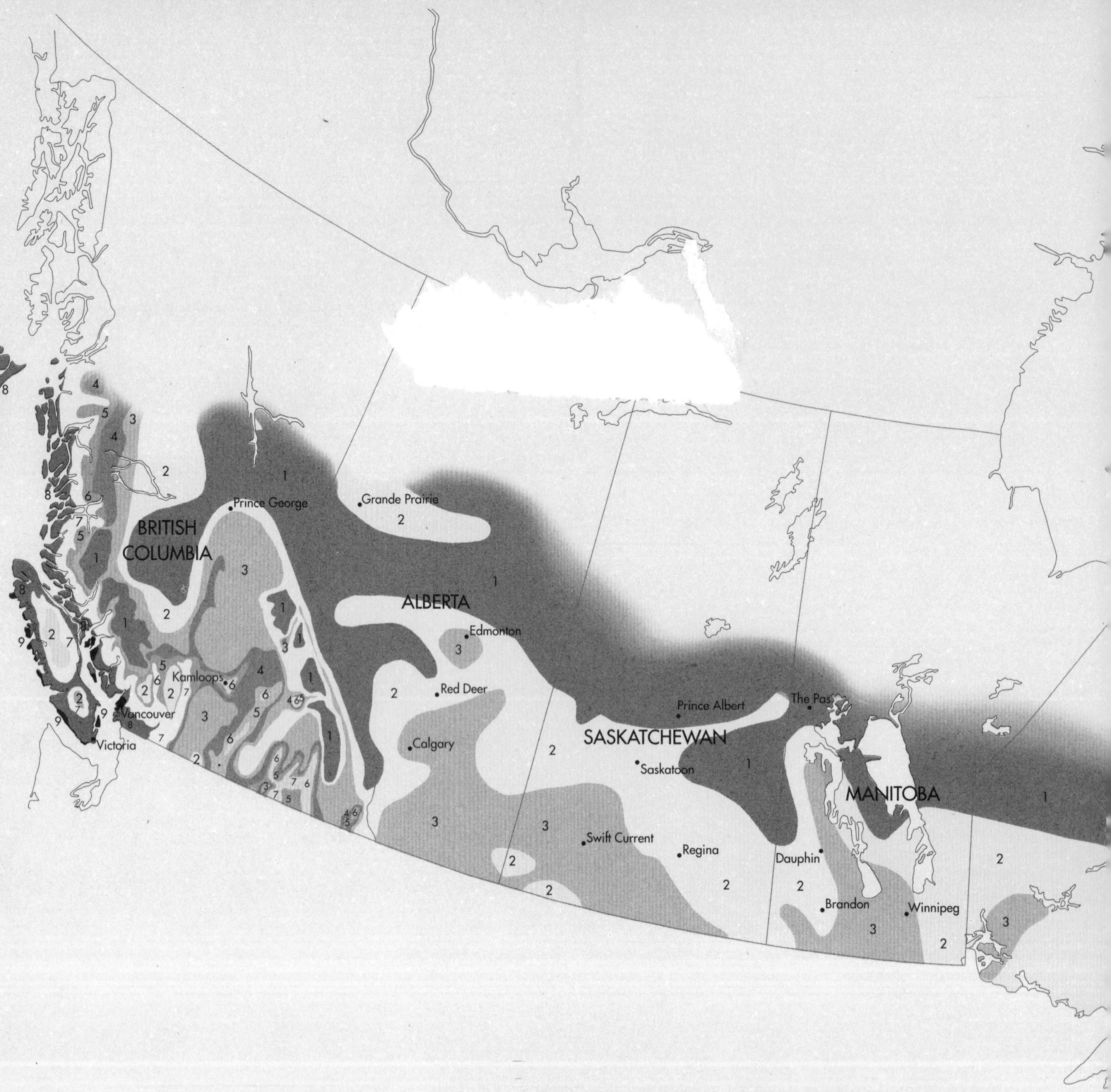

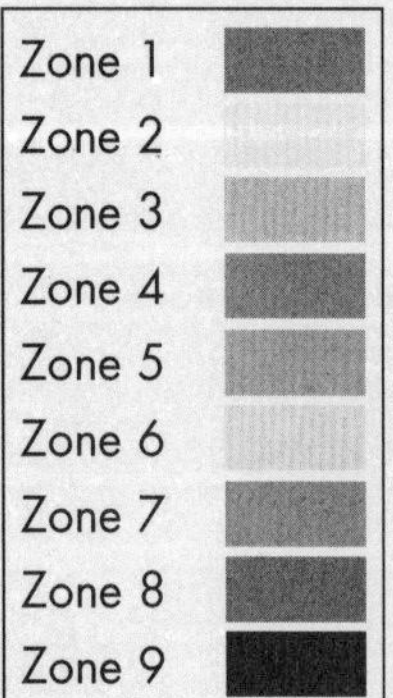

Hardiness Across Canada

Plants that survive winters are called hardy, while those that succumb to cold weather are called tender. The nine Canadian hardiness zones define the areas in which a plant is likely to be hardy based partly on minimum winter temperatures. Each zone can grow plants from lower numbered zones. For example, if you live in zone 4 you can include plants from zones 3, 2, and 1 in your garden. The zones are only a guide however. Within each zone are microclimates, individual pockets that may be warmer or colder than the surrounding region. To find out in which zone your garden is, talk to experts at local garden centers.